HIGHROAD GUIDE
TO THE

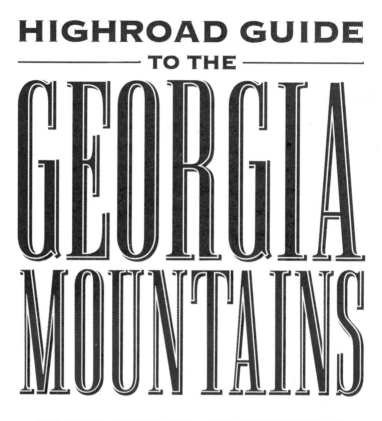

GEORGIA MOUNTAINS

BY THE GEORGIA CONSERVANCY
WITH FRED BROWN AND NELL JONES

FOREWORD BY JIMMY CARTER

CHARLES H. WHARTON, PH.D., SCIENCE ADVISOR

LONGSTREET
ATLANTA, GEORGIA

Published by
LONGSTREET PRESS, INC.
a subsidiary of Cox Newspapers,
a subsidiary of Cox Enterprises, Inc.
2140 Newmarket Parkway
Suite 122
Marietta, Georgia 30067

Printed by RR Donnelley & Sons, Harrisonburg, VA

1st Printing 1998

Library of Congress Catalog Number 97-76537

ISBN 1-56352-461-9

Book editing, design, and cartography
by Lenz Design & Communications, Inc., Decatur, Georgia

Cover Design by Richard J. Lenz, Decatur, Georgia

Illustrations by Danny Woodard, Loganville, Georgia

Some Things Never Change

In Memory of Byron Herbert Reece, Georgia Mountain Poet
September 14, 1917–June 3, 1958

Some things never change—
Madrigals still wake soft under rains;
The green of the mountains far fades into blue
As a bird flying close gives its music to you.

The creeks in their shallows still ripple along
Making from every stone a song,
While the dapple of light on a single tree
Is more splendor than needed for any who see.

Deer gaze out in mild surprise
Then turn to shadow before your eyes;
In Elder's Wood and Hughly's Glen
They call us now, as they called you then.

The flowers in bloom on the valley floor
Were surely the same by your mother's door.

The breezes that drift down Dooley's glades
Still whisper to lovers in Pindar's shades;
The message they breathe is as old as new
(I'm so glad I can tell these things to you)—
Some things never change.

Oh, it's true some have come to change what they can
But the mountains, in time, will say "No!" to man;
In vain they move boulders, in vain alter streams—
They never will ever learn how to pave dreams.
For your words bear them witness as time passes by
And the mountaintops still define the whole sky.

The mountaintops still define the whole sky.

— Mildred Greear

Contents

Georgia

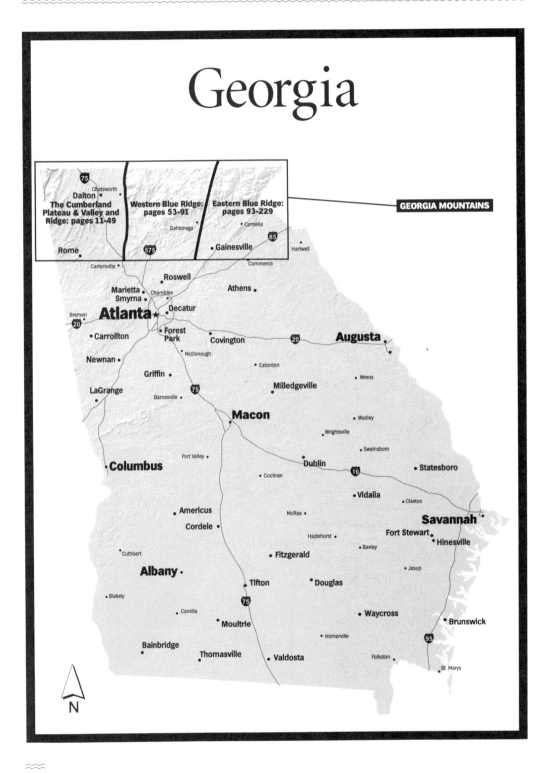

GEORGIA MOUNTAINS

The Cumberland Plateau & Valley and Ridge: pages 11-49

Western Blue Ridge: pages 53-91

Eastern Blue Ridge: pages 93-229

How To Use Your Highroad Guide

The *Highroad Guide To Georgia* includes a wealth of detailed information about the best of what the Georgia mountains have to offer, including hiking, camping, fishing, canoeing, mountain biking, and horseback riding. The *Highroad Guide* also presents information on the natural history of the mountains, plus interesting facts about Georgia's flora and fauna, giving the reader a starting point to learn more about what makes the mountains so special.

This book is divided into two major sections using Georgia's physiographic regions, plus two additional sections. One is an introduction to the natural history of the mountains and the other details long trails. Georgia's major provinces include the Appalachian Plateau, the Valley and Ridge, and the Blue Ridge. Because of the volume of information, the Blue Ridge province is divided into two subsections, the western Blue Ridge and the eastern Blue Ridge, to help the reader.

The maps in the book are keyed by figure number and referenced in the text. These maps are intended to help orient both the casual and expert mountains enthusiast. Below is a legend to explain symbols used on the maps. Remember, hiking trails frequently change as they fall into disuse or new trails are created. Serious hikers may want to purchase additional maps from the US Geological Service before they set out on a long hike. Sources are listed on the maps, in the text, and in the appendix.

A word of caution: the mountains can be dangerous. Weather can change suddenly, rocks can be slippery, and wild animals can act in unexpected ways. Use common sense when in the mountains so all your memories will be happy ones.

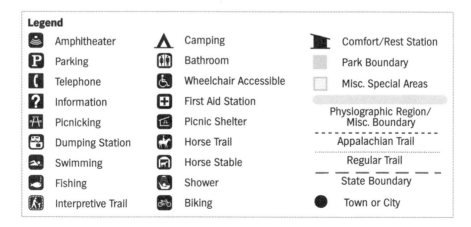

Legend

Amphitheater	Camping	Comfort/Rest Station	
Parking	Bathroom	Park Boundary	
Telephone	Wheelchair Accessible	Misc. Special Areas	
Information	First Aid Station	Physiographic Region/ Misc. Boundary	
Picnicking	Picnic Shelter	Appalachian Trail	
Dumping Station	Horse Trail	Regular Trail	
Swimming	Horse Stable	State Boundary	
Fishing	Shower	Town or City	
Interpretive Trail	Biking		

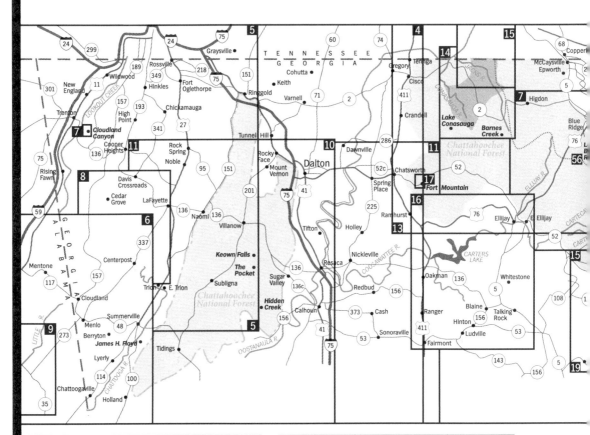

KEY TO THE MAPS

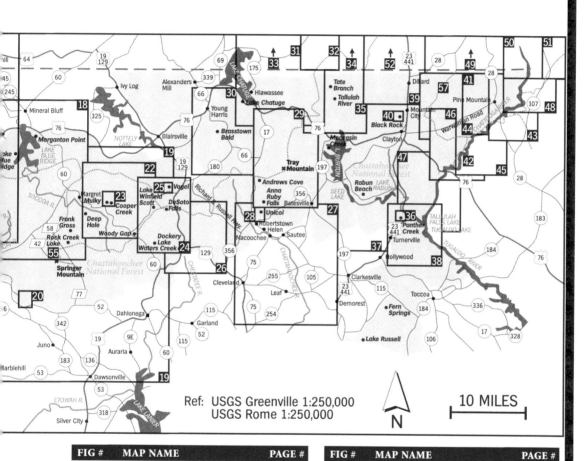

Ref: USGS Greenville 1:250,000
USGS Rome 1:250,000

10 MILES

N

Foreword

Looking out from our little log cabin on Turniptown Creek, which flows out of the Rich Mountain Wilderness, Rosalynn and I behold the breathtaking beauty of another Georgia mountain spring. The mountain laurel—which locals call "ivy"—is bursting forth with its delicate, pale pink blossoms. The waterfalls outside my window are brimming with spring's fresh rains, rapidly rushing downstream to their rendezvous with the Ellijay River. The hardwood forest surrounding us is clothed in nature's fresh green habit, and the cool spring air is sweet and clean. Phoebes are building a nest nearby in anticipation of the new life soon to appear. In the stream, rainbow trout chase stoneflies emerging to begin their brief mating flights. Everywhere there is evidence of the renewal of life.

Here in this natural setting Rosalynn and I have found peace and serenity we seldom enjoyed in our earlier years. For us, Washington, D.C., was an extraordinary

> In a remote cove or on a high windswept ridge, thoughts and cares
>
> of the modern world drop away, letting us for a little while become
>
> children of the earth.

center of temporal power, international politics, and human sophistication. These mountains are the antithesis of the political and military power embodied in the statehouses of man's government. Here in the Georgia mountains we enter an earth-centered consciousness where nature's laws are in charge. Here, we return to the physical source of our nurturing—nature's management of our air, water, and soil, without which our civilization could not survive. We return also to a great spiritual resource, amidst God's handiwork.

Our cabin in the Rich Mountains has been a refuge from the press of civic duties. Here, the rumble of thunder over our mountain hideaway has replaced the 21-gun salute in some foreign port of call, and the water music of a trout stream, the sound of public ovation.

Both Hernando De Soto, in the sixteenth century, and William Bartram, in the late eighteenth century, found these Georgia mountains clothed with verdant forests and crystal streams and peopled with the proud Cherokee. Later, Americans of European origin settled far back in the mountain coves, treasuring the solitude and the ability to sustain themselves on the rich mountain soils and forests. Today, our citizens crave these qualities that gave the early Americans spiritual strength and fierce independence. We steal back to the mountains at every opportunity to revel in the pure air and water and untrammeled wildness. This closeness to nature restores us in body and soul. We sit once again by an eternal pool and stare in wonder at the diversity of a forest that has endured the great ice ages—a forest that remembers the howl of the wolf, the bugle of the elk, the thunder of the bison, and perhaps even the cautious footfall of the first humans many years ago.

For over two centuries we have wrested from our mountains the wealth that made our nation strong—mica, corundum, coal, iron, gold, and timber. Our cities have flourished on the water from mountain rivers, filtered and purified by mountain soils. Now is the time for us to acknowledge that we can no longer live without respecting and understanding our mountain forests and the other great ecosystems of the earth which have for millennia supported the habitat of man.

This guide, painstakingly produced by many volunteers of The Georgia Conservancy, opens the door to adventure in a cherished part of our natural heritage. In addition, it introduces the remarkable diversity of mountain environments whose vital functions are powered only by the sun. Here, we stand in awe of divine forces that have shaped our planet. In a remote cove or on a high windswept ridge, thoughts and cares of the modern world drop away, letting us for a little while become children of the earth.

Having known the fine work of The Georgia Conservancy for over 30 years, Rosalynn and I are not surprised that this strong conservation organization has produced another excellent publication for those who enjoy nature's wonders. As one of the Conservancy's founding members in 1967, I recall very favorably participating in its annual conferences in the early 1970s. Rosalynn joins me in recommending this valuable guide to all those who seek to discover the natural treasures awaiting them in the Georgia mountains.

— Jimmy Carter

Preface

What you have in your hands is the best single guide ever assembled for anyone who wants to explore, really explore, and understand the Georgia mountains. I say that after living in Georgia for over 50 years and spending a good part of that time involved somehow with the northern part of the state—driving it or walking it, or writing about it, or editing the material that others had written about it.

The process of helping compile and edit earlier editions of this book has shown me plenty I didn't know about the mountains, and I promise that reading and using it will do the same for you.

The book looks at the mountains the way everyone should, but few people do: as two separate and distinct mountain ranges—the Cumberlands in the west and the Blue Ridge in the east—separated by three regions of valleys and ridges. This geology is what accounts for the tremendous diversity of terrain from one side of the state to the other and for the intense interest in the area by botanists and geologists. Those readers who come to terms with the mountains' geology, botany, and wildlife as described and illustrated throughout the book will know more about the basic structure and the natural environments of the Georgia mountains than most people ever do.

In addition, the exploration of the Georgia mountains in this book follows "nature's organization" rather than political boundaries; it doesn't stop at the state line, but follows the natural terrain where it leads, be that into Alabama, Tennessee, North Carolina, or South Carolina. As a result, readers who drive the Lookout Mountain Parkway from Gadsden, Alabama, across the northwestern tip of Georgia to Chattanooga will gain a clearer perspective of the dramatic 100-mile sweep of this flat-topped mountain. Likewise, visitors who discover the corundum deposits of Rabun County can trace them to Franklin, North Carolina, and see the mines that have produced some of the world's finest rubies and sapphires. This guidebook contains much "new" information never before assembled in one place. This happened because a large number of very knowledgeable and dedicated people contributed research, articles, maps, and notes about trails, rivers, vistas, or waterfalls that they have collected personally over the years or, in some cases, specifically for this book. Al Tate, for example, is a professional ecologist who, in these pages, leads readers on several hikes in the Raven Cliffs area. Mildred and Philip Greear, both recognized experts on the geology, botany, history and wildlife of the area, tell readers where to find fossils in northwest Georgia. Botanist Chick Gaddy and Hugh and Carole Nourse share wonderfully detailed information about exploring the escarpment gorges, an area Chick has hiked for many years. Few people know more about Georgia's rivers or write about them with more feeling than Reece Turrentine, longtime canoeing editor of *Brown's Guide to Georgia.* In this book, Reece's guide to Lakes Rabun, Seed, Burton, and Tallulah is a gem of guidebook journalism.

Chief among those contributing to this book is Charles Wharton, adjunct research associate at the University of Georgia's Institute of Ecology, for 20 years professor of biology at Georgia State University, and author of *The Natural Environments of Georgia.* I believe Charlie knows more about Georgia's mountains, their geology, trails, trees, flowers, wildlife, rivers, and vistas than any single person alive. Much of the new information in this volume was until now in his files, library, and brain—it was Charlie's private stash—and he has now generously and lovingly shared it with all of us. Many of the others who contributed bits and pieces of hard-earned information from their personal data bank or did original research specifically for this book are listed in the acknowledgments.

The most gratifying thing for an editor is to witness the pooling of information from a variety of sources into something that is bigger than any one of the contributors could have done on his or her own. I have never been associated with a project that did that more successfully than this one. This book has been compiled and designed for both the casual reader and for those committed to more serious explorations. It is not a guide to the more obvious tourist attractions of the mountains, although some of those attractions are included when they add to our understanding of the natural development, history, or culture of the region. It is a book filled with detail, directions, and maps. To some readers it may appear at first somewhat intimidating. But I promise you that no matter how well or how little you know the mountains, whether you are taking a Sunday drive, introducing young children to their first hiking trail, or setting off on a week-long backpacking trek, if you read and use this guide, it will open up a world of mountain experience that will surprise and amaze you.

— Fred Brown

Acknowledgments

The Georgia Conservancy gratefully acknowledges the following sponsors who made the publication of the original guidebook possible: Georgia Department of Natural Resources, Georgia Power Company, Nell H. Jones, The Lyndhurst Foundation, Thomas D. Perrie, Charles and Deen Day Smith, Charles A. Smithgall, and Charles H. Wharton.

Any project attempting to cover an area as expansive and complex as the Georgia mountains naturally requires a great deal of effort and cooperation from many sources. This mountain guidebook is certainly no exception. So many individuals gave of their time and talents to make the guidebook a reality that it would be impossible to recount every contribution. Without certain dedicated Georgia Conservancy volunteers, however, this mountain guide could not have been published.

Foremost among these was Dr. Charles Wharton, adjunct research associate at the University of Georgia's Institute of Ecology and acknowledged expert in the field of natural environments in the Southeast. We are most grateful for his unflagging dedication and support, which were an inspiration to all who worked with him.

Other steering committee members worked to shepherd the guide on its perilous passage from planning to publication. Committee members Donna Wear Veal, Frank McCamey, and Jack Byrne served tirelessly as team leaders of more than 150 volunteers who went enthusiastically into the field to obtain much of the basic data used in the book. Priscilla Golley spent months organizing, further researching, consolidating, and writing text from reports as they were received. Tom Perrie displayed infinite patience in setting up computer forms and formatting graphs, memos, and agendas. Other invaluable committee members included Steve Bowling and Bob Kerr, who participated in every phase of the book's development and production.

The Georgia Conservancy is especially grateful to Mildred and Philip Greear, who diligently reviewed site selections and data and wrote and rewrote several portions of the text. Other volunteers contributed reports and graphics, wrote and proofread text, and carried out numerous special assignments. These included Miriam Talmadge, Chick Gaddy, Judy Alderman, Edwin Dale, Anthony Lampros, Jim Renner, Tracy Battle of Gainesville Whiteprint, Jim Mackay, Kathy Mackay, George McGee, Pat Marcellino, Bill Mitchell, Michael Terry, Sherri Smith, and Bob Humphries.

Acknowledgments are also made to the Georgia Department of Industry, Trade and Tourism; the Northwest Georgia Travel Association; the Georgia Department of Natural Resources; Georgia Power Company, and the U.S. Forest Service, Chattahoochee-Oconee National Forests, for providing and testing key information.

As subsequent editions of the book have required revisions and updates to the original text, the assistance from Georgia Conservancy volunteers, staff members, and others who are knowledgeable about the mountains has continued with the same dedication and enthusiasm that was the hallmark of the first edition: Brian Boyd revised the Chattooga River text; Jack Byrne improved the Tallulah Gorge material; Darcy Douglas added a new section to the Benton MacKaye Trail; Peter Kirby provided important current information about mountain wilderness areas; Anthony Lampros added to the material on Black Rock Mountain State Park, Rabun Bald, and the physiography of north Georgia; Jim and Kathy Mackay reorganized the material on Lookout Mountain; and Dan Pitillo improved the Bartram Trail information.

Mike Palmeri of the Cartecay River Bicycle Shop in Ellijay provided the descriptions of the biking trails. Tim Homan, author of *The Hiking Trails of North Georgia*, reviewed the text and allowed us to use some of the information from his excellent resource. Billy Grimes, Cecil Philips, and Bob Lipscomb provided the photographs in the book.

The Georgia mountains are filled with many breathtaking vistas. Above, Black Rock Mountain State Park.

U.S. Forest Service employees in the field and in administrative offices in Atlanta and Gainesville who were extremely helpful in reviewing and updating information include Steve Bailey, Bill Black, Karen Braddy, Erin Bronk, Virginia Brown, Tom Fearrington, Tom Hawks, Dave Jensen, Joe King, David Kuykendall, Larry Luckett, George Martin, Terry McDonald, Jeff Owenby, Jerry Pless, Janet Thomas, Larry Thomas, and Michael Wilkins.

Others who assisted with revisions by providing current information about the mountains include Bob Beck, Arthur Blakenship, Marcie Diaz, Kim Coons, Ann Gale, Ame Gasque, Bruce Hare, Joe King, Mike Magley, Kristi Ogle, Shirl Parsons, Joe Patterson, Bill Porter, David Schubert, Stewart Stoker, Ken Thomas, and Susanna Wallace.

All the volunteers listed on the next page who walked trails, researched destinations, and provided insight and information for the first and subsequent editions of *The Georgia Conservancy's Guide to the North Georgia Mountains*, now known as *The Highroad Guide to the Georgia Mountains*, have helped make it the finest resource of its kind ever published.

Mountain Guidebook Volunteers

Cary Aiken
Judy Alderman
Walter Allen
John Ambrose
Pat Axsiom
Crawford Barnett
Tracy Battle
Peter Beney
Joseph Biesbrock
Toby Blalock
Polly Boggess
Steve Bowling
Brian Boyd
Gary Breece
Fred Brown
J. Marion Brown Jr.
John M. Brown
Barbara Burch
Elmer Butler
Jack Byrne*
Larry Caldwell
Darcy Camp
Chris Canalos
Terry Centner
Linda Chafin
Henry Chambers
Bob Clark
Linda Cobb
Nancy Coile
Taylor Crockett
Edwin Dale
Tony Darnell
Lisa Davis
Chris deForest
Jeanne deSana
Jim deSana
Huck DeVenzio
Harriett DiGioia
Mary Lou Dixon
Marty Dominy
Frank Drago
Diana Durden
Lisha Duvaritanea
Bo Edwards

Lamar Edwards
Bud Elsea
Betty Fairley
Willard Fairley
Larry Farist
Elaine Fatora
Pat Fincher
Henry Finkbeiner
Louise Franklin
Dave Funderburk
Mozelle Funderburk
Chick Gaddy
Jerry German
Frank Golley
Priscilla Golley
David Gomez
Norma Gordon
Vernon Gordon*
Tom Govus
Alyce Graham
Delbert Greear
Mildred Greear
Philip Greear
Wilson Hall
Fran Hallahan
Jane Harrell
Baker Harrison
Mahala Harrison
Anne Heath
Maryann Herbermann
Linda Hinton
Jan Holland
Amy Horne
Carol Howel-Gomez
Bob Humphries
Dick Hurd
Janet Hurlburt
Mary Ann Johnson
Nell Jones
Bill Kaliher
Lorraine Kaliher
Eleanor Kelly
Bob Kerr
Carolyn Kidd

Jim Kidd
Reggie Kimsey
Mark Kinzer
Peter Kirby
Tom Knight
Christy Lambert
Anthony Lampros
Bobby Ledford
Debra Lee
Terry McCallum
Frank McCamey
Jerry McFalls
George McGee
Ed McGowin
Lucia McGowin
Gwyn McKee
Jim Mackay
Kathy Mackay
Pat Marcellino
Brian Markwalter
Holly Markwalter
Frances Mason
Barbara Massey
Marie Mellinger
Bill Mitchell
Michelle Moran
Ed Morgan
Marilou Morgan
Mark Morrison
Paul Nelson
Sharon Nelson
Hans Neuhauser
Steve Nix
Carolyn Nourse
Hugh Nourse*
Mark Ogilvie
Martha O'Kelley
Steven Pagano
Dan Patillo
Tom Perrie
Ray Pierotti
Annette Ranger
Scott Ranger
Ted Reissing
Jim Renner

Ann Rhea
Rope Roberts
Carol Schneier
Damaris Schotsmans
Diana Shadday
Ed Shanahan
Sandy Shobe
Nancy Shofner
Becky Shortland
Judy Silverman
Bob Slack
Andy Smith
Cina Smith
Sherri Smith
Betty Smithgall
Brian Smithgall
Annice Snyder
Lloyd Snyder
Marvin Sowder
Rosalie Splitter
Mary Jane Warren Stone
Kathryn Stout
Allen Stovall
Miriam Talmadge
Al Tate
Alice Taylor
Claude Terry
Michael Terry
Dale Thorpe
Bill Timpone
Dawn Townsend
Richard Tunkle
Ann Vanderbeek
Glen Vanderbeek
Donna Wear Veal
Sheila Ward
Richard Ware
Burt Weerts
Charles Wharton
Endra Widianarko
Kristin Williams
Sue Worley
Janie Yearwood
Bob Zahner
Glenda Zahner

* Team Leaders

The Natural History of the Georgia Mountains

By Charles Wharton, Ph.D., Institute of Ecology, The University of Georgia

Our north Georgia mountains are masses of ancient rock on which life has but a tenuous foothold. A short history of the area's geology helps us appreciate nature's management of such finite entities as water, air, and soil in such remarkably beautiful surroundings. Moreover, greater knowledge of the function of ecological systems like the southern Appalachian bioregion is essential for the survival of man as a part of—not apart from—the natural world. This understanding, transcending economic and political considerations, now becomes the major bridge uniting peoples of the earth. Compared with the youthful Rockies or Himala-

[*Above*: Rock Town on Pigeon Mountain]

yas, Georgia's mountains are hoary with age. Some of the basement rocks, or roots, of the early Blue Ridge formed over a billion years ago. The bulk of our mountains, however, was derived from ancient marine sediments between 200 and 450 million years ago. These sediments, such as sands and silts, were transformed or metamorphosed into the hard rock that forms the backbone of the Blue Ridge. This was accomplished by uplift, heat, and pressure resulting from enormous forces generated by the collision of North America with other drifting continents.

Look at any rock face exposed in highway cuts such as at Hog Pen Gap on the Richard Russell Scenic Highway or at Woodall Shoals on the Chattooga River. Here it can be seen how heat and pressure deep within the earth caused near-molten rock to flow and fold into visible contortions. In the western part of the Blue Ridge, the rocks were less metamorphosed by these processes.

Least changed of all were the thick beds of sediments in northwest Georgia. Here, sands hardened into sandstone, and mud or silt into shale, while the shells of minute marine life became limestone. These rocks show little of the folding and distortion that you see east of the great fault line between Chatsworth and Cartersville which divides the Valley and Ridge from the Western Blue Ridge.

Regardless of bedrock type, however, most forest communities form soils that are remarkably similar. Normally, about 22 minerals occur in most rock types; two or three others are supplied by atmospheric fallout. These minerals are carefully concentrated and recycled by the forest. Occasionally, where carbonate rocks, such as limestone, outcrop near the surface, unique plants grow and require lots of calcium, as at Pigeon Mountain or Panther Creek. Sometimes, when rocks are low in some essential minerals, as at Buck Creek, a peculiar pine barren community develops.

Stripped of their forest cover, our Blue Ridge Mountains would resemble Stone Mountain. The thin skin of soil that hides their nakedness is made possible only by plant life, aided by abundant rainfall. Unless one has seen the bare rock where the entire side of a mountain has slid off, or gazed into Toxaway Gorge, it is hard to understand how important the vegetation cover is and how powerful the force of water is.

While collisions with other continents slowly raised the Appalachians, rains kept eroding them almost as fast as they were uplifted. Incredibly, geologists claim that a thickness of from 5 to 10 miles of Appalachian mountain rock has disintegrated and washed downhill in the last 300 million years. These sediments formed south Georgia, the coastal landforms and much of the continental shelf. Rains from the sun-powered water cycle are still trying to wash our mountains away, but nature has developed a remarkably tough and protective forest cover that slows down this process.

Ironically, the mountain forest cannot exist without this 5 to 8 feet of water that pours down in a single year. The mountain forests are expert in conserving and managing this precious substance through many millennia of trial and error. The forest operates as a soil-building and water-holding device, powered by solar energy.

The excess water not used by the system runs off as streams and rivers which we can, with wisdom, use ourselves. While there are mountain "products" other than water, we must never lose sight of the primary value of the mountains—the cost-free (to us) management of rock, soil, water, air, life, and sun energy. Anything that man does there must be prefaced with the question, "Are we compromising or damaging these vital life-support functions?"

Our mountains have been forested for at least 2 million years. Unglaciated during this time, they have stood as temperate-zone refuges for a diverse assemblage of terrestrial plants and animals, perhaps unequalled outside of the tropical rainforest. Biologically speaking, a trip up a 6,000-foot mountain is equivalent to driving 1,000 miles north. Because of this, many species of plants and animals can live in our mountains, especially in north-facing coves where it is always moist and cool. Once, boreal spruce-fir forests, such as now clothe much of Canada, covered our Georgia mountains, with alpine tundra on the highest peaks. When the climate warmed, these cold-adapted environments disappeared. Along the highest elevations of the Georgia Blue Ridge, they left behind some ice-age animal life—relicts such as the red-back vole and perhaps the red squirrel.

From the top of our highest peaks, as far as the eye can see, mountain slopes appear to be clothed in a uniform sea of green. Actually, this vista is not at all uniform, for what one sees is a remarkable mosaic of various combinations of rock, soil, plants, and animals organized into specific environments. Some of these combinations are considered by ecologists as communities, associations, or forest types. Each is adapted to certain slopes, temperatures, soil depths, compass exposures, and rainfall.

Described below are the major natural environments that occur in the Georgia mountains and are often encountered in the text.

Shrub Balds and/or Rock Balds. [Fig. 2(A)] Examples are Brasstown Bald [Fig. 30(6)], parts of Standing Indian [Fig. 34(15)], Pickens Nose [Fig. 39(11)], Tray Mountain [Fig. 29], and Blood Mountain [Fig. 24]. At the highest elevations, which were once alpine tundra, we now find Catawba rhododendron, mountain ash, and dwarf willow as plants characteristic of the shrub bald. Some mountains are called "balds" but have forested tops. Hightower Bald and Dick's Knob have, for example, dwarfed oak forests covering their summits. There may be a thick understory of beaked hazelnut or another shrub.

Boulderfields. [Fig. 2(B)] Lying just down slope from the summit of most of our peaks are boulderfields, which fill the top part of north- and northwest-facing coves, particularly if there is seeping or running water. The jumbled mass of boulders has resulted from ice-wedging during the Pleistocene period, perhaps 20,000 years ago. Boulderfields seldom extend below 3,200 feet. Although the moss-covered boulders are difficult to walk across, they are a photographer's delight and are most photogenic after leaf fall. In spite of the rocky nature of this environment, spring wildflowers are abundant. Trees such as yellow birch and basswood may occur. Perhaps the "best" boulderfield is on the north face of Tray Mountain [Fig. 29] between the summit and Corbin Creek Road. The one most accessible by car lies just above the parking area at Sosebee Cove [Fig. 24(5)] where, with diligent search, a few rare yellowwood trees may be found.

Northern Hardwoods. [Fig. 2(C)] This forest type usually lies between the boulderfields and the cove hardwoods (below), generally above 3,000 feet. Buckeye, basswood, and yellow birch are diagnostic. Sometimes beech and sugar maple may be present. This environment has exceptional wildflower displays. The dense, often knee-deep herb layer helps create a deep, black, loamy soil. Expect to find the mountain garlic or ramp (*Allium tricoccum*), spring beauty, ginseng, squirrel corn, Dutchman's breeches, waterleaf, and umbrella leaf. The giant hellebore (*Veratrum viride*) may be present. Three wood ferns are characteristic: Goldie's, marginal, and intermediate. The higher the elevation, the rarer the herbaceous plants.

To see the upper limit of the hardwood forest and a boulderfield, hike the old Wagon Train Trail [Fig. 30(1)] at Brasstown Bald. Around on the north face just below the tower are giant yellow birch festooned with "old man's beard" lichen and dripping with moisture from cloud condensation. This environment is Georgia's only cloud forest. This relict community is extremely vulnerable to fire or logging.

Cove Forests. [Fig. 2(D)] Below the northern hardwoods is the more extensive cove hardwood forest. There is a greater diversity of trees here, including various oaks, tulip poplar, ash, silverbell, and magnolia. Before the chestnut blight of the 1930s, many cove forests were full of chestnut trees. Since tulip poplars are present in most cove forests and have wind-borne seeds, they were able to seed in on the death of the chestnut.

Poplar also follows overintensive logging, as below the parking area in Sosebee's Cove. The whitish stumps of dead chestnut can still be seen in many coves. Old mountain pastures often reverted to almost pure stands of poplar. Near-original old growth cove forest can be seen in the northeast sector of the Cooper Creek Scenic Area [Fig. 22]. There, the dead chestnut logs were removed and sawed up on the spot. Some of the old poplars, some 18 feet in circumference, still remain, standing among huge white and red oaks. While shrubs are limited in cove forests, a variety of herbs is present, depending on soil depth and moisture.

Hemlock/Heath Forests. [Fig. 2(E)] Below the cove hardwood forest and often extending up the streams through it, grows the moisture-loving Canadian hemlock, with its delicate, evergreen foliage. It generally always has an understory of the common, evergreen rosebay rhododendron, which is a member of the heath family. Rhododendron may create nearly impenetrable thickets. This is one of the challenges facing trout fishermen where there are no trails. Few herbs are present. This environment may be seen along the lower reaches of Mulky Creek [Fig. 22(1)] near the Cooper Creek Scenic Area. A few large hemlocks remain on Soapstone Creek along the drive to Jack's Gap [Fig. 30(9)].

White Pine Forests. [Fig. 2(F)] There is some question as to the existence of stands of white pine prior to human clearing, logging, and fire prevention (white pine is very sensitive to fire). Some very beautiful open stands of white pine occur along the Chattooga River, especially above Burrell's Ford Bridge [Fig. 48(11)] and along the Reed Creek bottoms [Fig. 43(22), Fig. 44(26)] north of the Russell Bridge. Much white pine can also be seen from the Richard Russell Scenic Highway and near the Cooper Creek Scenic Area. It is believed that originally the white pine grew as scattered trees in fire-protected areas in places like the extensive bluffs along the Chattooga River. White pines are less prone to beetle attack than are the successional stands of Virginia pine which follow environmental disturbance at low elevations throughout much of the Blue Ridge.

Slope Forests. [Fig. 2(G)] These are mostly oak-hickory-chestnut forests and cover the most terrain of any environment. The chestnut—unfortunately for the wildlife which fattened for the winter on its nuts—is gone, except as sprouts and small trees at high elevations. Slope forests vary tremendously in species composition that, in turn, depends on soil depth, percent slope, compass exposure, and so on. Given sufficient soil moisture, white oak will dominate. Sourwood and black gum thrive on drier sites. Hickories are adaptable and widespread. While the herbaceous plants are not as rare and interesting as those in mountain coves, they are numerous. As distinguished from the cove forests, the slope forests have an abundance of shrubs. Blueberries are widespread under more open canopies here, as well as on ridges. Sweetshrub and buffalo nut (a favorite deer food) are common, as are azaleas. On drier sites horsesugar is outstanding.

Ridge Forests. [Fig. 2(H)] Among the types of ridge forests, the high elevation oak ridge forest is outstanding. This forest covers the higher ridges of the Blue Ridge, such as those traversed by the Appalachian Trail. This forest, mostly virgin red oak, has trees that are dwarfed and limby. A 12-inch-diameter tree may be 100 years old. These old growth ridge forests were rarely logged, since the trunks were too short. Sometimes, as in the Cohuttas, white oaks may dominate. High-altitude ridge forests have a variety of attractive understory plants. From Standing Indian [Fig 34(15)], one descends through tunnels of Catawba or purple rhododendron. Elsewhere, flame azalea dominates, or ferns (New York, hayscented), beautiful little wiry sedges, or grasses may carpet the ridgeline. In summer, dense herb growth may encroach, particularly white snakeroot (*Eupatorium rugosum*), one of the plants suspected of causing the "milk sick" that killed numerous settlers who grazed cattle in the mountains.

A variety of blueberries occupies mountain ridges, which are more open than cove forests. The highbush blueberry (*Vaccinium constablei*) is associated with high-elevation red oak forests. On rocky, white oak ridge forests, both deerberry (*V. stamineum*) and buckberry (*Gaylussacia ursina*) occur, while on lower, drier ridges the low blueberry (*V. vacillans*) forms thick ground cover. Grouse and bear feast on blueberries in summer and fall.

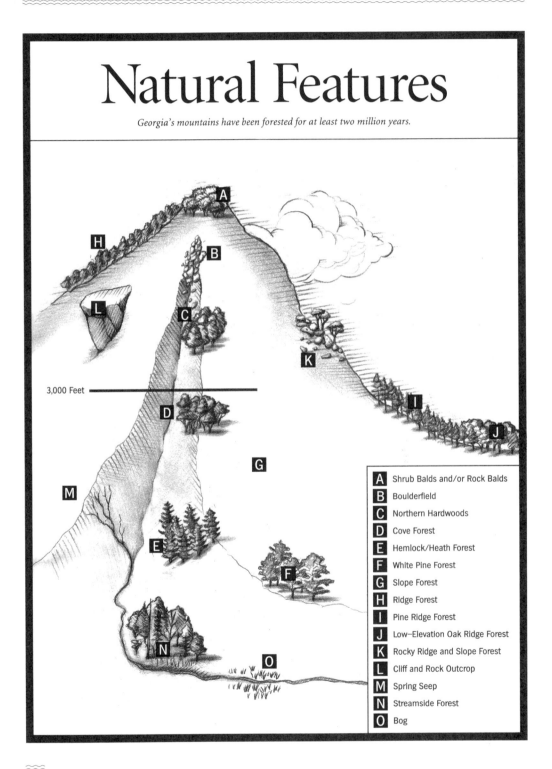

Natural Features

Georgia's mountains have been forested for at least two million years.

3,000 Feet

A	Shrub Balds and/or Rock Balds
B	Boulderfield
C	Northern Hardwoods
D	Cove Forest
E	Hemlock/Heath Forest
F	White Pine Forest
G	Slope Forest
H	Ridge Forest
I	Pine Ridge Forest
J	Low–Elevation Oak Ridge Forest
K	Rocky Ridge and Slope Forest
L	Cliff and Rock Outcrop
M	Spring Seep
N	Streamside Forest
O	Bog

Another type of ridge forest is a pine ridge forest. At higher elevations, the pines are chiefly table mountain pine, which seems to prefer rocks and cliff edges. It is common on ridges off the south face of Rabun Bald [Fig. 41(10)] and along the edge of the Cedar Cliffs along Big Creek [Fig. 44(3)] and occurs along the rim of Tallulah Gorge. At lower elevations, pitch pine is dominant, as on the scenic road across Patterson Gap [Fig. 38(25)], where the rare sweetfern grows in the herb layer. The soils of these pine communities appear drier and more acid. Various acid-loving heaths occur in the understory. There is a low-elevation hardwood ridge forest, a "dry" forest, which is widespread. Three oaks tend to predominate: scarlet, post, and southern red.

Rocky Ridges and Slope Forests. [Fig. 2(K)] Chestnut oaks tend to dominate on rocky ridges in the Blue Ridge and on slopes where the soil is thin and rocky. The upper, west-facing slopes of Lookout Mountain are often largely chestnut oak. On the western flank of Pigeon Mountain near The Pocket, in what can be called a limestone terrace environment, is a curious forest of chinquapin oak, red cedar, and the rather rare smoketree.

Cliffs and Rock Outcrops. [Fig. 2(L)] Our Blue Ridge is really solid rock with only a thin veneer of soil held by plant roots. When it is too steep for plants to stabilize, a naked cliff emerges. If the rock is perennially wet, very rare northern or tropical ferns and mosses may occur (Cullasaja Gorge [Fig. 49(2)], Escarpment Gorges [Fig. 51(1,2,3)]). Around drier cliffs (Tallulah Gorge [Fig. 38(2)], Satulah Mountain [Fig. 49], Cedar Cliffs [Fig. 44(4)]), you may see two rare conifers, Carolina hemlock and table mountain pine. Around and above cliffs on the north side of high ridges, rosebay rhododendron prevails; on the drier south side, mountain laurel. The highest rocky tops almost always bear the gorgeous purple rhododendron. In some moist, rocky areas at lower elevations (Tallulah Falls), Carolina rhododendron predominates. Big dense patches of evergreen heaths are known by the mountaineers as "slicks" or "hells." Mountaineers also call rhododendron "laurel" and mountain laurel "ivy." One of the most remarkable environments on an outcrop is called a cedar glade. In Georgia, it is found in the Chickamauga and Chattanooga National Military Park. It occurs on shallow-soiled, limestone slopes and low ridges. It is a shrub-free area thick with red cedars, along with old, dwarfed chinquapin oaks and with rare grasses and herbs allied to those of midwestern prairies. This is the only Georgia outlier of vast glades that cover central Tennessee. Red cedars are also common along the rocky bluffs in the Valley and Ridge and sometimes occur on rock outcrops in the Blue Ridge, as on top of Chimney Mountain [Fig. 29(58)].

Streamside Forests. [Fig. 2(N)] Along most of our rivers and larger streams, a streamside forest grows. This is distinguished by colorful and often rare trees and shrubs. Hemlocks and rosebay rhododendron are generally present. The rocky, more open bluffs support small trees such as the rare mountain camellia (*Stewartia*), serviceberry, and witch hazel. If moist enough, the environment supports mountain pepperbush, viburnums, and alders, either as shrubs or as small trees. Dense evergreen thickets of dog hobble, also known as leucothoe, are common. Characteristic herbs, such as yellowroot, may be present.

Bogs and Spring Seeps. [Fig. 2(O, M)] Bogs and spring seeps are wetlands. Bogs were formerly widespread on floodplains and on colluvial, or unflooded, flats. As in the "flats" near Rabun Bald [Fig. 41(1)] and in Horse Cove near Highlands, NC, landowners have unwittingly or intentionally destroyed their irreplaceable bogs. Bogs are often replete with rare boreal or arctic plant species and are the only known haunts of rare northern turtles. They are a habitat for several orchids and lilies such as the swamp pink (*Helonias*). The second largest bog complex south of the Pink Beds near Brevard, NC, is that along the Nantahala River south of White Oak Bottoms campground [Fig. 34]. These areas are under strict protection because man has eliminated most of them. They must not be disturbed.

Sagponds and Limesinks. Sagponds are northwest Georgia's equivalent of south Georgia's limesinks. Several sagponds occur on top of Pigeon Mountain. Scientists consider them valuable. They have drilled down through deep peat layers, which accumulate in sagponds, and identified ancient pollen that helped determine the vegetation of the area during the Ice Age. A large sagpond on the Chickamauga and Chattanooga National Military Park [Fig. 5] has a stand of large (36-inch diameter), buttressed willow oaks growing on it. A more famous sagpond on the park is called Bloody Pond, named after a Civil War battle.

Giant dry sinks found near Pigeon Mountain [Fig. 8] may have interesting plants, such as the glade fern, growing in them. Since there is no standing water, they contain a moist oak-hickory forest rather than the swamp black gum and marsh vegetation of wet sagponds. They are so large that going down inside one is like descending the slope of a mountain.

EASTERN MOLE (Scalopus aquaticus)

Spending most of its life underground, the mole feeds on earthworms and insect larvae in its passageway of tunnels 10 inches below the surface. It is identified by a pink snout, hairless tail, and furry body that grows to 6 inches.

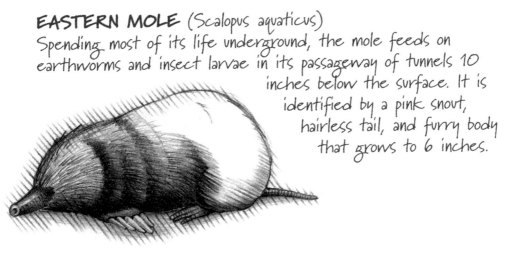

Geologic Time Scale

Era	System & Period	Series & Epoch	Some Distinctive Features	Years Before Present
CENOZOIC	Quaternary	Recent	Modern man.	11,000
		Pleistocene	Early man; northern glaciation.	1/2 to 2 million
	Tertiary	Pliocene	Large carnivores.	13 ± 1 million
		Miocene	First abundant grazing mammals.	25 ± 1 million
		Oligocene	Large running mammals.	36 ± 2 million
		Eocene	Many modern types of mammals.	58 ± 2 million
		Paleocene	First placental mammals.	63 ± 2 million
MESOZOIC	Cretaceous		First flowering plants; climax of dinosaurs and ammonites, followed by Cretaceous-Tertiary extinction.	135 ± 5 million
	Jurassic		First birds, first mammals; dinosaurs and ammonites abundant.	181 ± 5 million
	Triassic		First dinosaurs. Abundant cycads and conifers.	230 ± 10 million
PALEOZOIC	Permian		Extinction of most kinds of marine animals, including trilobites. Southern glaciation.	280 ± 10 million
	Carboniferous	Pennsylvanian	Great coal forests, conifers. First reptiles.	310 ± 10 million
		Mississippian	Sharks and amphibians abundant. Large and numerous scale trees and seed ferns.	345 ± 10 million
	Devonian		First amphibians and ammonites; Fishes abundant.	405 ± 10 million
	Silurian		First terrestrial plants and animals.	425 ± 10 million
	Ordovician		First fishes; invertebrates dominant.	500 ± 10 million
	Cambrian		First abundant record of marine life; trilobites dominant.	600 ± 50 million
	Precambrian		Fossils extremely rare, consisting of primitive aquatic plants. Evidence of glaciation. Oldest date algae, over 2,600 million years; oldest dated meteorites 4,500 million years.	

Cumberland Plateau & Valley and Ridge

This area is also called the "sedimentary region" because of rocky beds of sandstone, shale, coal, and limestone that were formed from deposits of the shallow seas that covered this area in Paleozoic times.

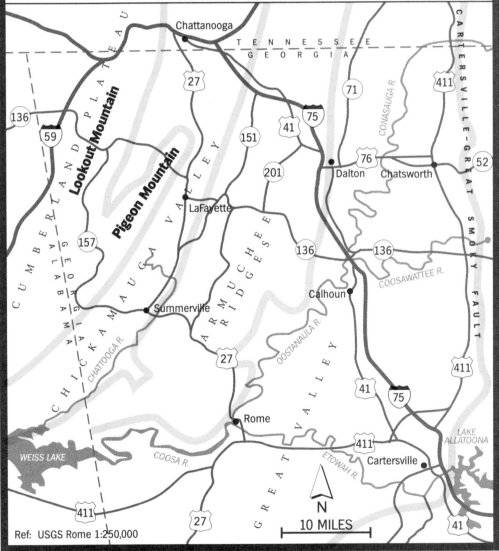

Ref: USGS Rome 1:250,000

The Cumberland Plateau and the Valley and Ridge

Northwest Georgia is here divided into four parts—the Cumberland Plateau, the Chickamauga Valley, the Armuchee Ridges, and the Great Valley. The Chickamauga Valley, Armuchee Ridges, and Great Valley are collectively known as the Valley and Ridge. Physiographers consider the Cumberland Plateau to be part of a larger area to the west, the Appalachian Plateau province, which extends from Alabama northeastward through Tennessee and Kentucky. Northwest Georgia is distinctly divided from the remainder of the Georgia mountains to the east by a great break in the earth's surface called the Cartersville–Great Smoky Fault. Strange-looking rocks, arranged in layers and often embellished with fossil sea life, tell the

[*Above*: Cloudland Canyon in the Cumberland Plateau Province]

visitor that he is in a quite different world from the more familiar Blue Ridge Mountains. Here in the northwest one finds long, linear ridges alternating with equally long valleys and straight streams—unlike the irregular mix of peaks and valleys in the Blue Ridge, where the drainage is dendritic like the branches of a tree.

This area is also called the "sedimentary region" because its rocky beds of sandstone, shale, coal, and limestone are clearly recognizable as having once been, respectively, sand, mud, plants, and marine life deposited in shallow seas that covered this area in Paleozoic times. The mountains may be flat-topped especially in the Cumberland Plateau, where the more nearly horizontal beds occur in "layer-cake" fashion, the younger ones lying on top.

This was an era of ancient life—largely marine invertebrates and primitive fishes. Between 300 and 425 million years ago (Mississippian and Silurian periods), these animals were entombed as fossils in various types of ocean floor materials—some in the limy shells of tiny organisms which formed limestone, and others in mud which became shale. These older animal fossils are most easily found in the Armuchee Ridges. During the Carboniferous or "coal measures" some 300 million years ago, the top of the Cumberland Plateau was the scene of swamps and fertile deltas. These deposits now yield plant fossils as well as coal deposits. Fossils are found in northwest Georgia because heat and pressure were not great enough to destroy them, as happened in the Blue Ridge.

The long, southwest-northeast-trending, limestone-floored valleys have been natural corridors for the passage of Coastal Plain life into the interior of Appalachia. Man, too, has used these fertile corridors in agriculture and in war. Because these plateaus, ridges, and natural passageways are coupled with extensive beds of mineral-rich carbonate rocks, one finds many plants and animals here which occur nowhere else in the Georgia mountains. The caves, springs, sinkholes, and animals (such as the cottonmouth water moccasin) of the Cumberland Plateau and Valley and Ridge are not what one would expect to find in the northern part of our state; hence, this area seems more closely allied with southwest Georgia than with the Blue Ridge. Also, a number of plants and animals that seem rare to us range into Georgia only here, representing species more commonly found to the west in areas such as the Cumberland Mountains of Tennessee and Kentucky.

Rugged and isolated, this is a region with its own geography, color, and personality. The landscape is dominated not only by the 84-mile-long Lookout Mountain, but also by the dramatic interplay of clouds and sunlight across the mountain and its valleys. Little wonder former residents chose place names like Cloudland, Craigsmere, Rocktown, and Lookout. This is a land relatively unknown until recently to tourists, casual visitors, or even outdoor recreational enthusiasts, who have long been attracted to the mountains in the eastern part of the state. It has remained the province of local inhabitants; summer residents around Mentone, Alabama; adventurous cavers; and hang gliders seeking the best takeoff point on the East Coast. Those who discover this region are soon under its spell and find themselves returning again and again.

The Cumberland Plateau

The Cumberland Plateau begins near Birmingham, Alabama, and crosses the extreme northwest corner of Georgia before entering Tennessee just to the west of Chattanooga. Northwest of Knoxville, the plateau becomes highly dissected due to erosion, and the region—although geologically still a plateau—is called the Cumberland Mountains.

The two principal features of the Cumberland Plateau in Georgia are Sand Mountain and Lookout Mountain, which are separated by 2-mile-wide Lookout Valley, in which the towns of Trenton and Rising Fawn are located.

From a physiographic standpoint, the flat-topped mountains of the Cumberland Plateau are quite different from the narrow Armuchee Ridges beyond the Chickamauga Valley to the east. Geologically, the Cumberland Plateau is transitional between the flat-lying sedimentary beds of central Tennessee and the ridges and valleys to the east in Georgia, which show more intensive folding and faulting.

The flat top of the Cumberland Plateau is sandstone which, while harder than limestone or shale, has nevertheless been carved and sculpted for millions of years by wind and water. Because of a tendency to fracture into squarish blocks, the sandstone has weathered into fantastic boulder formations in places like Rocktown and the Zahnd Tract, commercially called "rock cities." In addition, thick layers of soft, water-soluble limestone undergird the Cumberland Plateau. Because the top is actually slightly concave, surface water accumulates and seeps downward through cracks and crevices, where it dissolves the limestone and creates miles of underground passages or caves, issuing forth at numerous springs around the base of the mountain.

The great gulfs, or canyons, eroded in the sides of the Cumberland Plateau are spectacular in a geologic, biotic, and scenic sense. Two on Lookout Mountain are notable—a wide canyon known as Johnson's Crook, and a narrow one called Sitton's Gulch and renamed Cloudland Canyon.

Pigeon Mountain, a thumblike protrusion from Lookout Mountain, deserves special mention. It is a geological, botanical, and zoological treasure house. Happily, most of it was purchased by Heritage Trust funds under the farsighted Carter administration.

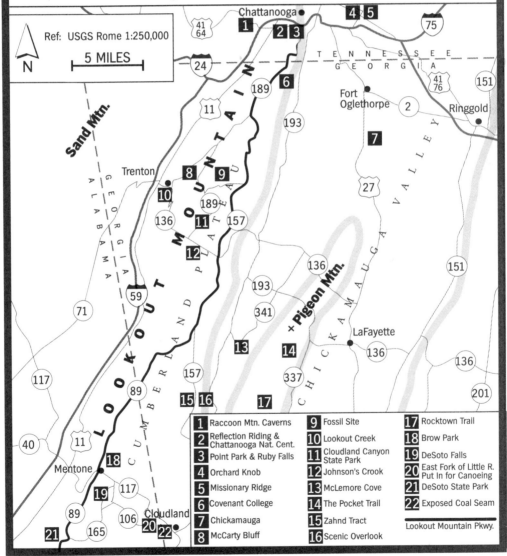

Cumberland Plateau North

*Two primary features of the Cumberland Plateau
in Georgia are Lookout Mountain and Sand Mountain.*

Ref: USGS Rome 1:250,000

5 MILES

N

Chattanooga
Trenton
Fort Oglethorpe
Ringgold
LaFayette
Mentone
Cloudland

Sand Mtn.
LOOKOUT MOUNTAIN PLATEAU
Pigeon Mtn.
CHICKAMAUGA VALLEY
CUMBERLAND

GEORGIA
ALABAMA
TENNESSEE
GEORGIA

1	Raccoon Mtn. Caverns	9	Fossil Site	17	Rocktown Trail
2	Reflection Riding & Chattanooga Nat. Cent.	10	Lookout Creek	18	Brow Park
3	Point Park & Ruby Falls	11	Cloudland Canyon State Park	19	DeSoto Falls
4	Orchard Knob	12	Johnson's Crook	20	East Fork of Little R. Put In for Canoeing
5	Missionary Ridge	13	McLemore Cove	21	DeSoto State Park
6	Covenant College	14	The Pocket Trail	22	Exposed Coal Seam
7	Chickamauga	15	Zahnd Tract		Lookout Mountain Pkwy.
8	McCarty Bluff	16	Scenic Overlook		

Lookout Mountain

Lookout Mountain is the southernmost extension of the Cumberland Plateau, which is parallel to but inland from the Blue Ridge Mountains. Long and relatively flat on top, it extends for 84 miles in a diagonal that cuts across Alabama, Georgia, and Tennessee. There are 3 miles of Lookout Mountain in Tennessee, 31 in Georgia, and 50 in Alabama. The mountain is in one of the world's richest cave regions.

LOOKOUT MOUNTAIN PARKWAY

[Fig. 5] The designation is sometimes confusing because the "parkway" includes several roads, not just one. Nevertheless, this multihighway driving route provides visitors to the region with an overview of the dramatic piece of geography between Gadsden, Alabama, and Chattanooga, Tennessee, that is Lookout Mountain. The route begins in Gadsden as AL 176 and runs in a northeasterly direction to Chattanooga. The mountain can be traversed not only in a north-south direction, but east-west as well. Visitors who explore county roads across the width of the mountain will have a better understanding of how this long, flat mountain of the Cumberland Plateau differs from the peaks and ridges of the Blue Ridge Mountains.

REFLECTION RIDING AND THE CHATTANOOGA NATURE CENTER

[(Fig. 5(2)] Reflection Riding is a 300-acre nature preserve along Lookout Creek at the base of Lookout Mountain. It adjoins 2,000-acre Point Park and Lookout Mountain Battlefield National Military Park. The area is maintained in the style of an English natural landscape and is crisscrossed by winding paths and graveled roads. It gains its name from Reflection Pond, a landmark on the property, and the English word "riding," which means an inviting pleasure path. The Great Indian War Path and the St. Augustine and Cisca Trail crossed Reflection Riding. Hernando De Soto's troops followed the Great Indian War Path over this area looking for gold. A gristmill operated by two Cherokees was on this site. Only the millstones remain today. In 1863 Union forces under General Hooker crossed Lookout Creek to engage the Confederate Army in the Battle of Lookout Mountain. Markers describing the battle are placed at many points along the drive.

Deep gorges, rock fields, and moss-covered boulders provide interesting topography as well as shelter for many species of birds and other wildlife. The edges of Lookout Creek furnish habitat for bog plants, frogs, and other small water creatures. Wildflowers and grasses cover the open meadows. Native rhododendron and azaleas have been planted on the mountain slope. The forest is predominantly oak with scattered groves of pine. The 12 miles of trails are well marked and make for relatively easy walking. All of the trails are interconnected, so a hike can be as long or short as desired and flexible in destination. From the park border trail and the driving loop, there are connections to the National Park Service trails. Maps are available at

Cumberland Plateau South

The top of the Cumberland Plateau is flat and composed of sandstone.

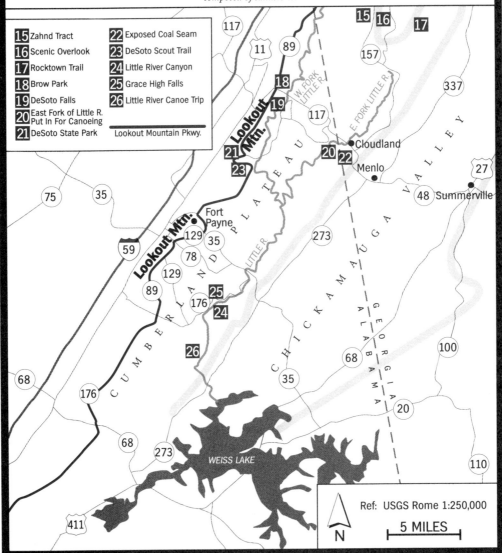

15 Zahnd Tract
16 Scenic Overlook
17 Rocktown Trail
18 Brow Park
19 DeSoto Falls
20 East Fork of Little R. Put In For Canoeing
21 DeSoto State Park

22 Exposed Coal Seam
23 DeSoto Scout Trail
24 Little River Canyon
25 Grace High Falls
26 Little River Canoe Trip

Lookout Mountain Pkwy.

Ref: USGS Rome 1:250,000

5 MILES

N

WEISS LAKE

Cloudland
Menlo
Summerville
Fort Payne

the nature center. The wetland walkway, accessible to handicapped visitors with wheelchairs, leads from the road in front of the nature center through the animal habitats to a lovely overlook beside the creek.

Along the 3-mile driving loop, most of the trees and shrubs are identified, as are points of historical interest. During the blooming seasons of spring, summer, and fall, a variety of wildflowers can be seen. Plant identification guides corresponding to the numbered plant labels are available at the nature center. There are frequent stopping places along the way. Surrounded by ferns, the secluded gazebo overlooking Siren Pool has benches and shade where visitors can sit quietly and relax. The screened pavilion at the fragrance garden has benches and outside picnic tables.

Located at the gateway to Reflection Riding, the nature center features passive solar-designed buildings containing a wildlife diorama, exhibits, a library, resource collections, and a gift shop. An auditorium and solar greenhouse are next to the wildlife rehabilitation laboratory, where visitors can visit injured and orphaned wild animals, including hawks and owls. On weekends, programs including workshops, films, classes and interpretive walks are offered. Special programs are available upon request. Hand-fed Canada geese, mallards, and wood ducks are year-round residents of Reflection Pond. Visitors are allowed to feed them. The nature center also offers a summer day camp and an annual wildflower walk in mid-April.

Directions: From I-24 in Chattanooga take Brown's Ferry Road Exit south onto US 41; turn left onto TN 318; right onto Garden Road; right (south) into Reflection Riding and Nature Center. Garden Road is also reached from Scenic Highway 148.

For more information: Reflection Riding and Chattanooga Nature Center, 400 Garden Road, Chattanooga, TN 37419. Phone (423) 821-1160 or (423) 821-9582.

CAVES OF LOOKOUT MOUNTAIN

Here in the northwest corner of Georgia, the northeast corner of Alabama, and the southern part of Tennessee, cavers have discovered a region linked by the Cumberland Plateau and characterized by a vast network of caves cut through limestone rock. To cavers this region is not Tennessee, Alabama, and Georgia, but "TAG." They come from all over the world to explore its labyrinthine underground passages. Tennessee alone has more than 5,500 caves—more than any other state. Ellison's Cave on Georgia's Pigeon Mountain is the deepest cave east of the Mississippi River.

A few caves in the region are commercial, open to the public for a fee. These include famous caves such as Ruby Falls in Lookout Mountain and lesser-known sites such as Sequoyah Caverns near Valley Head, Alabama. Business volume varies greatly at different caves. Raccoon Mountain Caverns estimates some 10,000 visitors a year, while perhaps 350,000 annually see Ruby Falls.

RACCOON MOUNTAIN CAVERNS

Fig [5(1)] The absence of props such as dramatic music and sophisticated lighting allows the visitor to experience the natural environment of the cave. Visitors may receive a personal tour by a knowledgeable caver. Wild tours—explorations of parts of the cave not normally seen by those taking commercial tours—last from two hours to overnight and are available by appointment only. Hard hats, lights, and other necessary caving equipment are furnished.

Directions: From I-24 at Tiftonia/Lookout Mountain Exit, go north on US 41 and follow signs. From Lookout Mountain, follow US 41 north.

For more information: Raccoon Mountain Caverns, 319 Hills Drive, Chattanooga, TN 37419. Phone (423) 821-9403.

RUBY FALLS

[Fig. 5(3)] This is the most heavily promoted and commercially successful cave in the Southeast. Visitors ride an elevator 260 feet down into the cavern. They then walk .4 mile one-way, past a variety of rock formations to Ruby Falls, with its 145-foot cascade lighted from below with multicolored spots and accompanied by the theme from the movie *2001*. Tour guides are cheerful and enthusiastic college students.

Facilities: Gift shop and lookout platform with good views of Chattanooga.

Directions: Main entrance is on TN 148, .5 mile off US 41, 11, 64, and 72. From I-24, take Exit 178 (Lookout Mountain Exit) and follow signs.

For more information: Ruby Falls, Scenic Highway, Chattanooga, TN 37409. Phone (423) 821-2544.

COVENANT COLLEGE

[Fig. 5(6)] Called the "Castle in the Clouds," a name first applied to the luxury hotel and gambling casino that occupied this site in the late 1920s, Covenant is a four-year, Presbyterian-affiliated college. A visit to the campus affords the visitor with the only unobstructed, 360-degree panorama of the country beyond the mountain.

Directions: Covenant College is on the Lookout Mountain Parkway, just south of the Tennessee/Georgia border. If approaching from Chattanooga, take Exit 178 on I-24 and follow the "See Rock City" signs until the Lookout Mountain Parkway signs and Covenant College signs are apparent. Approaching from the south on either GA SR 157 or GA SR 189, continue north and follow the Covenant College direction signs.

SUGAR MAPLE
(Acer saccharum)
Sugar maple's sap is the source of maple syrup and sugar.

MCCARTY BLUFF

[Fig. 5(8)] (Lookout Mountain Flight Park and Training Center). Sixty miles of ridgeline and the unique thermal-producing qualities of the valley floor make this the premier hang gliding site on the East Coast. Pilots from all over the world sail high above the Lookout Mountain Ridge and fly for hours up and down the valley. There is usually activity every day, and spectators get a close-up, breathtaking view of winged participants jumping off the sheer cliffside. The local flight-distance record is 154 miles. The pilot launched here and landed 70 miles east of Atlanta at Swords, Georgia. National and regional competitions are held here on a regular basis.

Directions: South of Chattanooga on GA 189, 7 miles north of GA 136.

For more information: For information on flight training and equipment, contact Lookout Mountain Flight Park and Training Center. Phone (706) 398-3541.

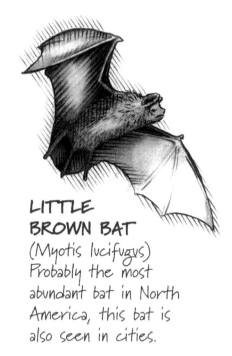

LITTLE BROWN BAT (Myotis lucifugus) Probably the most abundant bat in North America, this bat is also seen in cities.

FOSSIL SITE

[(Fig. 5(9)] Pennsylvanian plant fossils. Fossils to be found include tree fern–like plants called Sigillaria; small ferns such as Pecopteris, Alethopteris, Neuropteris, Archeopteris; and others.

Directions: From the intersection of GA 136 and GA 157 west of LaFayette, go north on GA 157 for 5.7 miles. Turn left on Durham Road and go .6 mile. There are large spoil banks on the right made up of minerals taken from coal mines nearby.

LOOKOUT CREEK

[Fig. 5(10)] Lookout Creek runs through Lookout Valley, along the base of Lookout Mountain. It begins just across the state line near the little town of Valley Head, Alabama. It then flows northeastward, slicing across the extreme northwestern corner of Georgia, then into Tennessee, where it empties into the mighty Tennessee River at the base of Lookout Mountain in Chattanooga. It weaves its way through Georgia for 30 miles, in and out of wilderness areas and pastureland, offering the canoeist briskly flowing flat waters and a moderate number of Class I shoals. Scenery varies dramatically during the 9-mile run between the put-in and take-out points described here. At one moment canoeists pass through heavy forests, the next through open pastureland that offers impressive views of Lookout Mountain, a constant companion to the east. Although the headwaters of Lookout Creek are

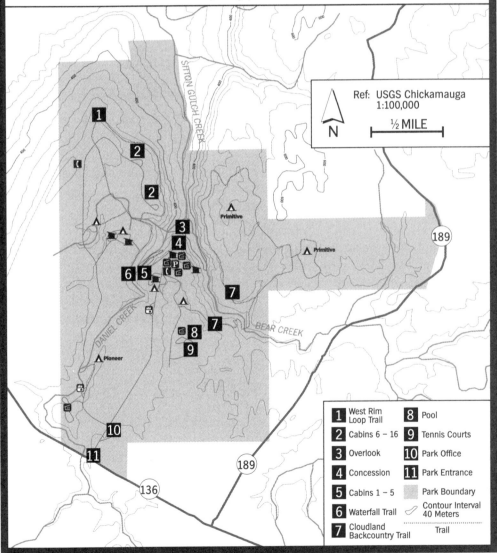

Cloudland Canyon State Park

The steepest cliffs in Cloudland Canyon were formed out of sandstone over 200 million years ago from an ancient shoreline.

Ref: USGS Chickamauga
1:100,000

½ MILE

N

1 West Rim Loop Trail		**8** Pool	
2 Cabins 6 – 16		**9** Tennis Courts	
3 Overlook		**10** Park Office	
4 Concession		**11** Park Entrance	
5 Cabins 1 – 5		Park Boundary	
6 Waterfall Trail		Contour Interval 40 Meters	
7 Cloudland Backcountry Trail		Trail	

scarcely a mile from the headwaters of Little River, these two neighboring rivers flow in opposite directions. The former flows north, placidly winding through Lookout Valley. The latter flows south, roaring violently down the spine of the mountain. The explanation is that although born in the same neighborhood, the streams belong to different watersheds. Lookout Creek belongs to the Tennessee Valley watershed; the Little River, to the Coosa Valley watershed. This fact also explains why Lookout Creek can maintain its water level, since it is filled by water running off the western slopes of the entire Lookout Mountain Plateau, while its rocky-bottomed neighbor up on the mountain, fed by a smaller watershed, can quickly run dry.

Directions: The take-out bridge is on GA 136, .7 mile east of where 136 meets US 11 in Trenton [Fig. 5(10)]. The best take-out spot, however, is not at the bridge but down a dirt road that runs south along the west side of the creek for .2 mile to a good access point above an old mill dam. To reach the put-in, return to Trenton on GA 136, turn left (south) on US 11 and drive 7.5 miles to Rising Fawn. Turn left (east) on Newsome Gap Road (County Road 197) and drive .3 mile to the put-in bridge.

CLOUDLAND CANYON STATE PARK

[Fig. 5(11), Fig. 7] Located on the western edge of Lookout Mountain, Cloudland Canyon is one of the largest and most scenic state parks in Georgia. The park provides visitors with beautiful vistas of the rugged geology of this area, and it is an excellent outdoor setting for the camper or hiker wanting to experience the beauty of the natural world. Cloudland was established in 1939 when the state of Georgia began the acquisi-

tion of land from several private landowners. Today it encompasses some 2,350 acres of beautiful mountain land. Until 1939, when construction of a Georgia highway through this area was finally completed, the only access was through Alabama or Tennessee. The park is perhaps one of the best places to view and understand the geology of northwest Georgia. An excellent guidebook, the *Geologic Guide to Cloudland Canyon State Park,* by Martha Griffin and Robert Atkins, is available at the park office. It discusses the fascinating geology of this area at ten stations around the rim trails and along the trails to waterfalls on Daniel's Creek.

SPRING PEEPER
(Hyla crucifer)
This treefrog is identified by an X on its back.

The park straddles a deep gorge cut into the west side of Lookout Mountain by Sitton Gulch Creek. The elevation here drops from 1,800 to 800 feet above sea level at the bottom of the gorge. The rimrock and steeper cliffs are resistant sandstone formed over 200 million years ago from beach and dune sands of an ancient shoreline. Shale layers below the sandstone are marked by a growth of pines. At the canyon bottom is a slope of rock fragments called "talus" that is now heavily forested. The valley floor and gentle slopes seen in the distance are formed of fossil-bearing limestone. Special events at this site include Crafts in the Clouds during the third weekend in May, a wildflower program in May, and a backpacking trip in October.

Directions: Located on GA 136, 8 miles east of Trenton and I-59, 18 miles northwest of LaFayette.

Facilities: 75 tent and trailer sites, 16 rental cottages, 40-person group camp, winterized group shelter, tennis courts, swimming pool, 30 walk-in campsites.

For more information: Cloudland Canyon State Park, Georgia Department of Natural Resources, Route 2, Box 150, Rising Fawn, GA 30738. Phone (800) 864-PARK or (770) 389-PARK in metro Atlanta, for individual reservations.

HIKING TRAILS OF CLOUDLAND CANYON STATE PARK

The canyon's rugged beauty is a joy year-round, each season offering special sights and sounds for visitors. A hike down Cloudland's trails to the canyon floor is a walk through millions of geologic years. Trails are well marked and easy to follow. The park provides good interpretive information about the history and geology of the area. Maps and directions to the trailheads are available in the park office.

WEST RIM LOOP TRAIL. [Fig. 7(l)] 4.9 miles. Part of the trail follows the canyon rim close to its edge. An overlook provides views into the three park gorges.

WATERFALL TRAIL. [Fig. 7(6)] .3 mile. Walk to two waterfalls on Daniel Creek.

CLOUDLAND BACKCOUNTRY TRAILS. [Fig. 7(7)] 5.4-mile loop. Backpacking and camping are permitted on this trail. Stop by the park office to obtain a permit and pay the $3-per-person fee.

JOHNSON'S CROOK

[Fig. 5(12)] Johnson's Crook is a deep indentation or cove on the west side of Lookout Mountain, located entirely in Dade County, Georgia. The valley of the crook is about 1,100 feet above sea level, and the brow around it ranges from 1,900 to 2,100 feet. The village of Rising Fawn and impressive Fox Mountain are immediately to the west of the crook.

In September 1863, shortly before the Battle of Chickamauga, an epic event occurred when 40,000 Union troops marched from Rising Fawn east into the crook and up, over, and down Lookout Mountain, building a road as they advanced and carrying with them all of the equipment of war.

ZAHND TRACT

[Fig. 5(15), Fig. 6(15)] This is an area of large, unusual rock formations characteristic of this region. Also present is a mixture of mesic (liking moist conditions), xeric (liking dry conditions), and Coastal Plain plants. Most visible from the road is the mountain laurel, which is especially abundant and blooms in May. The plot is owned by the state of Georgia. The rocks are about 200 feet off the road, east of GA 157.

Directions: From the intersection of GA 48 and GA 157 in Cloudland, go north 12.9 miles on GA 157; or from GA 136 go 9.7 miles south on GA 157.

SCENIC OVERLOOK

[Fig. 5(6), Fig. 6(16)] On GA 157, look for a metal highway rail about 11.9 miles north of GA 48 (or 10 miles south of the intersection of GA 136 and GA 157 south) which overlooks McLemore Cove [Fig. 5(13)], a breached, eroded, anticlinal valley between Pigeon and Lookout mountains.

EXPOSED COAL SEAM

[Fig. 5(22), Fig. 6(22)] Just before the brow of the mountain, a thinly bedded seam of coal is visible under massive sandstone and over shale. During the millions of years of the Carboniferous period, huge tree ferns and giant horsetails which were 1 to 2 feet in diameter and 60 or more feet high lived in the great swamps and river deltas that circled the northern hemisphere. As these plants died and fell to the earth, the swamp water prevented them from losing their carbon by oxidation. After eons of peat formation, these carbonized remains were compressed into layers of coal, which has powered mankind ever since. To split a piece of coal and find the imprint of the leaves of these ancient forests is one of the most significant experiences in the study of natural history. Birmingham, Alabama, became a great metallurgical center because of its combination of coal and iron deposits somewhat similar to those around Lookout Mountain.

Directions: 2 miles west of Menlo on the south side of GA 48. One must climb the bank to see it.

CHRISTMAS FERN
(Polystichum acrostichoides)

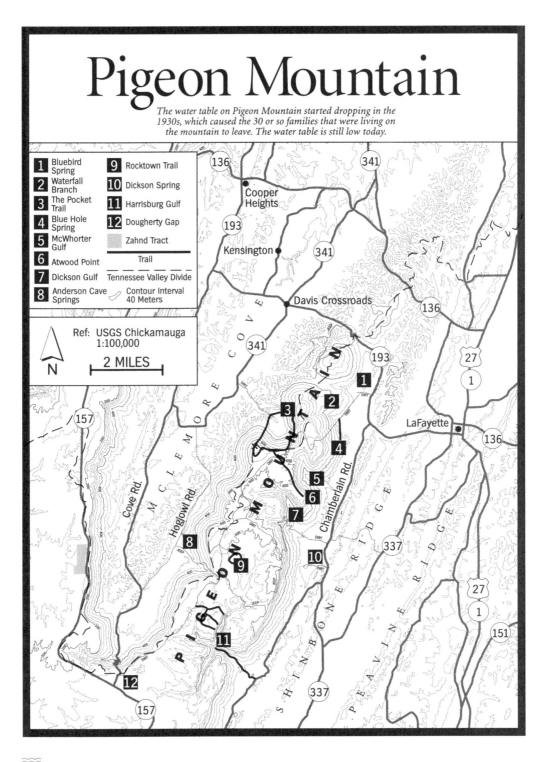

Pigeon Mountain

The water table on Pigeon Mountain started dropping in the 1930s, which caused the 30 or so families that were living on the mountain to leave. The water table is still low today.

1 Bluebird Spring	**9** Rocktown Trail
2 Waterfall Branch	**10** Dickson Spring
3 The Pocket Trail	**11** Harrisburg Gulf
4 Blue Hole Spring	**12** Dougherty Gap
5 McWhorter Gulf	Zahnd Tract
6 Atwood Point	Trail
7 Dickson Gulf	Tennessee Valley Divide
8 Anderson Cave Springs	Contour Interval 40 Meters

Ref: USGS Chickamauga 1:100,000

N

2 MILES

Pigeon Mountain

Pigeon Mountain [Fig. 4, Fig. 5, & Fig. 8] and Lookout Mountain form a V, like the thumb and index finger of a person's left hand held palm down, with Lookout being the index finger and Pigeon being the thumb. Nestled in the V shape is the Chickamauga Valley's lovely McLemore Cove, a National Historic District [Fig. 5(13)]. The northern tip of Pigeon Mountain lies about 3 miles west of LaFayette and stretches southwest for 10 miles, where it joins with Lookout Mountain. The mountain was named for the passenger pigeon, now extinct, which in the 1800s roosted there by the thousands. In the 1920s and 1930s some 30 families lived on Pigeon Mountain, working small farms and perhaps making moonshine liquor. Their names have stayed behind as part of the landscape, as in Rape Gap, Ellison's Cave, and Pettijohn's Cave. The 1930s saw a lowering of the water table on the mountain, causing all the wells to dry up and the families to abandon their homes. The water table has yet to return to its former level.

This is an area with many natural features of exceptional value for wildlife, recreation, and historical, archeological, and educational purposes. For years it has been studied by scientists, who are still finding new and exciting plants, animals, and natural environments. Some 21 rare plants and several rare salamanders are found here. The area was leased by the Georgia Department of Natural Resources in 1969. Since that time, the state has purchased more than 13,000 acres of the mountain. The land is managed as the Crockford–Pigeon Mountain Wildlife Management Area, primarily for wildlife and the protection and enhancement of the mountain's many natural features.

Activities: Hiking, caving, rock climbing, hang gliding, all-terrain bike riding, horseback riding, primitive camping, hunting, and fishing.

For more information: The Georgia Department of Natural Resources, 2592 Floyd Springs Road NE, Armuchee, GA 30105. Phone (706) 295-6041.

CAVES OF PIGEON MOUNTAIN

Like Lookout Mountain, Pigeon Mountain is laced with caves that wind all through the limestone rock. There are many cave entrances on the mountain, and it is an important location for cavers throughout the Southeast. Ellison's Cave contains two exceptionally deep pits—Fantastic Pit at 586 feet and Incredible Dome Pit at 440 feet. About 13 miles of Ellison's Cave have been explored and mapped. In fact, it is likely that Pigeon Mountain is a vast system of underground caverns and stream channels. Pettijohn's Cave was first described in 1837. Approximately 6 miles of passageways in this cave have been mapped, and new passages are still being discovered. This cave has seen much more use than Ellison's and has sustained more damage to its mineral formations.

It should be emphasized also that the underground can be an extremely dangerous area to explore for individuals unfamiliar with the skills required in caving. Caves should be explored only in the company of well-equipped, experienced cavers.

For more information: Because of the danger of caving and the fragile nature of caves, directions are not provided. For information on the sport of caving, contact the National Speleological Society, 2813 Cave Avenue, Huntsville, AL 35810-4431. Phone (205) 852-1300. Fax (205) 851-9241. E-mail nss@caves.org. World Wide Web http://www.caves.org

PIGEON MOUNTAIN SITES

WATERFALL BRANCH. [Fig. 8(2)] A small stream containing a scenic waterfall. Several rare plants have been recorded on the east- and northeast-facing slopes in the vicinity of this stream, including the hairy mock-orange, hedge nettle, Alabama snow-wreath, wild hyacinth, nodding spurge, celandine poppy, and state-protected twinleaf.

BLUE HOLE. [Fig. 8(4)] This is a large spring located at the base of the eastern slope of Pigeon Mountain. The unusual bluish color of its waters, its constant 56-degree Fahrenheit temperature, and the fact that it represents a hydrological discharge of the extensive Ellison's Cave system make this a significant feature. It is accessible by vehicle. No camping is allowed within 100 feet of the spring.

MCWHORTER GULF, DICKSON GULF, AND HARRISBURG GULF. [Fig. 8(5, 7, 11)] These gulfs contain the important and rare Pigeon Mountain salamander, a species known from only four sites, all located along the eastern slope of Pigeon Mountain. The green salamander has also been collected from this area. Collecting is prohibited except by specific permit.

SAGPONDS. These are water-filled depressions formed when underlying limestone strata are dissolved by groundwater and "slumping" occurs. Many of these sagponds serve as important groundwater recharge areas, slowly adding water to underground reserves. Several natural sagponds are found atop Pigeon Mountain. Some of these have been valuable to scientists who drilled through deep layers of peat, which accumulates in sagponds, and found ancient pollen samples which enabled documentation of the vegetation that covered the area during the Ice Age.

HIKING ON PIGEON MOUNTAIN

ROCKTOWN TRAIL. [Fig. 6(17), Fig. 8(9)] 1 mile one-way. Exploration of the massive boulders within the 150 acres of Rocktown can easily consume the better part of a day. The biggest mistake visitors can make is not to allow enough time to inspect this unusual site. Some of the boulders are as large as three-story office buildings; a narrow pedestal supporting a caprock resembles a 25-foot-tall champagne glass; and deep inside a narrow, dark crevice it is cool enough for hikers to see their breath even though the outside temperature may be close to 80 degrees Fahrenheit.

The reddish rocks of this ancient river delta that hikers see along the trail or imbedded in the sandstone formations of Rocktown are iron ore deposits. At one time there were 10 iron mines on the mountain. These deposits add a special visual interest to the Rocktown environment, because the softer sandstone erodes around them. Rocktown is easy to reach and would be a suitable hike for those of almost any age or physical condition. Children could, however, accidentally stray from the trail. The trail is marked with pink blazes.

Directions: From US 27 in LaFayette, go west 2.8 miles on GA 193 to Chamberlain Road; turn left and go 3.4 miles; turn right (marked by a wooden sign for Crockford–Pigeon Mountain WMA). Pass the Department of Natural Resources's check station and continue straight on the gravel road. Where the road forks, 4.2 miles from the check station, continue on the right fork. Past some cleared fields on the left, there is a good gravel road to the left 1.3 miles after the fork. Turn left there and go .7 mile to a clearing near the trailhead.

THE POCKET TRAIL. [Fig. 5(14), Fig. 8(3)] This is a loop trail about 9.5 miles long. This steep trail climbs Pigeon Mountain and follows the ridgeline for 2.3 miles. The view to the northwest looks down on McLemore Cove, a valley of farmland between Pigeon and Lookout mountains, and across to Lookout Mountain itself. Here the hiker has an excellent opportunity to observe and carefully climb on the unusual rock formations typical of this portion of the Cumberland Plateau. The fractured sandstone has been weathered and eroded over thousands of years into spires and teetering boulders that are most dramatic, particularly when perched—as many of them are—on the edge of the mountain.

Several rare or uncommon plant species have been recorded here, making it one of the most remarkable botanical areas in northwest Georgia. There are at least 11 significant species, found almost nowhere else in Georgia, present in the small patch of mesic hardwood forest below the wet-weather falls. These include celandine poppy, Ohio buckeye, bent trillium, nodding spurge, lanceleaf trillium, wild hyacinth, log fern, harbinger of spring, Virginia bluebells, hairy mock-orange, and blue ash. When the plants are in bloom, the forest below the waterfall near the start of the trail is truly remarkable, with some species occurring in quite thick beds. The rocky slopes above The Pocket contain an unusual open forest community dominated by red cedar and chinquapin oak. The forest also includes the smoketree, a rarity in Georgia. Hedge nettle, another new occurrence for the state, was first observed on slopes above the open meadow.

Directions: From LaFayette, take GA 193 west 8 miles to Davis Crossroads. Turn left on Hog Jowl Road and go about 2.7 miles. When the road forks, take the left fork and pass Mt. Hermon Baptist Church on the left. At the top of the hill, just past the church, a paved road turns left. Turn there and follow the road (it is paved only for about .5 mile) into The Pocket. The road winds 1.6 miles past several fields to a parking area at a gate. From there the trail continues up the narrow mountain track for .3 mile past falls on the right. In dry months the falls dries up completely. Just above the falls on the right is the beginning of the South Pocket Loop; straight ahead is the beginning of the North Pocket Loop. Begin the hike at either trailhead.

MCLEMORE COVE

[Fig. 5(13)] Before leaving this area, the reader may wish to visit nearby McLemore Cove, located in the Chickamauga Valley. (*See* McLemore Cove, page 33.)

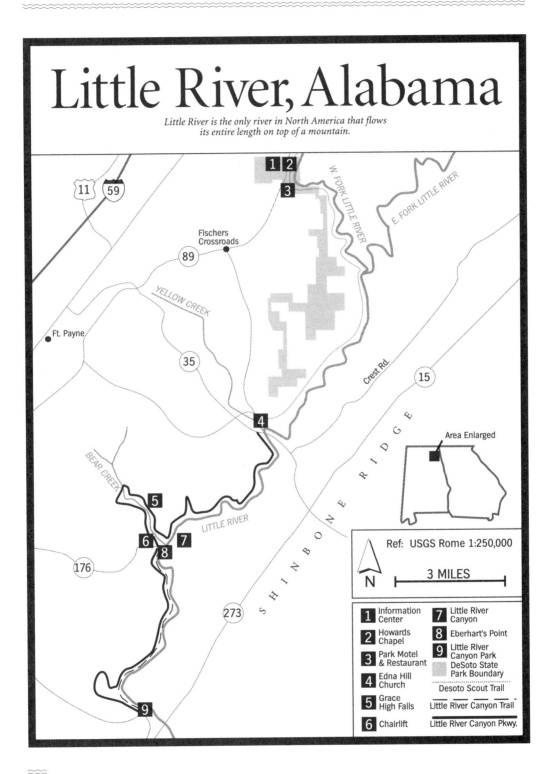

Little River, Alabama

Little River is the only river in North America that flows its entire length on top of a mountain.

11   59

1 **2**
3

W. FORK LITTLE RIVER

E. FORK LITTLE RIVER

Fischers
Crossroads

89

YELLOW CREEK

Ft. Payne

35

Crest Rd.

15

4

Area Enlarged

BEAR CREEK

5

LITTLE RIVER

6   **7**
8

176

S H I N B O N E   R I D G E

273

Ref: USGS Rome 1:250,000

N   **3 MILES**

1 Information Center
2 Howards Chapel
3 Park Motel & Restaurant
4 Edna Hill Church
5 Grace High Falls
6 Chairlift
7 Little River Canyon
8 Eberhart's Point
9 Little River Canyon Park
DeSoto State Park Boundary
Desoto Scout Trail
Little River Canyon Trail
Little River Canyon Pkwy.

9

Little River, Alabama

BROW PARK
[Fig. 5(18), Fig. 6(18)] Here visitors can get a representative sample of what the views are like along the entire length of Lookout Mountain. Picnic tables, good sunset views.

Directions: .2 mile north of Mentone, AL, on County Road 89.

DESOTO FALLS
[Fig. 5(19), Fig. 6(19)] In addition to a beautiful 100-foot waterfall, there is a dam creating a lovely mountain lake which provides swimming, fishing, and boating.

DESOTO STATE PARK
[Fig. 5(21), Fig. 6(21)] This fine Alabama state park has approximately 8 miles of easy-to-follow, well-marked hiking trails within the main area of the park. Rustic foot bridges span many of the streams; unusual rock formations and rare forms of plant life are found along these trails.

Directions: On Alabama County Road 89. Follow signs from Mentone, AL.

Facilities: A variety of lodging, including rustic log cabins, mountain chalets, a lodge, and a 25-unit motel, as well as primitive and developed campgrounds. The information center has a coin-operated laundry, restrooms, country store, and a local craft and gift shop. The store is stocked with all items necessary for camping, picnicking, and housekeeping in the cottages. Additional facilities include a picnic area with rustic stone shelter, picnic tables and grills, volleyball court and ball field (equipment may be checked out at the country store), Olympic-size pool, and two unlighted tennis courts.

Dates: Pool open Memorial Day weekend–Labor Day weekend.

For more information: For general information on DeSoto State Park camping, hiking, and picnicking, contact DeSoto State Park Country Store, Rt. 1, Box 210, Fort Payne, AL 35967. For information on the lodge or reservations for cottages or rooms, contact DeSoto State Park, Route 1, Box 205, Fort Payne, AL 35967. Phone (205) 845-5380.

DESOTO SCOUT TRAIL
[Fig. 5(21), Fig. 6(21)] This is a 16-mile trail that begins at Comer Scout Camp and follows the West Fork of Little River to a spot north of AL 35. The trail has been poorly maintained in recent years. Inquire at the DeSoto State Park Country Store for trail conditions and detailed directions to the trailhead.

Dates: The trail is closed during Nov., Dec., and Jan.

For more information: (205) 845-5075.

LITTLE RIVER CANYON

[Fig. 6(24), Fig. 9(7)] Little River Canyon on long, flat Lookout Mountain is one of the deepest gorges in the eastern United States. With an average depth of 400 feet, it is 700 feet at its deepest point and .75 mile across. Little River flows right down the middle of the canyon and, therefore, down the spine of Lookout Mountain, making it the only river in North America to flow its entire length along a mountaintop.

Geologists have devised two theories to explain the canyon's formation, neither of which has been proved or disproved. One is that the river may have once flowed underground until its roof overhead caved in and exposed it. Or perhaps an upheaval within the earth opened up a crevice which was enlarged over time by the erosive action of the river formed within it.

GRACE HIGH FALLS. [Fig. 6(25), Fig. 9(5)] The highest waterfall in Alabama, it is located on the south side of Bear Creek Canyon but can be seen only from the north side of the canyon.

LITTLE RIVER CANYON PARKWAY—RIM DRIVE. [Fig. 9(7)] This is a spectacular 22-mile drive along the western rim of Little River Canyon. The road passes a dozen lookout points and is a rewarding route to experience one of the most outstanding natural landscapes in the Southeast.

CANOEING ON LITTLE RIVER

LITTLE RIVER. [Fig. 6(20)] Little River is classified as an Alabama Wild and Scenic River. It would have qualified as a National Wild and Scenic River had it not been for the now-abandoned chairlift near the intersection of AL 176 and Rim Road. It is the only river in North America that flows its entire length on top of a mountain. Etched deep in the spine of the long Alabama portion of Lookout Mountain, it flows through one of the deepest canyons east of the Rockies.

Born in the uplands around Mentone, Little River grows until it reaches the dramatic 100-foot DeSoto Falls at DeSoto State Park. It is a pretty Class II run until it is joined by its east fork just above the AL 35 Bridge. Just below the bridge it takes a lethal, 60-foot plunge downward and the Little River Canyon is dramatically born.

When the water level is right, the river is a fast and heavy whitewater run of repeated Class II, III, and IV rapids. Only experienced canoeists should attempt it. Even then, it should be run only after careful preparation and on-the-spot information checks with the DeSoto State Park information office. There are no water gauges in Little River, and levels can change from unrunably bumpy in low water to suicidally heavy in high water. This river requires a support team of at least three canoes equipped with heavy throw ropes, life vests, and helmets. The canyon section of the river runs 16 miles from the AL 35 Bridge to Canyon Mouth Park, but only half of this is suitable for canoeing.

The run from Eberhart's Point to Canyon Mouth Park is approximately 8 miles, but the distance is deceptive. Canoeists will need all the daylight hours available for unpredictable portages and unavoidable delays. Once in the canyon, one has no way out but downriver. In moderate water some of the rapids must be portaged. Do not try to run the section of the river from AL 35 to Eberhart's Point. According to park officials, most who try this end up having to rope themselves and their damaged canoes up the 500-foot cliffs to get out. Consider coordinating a canoe trip with an accompanying hiking party. This will provide additional support for the put-in portage and other necessary portages around unrunable rapids.

Directions: To put in and take out, from Rome go west on GA 20 into Alabama. About 10 miles into Alabama, turn north on AL 35, continuing to the Little River Canyon Bridge. At the northwest corner of the bridge begins the Canyon Rim Parkway. Follow this for approximately 15 scenic miles to Eberhart's Point, the site of a now-defunct chairlift. Several trails lead down the canyon wall to the put-in. Each is tortuous and long, a portage of almost 600 feet virtually straight down. Only the most determined of paddlers will attempt it. Canoeists should drop their shuttle vehicle at the take-out at AL 273.

EAST FORK OF THE LITTLE RIVER. [Fig. 5(20), Fig. 6(20)] The East Fork of Little River provides the average canoeist with a safe yet exciting way to experience this canyon area without having to face the dangers and difficulties of Little River Canyon farther downstream. Located north of the actual canyon area, the East Fork is a canoeable Class I–III tributary for paddlers of beginner and intermediate skills. It begins in the southwest corner of Georgia's Walker County and flows into Alabama for a distance of 16 miles before it joins with the West Fork to form Little River. The information here covers the last 6 miles of the East Fork (from Lake Lahusage to the confluence with the West Fork) and the first 5 miles of the Little River (down to the AL 35 Bridge). It is just beyond this bridge that the Little River takes its dramatic plunge into the canyon. The total canoeing distance for this run is 11.2 miles, a distance that can be covered in one full day of paddling.

Directions: For the shortest and fastest shuttle, leave the take-out bridge on AL 35 and go south on this road for 3 miles until it meets County Road 15 at Blanche, AL. Turn left (northwest) on County Road 15 and go 11 miles (crossing back into Georgia) to Menlo.

There, turn left onto GA 48 and go 4 miles to the Alabama state line. At 200 yards past the state line sign is a paved road to the left, the Old Dam Road. Turn left here and go 1.4 miles to the dead end at the put-in.

For a more scenic shuttle, only 4.8 miles longer than the one above, go north from the take-out bridge on AL 35 for 5.4 miles, then turn right on AL 89 (the DeSoto State Park Road) and follow this road through the state park, past DeSoto Falls, for 11.4 miles to Mentone. In Mentone, turn right on AL 117 and go 6 miles, arriving at the Old Dam Road leading off to the right, about 200 yards before the Georgia state line. Follow the Old Dam Road 1.4 miles to the put-in.

NOCCALULA FALLS PARK AND CAMPGROUND

A rushing waterfall on Black Creek is the centerpiece of Noccalula Falls Park and Campground, located at the southwestern end of the Lookout Mountain Parkway. A re-created pioneer community depicts life of early settlers in the Appalachian foothills. Some of the buildings were moved from their original sites to be preserved here. Among these are a house built in 1877 and a large cotton warehouse built in 1888. From March until September, a train circles the edge of the park, which includes a botanical garden. A stairway leads to the gorge below the falls and the Gorge Trail. Interesting rock formations are found in the center of the park. Special events include Art on the Rocks the first Sunday in May and the Fall Fest the first Sunday in October.

Directions: East of 1-59 on AL 211, Noccalula Road, at Gadsden, AL.

Activities: Swimming, camping, picnicking, tennis.

Facilities: Restrooms, concessions, restaurant, playground, dump station, store, laundry facilities.

For more information: Noccalula Falls Park and Campground, City of Gadsden, PO Box 267, Gadsden, AL 35999. Phone (205) 543-7412 (campground) or (205) 549-4663 (park).

Map References: USGS 1:100,000 series: Chattanooga–Chickamauga–Rome.

FLOWERING DOGWOOD
(Cornus florida)
The dogwood's wood is shock resistant and used in tools and as shuttles in cotton mills. The energy-rich berries provide fuel for birds and squirrels.

The Chickamauga Valley

The Chickamauga Valley lies between the Cumberland Plateau's Lookout Mountain to the west and the Armuchee Ridges to the east. Where it divides the "thumb" of Pigeon Mountain from Lookout Mountain is the famed McLemore Cove. The Chickamauga Valley forms a natural passageway between the high ridges on either side. Because it gives access to both Chattanooga and the Tennessee River and contains a few low ridges, it was the site of much movement and conflict during the Civil War.

The Chickamauga Valley is not just one valley but a series of northeast-southwest trending valleys with limestone floors and ridges some 200 to 300 feet high, capped with more weather-resistant rock. Down through these valleys and across the ridges between Chattanooga and Atlanta, Union army forces under General William Sherman pursued Confederate troops during the fighting which led to the Battle of Atlanta near the end of the Civil War. Visitors to the military parks at Chickamauga, Missionary Ridge, and Orchard Knob, as well as other areas such as the lovely and serene McLemore Cove, will come away with a clearer understanding of how the natural geology of the region has helped shape recent human history.

From the Chickamauga Valley, especially GA 337, one can reach a variety of natural features lying at the base of the Pigeon Mountain escarpment. These include giant, dry, forest sinkholes; Blue Hole; and the entrances to the enchanting Dickson and McWhorter gulfs, deeply eroded into Pigeon Mountain's east wall.

MCLEMORE COVE

[Fig. 5(13)] A postcard-pretty valley nestled in the V formed by Lookout Mountain and Pigeon Mountain, the McLemore Cove Historic District was listed in the National Register of Historic Places in 1994. The steep limestone and sandstone walls of the mountains form a dramatic backdrop for a scenic drive through the cove. The area is almost exclusively agricultural, with small dairy farms taking up most of the land. At the southwest end of the cove is a portion of the picturesque 11,500-acre Mountain Cove Farm. Red cedars which thrive on the limestone soil here are profuse throughout the cove, particularly along West Cove Road, as indicated by the names of the natural features and landmarks: Cedar Grove Creek, Cedar Grove community, and Cedar Grove Church and Cemetery. Perhaps nowhere else in Georgia are so many cedars concentrated in such a small area.

The cove, which was named for Robert and John McLemore, sons of a white trader and a Cherokee mother, is just south of Chickamauga Battlefield. One of the Civil War battles took place at Davis Crossroads.

Near Cedar Grove Methodist Church, a large number of Union soldiers spent the night of September 17, 1863, immediately prior to the historic Battle of Chickamauga. Another antebellum structure is the 130-year-old, plantation-plain style farmhouse where the Hise family has lived for generations. It is located .5 mile south of Mt. Hermon Church on Hog Jowl Road. Most of the other old houses and buildings in the cove are not antebellum but date from the 1890s, when the railroad was built through the northern part of the cove.

Directions: Take GA 193 west from LaFayette 8 miles to Davis Crossroads. Note that the best view of McLemore Cove is from GA 157 atop Lookout Mountain.

CHICKAMAUGA AND CHATTANOOGA NATIONAL MILITARY PARK

This park is comprised of four separate battlefield sites—Chickamauga, Point Park, Orchard Knob, and Missionary Ridge. The park became the first of four military parks established by Congress between 1890 and 1899, the others being Shiloh, Gettysburg, and Vicksburg.

CHICKAMAUGA. [Fig. 5(7)] The Civil War battle of Chickamauga, in the northwest corner of Georgia, was the first of a series of decisive battles that culminated in the fall of Atlanta and brought the Civil War to a close. A Union force of about 58,000 men and a Confederate force of about 66,000 men clashed on the battlefield at Chickamauga September 19–20, 1863. The result, after 34,000 casualties (3,969 dead), was that the Union army retreated north to Chattanooga, then a town of about 2,500 people, and the Southern forces occupied Missionary Ridge and Lookout Mountain, which bordered the town. Troops from 29 of the 33 states east of the Rockies engaged in the campaign; four states had troops on both sides.

The Chickamauga Battlefield visitor center has an excellent small museum containing artifacts related to the Civil War. It also houses the Fuller Gun Collection, which consists of 355 weapons dating from the Revolutionary War period through World War II. A 26-minute, multimedia show is presented daily. Books on Civil War history and four rental audiocassettes are available.

The major points of interest on the Chickamauga Battlefield, which when the battle was fought consisted of small fields, dense woods, and thick

EASTERN REDCEDAR
(Juniperus virginiana)
Cedar chests are made from the fragrant wood of this tree.

underbrush, can be reached by following a 7-mile driving tour. Monuments and markers along the road indicate the locations of units and batteries engaged in the battle.

Chickamauga contains remarkable natural environments. In the eastern portion is Georgia's best example of the remarkable cedar glades, where red cedars dominate an open forest community. The thin soil over a limestone outcrop supports rare and unique prairie plants, some found nowhere else in the state. There are late-summer displays of showy coneflowers and black-eyed susans. The only year-round stream, Cave Springs Creek, has rich aquatic fauna; large shell-bark hickories grow along it. Two quarry ponds lie just east of US 27 near its junction with Viniard Road. Several limesinks, or sagponds, occur. The most historic is Bloody Pond, near the southwestern corner of the park. The largest and most interesting limesink is just north of Alexander's Bridge over Chickamauga Creek in the southeast corner of the park. It contains huge, 36-inch-diameter willow oaks buttressed at the base. Staff is not available to assist in nature tours.

Directions: Exit I-75 at GA 2 and go west about 6 miles to US 27; go south to the park 1 mile from the town of Fort Oglethorpe.

Facilities: Museum, orientation program, bookshop, guided tours, maps, brochures, driving tour.

Dates: Open daily, closed Christmas.

POINT PARK. [Fig. 5(3)] Point Park, although located in the Cumberland Plateau, is more conveniently discussed here, in the Chickamauga Valley section. After the Battle of Chickamauga, the Union army retreated to Chattanooga, and the Confederate army reformed battle lines around the city with the intention of starving and freezing the Union troops into submission. Point Park, strategically positioned on top of Lookout Mountain, was the location of one of those battle lines. The dominance of the location over the city below cannot be fully grasped until one stands on the edge of Point Park and looks down on Chattanooga.

A visit to this park is an opportunity to visualize the grand strategy of a major Civil War battle. During the Battle of Lookout Mountain, termed the "Battle Above the Clouds" because during the fighting a band of mist and fog hung around the middle of the mountain, the Union army drove the Confederates from their position and effectively gained control of the city.

Point Park is on the northeastern tip of Lookout Mountain. The welcome center contains a fine 13-foot-by-30-foot mural painted by James Walker, an eyewitness to the battle. A tape recording provides a narrative that describes the scene and effectively draws the visitor into the action. The small Ochs Museum in the park has an observation deck which affords a commanding view of the area.

Directions: From I-24 in Chattanooga, take the Lookout Mountain Exit and follow the signs for Lookout Mountain Parkway (which is Broad Street and also

Highways 11, 41, 64, and 72). Follow the signs for Ruby Falls (Point Park is past that), and when past the falls, pick up the signs for the Cravens House and Point Park. The route goes up the mountain on TN 148 (Scenic Highway).

ORCHARD KNOB. [Fig. 5(4)] This hill in front of Missionary Ridge was initially the forward position of the Confederate defense line. It was taken by Union forces, and from here General Ulysses Grant commanded the assault on Missionary Ridge. On November 25, 1863, six cannon shot from this hill signaled the beginning of the battle for the ridge. Visitors will find a half dozen state monuments and a number of cannon, but the real reason to visit Orchard Knob is the geographical perspective it gives to the fighting between Lookout Mountain and Missionary Ridge.

Directions: Follow Broad Street in Chattanooga to Fourth Street. Turn right and pass the Erlanger Medical Center. Turn right onto Orchard Knob Avenue. Note that just before Orchard Knob Avenue is Holtzclaw; turn right there to see the National Cemetery.

MISSIONARY RIDGE. [Fig. 5(5)] Missionary Ridge was occupied by the Confederate forces after the Battle of Chickamauga and was part of the battle line around Chattanooga. During the battle for the city, Union troops attacked and captured the ridge. Along the ridge are remarkable views of Orchard Knob, Chattanooga, and Lookout Mountain. Markers, plaques, and gun positions give details of troop positions and describe the action in which various units participated. The historical markers are dispersed among elegant houses.

Directions: From Orchard Knob continue on Third Street. Turn right on Glenwood and left on Oak, which merges with Shallowford and then intersects with Crest Road to run along Missionary Ridge.

For more information: Chickamauga and Chattanooga National Military Park, Point Park and Lookout Mountain, National Park Service, PO Box 2128, Fort Oglethorpe, GA 30742.

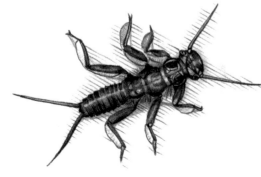

STONEFLY NYMPH
(Family Perlidae)
The adult stonefly is found near mountain streams in late spring and summer. Nymphs, or naiads, take as long as three years to develop into adults and are important food for fish.

The Armuchee Ridges

Unlike the Cumberland Plateau's broad, flat-topped mountains complete with streams, the Armuchee Ridges are true ridges, relatively narrow and linear. The principal ridges are Taylor Ridge, John's Ridge, Horn Mountain, and Rocky Face. Roadside ditches along Taylor Ridge are filled with multimillion-year-old fossils from former sea floors. There are also "pockets" or coves, outcrops of iron ore, and attractive waterfalls to provide visitors with pleasant travel destinations.

Instead of both sides of these ridges being similar, as in the Cumberland Plateau, here opposite sides are different. For example, on Taylor Ridge the western summit face is sandstone, while the east-face cliffs are hard chert, a noncrystalline quartz. Rocky Face is similar, except that siltstone instead of limestone underlies its western flanks. These differences lead to changes in both topography and plant communities. Interstate 75 crosses Rocky Face in a deep notch just west of Dalton and continues, crossing Taylor Ridge at the famous Ringgold Cut, where the subsurface rocks are highly visible and fossils are found in the wall of the highway cut adjacent to the southbound lane.

TAYLOR RIDGE

[Fig. 10] Taylor Ridge extends as one geological unit from the village of Holland on GA 100 in Chattooga County northwestward beyond the Tennessee line. A remnant of an ancient larger ridge which once reached all the way to Lookout Mountain, it eroded over a period of some 200 million years. In the valley between Taylor Ridge and Lookout Mountain are located the towns of Summerville, LaFayette, and Ringgold. The ridge is broken by a gap at Ringgold, the Ringgold Cut, where its name is changed to Whiteoak Mountain, although it is the same structure geologically. GA 100 passes the southwest tip of the ridge. It is crossed by US 27 between Gore and Summerville, by GA 136 between Villanow and LaFayette, by I-75 at Ringgold, and by several U.S. Forest Service roads. Because of federal ownership, both John's and Horn mountains are in a wildlife management area. Gate closure is seasonal; some gates are open only for hunting.

Geological time periods which can be observed in road cuts are Silurian (the age of fishes) and Mississippian (the carboniferous "coal age" and the age of amphibians).

TAYLOR RIDGE TRAIL. [Fig. 10(1)] 2.4 miles. The trail, for foot traffic only, runs along the ridge to FS 635-A.

Directions: Take GA 136 east from LaFayette for about 7 miles to the top of Taylor Ridge. Turn right (south) onto FS 217 (at gate). The trail begins at this point in the left fork of the road.

CHICKAMAUGA CREEK TRAIL. [Fig. 10(3)] 6.2 miles. A loop trail which

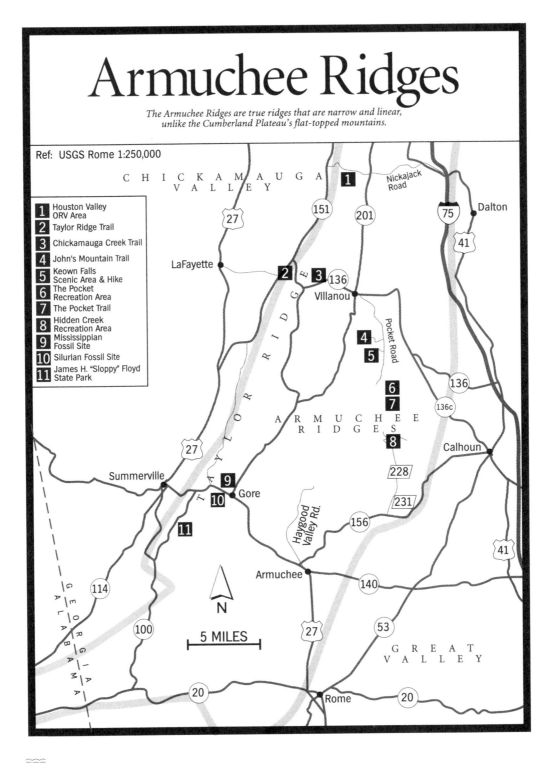

Armuchee Ridges

*The Armuchee Ridges are true ridges that are narrow and linear,
unlike the Cumberland Plateau's flat-topped mountains.*

Ref: USGS Rome 1:250,000

1 Houston Valley ORV Area
2 Taylor Ridge Trail
3 Chickamauga Creek Trail
4 John's Mountain Trail
5 Keown Falls Scenic Area & Hike
6 The Pocket Recreation Area
7 The Pocket Trail
8 Hidden Creek Recreation Area
9 Mississippian Fossil Site
10 Silurian Fossil Site
11 James H. "Sloppy" Floyd State Park

begins and ends at the end of Ponder Creek Road. Foot travel only.

Directions: Take GA 136 east from LaFayette for 9 miles. Turn left onto Ponder Creek Road and go about .6 mile. Take the right fork onto FS 219 to the end of the road. The trail can also be reached along FS 250, located at the intersection of GA 136 and Taylor Ridge.

▓ HOUSTON VALLEY ORV AREA

[Fig. 10(1)] This 2,600-acre, off-road-vehicle area has a network of trails for motorbikes and all-terrain vehicles. Timbering is conducted in this area, so visitors are asked to stay on the trails.

Directions: From I-75 take the LaFayette Exit 133 west onto GA 136 connector and go 7 miles. Turn right at GA 136 and go 11 miles. Turn right onto GA 151 and go 6 miles to Nickajack Road, located beside Wood Station Volunteer Fire Department. Follow Nickajack Road for 2 miles, crossing Taylor Ridge. At the base of Taylor Ridge, turn right onto Capehart Road and go 1 mile until the pavement ends. A parking area for Houston Valley is on the left at the beginning of a FS gravel road.

▓ KEOWN FALLS SCENIC AREA AND HIKE

[Fig. 10(5)] This scenic area was set aside because of the unique rock bluffs and high elevation swampy areas formed from springs. Keown Falls, named for land surveyor Gordon Keown, are twin falls located along two spring-fed streams within the 218-acre scenic area. The larger one free-falls 60 feet and the smaller about 40 feet. During summer the streams may become dry. A sign posted at the trailhead informs visitors whether the falls are flowing. The area is scenic even when the falls are dry. The 1.8-mile Keown Falls Loop Trail begins and ends at the picnic area parking lot. It is unmarked but easily followed. The northern part of the loop provides views of moisture-loving cove hardwood tree species, and the southern portion gives views of tree species indicative of dry ridges. This trail may be used to access the 3.5-mile John's Mountain Loop Trail, which is marked with white blazes. An overlook at the top of John's Mountain offers a scenic vista of Taylor Ridge, Lookout Mountain, and the surrounding valley. Keown Falls Recreation Area, located adjacent to the scenic area, offers an abundant variety of colorful wildflowers and shrubs. Mountain laurel blooms throughout the late spring and early summer months; both the pink and white varieties bloom in June. Azaleas and dogwood add to the springtime color. The mixture of hickory, sourwood, oak, beech, and yellow poplar presents a brilliant spectrum for autumn leaf watchers. The picnic area located in a forest at the foot of John's Mountain has a flowing creek where children can wade and tired hikers can cool their feet.

Directions: Take GA 136 east from LaFayette 13.5 miles; turn right (south) at Villanow onto Pocket Road; go approximately 5 miles to the Keown Falls entrance road, FS 702.

Facilities: Parking, picnic area with tables and pedestal grills, restrooms, hand pump for water, hiking trail. Information is available at the U.S. Forest Service office.

For more information: Keown Falls Recreation Area, U.S. Forest Service, PO Box 465, LaFayette, GA 30728. Phone (706) 638-1085.

JOHN'S MOUNTAIN LOOP TRAIL

[Fig. 10(4)] 3.5 miles. This loop trail begins and ends at the John's Mountain Overlook located at the end of FS 208. The trail connects with the Keown Falls Loop Trail above the falls.

Directions: Take GA 136 east from LaFayette for 13.5 miles. Turn right (south) past Villanow onto a county road (Pocket Road) and go about 4 miles. Turn right onto FS 208 to the observation deck.

THE POCKET RECREATION AREA

[Fig. 10(6)] Not to be confused with The Pocket on Pigeon Mountain, this pocket got its name because it lies in a low pocket created by the steep ridges of Horn Mountain, which surrounds it on three sides. From 1938 through 1942, it was the site of a Civilian Conservation Corps camp. The foundations of the old structure are still visible. A large, clear, ice-cold spring bubbles up in the middle of the picnic area and flows through the recreation area as a refreshing creek for wading.

Directions: Exit I-75 onto GA 136 north of Calhoun; go approximately 14 miles west toward Villanow; .5 mile east of Villanow, turn left (south) on Pocket Road (County Road 230) and go approximately 7 miles past Keown Falls.

Facilities: Restrooms (handicapped facilities), drinking water.

Activities: Camping, picnicking, hiking.

THE POCKET TRAIL. [Fig. 10(7)] A well-maintained and clearly marked hiking trail makes an easy 2.5-mile loop from the picnic area along low-lying streambeds and back to the campgrounds. When spring arrives, azaleas, dogwood, sourwood, and mountain laurel enliven the area with color. In the fall it is brilliant with the leaves of hickory, maple, oak, beech, and yellow poplar. The soil's subsurface in this area, made up of white limestone, erodes more easily than the harder rocks which make up the higher elevations in northwest Georgia. This erosion has resulted in the area's unusual topography.

HIDDEN CREEK RECREATION AREA

[Fig. 10(8)] The recreation area is located on a creek which appears and runs clear and cool for a day or so, then disappears. The area is a prime example of an oak-hickory forest, with a few beech trees in low-lying areas. There is a wide variety of flowering shrubs and plants. Dogwood, sourwood, hickory, maple, yellow poplar, and red oak abound. The varied forest conditions offer excellent opportunities for the birder. There are no hiking trails but many dirt roads to walk.

Directions: From Calhoun take GA 156 southwest for 7.5 miles. Turn right (northwest) on Everett Springs Road and go 2 miles. Turn right (southwest) on Rock Creek Road and go 3 miles. Turn right on FS 955 and follow signs to the recreation area.

Facilities: 16 campsites with tent pads, picnic tables, and fire rings are seldom full, even on weekends; water pump near the entrance; sanitary facilities.

For more information: Hidden Creek Recreation Area, U.S. Forest Service, Armuchee Ranger District, 806 E. Villanow Street, LaFayette, GA 30278. Phone (706) 638-1085.

FOSSIL SITES

This region of Georgia contains numerous fossil deposits. Many are exposed in road cuts which are accessible to the public.

MISSISSIPPIAN SITE. [Fig. 10(9)] From Rome take US 27 north 18.8 miles to the Gore intersection. Go .3 mile from Gore, turn right (north) onto a Forest Service road, and park almost immediately by a gate. Walk up an old woods road to the left. There are many crinoid stems, some brachiopods, some bryozoa, and rare small geodes. At this site the best picking is after a hard rainfall, which tends to expose the fossils.

SILURIAN SITE. [Fig. 10(10)] From Rome take US 27 north 18.8 miles to the Gore intersection. Go an additional 1.5 miles; turn left at the top of Taylor Ridge on a Forest Service road; go .2 mile. In the road bank on the right, find chunks of iron ore containing Silurian cephalopods such as Homotoma. Usually one must break open the ore to find the fossils. They are very small—5 to 15 millimeters long and 2 to 3 millimeters in diameter.

JAMES H. "SLOPPY" FLOYD STATE PARK

[Fig 10(11)] The park covers 545 acres at the base of Taylor Ridge. It was named for a Georgia state representative who served in the legislature from 1953 until his death in 1974. Two fishing lakes have wooden porch swings along their shorelines where visitors can sit and relax. Trails circle each lake. Rental boats are available and private boats are welcome. Only rowing, paddling, or trolling motors are permitted. The lakes are stocked with channel catfish, bream, and bass and are open for fishing year-round. The park has a program of wildflower planting and an ongoing program for restoring the bluebird population.

Directions: 2 miles south of Summerville on US 27, turn south onto well-marked road to the park.

Facilities: 25 shaded tent and trailer campsites with water and electrical hookups, within walking distance of the lake; a primitive camping area with only water and pit toilets, available for organized groups; 2 picnic shelters; fishing; boat ramps and docks; boat rental; hiking trails; playground; trailer dump station.

For more information: James H. "Sloppy" Floyd State Park, Georgia Department of Natural Resources, Route 1, Box 291, Summerville, GA 30747. Phone (706) 857-0826.

Great Valley

The Great Valley is between the Armuchee Ridges and the Cohutta Mountains, and it has provided an easy route for wildlife to travel north from the coastal lowlands of Alabama to the north Georgia mountains.

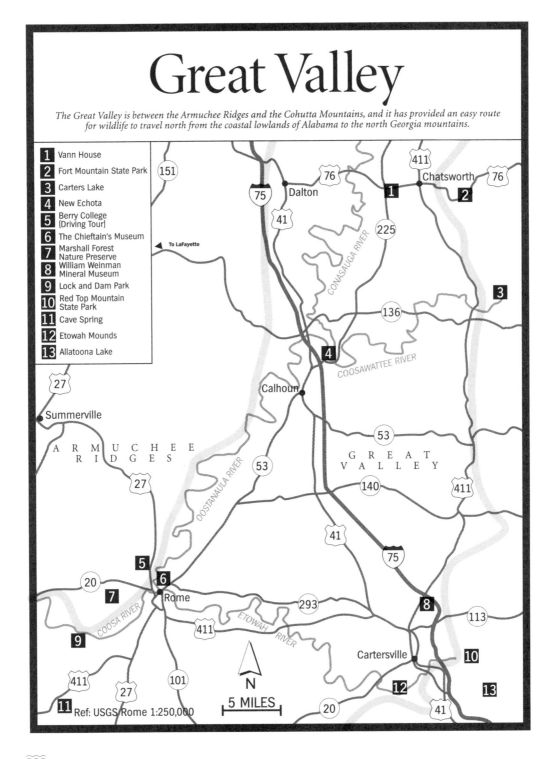

1 Vann House
2 Fort Mountain State Park
3 Carters Lake
4 New Echota
5 Berry College (Driving Tour)
6 The Chieftain's Museum
7 Marshall Forest Nature Preserve
8 William Weinman Mineral Museum
9 Lock and Dam Park
10 Red Top Mountain State Park
11 Cave Spring
12 Etowah Mounds
13 Allatoona Lake

To LaFayette

Chatsworth

Dalton

Calhoun

Summerville

ARMUCHEE RIDGES

GREAT VALLEY

Rome

Cartersville

N
5 MILES
Ref: USGS Rome 1:250,000

The Great Valley

The Great Valley, situated between the Armuchee Ridges and the Cohutta Mountains, has long presented to all types of life an easy route from the coastal lowlands of Alabama to the north Georgia mountains and farther north into Tennessee and possibly North Carolina. This was true even in prehistoric times, when such animals as barking tree frogs and cottonmouth moccasins moved northward along the sluggish streams, swamps, and oxbow lakes of the Coosa River. These watery roads were probably main trading routes between Creek and Cherokee nations. The names of great rivers like Conasauga, Oostanaula, Coosawattee, and Etowah attest to their Indian heritage. Etowah Mounds, Georgia's best-known Indian village, is near the junction of the Etowah River and Pumpkinvine Creek. The wide bottomlands of the valley, their timber already killed in many areas by beaver, presented fertile settings for the corn-bean-squash agriculture of the Mississippian period of Indian culture (1000 A.D.–1500 A.D.). In this region Indians trapped great spawning runs of fish such as the small-mouth buffalo and the freshwater drum. Tons of these fish were captured, smoked, and dried. The unpolluted rivers were also full of large freshwater clams. Chestnuts, black walnuts, and acorns of the lush valley forest, together with abundant game, supplemented the Indian diet.

The first white settlers must have eyed the Great Valley as a land of Eden when they arrived. As settlement of the territory continued, the Coosa River system opened up a large market for the goods grown here.

THE CHIEFTAIN'S MUSEUM

[Fig. 11(6)] Located on the banks of the Oostanaula River, this was the nineteenth-century home of Major Ridge, a prominent Cherokee Indian who, along with his family, operated a ferry boat, owned a store, and lived as slaveowner planters. The museum in the white clapboard plantation house contains exhibits describing Ridge's life and the history of Rome and northwest Georgia. Visitors can walk on a paved trail along the river. There is also an archeological dig at the site.

Directions: Located in Rome on Riverside Parkway between GA 53 spur and US 27.

For more information: The Chieftain's Museum, 501 Riverside Parkway, PO Box 373, Rome, GA 30162. Phone (706) 291-9494.

MARSHALL FOREST NATURE PRESERVE

[Fig. 11(7)] Marshall Forest, an old growth forest with remnants of virgin forest, was designated Georgia's first National Natural Landmark in 1966. The 104-acre forest was donated to The Nature Conservancy in 1976 by the Marshall family, who had owned and protected it for nearly a century. About 300 plant species, including

46 tree species, grow here. The trees are a mixture of northern and southern species. Northern red oak and chestnut oak are near the southern limits of their ranges, while longleaf pine is near its northern limit. The forest is home to several rare and unusual species. Access to the area is by special permission or guided tour only. Tours are provided by the Marshall Forest Stewardship Committee and may be arranged by calling the office. Students from several colleges and universities in the state have used the forest as a research site.

There are five trails, but most tours are conducted on the braille trail, which was designed for the visually impaired. Unfortunately, all of the trails are unkept. Lists of plants, birds, and trees are available.

Directions: In Rome go west on Shorter Avenue (GA 20); turn south (left) on Horseleg Creek Road. Forest begins approximately .5 mile from Rome city limits.

Facilities: Tours, braille trail, other trails. Note: Access to the forest is by reservation only.

For more information: Marshall Forest Nature Preserve, The Nature Conservancy, Chamber of Commerce, Rome, GA 30161. Phone (706) 291-0766.

LOCK AND DAM PARK

[Fig. 11(9)] Mayo's Bar Lock and Dam were built on the Coosa River at Horseleg Shoals to facilitate the movement of steamboats and barges upstream from Alabama to Rome. As many as 50 steamboats operated on the Coosa River between Rome and Greensport, Alabama, during the mid- to late 1800s. These steamboats had difficulties navigating through shoals located throughout the river. At Horseleg Shoals, the worst of these shallow sandbanks, local citizens built temporary dams to create a deeper pool of water. Congress ordered a survey of the Coosa River in 1870, but it was not until 1913 that the lock and dam near Rome was completed. By the time of its completion, only three commercial boats remained on the river, and one of these was the Corps of Engineers' dredge. The steamboats turned to transporting passengers for picnics, parties, and hunting and fishing trips. River traffic dwindled until the lock was finally closed in 1941.

Directions: On the Coosa River 7.5 miles south of Rome. Take US 27 to Walker Mountain Road; turn west; go 3.4 miles to the park.

Facilities: 25 campsites equipped for recreational vehicles, boat launch ramp, boat dock, fuel and supplies, restrooms, canoe rental, trail, handicapped facilities, brochures, maps, restaurant, dump station.

Activities: Fishing, hunting picnicking, hiking.

For more information: Lock and Dam Park, Rome–Floyd County Parks and Recreation Authority, 181 Lock and Dam Road, Rome, GA 30161. Phone (706) 234-5001.

CAVE SPRING

[Fig. 11(11)] Cave Spring, settled in 1829, is a picturesque village in beautiful

Vann's Valley. Definitely off the beaten track (about 8 miles east of the Alabama border, 15 miles south of Rome), the small community has been able to preserve its charm and integrity from modern development. Over 90 structures in Cave Spring are listed on the National Register of Historic Places.

Cave Spring's original claim to fame is its namesake mineral spring, flowing from a cave in Rolater Park, which covers 29 acres of natural landscape inside the village. Little Cedar Creek flows through the park and village. The park has covered pavilions and picnic tables under beautiful trees. The large limestone cave is a popular attraction. It is open to the public during the summer and boasts a cool temperature of 56 degrees. The mineral spring has a capacity of about 4 million gallons a day of the "purest water in Georgia," which is now being bottled and sold in stores. There is a 1.5-acre swimming pool, the second largest in Georgia, which is fed by spring waters. The Hearn Academy Inn is also on park grounds. Begun in 1839 as a dormitory for the Hearn Manual Labor School, it has been restored by the Cave Spring Historical Society, which offers tours of the building during Country Festival Week. Bed and breakfast are available here, as well as catered parties and weddings by reservation.

Also in Cave Spring is the Georgia School for the Deaf. Its first five students were admitted in 1846. The school is still in its original location. During the second weekend in June, the Annual Country Festival and Road Race includes tours of Hearn Academy and an arts festival.

Directions: On US 411 about 15 miles south of Rome.

Facilities: Historic village with many old buildings; 29-acre Rolater Park with limestone cave, mineral spring, swimming pool, and picnic tables. Hearn Academy Inn features bed and breakfast; antique shops

CHESTNUT OAK (Quercus prinus) This is also called rock oak because of its preference for a rocky habitat.

in village, including Country Roads Antique Mall, 14,000 square feet; 2 village restaurants feature home cooking.

For more information: Hearn Academy and Rolater Park, phone (706) 777-8439.

🌸 BERRY COLLEGE DRIVING TOUR

[Fig. 11(5)] Berry College was founded around the turn of the century by the remarkable Martha Berry. She lured industrialists such as Henry Ford and politicians such as Teddy Roosevelt here and convinced them to support her efforts to educate rural mountain children getting their first chance at formal schooling.

Berry is one of the largest campuses in the world (28,000 acres). In the early years studies were conducted in log cabins which still stand, well preserved, but now Berry students use 40 more-modern buildings. Most of the property owned by the college is farmland which is worked by students in accordance with the founder's idea that every student should work part time on campus to help defray tuition costs.

The campus is testimony to one woman's determination to bring education to children of the mountains. A tour of its grounds and buildings provides the visitor with insight into the isolated, hard, determined and proud nature of life in these hills during the first half of the century. The guard at the main entrance has maps for a self-guided tour. Highlights of this tour include the Gothic architecture of the Ford Quadrangle; the old mill wheel, one of the largest overshot waterwheels in the world; and picturesque agricultural buildings.

NORTHERN RED OAK
(Quercus rubra)
Red oaks can be identified by tiny bristles on the tip of each leaf.

Directions: From Rome, follow US 27 north to the Berry College campus on the left.

For more information: Phone (706) 236-2213.

VANN HOUSE

[Fig. 11(1)] The house built by the Cherokee chief James Vann in 1804 and called "Showplace of the Cherokee Nation" is preserved as the Vann House Historic Site. James Vann, son of a Scottish trader and a Cherokee woman, helped establish the Moravian mission at Spring Place in 1801. In sponsoring the mission school, he contributed to the education of the Cherokee young, including several of the nation's future leaders. He was reputed to be generous when sober and pugnacious when drinking—which he did often. He was shot at Buffington's Tavern on February 21, 1809, at age 41. He had expected to leave his vast holdings to his young son, Joseph, but the Council of Chiefs intervened to divide the property between his widow and all of his children.

Joseph Vann managed nevertheless to acquire the house and much of his father's other property. An even better businessman than his father, he became known as "Rich Joe Vann" by the Indians and whites alike. During the 1830s push for Indian removal in Georgia, Vann made the mistake of hiring a white man as overseer of his plantation. Thus he unwittingly violated a new Georgia law declaring it illegal for a white man to work for an Indian. Because of this, his house and land were claimed by the state. During a dispute over ownership between a white boarder in the house and the Georgia Guard, the stairway was set on fire. The charred flooring is still visible.

When turned out of their home in Georgia, the Joseph Vann family moved first to a farm he owned in Tennessee and then traveled by steamboat to Webbers Falls, Oklahoma, where he built a duplicate of the Georgia Vann House. That house was destroyed by Union forces during the Civil War. In the 1840s, after much litigation, the federal government later paid Joseph Vann $19,605 for his property in Georgia: a fine brick house, 800 acres of cultivated land, 42 cabins, 6 barns, 5 smokehouses, a grist mill, a sawmill, a blacksmith shop, 8 corn cribs, a shop and foundry, a trading post, a peach kiln, a still, 1,133 peach trees, 147 apple trees, and more.

Joseph Vann operated a steamboat line after he moved to Oklahoma. He met his death in October 1844 when an overheated boiler on his steamboat exploded during a race with another vessel on the Ohio River.

After deteriorating for 150 years, the house and three acres were purchased by the community and presented to the Georgia Historical Commission in 1952. The house was restored and dedicated in July 1958. Many priceless relics of the family were returned to the house as exhibits.

Directions: Located on the outskirts of Chatsworth between Dalton and Chatsworth at the intersection of GA 225 and GA 52-A.

Facilities: Restrooms and picnic area; brochures and tours available.

For more information: Vann House Historical Site, Georgia Department of Natural Resources, Route 7, Box 7655, Chatsworth, GA 30705. Phone (706) 695-2598.

NEW ECHOTA

[Fig. 11(4)] By 1825 the Cherokee Nation had discarded the tribunal Council of Chiefs as a ruling body and patterned their government on the republican form of the United States. In November 1825 the legislature of the Cherokee Nation, which covered the area from eastern North Carolina westward through northern Georgia into northeastern Alabama and eastern Tennessee, established its capital at New Echota. Among the many buildings constructed there were a number of commercial buildings, a legislative hall, a supreme court building, and a mission station.

Prior to 1827, Sequoyah created the first written form of the Cherokee language. In response to his syllabary, the American Board of Commissions for Foreign Mission, which was based in Boston, underwrote most of the cost of establishing a print shop in New Echota. A member of the board, Samuel A. Worcester, settled in the community in 1827. Thirteen years after the establishment of New Echota, the U.S. Congress ordered the removal of the Cherokees to the West. This forced march in the winter of 1838–39 caused the death of 4,000 people and became known as the Trail of Tears. After this march, the town quickly fell into disrepair, and by the twentieth century the site was lost.

In the early 1950s, a group of Calhoun citizens purchased 200 acres of the original site and deeded it to the state of Georgia. Thirteen buildings have been restored or reconstructed, and guided tours are available.

Directions: From I-75 take Exit 131 (north of Calhoun) onto GA 225 and go east 1 mile.

Facilities: Guided tours, museum with video presentation, nature trail, and bus parking.

For more information: New Echota State Historic Site, Georgia Department of Natural Resources, 1211 Chatsworth Highway NE, Calhoun, GA 30701. Phone (706) 629-8151.

WILLIAM WEINMAN MINERAL MUSEUM

[Fig. 11(8)] This museum, the largest mineral museum in the Southeast, was established in 1983 by the Cartersville Tourism Council with a donation from the family of William J. Weinman, a pioneer in barite mining in Bartow County. It is dedicated to the collection and exhibition of minerals, rocks, gemstones, and fossils from Georgia and around the world. It provides lapidary and identification services. Part of the facility is set aside for lapidary research and classroom activities. A new wing and a library were added in 1987.

The Georgian Exhibit Hall features a simulated limestone cave with a waterfall that dramatizes the dynamics of cave formation. The hall also houses a local mining display, local fossil finds, and other specimens from Georgia. Many of the exhibits throughout the museum may be touched.

Lectures by a museum consultant on a variety of topics including rock and mineral identification, birthstones, fossils and fossilization, and the solar system may be scheduled by appointment. On the second Saturday in June, the museum hosts its annual rock swap.

Directions: On the southwest side of the intersection of US 411 and 1-75, Exit 26.

Facilities: Touch-and-feel exhibits, guided tours on request, film, special lectures by appointment, library, handicapped access, gift and book shop.

For more information: William Weinman Mineral Museum, Cartersville Tourism Council, PO Box 1255, Cartersville, GA 30120. Phone (770) 386-0576.

ETOWAH MOUNDS

[Fig. 11(12)] The Etowah Mounds and Village of the Mississippian Indians were occupied between 1000 A.D. and 1500 A.D. Several thousand Indians may have lived in this fortified town at the peak of its prosperity. It was the center of political and religious life in the valley and home to the chiefs who directed the growth, storage, and distribution of food.

Three flat-topped ceremonial mounds that served as platforms for temples or residences for chiefs and priests are located on the floodplain at the juncture of the Etowah River and Pumpkinvine Creek. The village was surrounded by a stockade and deep ditch on all but the river side. It was linked to other Mississippian towns by the Etowah River. Visitors may take a self-guided tour of the mounds. The entire walk is a little over .5 mile.

An excellent museum explains the archeological interpretations of the lives of people of the community. Many artifacts, including ceremonial objects, pottery tools, and many shell beads, are on display. This is the only archeological site in northwest Georgia open to the public. Special events at this site include an Indian skills day in the spring, artifacts identification days (April and November), and astronomy programs.

Directions: From I-75 take Exit 124 onto GA 61, go through Cartersville to Indian Mound Road; follow signs to the mounds, 6 miles.

Facilities: Archeological site, museum with audiovisual show, maps and brochures, nature walks, bus parking, benches by the river.

For more information: Etowah Mounds Historic Site, Georgia Department of Natural Resources, 813 Indian Mounds Road SW, Cartersville, GA 30120. Phone (770) 387-3747.

Map References: USGS 1:100,000 series. Chattanooga–Rome–Chickamauga–Cleveland–Dalton–Cartersville.

The Blue Ridge

The Blue Ridge, the Cumberland Plateau, and the Valley and Ridge are all part of the Appalachian Mountains—also known as Appalachia. The part of Appalachia known as the Blue Ridge is technically called the Blue Ridge province, which should be distinguished from the Blue Ridge Mountains. The Blue Ridge province, which stretches from northern Georgia to southern Pennsylvania, contains many different mountain ranges. Together, these ranges form what is literally the rooftop of eastern North America. The Blue Ridge province is shaped somewhat like an elongated teardrop; it is 12 to 15 miles wide in northern Virginia, but becomes much wider toward the southern end of the region where, across Georgia, North Carolina, and Tennessee, the province is more than 70 miles wide.

Running down the eastern edge of the province is the region's namesake range, the Blue Ridge Mountains. This historic mountain range forms an almost unbroken

[*Above*: Tallulah Gorge in Georgia's Blue Ridge Province]

wall which stretches from Georgia through Virginia. For much of its length, the crest of the Blue Ridge Mountains forms the drainage dividing line—known as the Eastern Continental Divide—which separates rivers flowing eastward into the Atlantic Ocean from those flowing westward to the Gulf of Mexico.

The western part of the Blue Ridge province is made up of several other ranges known collectively as the Unaka Mountains. The Unakas include the Iron Mountains in southwestern Virginia and northeastern Tennessee, the Bald Mountains and Stone Mountains along the Tennessee/North Carolina border, and, farther south, the famous Great Smoky Mountains. South of the Smokies are the Unicoi Mountains and, in Georgia, the southernmost component of the Unaka Range—the Cohutta Mountains.

While the Cohuttas, as one segment of the Unaka Range, are part of the Blue Ridge province's western side, they are geologically and geographically independent of their counterpart range to the east—the Blue Ridge Mountains.

Geologically, the Eastern Blue Ridge and Western Blue Ridge sections are divided by a break in the earth's surface called the Hayesville Fault. The Eastern Blue Ridge has more highly metamorphosed rocks (mostly schists and gneisses) than its counterpart. In addition, the Eastern Blue Ridge is more or less one continuous high ridge, while in the Western Blue Ridge the mountains tend to be in isolated groupings. Also, the Western Blue Ridge has a unique feature called the Murphy Syncline, a great trough stretching from the marble quarries near Tate through Ellijay to Blue Ridge, Georgia. This syncline is a long, low, straight pass through the mountains and the easiest major access to the valleys and Tennessee River tributaries lying north of the Blue Ridge.

The Blue Ridge enjoys a botanically rich mixture of temperate climate plants. North meets South in Georgia's mountains, with northern species mixing with their southern kin. Many northern species are at their southern limits here. The Southern Highlands contains the greatest mixture of temperate climate plants in the world, save eastern temperate Asia, located at about the same latitude. The Blue Ridge is generally part of the Appalachian flyway for birds, especially warblers, tanagers, thrushes, and vireos. Because the climate more resembles that of New Jersey than of Georgia, birds nest here that do not nest in the valleys below. Rose-breasted grosbeak, scarlet tanager, dark-eyed junco, chestnut-sided warbler, black-throated blue warbler, and black-throated green warbler are but a few examples. These are all birds that nest in the North or in mountainous regions of the South.

Most of the mountain forests managed by the Forest Service lie in the Western Blue Ridge and Eastern Blue Ridge, as do all of the wildernesses. For details of the history and use of wildernesses, please consult Appendix H. Appendix I addresses the management plan by which the Chattahoochee-Oconee National Forest is currently administered. There the reader will find a brief explanation of how our national forest is zoned in Management Area categories, some being potential wildernesses and others lying adjacent to established wildernesses.

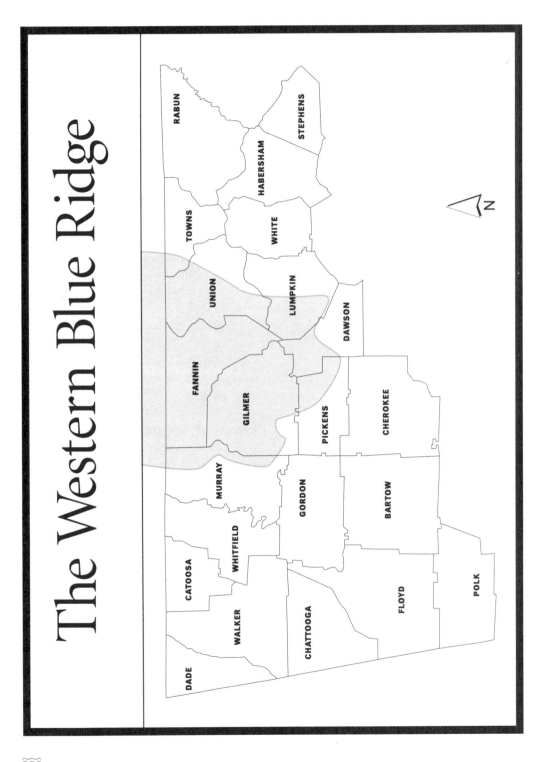

The Western Blue Ridge

The Western Blue Ridge

The area known as the Western Blue Ridge includes the Cohutta Mountains and Wilderness, Big Frog Wilderness, Lake Conasauga, Carters Lake, Fort Mountain State Park, Copper Basin, the Rich Mountains, and much of the area drained by the lower reaches of the Etowah and Toccoa rivers. Positioned between the Great Valley and the Eastern Blue Ridge, the Western Blue Ridge section of the Georgia mountains has a character and wildness all its own. Geologically, as part of the southern Unaka Range, some of these mountains have more in common with the Great Smokies to the north than with their immediate sandstone and limestone neighbors to the west or the highly metamorphosed crystalline rock to the east. Because of its diversity, this region offers some of the greatest possibilities for ecological rambling found anywhere in the mountains.

The Cohutta Wilderness

The Cohutta Wilderness covers 36,977 acres (about 60 square miles) that spill over the Georgia/Tennessee border and lie within the 95,265-acre Cohutta Wildlife Management Area. It was designated as a wilderness in 1975. Hemp Top was added in 1986, making this the third largest mountain wilderness area in the East.

The Cohuttas share a unique distinction with the Rich Mountains in having round, flat-topped ridges and peaks covered with deep, black soils. In most of the Eastern Blue Ridge, on the other hand, the higher the elevation, the rockier and thinner the soils. This characteristic of the Cohuttas profoundly affects the plant communities. Rich-soil ridges are often carpeted with lush ferns and knee-high herbs. The wilderness is home to a variety of wildlife. Deer and black bears make their home here, as do wild boar and a variety of smaller creatures such as bobcats and squirrels.

T.P.'s Country Store (*see* Eton Access, page 55) and Greg's General Store (*see* Cisco Access, page 57) display the trophies of local hunters and are good places to get a close-up look at some of the kinds of creatures that inhabit the wilderness.

Few of the visitors who enjoy the Cohutta Wilderness realize its history of logging; 70 percent of the area was logged between 1915 and 1930. Three or four logging camps, each with 80 to 100 men, were operated simultaneously in the area. Railroads were built by hand and ran up the Jacks and Conasauga rivers. Trestles built over the river often were washed away by floods. Bunk cars were winched up hillsides. Logs were skidded out with horses, and cable logging was done in the areas inaccessible by horses.

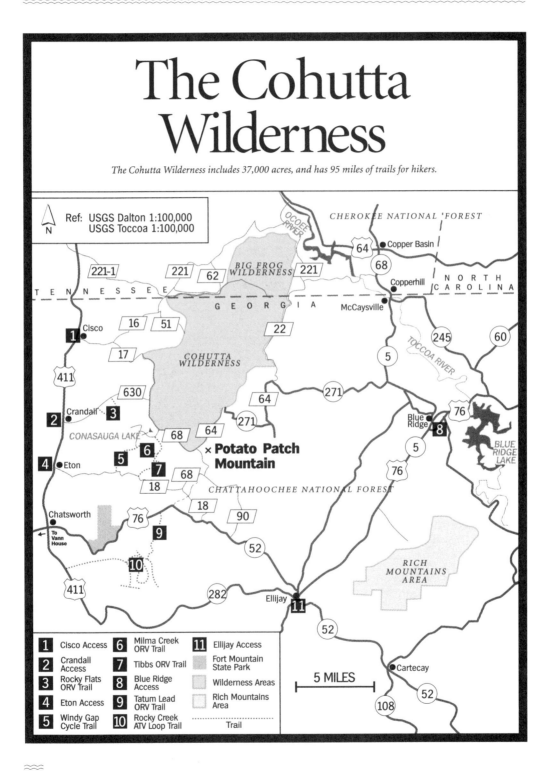

The Cohutta Wilderness

The Cohutta Wilderness includes 37,000 acres, and has 95 miles of trails for hikers.

Ref: USGS Dalton 1:100,000
USGS Toccoa 1:100,000

N

CHEROKEE NATIONAL FOREST

OCOEE RIVER

64 ● Copper Basin

68

BIG FROG WILDERNESS

221   62   221   Copperhill

NORTH CAROLINA

TENNESSEE

GEORGIA   McCaysville

221-1   221   62

1 Cisco   16   51   22

17

245   60

COHUTTA WILDERNESS

TOCCOA RIVER

411   5

630   271

2 Crandall   **3**   64

271

4 ● Eton   **5**   **6**   68   64   271

Blue Ridge   76

8

CONASAUGA LAKE   × **Potato Patch Mountain**

BLUE RIDGE LAKE

7   68   5

18   76

CHATTAHOOCHEE NATIONAL FOREST

Chatsworth   76   18   90

← To Vann House   **9**

52   RICH MOUNTAINS AREA

10

411   282   52

Ellijay **11**

52

● Cartecay

5 MILES

52

108

1 Cisco Access	**6** Milma Creek ORV Trail	**11** Ellijay Access		
2 Crandall Access	**7** Tibbs ORV Trail	Fort Mountain State Park		
3 Rocky Flats ORV Trail	**8** Blue Ridge Access	Wilderness Areas		
4 Eton Access	**9** Tatum Lead ORV Trail	Rich Mountains Area		
5 Windy Gap Cycle Trail	**10** Rocky Creek ATV Loop Trail	⋯⋯ Trail		

Logging was completed in the Conasauga River drainage in 1928 and started along the Jacks River in 1929. The Depression halted logging for about three years. During that time the loggers worked in the Civilian Conservation Corps building some of the facilities still used in the area. After the Depression, the Beech Creek, Rough Creek, Rock Wall, Poplar Creek, and Penitentiary Creek areas were logged.

The railroads were dismantled and the rails removed in 1937. Remnants of ties and trestles can be found today. Also one can occasionally find dynamite drills in rocks, spikes, cables, steel support rods, horseshoes, and old building foundations. While in operation, the Conasauga River Lumber Company sawed 80,000 board feet a day. It was from this company that the U.S. Forest Service acquired a large portion of the area in 1934 and 1935. Farms have reverted back to forests, roads have been turned into hiking trails, and the area is returning to the way it was when only Native Americans lived here.

ACCESS TO THE COHUTTA WILDERNESS

The following pages provide an overview of the Cohutta Wilderness, a way to approach the endeavor before beginning a detailed exploration of any one trail. The map provides information on access roads to the wilderness. Also shown are Forest Service roads bordering the area and designated trails which cross it. Trailheads are generally well marked and parking areas are provided. All of the roads that border the wilderness are one-lane dirt, sometimes with a coating of loose gravel. They are wide enough for two cars to pass cautiously. Curves are sharp and hard to see around.

Often rock breaks through the road surface, creating a washboard ride. Although a four-wheel-drive vehicle would be the ideal transportation on these surfaces, most cars in good condition will have little trouble. Some roads are closed depending on weather conditions, so it is recommended that one call the Cohutta Ranger District of the U.S. Forest Service at (706) 695-6737 in advance of a trip to check road conditions.

ELLIJAY ACCESS. [Fig. 13(11)] From the Ellijay Square, travel west on GA 52 for 9.5 miles to FS 18. There is a sign for Lake Conasauga Recreation Area; turn right. After 1.3 miles the pavement ends. At the fork, bear left over a one-lane bridge. At 3.5 miles turn sharply to the right onto FS 68. At 4.5 miles is a level picnic area, and at 5.7 miles is Holly Creek Checking Station. At 6 miles is a three-way junction with FS 64. Stay on FS 68 (to the left). Barnes Creek Picnic Area for day use is at 7.2 miles; a wooden platform extends out over a small waterfall. At 9.5 miles is the intersection marked Potato Patch Mountain on the map.

ETON ACCESS. [Fig. 13(4)] If there is time for exploring only one access point to the Cohutta Wilderness, this should be it. The valley drive and the drive along the creek make this one of the most visually rewarding ways to approach the wilderness. From Chatsworth take US 411 4.2 miles north to Eton. Turn right at the traffic light onto Fourth Avenue (GA 286 ends here). At 1.1 miles, Grassy Mountain intersects

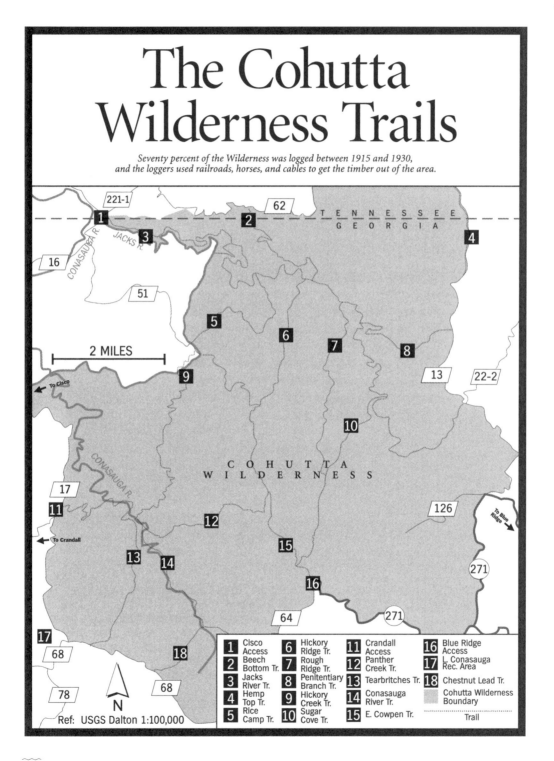

The Cohutta Wilderness Trails

*Seventy percent of the Wilderness was logged between 1915 and 1930,
and the loggers used railroads, horses, and cables to get the timber out of the area.*

221-1

62

1

2

TENNESSEE
GEORGIA

3

16

4

51

5

6

7

8

To Cisco

2 MILES

9

13

22-2

10

COHUTTA
WILDERNESS

17

126

11

To Blue
Ridge

To Crandall

12

271

13

14

15

16

64

271

17

68

18

78

68

N

Ref: USGS Dalton 1:100,000

1	Cisco Access	**6**	Hickory Ridge Tr.	**11**	Crandall Access	**16**	Blue Ridge Access
2	Beech Bottom Tr.	**7**	Rough Ridge Tr.	**12**	Panther Creek Tr.	**17**	L. Conasauga Rec. Area
3	Jacks River Tr.	**8**	Penitentiary Branch Tr.	**13**	Tearbritches Tr.	**18**	Chestnut Lead Tr.
4	Hemp Top Tr.	**9**	Hickory Creek Tr.	**14**	Conasauga River Tr.		Cohutta Wilderness Boundary
5	Rice Camp Tr.	**10**	Sugar Cove Tr.	**15**	E. Cowpen Tr.		Trail

CONASAUGA R.

JACKS R.

CONASAUGA R.

from the left. At 1.5 miles, the road forks at T.P.'s Country Store; bear left on the CCC Camp Road. At 5.1 miles, the road passes through a scenic valley with Fort, Beaver, and Tatum mountains in the background. The pavement ends at 6 miles and the road becomes FS 18. At 7 miles is the start of a nice drive along a creek. At 7.2 miles, the view looking upstream through the trees at Holly Creek is a fine sight. At 10 miles is the intersection of FS 18 and FS 68. From this point, refer to the Ellijay Access (above) beginning at 3.5 miles.

CRANDALL ACCESS. [Fig. 13(2), Fig. 14(11)] From Chatsworth take US 411 north 7.5 miles through Eton to Grassy Street; turn right. Cross railroad tracks and turn right. Take the first left at .1 mile (Mill Creek Road, FS 630). There is a sign for Lake Conasauga. The paved road ends at .5 mile. At 6.7 miles is Hickey Gap. At 8.9 miles is intersection with FS 17.

CISCO ACCESS. [Fig. 13(1), Fig. 14(1)] From Chatsworth take US 411 north 13.2 miles to Cisco community and intersection with Old Highway 2 (also known as FS 16). At .7 mile pass County Road 169 on the right. The pavement ends at 1 mile. Take the right fork at the Y intersection at 1.6 miles. (County Road 210 bears left.) At 3.2 miles, FS 17 comes in from the right, FS 16 goes left. Follow FS 16 just across the Tennessee state line to the northwestern trailhead of the Jacks River Trail. (Note that FS 51 branches to the right just after crossing the river. Stay left on FS 16.)

BLUE RIDGE ACCESS. [Fig. 13(8), Fig. 14(16)] From the intersection of US 76 and GA 5 just north of Blue Ridge, travel north 7 miles on GA 5 to Old Highway 2 and turn left. At 6.9 miles are Fightingtown Creek and McKinney Crossing. At 9 miles the pavement ends. At 10.5 miles, after a long climb up the mountain, look for the sign "Cohutta Wildlife Management Area, Watson Gap." Bear left on FS 64. Dyer Gap is 17.6 miles to the left on FS 64. Continue on FS 64. Where FS 64-A forks to the left, stay on FS 64 to the right. At 18.3 miles, cross the south fork of the Jacks River. At 18.4 miles, FS 64-B intersects on the left. At 20.2 miles, the Mountain Town Creek trailhead is on the left. At 22.9 miles are the Three Forks and East Cowpen [Fig. 14(15)] trailheads.

HIKING TRAILS OF THE COHUTTA WILDERNESS

With 95 miles of trails, the Cohutta Wilderness is a hiker's dream come true. After heavy rains, both the Jacks and Conasauga rivers can become raging torrents, virtually impossible to cross safely. Those planning a hike to the Cohutta Wilderness should watch weather forecasts carefully. Use a walking stick or staff to help cross rivers, and if water is raging, do not even try. In bad weather a trip may get extended. Be prepared for this possibility with extra food. Make sure people know the route of the hike and expected time of return. Even in low water, plan on getting wet. For example, the Conasauga River Trail between Betty Gap and FS 17 has 38 river crossings. Hiking boots will quickly become soggy foot weights. Many experienced hikers on the Conasauga and Jacks River Trails wear old tennis shoes and simply resign themselves to having wet feet. Bring dry shoes for camp.

Camping is permitted anywhere except in the trails and at trailheads. The trick is to find a spot flat enough. Fires are permitted using dead and down wood only. No permits are required. Please obey wilderness regulations posted on bulletin boards at trailheads. Horses are prohibited on certain trails. These trails are also posted on bulletin boards.

Text mileages that follow are from Tim Homan's book, *The Hiking Trails of North Georgia*. Homan's figures are regarded as accurate, since he walked and rewalked the trails using a measuring wheel.

Wilderness maps are available from the U.S. Forest Service District Office in Chatsworth or from patrolling Forest Service officers.

CONASAUGA RIVER TRAIL. [Fig. 14(14)] 13.1 miles. Marked by yellow blazes, a moderately difficult hiking trail that fords the river 38 times. Large Eastern hemlock trees are a feature of this trail, which is the roadbed of an old railroad. Bray Field is a popular, but sometimes crowded, camping area.

Directions: *See* Ellijay access (page 55) for southeastern trailhead at Betty Gap. From the FS 68/FS 64 three-way junction, turn right onto FS 64 and travel 1.4 miles to the Conasauga River Trail sign and parking area. *See* Cisco Access (page 57) for northwestern trailhead. At 3.2 miles, turn right onto FS 17 at the Conasauga River Trail sign. Go straight on FS 17 for 3.6 miles and turn left at FS 17-B and another Conasauga River Trail sign. FS 17-B ends shortly at the trailhead and parking area.

TEARBRITCHES TRAIL. [Fig. 14(13)] 3.2 miles. A moderately difficult to strenuous, orange-blazed trail, which climbs Bald Mountain (over 4,000 feet elevation) and then descends steeply to Bray Field—the junction for the Conasauga River and Hickory Creek trails and nearby Panther Creek Trail.

Directions: *See* Ellijay Access (page 55). At the FS 68/FS 64 three-way intersection, turn left toward Lake Conasauga. Pass Chestnut Lead trailhead. Trailhead is 3.5 miles from intersection.

CHESTNUT LEAD TRAIL. [Fig. 14(18)] .14 mile. An easy to moderately difficult, blue-blazed trail which provides a good look at skeletons of giant chestnut trees that thrived in this forest before the chestnut blight.

Directions: *See* Tearbritches Trail, *above*. Trailhead is 2 miles past FS 68/FS 64 three-way intersection on FS 68. Parking at trailhead.

PANTHER CREEK TRAIL. [Fig. 14(12)] 3.4 miles. A moderately difficult to strenuous, blue-blazed trail, very popular and scenic, passing a high waterfall. This trail has some very rugged, rocky sections.

Directions: *See* East Cowpen Trail (page 59) for eastern end. Trail is 2.3 miles from East Cowpen's southern trailhead. See Conasauga River Trail above for western end. Trail is 4.9 miles from Betty Gap.

HICKORY CREEK TRAIL. [Fig. 14(9)] 8.6 miles. An easy to moderately difficult, white-blazed trail, used as access to the Conasauga River, which can be reached from either trailhead. From the western trailhead, the Conasauga is a little more than 1.5 miles.

Directions: *See* Crandall Access (page 57) for western trailhead. Continue through the FS 630/FS 17 intersection on FS 630. The trailhead is .3 mile. *See* Cisco Access (page 57) for northern trailhead. After crossing the Conasauga River, turn right on FS 51. Travel 4.8 miles to the trailheads of Rice Camp and East Cowpen. Hickory Creek Trail starts about 140 yards along East Cowpen Trail.

EAST COWPEN TRAIL. [Fig. 14(15)] 7 miles. This moderately difficult to strenuous trail is a good, high-elevation trail, which follows the former route of Old Highway 2, on which erosion control was done before it was closed. Though not necessarily a good destination trail, it can provide relatively quick access to other trails.

Directions: *See* Hickory Creek Trail, northern trailhead (*above*), for northern trailhead. *See* Ellijay Access (page 55) for southern trailhead. At the three-way junction, take FS 64 right for 4.4 miles to the East Cowpen parking lot.

JACKS RIVER TRAIL. [Fig. 14(3)] 16.7 miles. This moderately difficult, orange-blazed trail is the roadbed of an old railroad. It is the longest and wettest trail in the Cohutta Wilderness, crossing the river 42 times. It is often crowded at the falls. The least-used portion of the trail is from Alaculsy to Jacks River Falls. In the middle of Horseshoe Bend are several beautiful spots to camp.

Directions: *See* Cisco Access (page 57) for northwestern trailhead. *See* Blue Ridge Access (page 57) for southeastern trailhead. At Watson Gap turn right on FS 22 and travel 3.6 miles to Dally Gap and Jacks River trailhead.

SUGAR COVE TRAIL. [Fig. 14(10)] 2.2 miles. A moderately difficult to strenuous, white-blazed, interior trail to Jacks River. Trail descends through a hardwood cove.

Directions: *See* Rough Ridge Trail, (*below*). Walk 2.1 miles on Rough Ridge Trail to sign at start of Sugar Cove Trail.

PENITENTIARY BRANCH TRAIL. [Fig. 14(8)] 3.6 miles. An easy to moderately difficult interior trail with its start on Hemp Top Trail. It ends at Jacks River.

Directions: *See* Jacks River Trail, southeastern trailhead at Dally Gap (*above*). Walk 2.3 miles on Hemp Top Trail to junction with Penitentiary Branch Trail.

ROUGH RIDGE TRAIL. [Fig. 14(7)] 7 miles. A moderately difficult to strenuous, blue- or white-blazed trail, providing access to Jacks River. Ridge trail that descends to a hardwood cove and then becomes very steep and sometimes rocky as it continues to descend to the river.

Directions: *See* East Cowpen Trail, *above*. Rough Ridge Trail begins .4 mile on East Cowpen Trail starting at its southern end.

HICKORY RIDGE TRAIL. [Fig. 14(6)] 3.6 miles. A moderately difficult to strenuous, yellow-blazed, interior trail to Jacks River and Jacks River Falls.

Directions: *See* East Cowpen Trail, *above*. From East Cowpen Trail's northern trailhead, walk 2.6 miles to the junction with Hickory Ridge Trail.

BEECH BOTTOM TRAIL. [Fig. 14(2)] 4 miles. An easy to moderately difficult, heavily used, access trail to Jacks River and Jacks River Falls.

Directions: *See* Cisco Access (page 57). From the Jacks River trailhead, take FS 221 in Tennessee (FS 16 in Georgia) 1 mile to FS 62. Turn right and continue 4.5 miles to a parking lot at trailhead.

RICE CAMP TRAIL. [Fig. 14(5)] 3.9 miles. An easy to moderately difficult, yellow-blazed access trail to Jacks River with several stream crossings.

Directions: *See* Hickory Creek Trail, northern trailhead (page 58).

HEMP TOP TRAIL. [Fig. 14(4)] 6.2 miles. A moderately difficult to strenuous, white-blazed, lesser-used trail that continues into the Big Frog Wilderness in Tennessee. The trail climbs up Big Frog Mountain.

Directions: *See* Jacks River Trail, southeastern trailhead at Dally Gap (page 59).

🐾 OFF-ROAD-VEHICLE TRAILS ON THE COHUTTA RANGER DISTRICT

WINDY GAP CYCLE TRAIL. [Fig. 13(5)] 5 miles. Designed for experienced trail bikers. Take US 411 north from Chatsworth for 4 miles. Turn right (east) at the traffic light in Eton and go about 5 miles. Turn left on FS 218 (Muskrat Road) and travel 2 miles to the trailhead. The northern portion is unsuitable for three- and four-wheelers. They must use Milma Creek to Tibbs ORV Trail.

MILMA CREEK ORV TRAIL. [Fig. 13(6)] 3.4 miles. Suitable for all-terrain vehicles. Connects Windy Gap Cycle Trail and Tibbs Trail. Access is by Windy Gap Cycle Trail. *See* directions above.

TIBBS ORV TRAIL. [Fig. 13(7)] 5 miles. Suitable for all-terrain vehicles. Note that this trail is closed by a gate at both ends. Access through Windy Gap Cycle Trail and Milma Creek ORV Trail. *See* directions above.

ROCKY FLATS ORV TRAIL. [Fig. 13(5)] 5 miles. Suitable for four-wheel-drive vehicles. Trail is 3 miles east of Crandall off Mill Creek Road (FS 630) on the right.

TATUM LEAD ORV TRAIL. [Fig. 13(9)] 7 miles. Both ends of trail are on private property. Trail begins 2.5 miles south of Tatum Lead Road and GA 52 (10 miles east of Chatsworth, .95 mile past Cohutta Lodge). Cross this 2.5 miles of private property in vehicle, and park on marked portion of trail. The trail dead-ends with no outlet.

ROCK CREEK ATV LOOP TRAIL. [Fig. 13(10)] 4.7 miles. Reached from GA 52 off the Tatum Lead ORV Trail, or take FS 3 past Peeples Lake. The trail is about .25 mile south of the low water bridge on Rock Creek. Suitable for all-terrain vehicles and cycles.

Lake Conasauga

Seventeen-acre Lake Conasauga [Fig. 14(17)], located at 3,150 feet, near the summit of Grassy Mountain, is the highest lake in Georgia. The name "Conasauga" is derived from the Cherokee word *kahnasagah*, meaning "grass," "sparkling water," or "strong horse," according to various sources. Grassy Mountain, at 3,682 feet, is one of the higher mountains in the area, and the grassy Ball Field is nearby.

Conasauga River and Lake Conasauga do indeed sparkle. The river has been compared to a strong horse because it overflowed its banks and flooded after heavy rain. Whatever the source of the name, a river, lake, and several Indian settlements in the area are called "Conasauga."

Lake Conasauga, the picnic area, and U.S. Forest Service roads 17, 18, and 68 were constructed by the Civilian Conservation Corps during the administration of Franklin D. Roosevelt.

A fully developed Forest Service campground is available. The 35 campsites have tent pads. Restrooms and cold running water are centrally located. Most of the sites are not on the lake, but are very close. This is a heavily used campground, and on busy summer weekends it is likely to be full. There is an overflow camping area. No water is available but there are portable toilets. The group camping area is a large grassy field without tables, grills, or water.

The entire recreation area is accessible from the day-use area, which has a restroom, water, tables, grills, two covered shelters, and a parking lot. The large, heavily used

SCARLET TANAGER
(Piranga olivacea)

This bird has a distinctive "chick-kurr" call.

but rarely full picnic area offers quiet solitude a short walk from the car. Food and equipment must be carried to the picnic tables and shelters that are some distance from the parking area. At the lake there is a developed swimming area with a pea-gravel bottom and a dock. There is no beach for sunbathing, but a pleasant, grassy ledge instead. Swimming is restricted to the marked swimming area. The water remains cool most of the summer, though by July 4 it is quite comfortable.

Off the picnic road is a boat ramp and parking lot access road. The lake is limited to electric motors, rowing, and paddling. It is a great place to canoe or raft.

Although the lake is heavily fished, some very large bass live in the deeps. Rainbow trout are stocked, and good populations of bream are also present.

LAKE CONASAUGA RECREATION AREA

[Fig. 14(17)] This is a Song Bird Management Area, where the trees and other vegetation are managed to provide the best bird habitat. Over 100 species of birds have been seen. These include hawks, owls, woodpeckers, kinglets, thrushes, vireos, warblers, cuckoos, phoebes, flycatchers, chickadees, titmice, nuthatches, brown creepers, wrens, tanagers, grosbeaks, indigo buntings, and red crossbills. A checklist of the birds is available from the Cohutta Ranger District Office.

Like most of Georgia's highlands, the elevation, climate, vegetation, and nesting birds of Lake Conasauga are similar to those in Pennsylvania. Georgia's mountains are the approximate southern limit for Eastern hemlock and Eastern white pine. This is an excellent area in which to see a wide range of trees, shrubs, herbs, and flowers representative of the southern highlands, including the yellow and black birch and mountain camellias. A plant list is also available from the ranger district office.

Directions: From Chatsworth, take US 441 north 4 miles; turn right (east) at traffic light at Eton; follow this country road making no turns until the pavement ends and it becomes FS 18; turn left (northeast) on FS 68 and travel 10 miles. From Ellijay take US 52 west from the square for about 7 miles to FS 18, marked with a sign for Lake Conasauga Recreation Area. Follow the paved road. Where the pavement ends, cross one-lane bridge. FS 18 marked here. Continue to the junction with FS 68; turn right and follow the signs to Lake Conasauga.

Activities: Hiking, camping, picnicking, swimming, boating (electric motors only), canoeing, fishing.

Facilities: Parking, trails, drinking water, restrooms.

For more information: U.S. Forest Service, Cohutta Ranger District, 401 Old Ellijay Road, Chatsworth, GA 30705. Phone (706) 695-6737.

HIKING TRAILS AROUND LAKE CONASAUGA

LAKE CONASAUGA TRAIL. 1.2-mile loop. An easy walk around the lake, passing through tunnels of rhododendron and crossing picturesque bridges. Interesting ferns, wildflowers, shrubs, trees, birds, and scenic views of the lake are found along the trail.

GRASSY MOUNTAIN TOWER TRAIL. 2 miles. From the dam on Lake Conasauga to the old fire tower atop Grassy Mountain, this trail makes an easy ascent along the ridge. To the west are excellent views of the wilderness and valley.

SONGBIRD TRAIL. 1.7-mile loop. This trail begins at the overflow, then runs along a small brook and around a beaver swamp through the Songbird Management Area, a series of clear-cuts which provide a variety of vegetation valuable to many songbirds.

Interpretive signs explaining songbird habitats lead hikers around the trail. Nature walks are offered on certain weekends between Memorial Day and Labor Day.

THE CONASAUGA RIVER

[Fig. 14] The Conasauga River is born deep in the Cohutta Wilderness. From its inception, it flows north through a series of rapids through almost inaccessible steep gorges before reaching the Alaculsy Valley. Here it appears to rest for a couple of miles before its confluence with the Jacks River. This upper section offers beautiful scenery and rough-country hiking.

Considered uncanoeable by most, at very high water levels the upper section provides a few hardy souls a wild-water experience hard to beat. The section beginning where the Conasauga leaves the valley at its confluence with the Jacks is more suited to recreational paddling. Here the river turns westward to cut across several ridges before bending south to join the Coosawattee and eventually become part of the Coosa River system.

This is a crystal-clear mountain stream which during the summer lacks sufficient water for easy navigation by canoe. On the section below the Jacks River confluence, most of the rapids are intricate Class I or Class II mazes—excellent water to help sharpen water-reading skills. There is one Class III rapid thrown into the middle of the run to keep paddlers alert on this exceptionally scenic river.

The Conasauga is normally high enough to run during the winter and spring months. Even at these higher levels it will remain clear. Since this river rises rapidly in times of flooding, avoid putting in if it is cloudy and turbid. There are no specific hazards for intermediate or advanced canoeists, although the one Class III rapid could cause problems for less-experienced paddlers. Cold-weather paddling trips are for experienced groups only. Full wet-suit protection and complete safety and first-aid gear are essential.

Directions: Travel north on US 411 over the Georgia state line. The Conasauga River bridge, which is the take-out point, is just a couple of miles across the line in Tennessee. To travel to the put-in, continue north on US 411 to the first paved road on the right next to a service station. This is Sheeds Creek Road; turn right. The pavement soon ends, but the roadbed is solid and will present no problems. Follow this same road for about 7 miles over several ridges until it drops down into a small valley. Several camping areas as well as the river will be visible on the right, followed by a large steel bridge. This is the Jacks River Bridge and marks the confluence of the Jacks and Conasauga rivers. There are several good launch sites in this area.

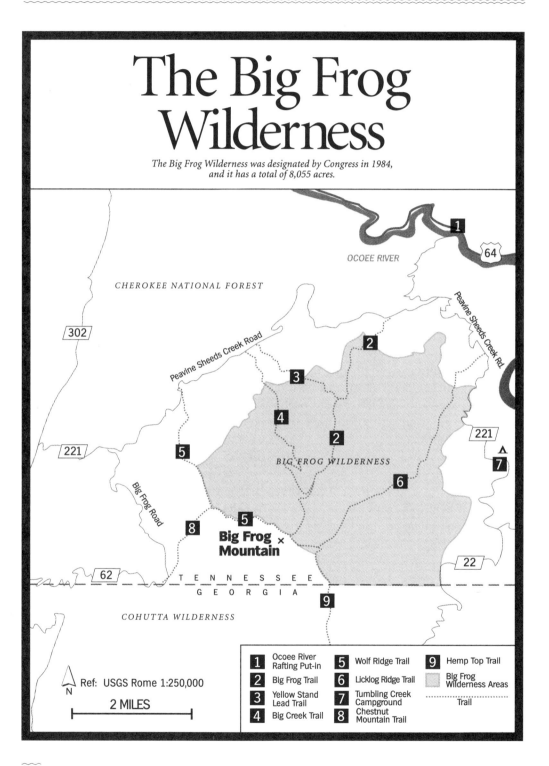

The Big Frog Wilderness

*The Big Frog Wilderness was designated by Congress in 1984,
and it has a total of 8,055 acres.*

OCOEE RIVER

64

1

CHEROKEE NATIONAL FOREST

Peavine Sheeds Creek Rd.

302

Peavine Sheeds Creek Road

2

3

4

2

221

221

7

BIG FROG WILDERNESS

6

Big Frog Road

5

5

8

Big Frog
Mountain ×

22

TENNESSEE
GEORGIA

9

COHUTTA WILDERNESS

62

Ref: USGS Rome 1:250,000

N

2 MILES

1	Ocoee River Rafting Put-in	5	Wolf Ridge Trail	9	Hemp Top Trail
2	Big Frog Trail	6	Licklog Ridge Trail		Big Frog Wilderness Areas
3	Yellow Stand Lead Trail	7	Tumbling Creek Campground		Trail
4	Big Creek Trail	8	Chestnut Mountain Trail		

The Big Frog Wilderness

The Cohutta Wilderness extends into Tennessee as far as the Eastern Continental Divide. Protruding from it is the isolated hulk of Big Frog Mountain [Fig. 15]. Big Frog is not a high mountain (4,224 feet), but, like Grassy Mountain (3,692 feet) in the Cohuttas, it appears more dominant because it stands alone. Lacking the protection of other mountains, it receives the full impact of cold fronts and other climatic events. In addition, it receives high rainfall. Big Frog is a scenic mountain. The top is forested; northern hardwoods are present, as is a boulderfield on the north side. Big Frog was designated a wilderness by Congress in 1984 and expanded in 1986. It totals 8,055 acres, 83 of which are in Georgia.

▓ ROAD ACCESS AND HIKING ACCESS TO BIG FROG WILDERNESS

COPPERHILL ACCESS. From Blue Ridge take GA 5 north to the Tennessee line. Pass through Copperhill and in about 2 miles take GA 251 west. Cross the Ocoee River and continue on GA 251 for 5.8 miles. Cross Tumbling Creek and intersect FS 221. Turn north on FS 221, Peavine–Sheeds Creek Road. Off this road, pass five trailheads to Big Frog Mountain. Note that at each trailhead, the distance from the trailhead to Big Frog Summit is given. At 2 miles, pass Tumbling Creek Campground [Fig. 15(7)]; at 5.6 miles reach Licklog Ridge Trail [Fig. 15(6)] (5.6 miles to summit); at 8.4 miles reach Big Frog trailhead [Fig. 15(2)] (5.2 miles to summit); at 13.1 miles reach Yellow Stand Lead Trail [Fig. 15 (3)], which ties into Big Frog Trail (5.4 miles to summit); at 13.2 miles reach Big Creek trailhead [Fig. 15(4)] (5.2 miles to summit); at 14.8 miles reach Wolf Ridge trailhead [Fig. 15(5)] (7.6 miles to summit); at 17.2 miles pass the turnoff on Big Frog Road (gated); and at 18.8 miles reach a fork in Alaculsy Creek Valley. Turn south on FS 221. Just north is the Sylco Campground. Continue down FS 221, but go straight when FS 221 turns west at 22.8 miles. One will reach Cisco on US 411 in 8 to 10 miles.

OCOEE RIVER ACCESS. From Copperhill north on TN 68, go 28 miles to US 64 intersection. Take US 64 west and go 8 miles. Take the first left road [Fig. 15(1)] after the highway begins running along the river. Just below this is the put-in for rafting the famous Ocoee River. After crossing the river one passes the USFS Thunder Rock Campground. Go 4 miles to intersect the Peavine–Sheeds Creek Road (FS 221) between Licklog Ridge (east) and Big Frog (west) trailheads. Note: It is well worth a few moments to drive down the Ocoee River Gorge just to watch the rafts go by. This whitewater trip rivals the Chattooga in excitement, but not as a wilderness experience, since US 64 closely follows the Ocoee.

CHESTNUT MOUNTAIN TRAIL. [Fig. 15(8)] Approximately 10 miles east of US 411 on FS 221 (Peavine–Sheeds Creek Road), turn east on FS 62 and go 6 miles to the trailhead. Hike 3.2 miles to Big Frog summit along Chestnut Mountain and Wolf Ridge.

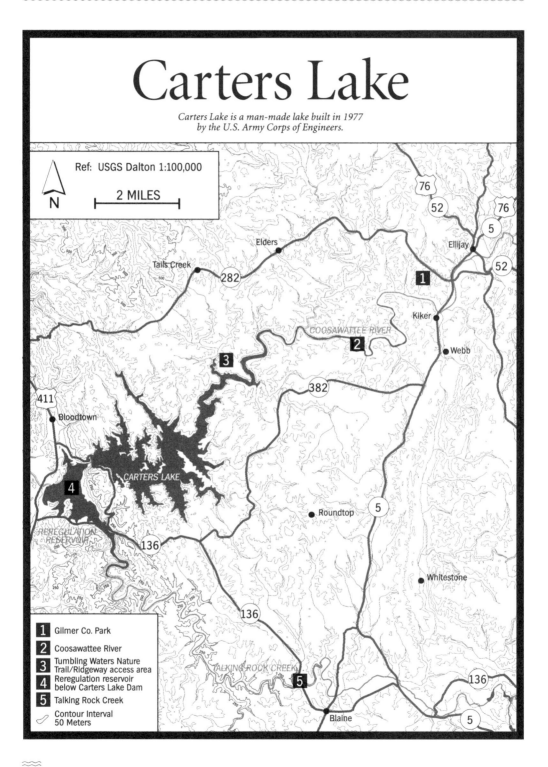

Carters Lake

*Carters Lake is a man-made lake built in 1977
by the U.S. Army Corps of Engineers.*

Ref: USGS Dalton 1:100,000

N

2 MILES

76
52
76
5
Elders
Ellijay
Tails Creek
282
52
1
Kiker
COOSAWATTEE RIVER
2
Webb
3
382
411
Bloodtown
CARTERS LAKE
4
Roundtop
5
REREGULATION RESERVOIR
136
Whitestone
136
TALKING ROCK CREEK
5
136
Blaine
5

1 Gilmer Co. Park
2 Coosawattee River
3 Tumbling Waters Nature
  Trail/Ridgeway access area
4 Reregulation reservoir
  below Carters Lake Dam
5 Talking Rock Creek

Contour Interval
50 Meters

Carters Lake

Located 12 miles south of Chatsworth off US 411, 3,500-acre Carters Lake [Fig. 16] was constructed by the U.S. Army Corps of Engineers in 1977. The lake provides many recreational opportunities including boating, swimming, camping, hiking, and fishing. A large area near the dam on the south shore has been developed by a concessionaire as the Blue Ridge Mountain Marina Resort. In a road cut below the dam one can see the Cartersville–Great Smoky Fault where Western Blue Ridge rocks rest against those of the Great Valley.

Directions: Access via GA 136 east from US 411. Follow signs.

Dates: The resource manager's office and visitor center is open year-round Mon.–Fri., and during the summer it is open daily.

For additional information: Contact the Resource Manager's Office, Carters Lake, PO Box 96, Oakman, GA 30732. Phone (706) 334-2248 or 2249.

CAMPING AT CARTERS LAKE

A map is available at the resource manager's office. Here, also, reservations can be made for campsites at Doll Mountain, Woodring Branch, and Harris Branch.

HARRIS BRANCH PARK. Group camping only. Shelter, 6 tables, large grill, 10 tent pads, running water, comfort station.

Dates: Public beach open daily May–mid-Sept. Closed Oct.–Mar.

DOLL MOUNTAIN PARK. 55 campsites, 39 with electrical and water hookups; 2 comfort stations with shower facilities and a recreational dump station.

Fees: There is a charge for campsites.

Dates: Closed Oct.–Mar.

RIDGEWAY PARK. 22 primitive campsites with pit toilets, boat ramp, and dock. Accessible by dirt road only. No charge.

WOODRING BRANCH. 32 campsites, all with electrical and water hookups; comfort station; and boat ramp. Another 12 campsites with pit toilets and a hand-operated water pump are available.

Fees: There is a charge for campsites.

Dates: Closed Nov.–Mar.

BLUE RIDGE MOUNTAIN MARINA RESORT. Cabins and rooms, rental house-boats, convenience store, pontoon and fishing boat rental, guided fishing trips, snack bar, and boat repair.

HIKING AT CARTERS LAKE

A map is available at the resource manager's office.

HIDDEN POND TRAIL. About .5 mile. The trail was constructed to provide access sites for bird watchers. Two bridges are part of the trail; one 20-foot bridge spans the stream near the entrance to the management area and a 210-foot structure crosses a beaver pond. An observation platform upstream at the edge of a second beaver pond provides a view of an active beaver lodge and offers an excellent opportunity for viewing waterfowl. Located near the entrance to the management area.

TUMBLING WATERS NATURE TRAIL. [Fig. 16(3)] Travels approximately 1 mile through a secluded valley carved by a mountain stream. The trail includes two viewing platforms located above a cliff from which hikers can view Tails Creek cascading into Carters Lake. Trailhead located in Ridgeway Park.

BIG ACORN NATURE TRAIL. About .2 mile. Easy trail along a wood-chip path. Signs identify trees and shrubs. The trailhead is at the Carters Lake Visitor Center.

BIKING AT CARTERS LAKE

RIDGEWAY MOUNTAIN BIKE TRAIL. The Ridgeway Recreational Area on Carters Lake is maintained by the Army Corps of Engineers. The trail is a 5.6-mile loop around Carters Lake that can be shortened or lengthened by taking the various trails branching off of it. The trail is narrow, fairly technical with a lot of ups and downs, and a good ridge for intermediate to advanced riders. Races are held here in the spring and fall, and downhill races are held at Carters Lake Dam. Be careful if you ride after a rain because the trail does get muddy, which is hard on the rider and the trail. Bathrooms, primitive camping, picnic tables, and drinking water are available near the trailhead. You can also take a swim in the lake to cool down after a hot ride. Camping with full facilities and beaches are available on the other side of the lake.

Carters Lake is a great place for a full-day outing of mountain biking, hiking, swimming, and boating. The overlook areas offer spectacular views, and the waterfall near the end of the trail is one of the most beautiful in Georgia.

Directions: Take GA 282 going west out of Ellijay approximately 8 miles. Turn left at the Ridgeway Recreational Area and Paw Paw Grocery signs.

For more information: Carters Lake, phone (706) 334-2248.

CANOEING TRIPS

THE COOSAWATTEE RIVER. [Fig. 16(2)] The Cartecay and Ellijay rivers meet in the town of Ellijay to form the Coosawattee, one of the largest rivers in north Georgia. Once out of town, the river turns west through the southern Cohuttas, carving downward more than 500 feet in 22 miles through a spectacular gorge and emerging through a narrow breach into what geologists call the Great Valley. The highest earthen dam east of the Mississippi now fills that breach, and Carters Lake has inundated more than half the river, including the biggest rapids and the highest cliffs.

This gorge was second only to Tallulah Gorge in grandeur. In fact, canoeing insiders believe that James Dickey's novel-turned-movie, *Deliverance*, which was filmed on the Chattooga, was actually written more with the Coosawattee in mind.

The upper section remains a fine run of intermediate difficulty, past forested bluffs. Because of the open nature of this river, with wide views of the surrounding trees, it is most scenic in April, when the woods are leafing out, and in October, during the fall color display. Although the river gradient is almost 30 feet per mile in places, the rapids do not exceed Class III and are separated by easy, flat sections which allow paddlers to relax and enjoy the scenery.

BROAD-WINGED KATYDID
(Microcentrum rhombifolium)
Heard more often than seen, these insects are named for their shrill song.

Directions: To find the put-in, first locate the GA 5 bridge over the Coosawattee south of Ellijay. On the north side of the bridge, turn west on Legion Road and drive about a mile to where the road comes just to the river's edge. To reach the take-out, go back out Legion Road to GA 5 up to GA 282 and west about 8 miles, watching for a large sign to the Ridgeway access area. Follow the signs to the boat ramp [Fig. 16(3)].

TALKING ROCK CREEK. [Fig. 16(5)] Talking Rock Creek is a beautiful, clear mountain stream deeply etched into the canyonlike foothills of the Cohutta and Blue Ridge mountains, just northwest of Jasper. Generally running northwest, it empties into the reservoir below Carters Lake Dam. Canoeists experience wild and remote country, high cliffs, and primitive mountain scenery, as well as Class I–III rapids.

Directions: The put-in and take-out are about 9 miles apart on GA 136. The put-in bridge is about 2 miles north of Blaine and the take-out bridge is where the creek runs into the reregulation reservoir below Carters Lake Dam [Fig. 16(4)]. Total distance from bridge to bridge is about 15 miles. Steady paddling by experienced canoeists makes a 6- to 8-hour trip feasible. Expect possible headwinds during the last 3 miles which could extend the length of the trip.

Map References: For Cohuttas, Rich Mountain, and Big Frog USGS 1:100,000 series: Cleveland–Dalton–Cartersville. USGS 1:24,000 series: Cashes Valley–Blue Ridge–Wilscot–Ellijay–Tickanetley Noontootla. For Big Frog, USGS 1:24,000 series: Epworth–Ducktown–Hemp Top–Caney Creek. County Highway Maps: Gilmer–Murray–Fannin–Gordon.

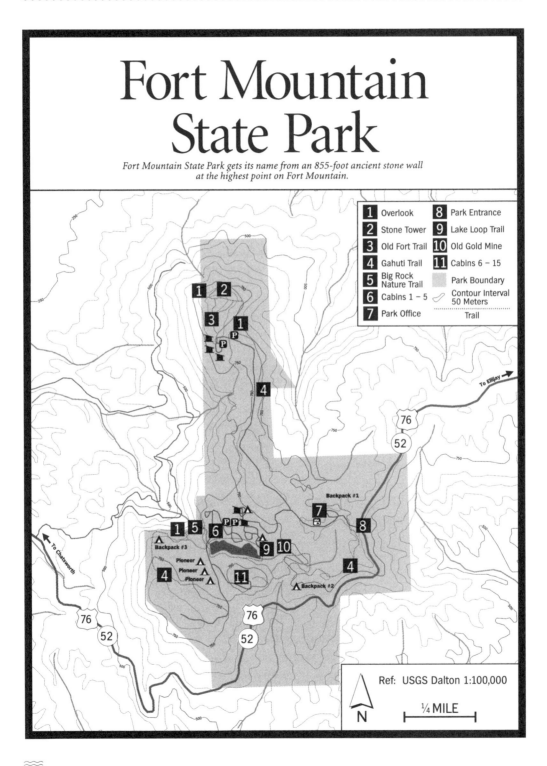

Fort Mountain State Park

Fort Mountain State Park gets its name from an 855-foot ancient stone wall at the highest point on Fort Mountain.

1	Overlook	8	Park Entrance
2	Stone Tower	9	Lake Loop Trail
3	Old Fort Trail	10	Old Gold Mine
4	Gahuti Trail	11	Cabins 6 – 15
5	Big Rock Nature Trail		Park Boundary
6	Cabins 1 – 5		Contour Interval 50 Meters
7	Park Office		Trail

Ref: USGS Dalton 1:100,000

¼ MILE

N

Fort Mountain State Park

Fort Mountain State Park [Fig. 17] is located on Fort Mountain, just southwest of the Cohutta Wilderness. The park derives its name from an ancient stone wall, measuring some 855 feet in length, which stands on the highest point of the mountain. Remains of circular depressions made of various-sized stones and measuring about 10 feet across occur in the wall at about 30-foot intervals. The wall ranges in height from 2 to 6 feet, although it was probably considerably higher in the past.

Archeologists and historians have been unable to solve the puzzle of who, if anyone, built the wall or why or when they built it. There are many theories. A favorite explanation is that the wall was built by the Woodland Indians around 500 A.D. The east-west orientation of its end points would result in alignment at sunrise and sunset at the solar equinox in both spring and fall.

The dramatic setting of the wall, offering expansive vistas to the east and west, could have added to its religious significance. Ceremonial centers similar to this one were built by the Woodland Indians at Old Stone Fort, Tennessee, and Rock Eagle Mound in Putnam County, Georgia. The Woodland Indians occupied the Southeast from several centuries B.C. to about 900 A.D.

A less probable but more romantic theory attributes the wall to a legendary Welsh prince named Medoc. He supposedly sailed into Mobile, Alabama, 500 years ago, then worked his way northward toward the Fort Mountain vicinity. Nothing else is known about Prince Medoc, except that his name is vaguely linked to several petroglyphs found in other parts of the Southeast.

Some geologists believe—and this is the least romantic explanation of all—that the "wall" is the result of natural weathering of a generally horizontal stratum of a hard caprock of quartzites and conglomerates.

In the 1930s the Civilian Conservation Corps built a 38-foot stone observation tower at the mountain's summit, 520 feet north of the wall. Its special feature is a heart-shaped stone which lies just above the east window.

A portion of Fort Mountain State Park's 3,268 acres was donated to the federal government in 1929 by Ivan Allen Sr. for the preservation of the stone wall and for the public's pleasure. In the 1940s it was turned over to the state of Georgia.

The hiking vistas and natural history are outstanding. The park has a spectacular cascade dropping 400 feet off the cliffs, an old gold mine [Fig. 17(10)] on streams feeding the lake, and an underlay of vast mineral deposits.

The visitor to Fort Mountain may hear the activity of commercial mines in the bowels of the mountain. Fort Mountain is probably Georgia's leading talc producer. Large companies moved in around 1900. Mines surround the mountain on three sides; two can be seen from the Chatsworth overlook.

Directions: Located 8 miles east of Chatsworth on GA 52. Take Exit 126 off I-75.

Facilities: There are 15 two- and three-bedroom cottages; 70 tent and trailer sites;

12 miles of foot trails; a swimming beach with bath house; paddle boats; 7 picnic shelters with 117 tables; and miniature golf.

For more information: Fort Mountain State Park, 181 Fort Mountain Park Road, Chatsworth, GA 30705. Phone (706) 695-2621. Call (800) 864-PARK, or (770) 864-PARK in metro Atlanta, for individual reservations.

FORT MOUNTAIN HIKING TRAILS

Inquire at the park office for detailed directions and a map.

GAHUTI TRAIL. [Fig. 17(4)] An 8.2-mile loop trail around Fort Mountain. Three limited-use camping sites are located along the trail for backpackers. An orange blaze, which is easy to see, designates the trail. Old logging roads crisscross the trail, and it is easy to mistake one of these for the trail. The first .3 mile looks out over the Cohutta Wilderness and is one of the finest views in Georgia. The trail begins at a gravel parking area marked "Cool Springs Overlook" in Fort Mountain State Park.

BIG ROCK NATURE TRAIL. [Fig. 17(5)] .6 mile. This trail provides hikers a glimpse of the rugged and diverse natural habitat found on Fort Mountain. Where the trail reaches the first branch, note the unusual occurrence of Catawba rhododendron. Then pass several rocky outcrops which form natural outlooks with chestnut oak as the dominant tree. One view is of a 400-foot cascade of Gold Mine Creek. Along this creek is ordinary rosebay, with mountain laurel, galax, and wild ginger.

LAKE LOOP TRAIL. [Fig. 17(9)] Approximately 1.2 miles. This trail follows along the edge of 17-acre Fort Mountain Lake. Enjoy the scenery and wildlife in the area including beautiful mountain overlooks and a gigantic boulderfield.

OLD FORT TRAIL. [Fig. 17(3)] 1.8 miles. This trail leads to the ancient stone wall from which Fort Mountain derives its name. The trail passes through a forest of alternating stands of scarlet oak, Virginia pine, and gnarled white oak. Past the wall there is a stone tower which children will love. West of the tower, a short trail leads to the Chatsworth Overlook platform.

GOLDMINE CREEK TRAIL. [Fig. 17(10)] 1.2-mile loop. Walk about .3 mile on the Lake Loop Trail and follow white blazes.

Note: As we go to press, 40 miles of mountain bike trails are planned for Fort Mountain State Park at various difficulty levels. Some of these trails will begin to open in early 1998.

The Copper Basin

At the junction where east Tennessee, northcentral Georgia, and southwest North Carolina meet, the Copper Basin stands out in startling contrast to its surroundings—the epitome of man's disregard for nature. Its denuded red hills shimmer with glowing colors ranging from soft pastels to dark copper and reddish hues, surrounded by a ring of lush green mountains, thus giving the illusion of a bowl or basin. Various ranges in the Blue Ridge province, some with elevations reaching 4,200 feet, can be seen in every direction.

Approximately 35,000 acres of rolling hills, the Copper Basin has been described as a moonscape, a red desert, or a beloved scar (by people who were born, raised, and continue to live in this area) and is damaging testimony to the long-term effect of acid rain. However, unlike present-day acid rain, that which produced the Copper Basin fell close to its point of origin, was highly visible, and had an immediate as well as long-range effect. Efforts to reclaim the proper balance of nature have been numerous and reportedly represent the most extensive reclamation project attempted in the United States.

Devastation of the Copper Basin is usually attributed to the copper mining industry. Other factors, however, also contributed. Burning by the Cherokee Indians, followed by early settlers' burning to clear land, established a pattern of land abuse early on. According to Tennessee historian J. B. Killebrew in 1874, the Copper Basin area was "a barren sterile region prior to 1850."

In the mid-1800s, the arrival of the copper mining industry was heralded with exuberance, as it provided much-needed livelihood for the local mountain people. During this period the Copper Basin was a veritable boom area, with people converging from every direction to participate in the mining, as well as the development of the railroad. The basin's forests were badly cut over to obtain fuel for copper smelting, then subjected to copper sulfide fumes generated by open-air roasting of copper ore. The fumes—spread farther when high smoke stacks were added after 1907—hung close to the ground or mixed with frost, fog, or rain, killing nearly every remaining tree, bush, shrub, weed, and growing plant in the 35,000-acre area. At that time little thought was given to the effect on the land. Even today, in spite of the ravaged land that remains as a result of copper mining, the people who worked in the mines and their families are fiercely proud of their barren hills.

The devastation was twofold when mining operations ceased. The land was exhausted, as was the morale of the people left with no source of income. Adding insult to injury, long after the copper smelting fumes were controlled, Tennessee law permitted open-range cattle grazing. Lowland farmers drove and later trucked cattle up into the basin for free grazing, having burned the land indiscriminately to encourage springtime growth of thin sedge pasturage.

Reclamation began with the help of the Civilian Conservation Corps in the early

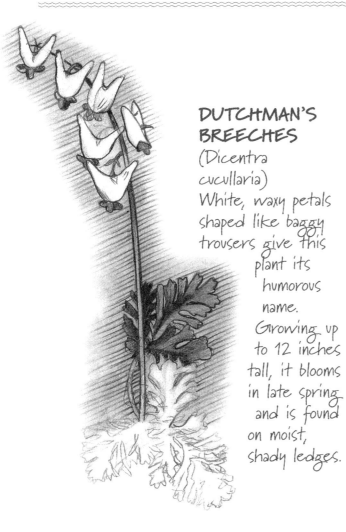

DUTCHMAN'S BREECHES

(Dicentra cucullaria)
White, waxy petals shaped like baggy trousers give this plant its humorous name. Growing up to 12 inches tall, it blooms in late spring and is found on moist, shady ledges.

1930s. It has continued through the efforts of at least three copper companies as well as the Tennessee Valley Authority (TVA), U.S. Soil Conservation Service, U.S. Forest Service, Tennessee Division of Natural Resources, other state agencies, and the Universities of Tennessee, Georgia, and North Carolina. The hillsides have been roughly regraded, partially terraced, and thickly planted with pines, bush clover, weeping lovegrass, clumps of Japanese knotweed, and kudzu. Rock check dams have been built and locust seedlings planted in the accumulated soil above the dams.

The Tennessee Chemical Company still operates a sulfuric acid plant in Copperhill, Tennessee. However, the area's future seems to point to tourism, with the proliferation of whitewater enthusiasts who pass through this area on the way to nearby rapids of the Ocoee River.

The Copper Basin is now listed on the National Register of Historic Places. The Tennessee Chemical Company has given the old abandoned Burra Burra mine, together with 17 hilltop acres with old buildings, to the Ducktown Basin Museum. In 1988 the state of Tennessee purchased the museum to commemorate the copper mining area as the state's first historical industrial site.

Directions: From Blue Ridge, Georgia, go north on GA 5 for 11 miles to Copperhill, then north on TN 68 to US 64, which bisects the area from east to west.

Map References: USGS 1:100,000 series: Cleveland.

The Rich Mountains

The 13,276-acre Rich Mountains [Fig. 18] are primarily wilderness (9,649 acres) and primitive backcountry (3,627 acres) that is not heavily used. The Rich Mountains are remarkable because many of the peaks and ridges are covered with a deep, black porter's loam, a characteristic these mountains share with the Cohuttas. In the Eastern Blue Ridge, such soils are confined to coves.

On the Rich Mountains, this soil covering results in spectacular wildflower displays. On ridges and slopes alike, one finds lush summer herb growth and forests of basswood, ash, and black cherry—trees that occur in the Eastern Blue Ridge mostly in high rich coves. Gaps—at least in the Turniptown area—have populations of the rare columbo, a most unusual plant. There is old growth timber south of Turniptown Mountain. North-facing coves have boulderfields and rare northern wildflowers at the southern limit of their range. There is a large bear population, and one can find "licks" where deer have eaten clay-rich soil.

About 60 inches of rain fall here each year, May usually being the wettest month and April and July the driest.

Sites of old Indian camps can be found along the high ridgelines. Remnants of white settlements dating from about 1910 are just north of this range's namesake peak, Rich Mountain [Fig. 18(6)]. The largest gold nugget ever found in Georgia came from a creek draining this area. Marble, which is mined at the famous quarries near Tate and Marble Hill, can also be found exposed in the bottom of the Murphy Syncline (*see below*).

Elevation varies from approximately 2,000 feet near Little Rock Creek to 4,081 feet on Big Bald Mountain [Fig. 18(7)]. High peaks and lookouts from the Old Road offer panoramic vistas after leaves fall. Rugged mountain terrain with rock outcrops and streams with many small waterfalls create a beautiful scenery.

US 76 between Ellijay and Blue Ridge, Georgia, generally follows the Murphy Syncline, which divides the highly metamorphosed rocks of the Blue Ridge proper from the moderately metamorphosed rocks of the Cohuttas.

This remarkable geologic trough is clearly visible in satellite photographs. It is likely, though, that the uninformed visitor driving up US 76 in the deep gash of the Murphy Syncline would pass the Rich Mountains area by, since the higher peaks and ridges are barely visible from the road. Hikers exploring the Rich Mountains area should be experienced and carry topographical maps, compass, and other survival gear.

Aska Trails Area. This area contains a 17-mile hiking and mountain biking trail system located on national forest land near Deep Gap and Stanley Gap south of Blue Ridge and east of Ellijay. Trails ascend to near 3,200 feet, providing vistas of mountain ridges, and descend to the shores of beautiful Lake Blue Ridge. They also pass through coves of mature hardwoods as well as traversing thickets of laurel and rhododendron.

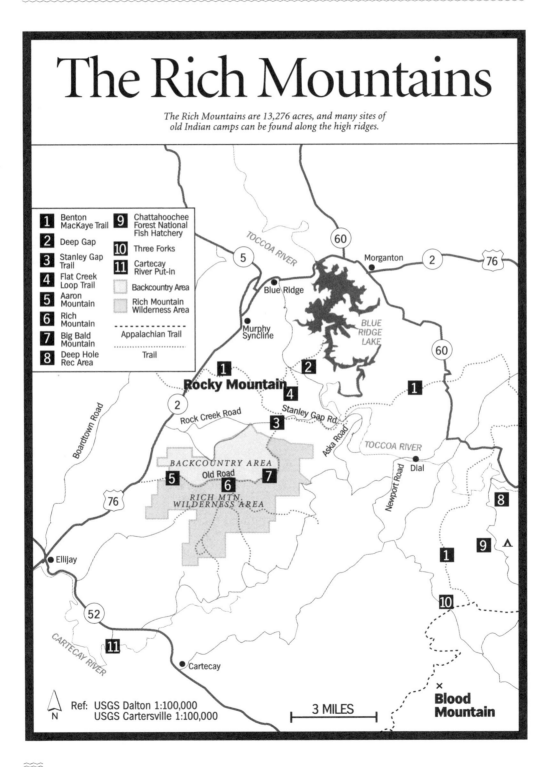

The Rich Mountains

The Rich Mountains are 13,276 acres, and many sites of old Indian camps can be found along the high ridges.

1 Benton MacKaye Trail
2 Deep Gap
3 Stanley Gap Trail
4 Flat Creek Loop Trail
5 Aaron Mountain
6 Rich Mountain
7 Big Bald Mountain
8 Deep Hole Rec Area
9 Chattahoochee Forest National Fish Hatchery
10 Three Forks
11 Cartecay River Put-in

Backcountry Area
Rich Mountain Wilderness Area

- - - - - Appalachian Trail
· · · · · · Trail

TOCCOA RIVER

60
5
Morganton
2
76

Blue Ridge
Murphy Syncline
BLUE RIDGE LAKE
60

1 **2**
Rocky Mountain
4
1

2
Rock Creek Road
Stanley Gap Rd.
3
Aska Road
TOCCOA RIVER
Dial

Boardtown Road

BACKCOUNTRY AREA
Old Road
5 **6** **7**
RICH MTN. WILDERNESS AREA

76

Newport Road
8

1
9 ⚐

1

10

52

11
CARTECAY RIVER

Ellijay

Cartecay

N
Ref: USGS Dalton 1:100,000
        USGS Cartersville 1:100,000

3 MILES

× Blood Mountain

Directions: From Blue Ridge travel 1.5 miles east on E. First Street to Aska Road. Go south on Aska Road 4.4 miles to Deep Gap. Park in the parking area on the west side below the gap. To reach Stanley Gap, continue south on Aska Road 3.7 miles to the intersection with Stanley Creek Road. Turn right (west) and go 4.2 miles to the parking area 100 yards below Stanley Gap.

STANLEY GAP TRAIL

[Fig. 18(3)] This trail offers a moderately strenuous 5-mile hike (one-way) or a difficult 12-mile bike ride (including the mileage along the roads to return to the trailhead) through a typical southern Appalachian hardwood forest with a variety of trees, shrubs, and wildflowers unmatched in their diversity throughout the country. Views of surrounding mountains, especially in winter on the overview of Lake Blue Ridge, add to the outdoor experience.

The trail begins at the corner of the parking lot at Deep Gap and starts as a gradual climb toward the summit of Davenport Mountain. There are several short, relatively steep ascents, but they are not strenuous. The trail along the south side of Davenport Mountain provides an overview of the mountains to the south and west. From the top of Rocky Mountain, the trail descends for 2.9 miles to Stanley Gap.

For the mountain biker, this is one of the most difficult bike rides in the area, but an incredible view greets you at the top, particularly in the winter and spring when there are fewer leaves. Once you descend to Stanley Gap, make a left off Stanley Creek for 2 miles, make a left on Aska Road, ride for 2.5 miles, and you are back at your car.

It's always important when you ride—particularly on a remote trail like this one—that you ride with someone and let someone know where you are going and when you expect to be back. In addition, the mountain biker survival motto is "always eat before you're hungry and drink before you're thirsty." Less-experienced riders on this trail especially should heed this bit of advice.

GREEN MOUNTAIN TRAIL

[Fig. 18] This 3.3-mile trail offers a very pleasant hike or bicycle ride, first over-looking and then alongside the shoreline of Lake Blue Ridge. The forest type is basic southern Appalachian hardwood with a variety of trees, shrubs, and wildflowers. Forest animals are rarely seen, but include deer and turkey. The trail begins on the east side of Aska Road at Deep Gap and starts as a gradual climb toward the summit of Green Mountain. On the trail there are five short, relatively steep ascents, but they are not strenuous. The ridge atop Green Mountain provides an overview of Charlie's Cove of Lake Blue Ridge. The trail then descends for 2.4 miles to its terminus on FS 711. Views of Lake Blue Ridge are found almost the entire way after cresting the mountaintop.

FLAT CREEK LOOP TRAIL

[Fig. 18(4)] This 5.8-mile, moderately difficult loop trail provides a range of forested settings as well as a short segment along a mountain creek. Beginning at Deep Gap on Aska Road, follow the white and dark green blazes west from the bulletin board at the parking lot. Within 100 yards the trail forks—bear left on the roadbed. At about .4 mile, take the side trail with the dark green blaze into the woods on the left. This trail goes through woods for about .25 mile. The trail follows an old logging roadbed before it rejoins a dug trail and gradually descends toward Flat Creek. After .5 mile, the trail joins an old road near the creek. Follow the road downhill to the creek, cross the creek, and go right at about 50 yards on an old road. Follow the road about 1 mile to the head of a valley with mature hardwoods in abundance. Cross the creek, again heading uphill, and gradually ascend to a gravel road. Follow the gravel road with the dark green blaze 2 miles back to the parking lot.

AARON MOUNTAIN

[Fig. 18(5)] This mountain has a rounded dome covered with rich, black soil and a wildflower display in spring. An old timber growth (129 years) lies on the south face of Aaron Mountain. At Horse Cove, there is a good boulderfield and a northern hardwood forest with some possibly record-sized, second-growth trees, especially silverbell.

RED & WHITE AND RIVER LOOP MOUNTAIN BIKE TRAILS

The Red & White and River Loop trails are sister trails located in the Cartecay Tract of the Rich Mountain Wildlife Management Area off Highway 52 East. The Red & White is a 2.6-mile, beginner/intermediate trail closest to the entrance of the management area. This trail is a single-track loop with occasional rocky or rooty sections. Dogwoods line this trail and brighten the trail in the spring. Be prepared for a long climb near the end of the trail. If you're looking for a short, relative easy ride, be careful not to turn on the River Loop or you might be out longer than you planned.

The River Loop is a 3.4-mile, intermediate/advanced trail just below the Red & White that follows the Cartecay River in sections. The single track is tight in spots, a few rocky descents challenge even the bravest riders to walk, a sand trap swallows your tires near the river, and an occasional windblown tree clutters the trail. Once you conquer the steep downhill, you can cool down with a dip in the Cartecay River or nap in the sun on the rocks. This is a beautiful ride, and it can easily be coupled with a ride on the Red & White or other trails in the area to make a full day of riding.

Directions: Travel east on Highway 52 going away from Ellijay. Approximately 4 miles outside the city, turn right on Mulkey Road and then right again into the Rich Mountain Wildlife Area. You will need to park your car and ride a short distance to the trailheads.

OWLTOWN CREEK MOUNTAIN BIKE TRAIL

The Owltown Creek Trail is the access point for the Owltown Mountain Trail, and, while only 4 miles long, the loop offers something for riders at every skill level: tight, rocky single track; a few creek crossings; some steep descents and ascents; grassy, double track; and a gravel road. The Ellijay Chapter of SORBA (Southern Off-Road Bicycle Association) and the Cartecay River Bike Shop, the bike shop in the area, hold beginner/intermediate bike clinics on this trail. True beginners might want to start the ride at the lower end of the trail where it crosses the bridge on Owltown Creek.

Directions: Take Highway 52 going east 3 miles outside Ellijay toward Amicalola Falls. The trailhead is at the Cartecay River Bike Shop and parking is free. Rental bikes and a bathroom are available on-site. Helmets are required on all group rides.

For more information: Call toll-free (888) 276-BIKE or visit the website www.mindspring.com/~gabikes.

LAKE BLUE RIDGE. [Fig. 18] The lake shimmers like a sapphire in a green granite setting. Most of the surrounding land is part of the Chattahoochee National Forest, which protects the lake from being overly developed. Except for a few water skiers, most of the visitors come to camp and fish. Although the prime fishing attractions are walleye, bluegill, and smallmouth bass, this is the only lake in the state where one can battle the mighty muskie, a large game fish of the pike family. Thirty-five fish attractors—man-made feeding covers—have been scattered around the coves and creeks. Lake Blue Ridge is fed by the north-flowing Toccoa River. The river flows gently for about 15 miles north of the dam, then changes its name to the Ocoee and froths into one of the Southeast's most exhilarating whitewater streams for rafting and kayaking.

For more information: Contact the U.S. Forest Service, Toccoa Ranger District, Suite 5, Owenby Building, Blue Ridge, GA 30513. Phone (706) 632-3031.

LAKE BLUE RIDGE TRAIL. .6 mile. A loop trail that follows the shoreline of Lake Blue Ridge and offers a beautiful view of the lake.

Directions: From Blue Ridge take old US 76 east for 1.5 miles to Dry Branch Road; turn right; go 3 miles to the entrance to the Blue Ridge Recreation Area. The trail begins and ends in the picnic area.

LAKE BLUE RIDGE CAMPSITES. 55 campsites in the area, several along the lake; bathrooms and showers; no hookups provided. For availability around the lake Memorial Day through Labor Day, contact the U.S. Forest Service, Toccoa Ranger District (*see* address above). Phone (706) 632-3031.

LAKE BLUE RIDGE BOAT RENTAL. Fishing boats can be rented at the Blue Ridge Lake Marina, phone (706) 632-2618, on the northern side, near the dam. It is the only commercial outlet on the lake for gas, food, and supplies. It also provides one of several boat launch ramps. Others are at Morganton Point and the more remote Lake Blue Ridge Recreation Area (also known as Dry Branch or Green Creek).

The U.S. Forest Service offers tent camping and picnic areas at both sites, phone (706) 632-3031. For additional information, contact the Fannin County Chamber of Commerce, PO Box 875, Blue Ridge, GA 30513. Phone (706) 632-5680.

MORGANTON POINT RECREATION AREA

Located on the shores of Lake Blue Ridge .5 mile from the town of Morganton, this campground contains 37 campsites, 8 picnic sites, a designated swimming area with a lifeguard on duty during the summer camping season, and a boat launch ramp. No showers or hiking trails are located within this recreation area, and electricity is available only in the bathrooms.

Directions: From Blue Ridge take old US 76 east and south of town to Lakewood Junction. Here GA 60 and US 76 join, with GA 60 continuing as the designated main road south and east to Morganton. It is approximately 5 miles from Blue Ridge to Morganton. The drive is scenic, crossing the TVA dam with a splendid view of Lake Blue Ridge to the southwest. Also between the dam and Lakewood Junction is a U.S. Forest Service boat launch ramp near Lakewood. At Morganton, look for the white-on-green sign to the recreation area on the right side of the road just before the road turns east and south.

DRIVING TOURS

ASKA ROAD TO NEWPORT ROAD. Starting from the intersection of old US 76 and Aska Road, go south 13.8 miles. Turn left at the dead end onto a paved road to Dial, Georgia. This road comes out on GA 60, where one can head for either Dahlonega or Morganton. For a picture-postcard alternative, turn right at the dead end onto Newport Road and go 4.5 miles to SR 1010. Turn right and go 12.2 miles to Cartecay.

BOARDTOWN ROAD BETWEEN ELLIJAY AND BLUE RIDGE. This 18.6-mile drive between Ellijay and Blue Ridge provides a good look at the intimacy and charm of the north Georgia countryside. Visitors will pass red barns and silver silos, small green fields with silver creeks running through them and cows wandering about, Christmas tree farms, double-wides, and cedar homes. Pickup truck drivers will lift an index finger off the steering wheel to say "howdy" as they pass.

Directions: From the town square in the center of Ellijay, take GA 52 and GA 2 west (Dalton Street) to Boardtown Road, about .4 mile from the center of town. There is a Beardtown Road sign, as well as a sign to Sugar Creek Raceway.

THE CARTECAY RIVER

[Fig. 18(11)] The Cartecay is a small, intimate river located east of Ellijay. Flowing out of a long valley and past farmlands, it passes over a series of tight drops around upland ridges. It then returns to its more placid nature just prior to its confluence with the Ellijay River, where the two become the Coosawattee. The

Cartecay is a narrow, clear mountain stream with almost continuous Class I and II rapids for the first 5.5 miles of this section. Although level, it is fast flowing along steep ridges and through shaded tree canopies for the final 6 miles. This is intermediate to advanced whitewater with one unavoidable Class III rapid. The river requires more skill than the upper Chattahoochee and Broad rivers. In places it is comparable to Section III of the Chattooga.

Directions: Put in on a dirt road located 2.5 miles east of Ellijay on GA 52 past Oak Hill Apple House. Turn right onto the dirt road and go 1.5 miles to the river [Fig. 18(11)]. Take out at a small roadside park along GA 52 east of Ellijay.

Map References: For Cohuttas and Rich Mt., USGS 1:24,000 series: Cashes Valley–Blue Ridge–Wilscot–Ellijay–Tickanetley–Noontootla. County Highway Maps: Gilmer–Murray–Fannin–Gordon.

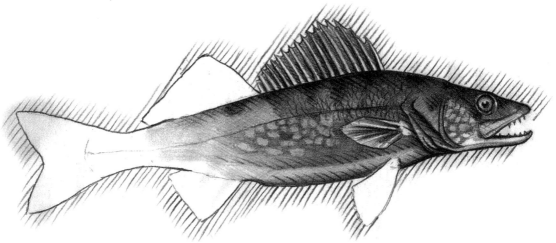

WALLEYE
(Stizostedion vitreum)

With a common name stemming from its large eye, the walleye is sometimes erroneously called a "walleyed pike." Walleye can grow to 2 feet long and up to 20 pounds.

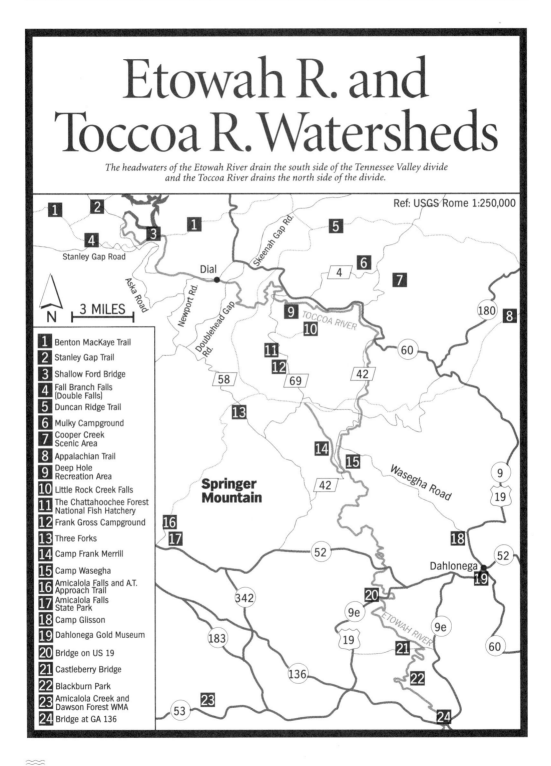

Etowah R. and Toccoa R. Watersheds

The headwaters of the Etowah River drain the south side of the Tennessee Valley divide and the Toccoa River drains the north side of the divide.

Ref: USGS Rome 1:250,000

N — 3 MILES

Stanley Gap Road

Aska Road

Newport Rd.

Doublehead Gap Rd.

Skeenah Gap Rd.

Dial

TOCCOA RIVER

Springer Mountain

Wasegha Road

Dahlonega

ETOWAH RIVER

1 Benton MacKaye Trail
2 Stanley Gap Trail
3 Shallow Ford Bridge
4 Fall Branch Falls (Double Falls)
5 Duncan Ridge Trail
6 Mulky Campground
7 Cooper Creek Scenic Area
8 Appalachian Trail
9 Deep Hole Recreation Area
10 Little Rock Creek Falls
11 The Chattahoochee Forest National Fish Hatchery
12 Frank Gross Campground
13 Three Forks
14 Camp Frank Merrill
15 Camp Wasegha
16 Amicalola Falls and A.T. Approach Trail
17 Amicalola Falls State Park
18 Camp Glisson
19 Dahlonega Gold Museum
20 Bridge on US 19
21 Castleberry Bridge
22 Blackburn Park
23 Amicalola Creek and Dawson Forest WMA
24 Bridge at GA 136

The Etowah River and Toccoa River Watersheds

The Etowah River and the Toccoa River flow in different directions. The Etowah drains the south side of the Tennessee Valley Divide, while the Toccoa drains the north side. In these watersheds, visitors will find the highest waterfall in Georgia, as well as the approach trail for the beginning of the Appalachian Trail. A fish hatchery allows one to see how the hundreds of thousands of rainbow trout stocked in Georgia's rivers and streams are raised to catching size. The two fine rivers provide canoeing opportunities for boaters of varying skills and experience.

▓ CANOEING

ETOWAH RIVER. The upper section of the Etowah River is ideal for beginning canoeists, families, and organized groups who want to run a brisk mountain river and also be close to the scenic and historical attractions of Dahlonega. A 12-mile stretch can be canoed in one day of steady paddling or two leisurely days. (Those opting for the two-day version can break the trip at Castleberry Bridge and camp at the nearby Blackburn Park [Fig. 19(22)] 1.3 miles south of Auraria on GA 9E or go into Dahlonega 7 miles south on 9E.)

One hazard is Etowah Falls, 1.5 miles from the put-in. The canoeist must land on the rocks on the right bank and portage over or around them. Below Castleberry Bridge [Fig. 19(21)] is an old mine tunnel about 7 feet in diameter and about .2 mile long. Scout this carefully. Run it only if light is visible at the other end; if the exit light is not clear and bright, the tunnel is likely to be too obstructed with debris and stumps to be safely passable.

Directions: Put in at the bridge on US 19 west of Dahlonega [Fig. 19(20)]. Castleberry Bridge [Fig. 19(21)] is a good take-out, or the trip may be continued to the bridge at GA 136 [Fig. 19(24)].

TOCCOA RIVER. Some knowledgeable canoeists have described the Toccoa [Fig. 17(18)] as Georgia's prettiest whitewater stream. It has its headwaters in Union County, flows into Fannin County, and becomes the major feeder stream for Lake Blue Ridge. It resumes its flow below Blue Ridge and travels into Tennessee, where it is known as the Ocoee.

The stream's first couple of miles illustrate the startling contrast between undisturbed river banks and those touched by human hands. In apparent efforts to squeeze a little more yield from floodplains, some farmers have cleared to the edge of the water, removing vegetation which holds the soil. The unhappy consequence is that the banks are rapidly eroding, dumping silt and any remaining vegetation into the water.

The river offers a variety of interesting forms of vegetation for each season. Early spring brings bluets in the moss, then azalea, laurel, and—all around Deep Hole Campground—wild strawberries. In late spring, abundant rhododendron garnishes the banks. Summer offers the richness of mature hardwood stands in full leaf. When autumn comes, the hardwoods take on an incredible glow. Alternate leaf dogwood and deciduous holly sport their bright red berries right on into winter. When upper-story trees provide enough shade, galax carpets the banks. The waxy leaves are dark green until December, then they thrive as coppery as pennies for the winter months. Galax is gathered frequently for use in floral arrangements. Sadly, this has led to its near-extinction in many areas.

The most beautiful section of the Toccoa River lies behind Toonowee Mountain. Small rapids, hemlocks trailing in the water, and the beautifully clear stream itself combine to saturate the senses.

Directions: Put-in for the upper section is at Deep Hole [Fig. 19(9)], a U.S. Forest Service campground on GA 60, 27 miles north of Dahlonega. Driving from Deep Hole, continue north on GA 60 for 4.5 miles and then left onto an unmarked, paved road that goes between two buildings and looks at first like a driveway. Continue on mixed gravel/paved roads to Dial, where there are two bridges. On the way is the Chastain House, the oldest home in Fannin County. The old bridge at Dial is blocked to traffic and so is the take-out (or, if you're running the lower section, the put-in). If the put-in is at Dial, the take-out is at the Shallow Ford Bridge, reached on the east side of the river by continuing on the gravel road along the river and bearing left at a fork about midway; or cross the Dial Bridge to the west side of the river. Continue on the paved road to the first road on the right, turn right, and continue until reaching the Shallow Ford Bridge [Fig. 19(3)].

WATERFALLS
LONG CREEK FALLS. Picturesque falls and trail. Requires a 20- to 30-minute walk in each direction.

Directions: From Blue Ridge follow old US 76 to Aska Road across from Harmony Church. Turn south and go 13.8 miles to the end of the road. Turn right on Newport Road, and go 4.3 miles to the end of the road. Turn left, cross bridge over Noontootla Creek, continue on gravel road. Pass a cemetery and come to an intersection .6 mile from the bridge. Turn hard right on FS 58 and go southeast into the forest along this road 6.6 miles to Three Forks [Fig. 19(13)]. Hike to the northwest up Long Creek to the falls. The trail corridor has an assortment of blazes designating three major hiking trails: the Appalachian (white vertical, 2 inches by 6 inches), the Duncan Ridge National Recreational Trail (blue vertical, 2 inches by 6 inches), and the Benton MacKaye Trail (white diamond, 5 inches by 7 inches). The distance to the falls is 1.1 miles, ascending gradually along the way. A side trail to the falls is indicated with vertical blue blazes.

FALL BRANCH FALLS. [Fig. 19(4)] A fine double waterfall.

Directions: From Blue Ridge follow old US 76 to Aska Road. Turn south and go approximately 8.2 miles to the intersection with Stanley Creek Road, entering from the right. Turn right onto Stanley Creek Road and go 3.2 miles to a small parking area just beyond an interesting farm owned by longtime Forest Service fire warden Garfield Stanley. Cross a wooden bridge over Fall Branch and park on the right. Hike up the hill on the Benton MacKaye Trail to double falls [Fig. 19(4)] on the right. There is a small picnic and/or camping spot 30 yards above the waterfall.

SEA CREEK FALLS.

Directions: From Blue Ridge follow old US 76 east 5 miles to the intersection with GA 60 South at Lakewood Junction. Continue 14.7 miles south on GA 60 through the small town of Morganton, past the entrance to Deep Hole Recreation Area, to the junction with FS 4 on left. Follow FS 4 an additional 3.3 miles to a right-hand curve in the road just inside the U.S. Forest Service boundary. The road to the immediate left before curve is the access to the falls. Park in the area at the end of this spur (about .3 mile) and walk upstream 150 feet to view the falls.

LITTLE ROCK CREEK FALLS. [Fig. 19(10)] There is a series of small falls just before reaching the main one. The walk is strenuous on a footpath leading along the left side of the creek and going only part of the way to the falls. Go no farther than this because of the dangerous, slippery rocks in the area.

Directions: From Blue Ridge follow the directions above for Sea Creek Falls, but only as far as the crossing of Skeenah Creek on GA 60 South. Skeenah Creek is located about 11.3 miles south of Morganton. There is an old but still-operational mill on the northeast side of the highway. A commercial campground is also located on this site. After crossing Skeenah Creek, continue south on GA 60 another 3.1 miles to the intersection with FS 69, Fish Hatchery Road, on the right. Turn onto this road and go about 3 miles to where the road crosses Little Rock Creek [Fig. 19(10)]. There is a bridge and a small pull-out area here.

CAMPING AND RECREATION

THE CHATTAHOOCHEE FOREST NATIONAL FISH HATCHERY. [Fig. 18(9), Fig. 19(11)] The hatchery produces rainbow trout for stocking in rivers, streams, and lakes of the Chattahoochee National Forest and other areas of north Georgia. While spawning operations are not conducted at this hatchery, fertilized eggs are shipped here and incubated under controlled conditions. Eggs hatch within three to four weeks, and the young fry are soon placed on a specially formulated dry feed. Upon reaching 2 to 3 inches in size, the fingerlings are moved to outside raceways for rearing to catchable size. The hatchery turns out about 850,000 trout each year. These fish are harvested from the hatchery's raceways and distributed by truck for stocking into streams, lakes, and reservoirs of north Georgia in cooperation with the State Game and Fish Department. There are signs located throughout the grounds to

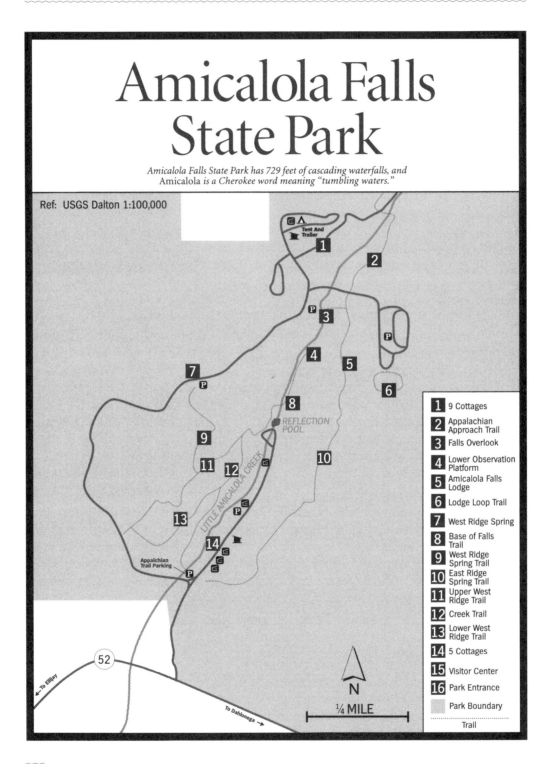

Amicalola Falls State Park

Amicalola Falls State Park has 729 feet of cascading waterfalls, and Amicalola is a Cherokee word meaning "tumbling waters."

Ref: USGS Dalton 1:100,000

Tent And Trailer

REFLECTION POOL

LITTLE AMICALOLA CREEK

Appalchian Trail Parking

52

← To Ellijay

To Dahlonega →

N

¼ MILE

1 9 Cottages
2 Appalachian Approach Trail
3 Falls Overlook
4 Lower Observation Platform
5 Amicalola Falls Lodge
6 Lodge Loop Trail
7 West Ridge Spring
8 Base of Falls Trail
9 West Ridge Spring Trail
10 East Ridge Spring Trail
11 Upper West Ridge Trail
12 Creek Trail
13 Lower West Ridge Trail
14 5 Cottages
15 Visitor Center
16 Park Entrance
Park Boundary
Trail

explain the hatchery and its operations, and there is a sheltered exhibit.

There is fishing in Rock Creek by the hatchery, and nearby Cooper Creek is an angler's paradise for trout fishing.

Directions: Located on Fish Hatchery Road (FS 69) 5 miles off GA 60, 27 miles northwest of Dahlonega, and 26 miles south of Blue Ridge. Direction signs are posted near Fish Hatchery Road.

Facilities: Group tours by arrangement, handicapped access, rooms.

Dates: Open daily.

For more information: U.S. Fish and Wildlife Service, Fish Hatchery Road (FS 69), Suches, GA 30572. Phone (706) 838-4723.

FRANK GROSS CAMPGROUND. [Fig. 19(11)] This is a small campground located along Rock Creek near the Chattahoochee National Fish Hatchery. Fishing is allowed (at no charge) in the adjacent Rock Creek and also in the 13.5-acre Rock Creek Lake, 1.7 miles farther west on the right side of Fish Hatchery Road. The lake is managed by the National Fish Hatchery, and the creek and lake are stocked periodically with 9-inch rainbow trout.

Directions: Take GA 60 north from Dahlonega for 27 miles; turn left (south) and go 5 miles on Fish Hatchery Road (FS 69).

Facilities: 11 campsites with picnic tables, drinking water, and 2 chemical toilets. Trailers up to 22 feet can be accommodated.

Dates: Open late spring to early fall.

Fees: There is a charge for camping.

For more information: Frank Gross Campground, U.S. Forest Service, Toccoa Ranger District, E. Main Street, Box 1839, Blue Ridge, GA 30513. Phone (706) 632-3031.

DEEP HOLE RECREATION AREA. [Fig. 19(9)] A small campground located in an attractive mountain setting on a bend of the Toccoa River just north of the fish hatchery. Its name comes from a deep hole in the river by the campground. This is an excellent canoe launch for the Toccoa River.

Facilities: 8 campsites suitable for tents or small trailers, restrooms, drinking water.

Dates: Open late spring through early fall.

Fees: There is a charge for camping.

Directions: The campground is 27 miles north of Dahlonega on GA 60.

Additional Information: Deep Hole Recreation Area, U.S. Forest Service, Toccoa Ranger District, E. Main Street, Box 1839, Blue Ridge, GA 30513. Phone (706) 632-3031.

AMICALOLA FALLS STATE PARK

Amicalola is a Cherokee word meaning "tumbling waters," an appropriate label since the park's beautiful falls [Fig. 19(16)] slide and plunge in seven cascades 729 feet, making it the highest waterfall in Georgia. It tumbles southwest through a cove of Amicalola Mountain and forms part of the Amicalola Creek watershed. This, in turn, feeds into the Etowah River, which joins the Oostanaula River to form the Coosa River near Rome.

PILEATED
WOODPECKER
(Dryocopus
pileatus)

The park, nestled along the southernmost edge of the Blue Ridge Mountain chain [Fig. 19(17)], consists of more than 1,440 acres surrounding the waterfall. The forest types include cove hardwood, upland oak-hickory, and mixed pine and hardwood.

Both mountain and Piedmont flora and fauna can be found, and most of the species native to this region inhabit the park. Here, a small colony of pink lady slippers grows, pileated woodpeckers nest, and the Eastern milk snake reaches its southernmost range.

All seasons are beautiful at Amicalola Falls. Spring and summer offer an abundance of wildflowers, including dogwood, mountain laurel, and rhododendron. Autumn offers brilliant colors in the forest, and the winter months hold a special magic as the deer and other wild animals seek refuge within the park. April and May are ideal times to enjoy the waterfall because of the unusually high volume of water. Little Amicalola Creek flows through the park and provides an opportunity for trout fishing.

Naturalist programs are provided year-round, Thursday through Sunday, on topics dealing with the area's natural, cultural, and historical resources. Other programs are featured throughout the year. A schedule is available in the park office.

Facilities: 1,600 acres; 17 tent and trailer sites; comfort station with hot showers, flush toilets, and laundry facilities; 57-room lodge with a restaurant and meeting center; 14 cottages; 3 playgrounds; 5 picnic shelters; and a walk-in lodge accommodating 40 persons with family-style meals. There is a 5-mile hike (3,000-foot elevation) from the park to the lodge. The trail crosses the Appalachian Approach Trail and passes near Cochran's Falls. A challenging ropes course is available for group team-building activities.

Directions: The park is 16 miles northwest of Dawsonville and 18 miles west of Dahlonega on GA 52.

For more information: Amicalola Falls State Park Lodge, Georgia Department of Natural Resources, Star Route, Box 215, Dawsonville, GA 30534. Phone (706) 265-8888. Call (800) 864-PARK or (770) 389-PARK, in metro Atlanta, for individual reservations.

HIKING TRAILS AT AMICALOLA FALLS STATE PARK
AMICALOLA FALLS HIKING TRAIL. [Fig. 20(8)] .25 mile. The most scenic trail in Amicalola Park leads to the base of Amicalola Falls. The easy walk, marked with red blazes, follows a rocky path uphill along cascading Amicalola Creek. Several large yellow poplars tower over the trail as it leads through a cove hardwood forest and ends at the lower observation deck.

Directions: The trailhead is in Amicalola Falls State Park near the reflection pool at the end of the main park road.

WEST RIDGE SPRING TRAIL. [Fig. 20(9)] A 2.6-mile, easy nature trail within the park. Virginia pine is the dominant tree along much of the trail.

Directions: There are 3 access points for the trail: 1) across the road and field from the visitor center; 2) to the right on the paved road to the top of the park; and 3) at the turnaround of the main park road, marked with nature trail signs. The access route across from the visitor center is the longest and most scenic, overlooking Amicalola Creek as it winds down the hillside.

APPALACHIAN TRAIL APPROACH TRAIL. [Fig. 20(2)] 8.1 miles. Springer Mountain (3,782 feet) [Fig. 19], the southern starting point/terminus for the Appalachian Trail (AT), is reached by this hike from Amicalola Falls State Park. The trail is strenuous, up and down along the peaks and knobs of Amicalola Mountain, and is a good testing ground for those contemplating longer hikes on the AT.

Directions: The trailhead begins at the back of the park visitor center.

LODGE LOOP TRAIL. [Fig. 20(6)] .25 mile. Easy, almost level, paved loop with interpretive signs. Trail passes beautiful vistas where frequently birds of prey may be seen sailing on thermal air currents over waterfall corridor.

Directions: The trailhead begins at the south end of the lodge parking lot.

BANDED
SCULPIN
(Cottus carolinae)
A bottom-dweller,
the sculpin walks
using leglike fins.

AMICALOLA CREEK & DAWSON FOREST WILDLIFE MANAGEMENT AREA

[Fig. 19(23)]. South of Amicalola Falls State Park, on Amicalola Creek in the Etowah River Basin, the Georgia Department of Natural Resources (DNR) operates a 4,700-acre wildlife management area. Knowledgeable canoeists and naturalists consider the Amicalola to be one of Georgia's most beautiful and exciting waterways. More river than creek in size, the Amicalola was one of the top three candidates in the nationwide search for a river to be designated as the first National Wild River Park. Georgia Highway 53 crosses the midpoint of the Amicalola, approximately 7 miles west of Dawsonville. Dawsonville can be reached from GA 400 by traveling west on GA 53.

On the southeast side of the GA 53 bridge is a guide marker which graphically depicts the river, access points, more prominent rapids, and difficulty ratings. First-time users in particular should pay close attention to the information on the marker.

There are several put-in points above the GA 53 bridge, including Six Mile and Devil's Elbow. Both are state-maintained. Some parking is available, camping is allowed, and launching is easy.

The take-out for boating above the GA 53 bridge (and put-in for boating below the GA 53 bridge) is near the DNR ranger's cabin on the northeast side of the bridge. Parking is not allowed at the cabin, but adequate parking is available on the shoulders of GA 53 at the bridge.

There are no access points on the Amicalola below the GA 53 bridge until one reaches the Etowah River. Take-out is on the Etowah, 2 miles below the confluence with Amicalola Creek, at a concrete ramp near Kelley Bridge. Access to Six Mile and Devil's Elbow is reached by proceeding west on GA 53 approximately 1 mile and turning north at the first paved road (County Road 192). Turn right at the first major intersection to reach Devil's Elbow. Continue north at the intersection and watch for the sign for the Six Mile put-in.

The GA Highway 53 bridge marks a dividing point in the Amicalola's difficulty. The section above the bridge is ideal for teaching and intermediate canoeing. This section begins as easy water and grows progressively more difficult.

Several long "rock gardens," a 5-foot drop, and a deceptive "roostertail" mark this section. Below the GA 53 bridge is the most difficult water on the river. Beginning with the "Edge of the World," a Class IV rapid about .5 mile below the bridge, there are several Class II–IV rapids which should be attempted only by expert boaters. Low-water conditions usually are present after June. A foot trail leads down the east side of the river to "Edge of the World."

The beauty of this river, with its steep banks, gorges, and mountain vegetation, cannot be overemphasized.

DAHLONEGA GOLD MUSEUM

[Fig. 19(19)] America's first major gold rush took place not in California, but in the southern Blue Ridge Mountains in the vicinity of Dahlonega during the late 1820s. The town's name, in fact, comes from the Cherokee word for gold, *talonega*, which translates literally as "precious yellow color." Gold was first discovered by white men near Dahlonega in 1828. Four years later, large discoveries of the precious metal were made in nearby Auraria. It was not until 1848 that gold was discovered in California and the gold rush occurred there.

From 1838 until 1861, the U.S. government operated a mint in Dahlonega which manufactured a total of $6 million worth of gold coins from locally mined ore. Samples of the precious metal, scale models showing old mining techniques, and other relics of Dahlonega's golden era are on display in the museum. Constructed in 1836, the museum is north Georgia's oldest public building.

Directions: On the town square in Dahlonega.

For more information: Dahlonega Gold Museum, Public Square, Dahlonega, GA 30533. Phone (706) 864-2257.

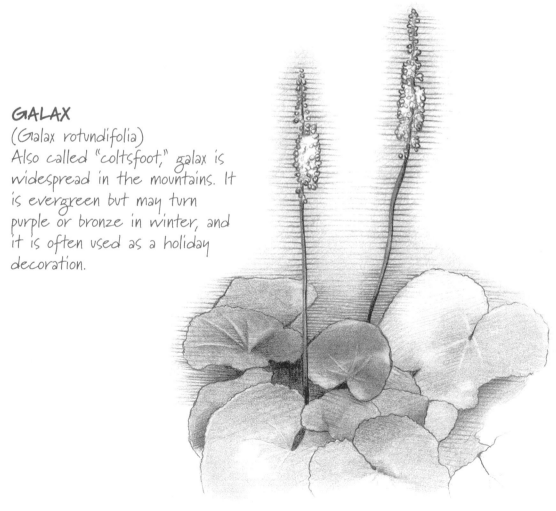

GALAX
(Galax rotundifolia)
Also called "coltsfoot," galax is widespread in the mountains. It is evergreen but may turn purple or bronze in winter, and it is often used as a holiday decoration.

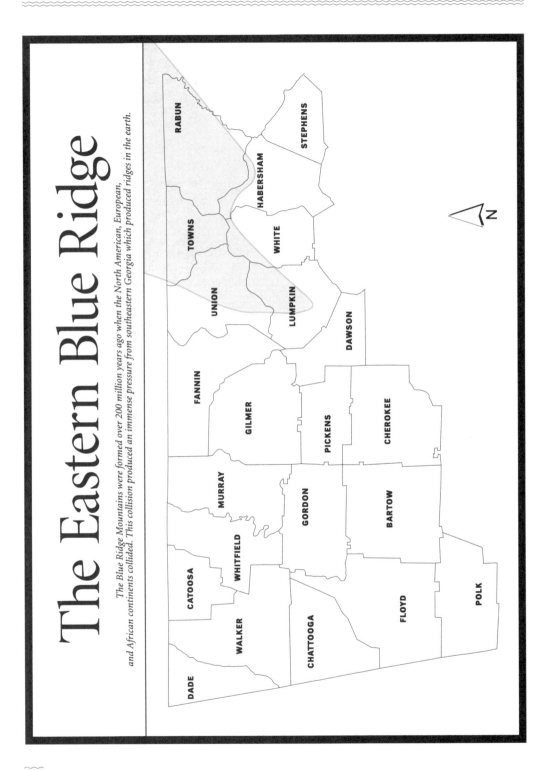

The Eastern Blue Ridge

The Blue Ridge Mountains were formed over 200 million years ago when the North American, European, and African continents collided. This collision produced an immense pressure from southeastern Georgia which produced ridges in the earth.

The Eastern Blue Ridge

The Blue Ridge Mountains, which form the spine of the Eastern Blue Ridge, were formed more than 200 million years ago when the North American, European, and African continents collided—a process called "plate tectonics." The movement of two continents against each other produced an intense pressure from the direction of what is now southeastern Georgia. Over millions of years, the forces of nature have worn as much as 5 miles off the mountains, shaping them into the peaks, cliffsides, and valleys we see today.

The changes that have gone on for millions of centuries continue today. For example, the Eastern Continental Divide running through much of Georgia, separating the waters that flow into the Gulf of Mexico from those that flow into the Atlantic, is currently moving northward at the rate of 3,000 feet every million years. Rivers continue to change course. Until recently (in geological terms), the Chattooga River, which originates in North Carolina and flows along the border between Georgia and South Carolina, was part of the headwaters of the Chattahoochee River and flowed into the Gulf of Mexico.

The Savannah River, gradually cutting a path northward, eventually intersected with the Chattooga and diverted its flow southeastward into the Savannah and eventually into the Atlantic. This "river capture," one of the most interesting and easily visualized phenomena of geological history, has occurred a number of times in Georgia and is an ongoing process. Topsoil—the thin, fragile covering of the hard gneiss and schist rock of the Blue Ridge—is forming at the rate of about 1 inch every 50 to 100 years. Visitors to the foot of Toxaway Dam can see how the flood of 1916 wiped away the topsoil down to bare rock in a matter of minutes.

Georgia's Blue Ridge Mountains, with their rich geological history and diverse recreational opportunities, are surprisingly undiscovered. When visiting the mountains, most of us stick to the main highways; towns such as Helen, Clayton, and Dahlonega are familiar. But few people have discovered the upper portions of the wild and scenic Chattooga River, much less explored the hundreds of scenic logging roads, or, even less, walked the unmarked hiking trails known mostly to hunters and fishermen.

The information on the Eastern Blue Ridge in the following pages is designed to help readers get off the main roads and onto the back roads and trails and to discover the diversity, beauty, and surprising fragility of these ageless mountains.

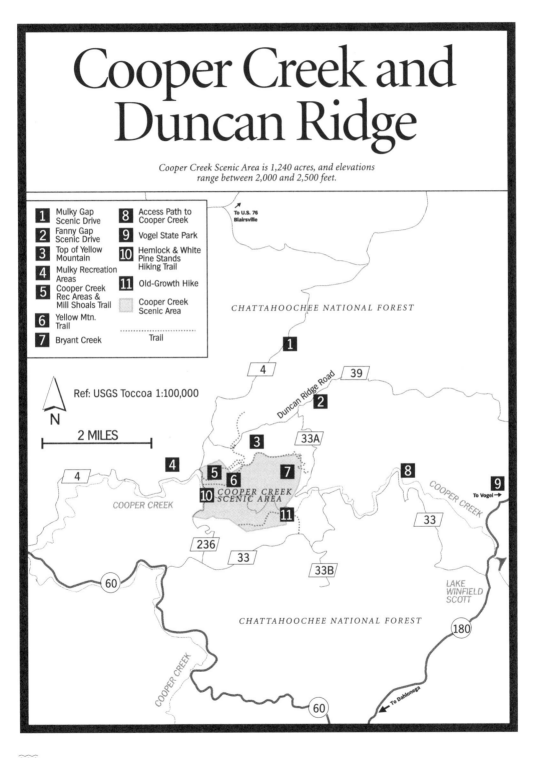

Cooper Creek and Duncan Ridge

Cooper Creek Scenic Area is 1,240 acres, and elevations range between 2,000 and 2,500 feet.

1 Mulky Gap Scenic Drive
2 Fanny Gap Scenic Drive
3 Top of Yellow Mountain
4 Mulky Recreation Areas
5 Cooper Creek Rec Areas & Mill Shoals Trail
6 Yellow Mtn. Trail
7 Bryant Creek
8 Access Path to Cooper Creek
9 Vogel State Park
10 Hemlock & White Pine Stands Hiking Trail
11 Old-Growth Hike

Cooper Creek Scenic Area

Trail

Ref: USGS Toccoa 1:100,000

N

2 MILES

To U.S. 76 Blairsville

CHATTAHOOCHEE NATIONAL FOREST

Duncan Ridge Road

39

COOPER CREEK SCENIC AREA

COOPER CREEK

To Vogel →

COOPER CREEK

33

236

33

33B

60

LAKE WINFIELD SCOTT

180

CHATTAHOOCHEE NATIONAL FOREST

COOPER CREEK

60

To Dahlonega →

Cooper Creek and Duncan Ridge

The 1,240-acre Cooper Creek Scenic Area [Fig. 22], which ranges between 2,000 and 2,500 feet in elevation, is surrounded by more than 34,000 acres of the Cooper Creek Water Management Area and the slightly larger, overlapping Cooper Creek Wildlife Management Area.

Within the latter are two U.S. Forest Service campgrounds, Cooper Creek [Fig. 22(5)] and Mulky [Fig. 22(4)] recreation areas. Cooper Creek Scenic Area is roughly 1.5 miles long by 1 mile wide. Cooper Creek, a cold mountain trout stream, runs approximately 2 miles down the center of the scenic area.

Numerous small branches join Cooper Creek. Two of these, Stillhouse Branch [Fig. 23] and Deep Cove Branch [Fig. 23], are completely contained within the boundaries of the scenic area. Bryant Creek [Fig. 22(7)], a larger tributary with its headwaters on the south face of Duncan Ridge, parallels the eastern boundary. There are stands of large hemlock and white pine, reaching 3 and 4 feet in diameter, along Cooper Creek (and, to some extent, Bryant Creek) and a short way up its tributaries. These are of special interest because here they are close to the southern geographical limit of the hemlock–white pine community. The only evidence of human occupation in the scenic area is a few rock piles on Deep Cove Branch, a possible former cabin site.

Cherry may have been cut for furniture manufacture in the past, and some dead chestnut was removed from among the giant poplars in the southeast corner. Fire has apparently only rarely touched the hemlock–white pine habitat. Dense growth of uniformly aged white pine on Chestnut Ridge and the ridge along the south boundary of the scenic area may attest to severe burns there in times past.

In an arc crossing the northern part of Figure 22 is Duncan Ridge, perhaps the longest continuous ridge projecting from the main Blue Ridge. Part of Duncan Ridge is traversed by Duncan Ridge Road, accessible from the scenic area or off Highway 180 at Wolfpen Gap. The Duncan Ridge Trail (*see* Blood Mountain, page 101) [Fig. 24(3)] is reached at several points off the Duncan Ridge Road or at Mulky Gap [Fig. 22(4)]. The north side of Duncan Ridge offers many opportunities to explore exciting environments such as boulderfields and northern hardwood forests in the coveheads, which also have spring wildflower displays.

Directions: From US 19 north of Dahlonega, turn left onto GA 60. Continue approximately 15 miles, through Suches, to FS 4 on right and go 6 miles.

For more information: U.S. Forest Service, Brasstown Ranger District, 1881 GA Highway 515 West, Blairsville, GA 30512. Phone (706)745-6928.

MULKY CAMPGROUND

[Fig. 22(4)] A small campground with 11 campsites. Camping is usually from the Wednesday before the last Saturday in March through October 31. There are sanitary facilities, drinking water, tent pads, picnic tables, and cooking grills.

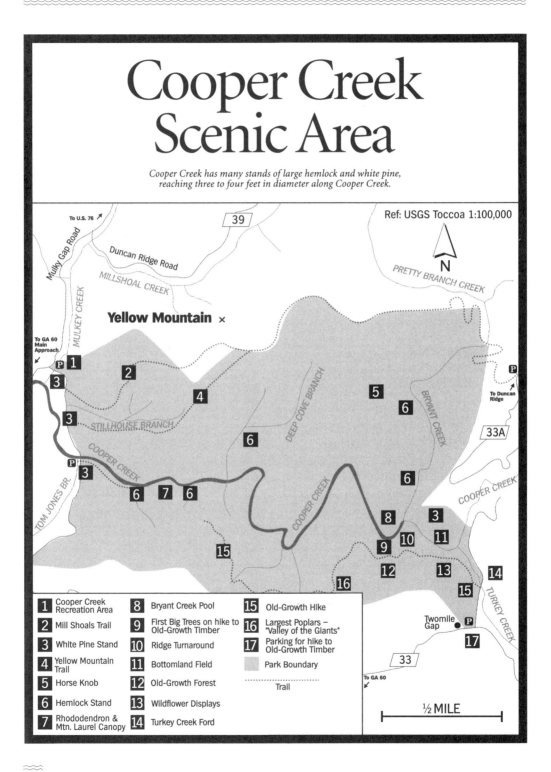

Cooper Creek Scenic Area

Cooper Creek has many stands of large hemlock and white pine, reaching three to four feet in diameter along Cooper Creek.

Ref: USGS Toccoa 1:100,000

To U.S. 76

39

Mulky Gap Road

Duncan Ridge Road

MILLSHOAL CREEK

MULKEY CREEK

PRETTY BRANCH CREEK

N

Yellow Mountain ×

To GA 60
Main
Approach

STILLHOUSE BRANCH

COOPER CREEK

TOM JONES BR.

DEEP COVE BRANCH

BRYANT CREEK

COOPER CREEK

COOPER CREEK

To Duncan
Ridge

33A

TURKEY CREEK

Twomile
Gap

33

To GA 60

1	Cooper Creek Recreation Area	**8**	Bryant Creek Pool	**15**	Old-Growth Hike
2	Mill Shoals Trail	**9**	First Big Trees on hike to Old-Growth Timber	**16**	Largest Poplars – "Valley of the Giants"
3	White Pine Stand	**10**	Ridge Turnaround	**17**	Parking for hike to Old-Growth Timber
4	Yellow Mountain Trail	**11**	Bottomland Field		Park Boundary
5	Horse Knob	**12**	Old-Growth Forest		Trail
6	Hemlock Stand	**13**	Wildflower Displays		
7	Rhododendron & Mtn. Laurel Canopy	**14**	Turkey Creek Ford		

½ MILE

Directions: Same as for Cooper Creek, above. Once on FS 4, continue on this dirt/gravel road entering and leaving national forest property once before reentering just before the campground sign. Distance is 4.9 miles from GA 60.

▨ COOPER CREEK RECREATION AREA

[Fig. 22(5)] Located along the banks of sparkling mountain streams stocked with trout, adjacent to the Cooper Creek Scenic Area. The 17 campsites can accommodate either tents or trailers up to 22 feet. There are sanitary facilities, drinking water, tent pads, and cooking grills. The Mill Shoals Trail originates in the Recreation Area and the Yellow Mountain Trail is nearby.

Directions: Same as for Cooper Creek and Mulky Campground, above. Cooper Creek Campground is 5.7 miles from GA 60.

▨ HIKING TRAILS

HEMLOCK AND WHITE PINE STANDS. A suggested walking route to see the streamside stands of hemlock-heath and white pine begins at the bridge over Cooper Creek on Cavender Gap Road, FS 236 [Fig. 22(10)], and follows the right (south) bank to at least the second small feeder branch coming in on the right side. Here is a rough trail made by fishermen. It passes through a grove of white pines [Fig. 23(3)], then under an almost solid canopy of rhododendron and mountain laurel [Fig. 23(7)]. After .25 mile, one begins to encounter the large hemlocks and white pines. At the second branch [Fig. 23(6)] is another intriguing grove in the tiny valley of the feeder stream. Farther up these small branch streams are cove hardwoods—oak, buckeye, hickory, cucumber tree, and yellow poplar.

OLD GROWTH FOREST HIKE. [Fig. 22(11)] About 1 mile. Park at a low gap [Fig. 23(17)] about .4 mile from the end of the pavement going east on FS 33. There will be an old road pitching steeply north, the first road to the left after leaving the pavement. Walk down this road and take the first left-hand log road [Fig. 23(13)] just before the Turkey Creek ford. This nearly level log road passes through several moist coves with wildflower displays. Across Cooper Creek is a 6-acre bottomland that has been continuously in cultivation since the time of white settlers and probably since Indian days.

After passing two small coves, watch for the first place where a vehicle could be turned around (the turnaround is on a ridge that leads down to a fine pool at the mouth of Bryant Creek [Fig. 23(6)]). From the turnaround ridge, the first of the big trees [Fig. 23(9)] is only several hundred yards along the old log road. The old growth forest has widely spaced specimens of large white and northern red oak and black birch, but the largest trees are giant tulip poplars with circumferences of up to 18 feet. Storms through the ages have broken the tops out of many of them. While many big trees can be seen from the log road, others must be searched for above and below the road. The log road continues, crosses a white pine ridge, and in about .25

mile reaches the "valley of the giants" where the largest poplars grow [Fig. 23(16)]. The trail continues to parallel Cooper Creek for an undetermined distance.

MILL SHOALS TRAIL. [Fig. 22(5)] This 3.4-mile, orange-blazed trail is considered moderate to strenuous. It begins north of the Cooper Creek Recreation Area; the starting point and the trail are blazed well. Stay to the right when entering the trail. It climbs steeply to a ridgetop, then descends through hardwoods to a jeep road, turns right onto the jeep road for 15 or 20 paces, then narrows and drops toward a stream on the left. It winds through an area with tall hemlock, white pine, and dense vegetation, crosses three small streams, turns right on an old road, and in about 50 feet turns left. At Duncan Ridge Road it turns right. Stay on the road until you reach Shope Gap, where it joins the Shope Gap Trail.

COOPER CREEK TRAIL. This is an easy, blue-blazed connector trail between Mill Shoals Trail and Yellow Mountain Trail. It can be accessed by hiking .6 mile from the Mill Shoals trailhead or 1 mile from the Yellow Mountain trailhead.

YELLOW MOUNTAIN TRAIL. [Fig. 22(6)] This yellow-blazed trail is mainly a ridge trail. It is 2.7 miles and is considered moderate to strenuous. The trail entrance is marked by a yellow post on the northeast side of Cavender Gap Road, FS 236. At the start of the trail, one passes through a shady grove of hemlock on a hillside above a small stream; later there are several large remnant oaks. This footpath splits into two trails 1.3 miles from the trailhead. The left fork (Shope Gap Trail) continues north and intersects with Duncan Bridge Road. The right fork (1.4 miles) continues on across Bryant Creek, ending at Addie Gap on Bryant Creek Road.

SHOPE GAP TRAIL. This green-blazed trail is accessed via the Yellow Mountain Trail 1.3 miles from the trailhead. The left fork is the beginning of the Shope Gap Trail, which is .9 mile long and rated moderate to strenuous. This trail continues north and intersects with the Duncan Bridge Road.

EYES ON WILDLIFE TRAIL. This is a 1.6-mile loop trail, created in 1993. Pick up the easy-to-moderate trail by crossing the Tom Jones Branch bridge and follow the directional arrows. Initially, look for tall Eastern white pines and saplings planted after salvage logging and a prescribed burn. Turn onto a logging road and watch for animal tracks. The last portion of the loop leads you through second-growth forest and back to the stream.

For more information: U.S. Forest Service Brasstown District, 1881 GA Highway 515 West, Blairsville, GA 30512. Phone (706)745-6928.

Note: These trails are located within the Cooper Creek Wildlife Management Area, open for hunting during the various hunting seasons throughout the year. Use extra caution during hunting seasons by wearing bright colors. The U.S. Army conducts training exercises in the vicinity; you may hear aircraft or small-arms fire, or see marching soldiers.

SCENIC DRIVES

There are three scenic drives that can be made through the area. Each drive begins at the entrance sign to Cooper Creek on FS 4.

MULKY GAP DRIVE. [Fig. 22(1)] The first drive continues on FS 4 north across Mulky Gap. It goes up along Mulky Creek, with a beautiful streamside zone of hemlock-heath. Soon after the gap, one can either turn right on FS 40—a dead-end road that in May and June will reward the visitor with a display of mountain laurel in bloom—or continue on FS 4, which winds down to US 76 west of Blairsville.

FANNY GAP DRIVE. [Fig. 22(2)] Turn right (east) from FS 4 onto FS 39. It passes Fanny Gap before turning sharply to follow Duncan Ridge past Buckeye Knob, Coosa Bald (4,271 feet), and Wildcat Knob. The road ends at GA 180, which goes east to Vogel State Park [Fig. 22(9)] and US 19/129, past Sosebee Cove Scenic Area, or goes west past beautiful, trout-stocked Lake Winfield Scott to GA 60 at Suches.

THE LOOP DRIVE. Turn right (south) near the Cooper Creek Recreation Area [Fig. 22(5)] onto the dirt Cavender Gap Road (FS 236) which winds through a forest of large Eastern white pine, Eastern hemlock, oak, hickory, and poplar and ends at paved FS 33 (Turkey Creek Road). Turn left (east) and proceed until the pavement ends after approximately 2 miles. Go on the gravel road for .4 mile to a low gap (Twomile Gap) where a narrow road dips steeply at the left. This is the main entrance to the east end of the scenic area and the starting point for the short hike to the virgin old growth area. The gravel road continues to the point where FS 33 makes a hairpin curve to the right. Here, go straight ahead onto FS 33A [Fig. 23], which crosses Cooper Creek, Addis Gap, and Bryant Creek before ending at FS 39. Turn left and go to the juncture with FS 4; turn left again and return to the starting point.

A CANOEING GUIDE TO COOPER CREEK

Cooper Creek flows from the base of the dam on Lake Winfield Scott [Fig. 22]. The dam is 14.5 miles south of Blairsville on GA 180. From its beginning, Cooper Creek twists and flows out of the mountains for 15 miles before it joins the Toccoa River along GA 60. The creek runs through the Chattahoochee National Forest and two areas within the Cooper Creek Wildlife Management Area and Cooper Creek Scenic Area. Cooper Creek has long been a popular trout-fishing stream and could well become one of Georgia's most popular canoeing streams as well.

The first 4 miles of Cooper Creek are too narrow and shallow to canoe, and the final 4 miles flow mostly through flat, privately owned farmland. The 7-mile stretch in between, however, is as interesting a run of Class II whitewater as Georgia has to offer. The average gradient of Cooper Creek is a steep 40-plus feet per mile, which puts it in the "gradient class" with such mighty rivers as the Chattooga Section IV (45 feet per mile) and Alabama's Little River Canyon (31 feet per mile). However, because Cooper Creek has a smaller watershed area and a lower level of water, it is less difficult to canoe than either of these rivers. Cooper Creek is within the Class II–

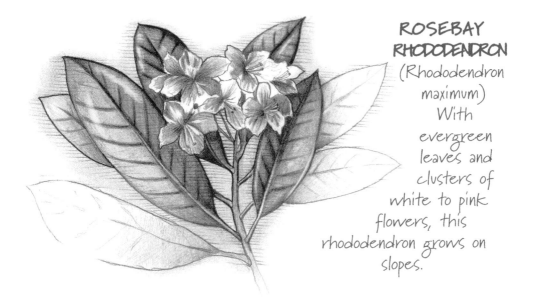

ROSEBAY RHODODENDRON (Rhododendron maximum) With evergreen leaves and clusters of white to pink flowers, this rhododendron grows on slopes.

III difficulty range. Nevertheless, the creek is a steep little stream that requires experience and skill to negotiate. There are two waterfalls—one drops 5 feet and the other 8 feet—which are good Class III runs. A long slide of twisting channels and barrier rocks, which descends more than 5 feet, is, in high water, a Class III run as well.

Directions: To reach the put-in on Cooper Creek, go north out of Dahlonega 9 miles on US 19/GA 60 to the point where the two roads separate. Bear left on GA 60, go 7 miles to Suches, and turn right (north) onto GA 180. Go north on 180 for 4.4 miles to Lake Winfield Scott Recreation Area. Turn left on FS 33 and go 5 miles. An access path leading down to the edge of the creek branches off FS 33 at the 5-mile point. Limited but adequate parking space is provided at this put-in. To reach the take-out, go west from the put-in on FS 33 for 1.4 miles to an intersection. (A right turn at this intersection and a .1-mile drive will lead to the Bryant Creek Road Bridge. The bridge offers a good view of the river and could serve as an alternate put-in, shortening the canoe trip by 1.7 miles.) At the intersection, turn left and continue 3.5 miles on FS 33 to where it meets FS 236; turn right (north) on FS 236 and go 2.3 miles to the Cooper Creek Scenic Area and the Tom Jones Creek Bridge over Cooper Creek; cross the bridge and continue .5 mile through the campground; turn left (west) on FS 4; and go another .5 mile to Mulky Creek Campground [Fig. 22(4)]. The total distance from put-in to take-out is about 7 miles.

Map References: 1:24,000 series: Suches–Neel's Gap–Mulky Gap–Coosa Bald.

Blood Mountain

Blood Mountain [Fig. 24] is the highest peak on Georgia's portion of the Appalachian Trail and the state's sixth highest mountain. The Blood Mountain Wilderness is the first designated wilderness area along the Appalachian Trail as the hiker heads north toward Maine. Some believe the name came from a bloody battle between the Cherokee Indians and Creek Indians long before white men arrived in the area. Other theories trace the name to red lichen or Catawba rhododendron growing on the rocky summit.

At 4,461 feet, it overlooks an area rich in streams, hiking trails, and scenic recreation spots, one of which—Sosebee Cove [Fig. 24(5)]—is probably Georgia's only north-facing cove traversed by a paved road at such a high elevation. It has a boulder-field, northern hardwoods, and large buckeyes and provides an example of how tulip poplar takes over following too-thorough logging of cove hardwood forests.

DESOTO FALLS SCENIC AND RECREATION AREAS

[Fig. 24(12,14)] DeSoto Falls was named for the Spanish explorer Hernando De Soto because a piece of armor attributed to his expedition was supposedly found in the area. The scenic area is located in rugged, mountainous country with exceptional views. Elevations in this 650-acre area of clear streams feeding Frogtown Creek vary between 2,000 and 3,400 feet. Visitors can hike to view two waterfalls.

Directions: Take US 129 north from Cleveland 15 miles.

Activities: Camping, picnicking, fishing, hiking.

Facilities: Parking, restrooms.

For more information: U.S. Forest Service, Brasstown Ranger District, 1881 GA Highway 515, Blairsville, GA 30512. Phone (706) 745-6928.

DESOTO FALLS TRAIL

[Fig. 24(13)] .8 mile. The trail passes by the two lower cascades of DeSoto Falls and is relatively easy. The trailhead is in the DeSoto Falls Recreation Area.

Directions: Follow the directions to DeSoto Falls Scenic Area (above). The trail begins at the bridge in the lower camping loop of DeSoto Falls Recreation Area.

DESOTO FALLS CAMPGROUND

[Fig. 24(15)] This is rugged, mountainous country with exceptional views and several beautiful waterfalls. It is adjacent to DeSoto Falls Scenic Area (*see* above).

Directions: Take US 129 north from Cleveland 15 miles.

Facilities: 24 campsites, 6 picnic sites, restrooms with cold showers, streams for wading and fishing.

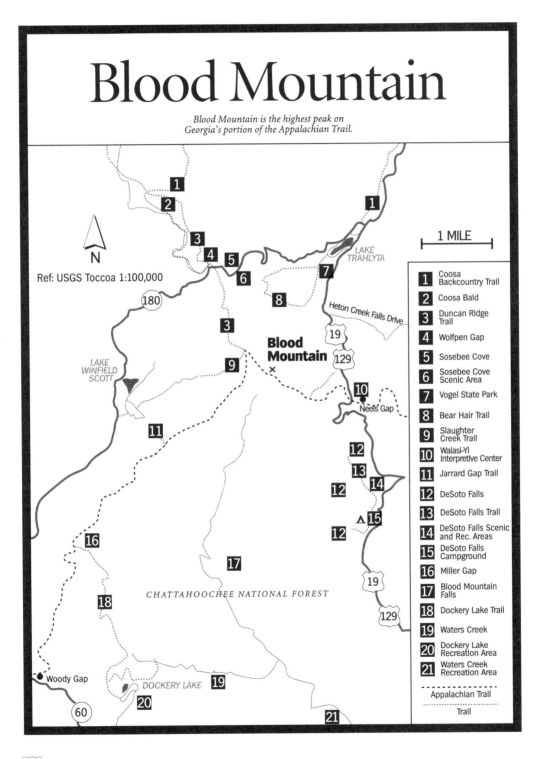

Blood Mountain

*Blood Mountain is the highest peak on
Georgia's portion of the Appalachian Trail.*

Ref: USGS Toccoa 1:100,000

N

**Blood
Mountain**

LAKE
TRAHLYTA

LAKE
WINFIELD
SCOTT

Heton Creek Falls Drive

Neels Gap

CHATTAHOOCHEE NATIONAL FOREST

DOCKERY LAKE

Woody Gap

180
19
129
19
129
60

1 MILE

1	Coosa Backcountry Trail
2	Coosa Bald
3	Duncan Ridge Trail
4	Wolfpen Gap
5	Sosebee Cove
6	Sosebee Cove Scenic Area
7	Vogel State Park
8	Bear Hair Trail
9	Slaughter Creek Trail
10	Walasi-Yi Interpretive Center
11	Jarrard Gap Trail
12	DeSoto Falls
13	DeSoto Falls Trail
14	DeSoto Falls Scenic and Rec. Areas
15	DeSoto Falls Campground
16	Miller Gap
17	Blood Mountain Falls
18	Dockery Lake Trail
19	Waters Creek
20	Dockery Lake Recreation Area
21	Waters Creek Recreation Area

- - - - Appalachian Trail

· · · · · Trail

WALASI-YI INTERPRETIVE CENTER

[Fig. 24(10)] This beautiful stone center was built from 1934 to 1938 of native rock by the Civilian Conservation Corps. It was placed on the National Register of Historic Places in 1977 and is now owned by the Georgia Department of Natural Resources. The breezeway is the only place where the approximately 2,135-mile-long Appalachian Trail goes through a man-made structure. Approximately 1,000 hikers each year pass through the breezeway, hoping to hike the entire length from Georgia to Maine. There is a store here (owned by Jeff and Dorothy Hansen since 1983) with outdoor books, mountain crafts, gifts, maps, clothing, and camping equipment.

Directions: At Neel's Gap on US 19 and 129, approximately 18 miles north of Cleveland and 21 miles north of Dahlonega.

For more information: Mountain crossing at Walasi-Yi Center, US 129, Route 1, Box 1240, Blairsville, GA 30512. Phone (706) 745-6095.

NEEL'S GAP TO BLOOD MOUNTAIN HIKE

About 2 miles. An enjoyable day trip with many scenic vistas is a climb up Blood Mountain (4,458 feet). The trail is generally steep and rocky in many places, but it is easy to follow. Near the summit hikers will be rewarded with several picnic rocks and superb vistas from rock outcrops, including views of Mount Yonah, Tray Mountain, Lake Winfield Scott, and Slaughter Mountain. An old stone cabin, built by the Civilian Conservation Corps in the 1930s as an Appalachian Trail shelter and listed on the National Register of Historic Places, sits near the top. This is the highest point on the Appalachian Trail in Georgia. It is the state's most-hiked portion of the Appalachian Trail.

Directions: To reach the trailhead, follow directions to the Walasi-Yi Center, above. Parking for day hikers is .5 mile north of the center at the Byron Herbert Reece parking area. Follow the blue blazes from the parking area along the Reece Access Trail. After about .8 mile the trail intersects with the white-blazed Appalachian Trail (AT) at Flatrock Gap (a 420-foot increase in elevation). Turn right onto the AT and proceed about 1.5 miles to the top of Blood Mountain.

VOGEL STATE PARK

[Fig. 24(7), Fig. 25] One of the prettiest state parks in all of Georgia. It is nearly 2,500 feet in elevation, usually affording cool temperatures even during hot summer months. The park can be crowded in summer, and campsites fill up quickly. There are short hiking trails in the park as well as the trailhead for the challenging 12.5-mile Coosa Backcountry Trail (*see* page 105).

Directions: 11 miles south of Blairsville on US 19/129.

Facilities: 36 cottages, 95 tent or trailer sites with water and electrical hookups (15 sites without), picnic shelters and tables, grills, restrooms, hot showers, stocked trout lake, swimming beach, paddle boats, playground, miniature golf course. Maps

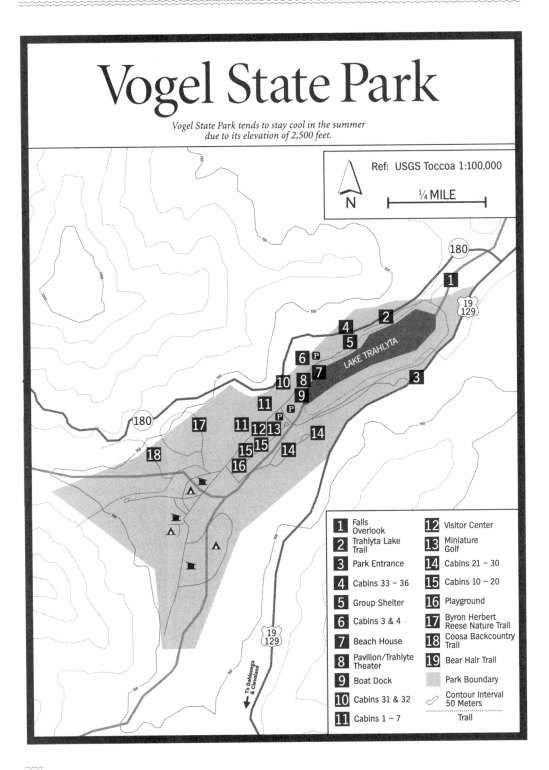

Vogel State Park

*Vogel State Park tends to stay cool in the summer
due to its elevation of 2,500 feet.*

Ref: USGS Toccoa 1:100,000

¼ MILE

N

180

19
129

LAKE TRAHLYTA

180

19
129

To Dahlonega
& Cleveland

1	Falls Overlook		**12**	Visitor Center
2	Trahlyta Lake Trail		**13**	Miniature Golf
3	Park Entrance		**14**	Cabins 21 – 30
4	Cabins 33 – 36		**15**	Cabins 10 – 20
5	Group Shelter		**16**	Playground
6	Cabins 3 & 4		**17**	Byron Herbert Reese Nature Trail
7	Beach House		**18**	Coosa Backcountry Trail
8	Pavilion/Trahlyte Theater		**19**	Bear Hair Trail
9	Boat Dock			Park Boundary
10	Cabins 31 & 32			Contour Interval 50 Meters
11	Cabins 1 – 7			Trail

are available at the visitor center near the entrance.

For more information: 7485 Vogel State Park Road, Blairsville, GA 30512. Phone (706) 745-2628. Call (800) 864-PARK, or (770) 389-PARK in metro Atlanta, for individual reservations.

HIKING TRAILS AT VOGEL STATE PARK

BEAR HAIR TRAIL. [Fig. 24(8)] This 3.6-mile orange-blazed loop trail is ideal for family hikes. It is of moderate difficulty, beginning and ending in Vogel State Park. Most of the trail is in the Chattahoochee National Forest.

Directions: Follow directions to Vogel State Park, (above).

COOSA BACKCOUNTRY TRAIL. [Fig. 24(1)] 12.5-mile loop. This strenuous trail is marked with yellow blazes and signs and for the most part is easy to follow. It fords streams on its lower part and traverses the high Duncan Ridge, including Coosa Bald [Fig. 24(2)] at over 4,000 feet. It is recommended that hikers take more than one day to hike the entire route, although it can be done in one long day, particularly during the longer daylight hours of spring and summer. A permit is required and is available free, together with a trail map, at the Vogel State Park Visitor Center.

Directions: The trail begins in Vogel State Park.

BYRON HERBERT REECE NON-GAME NATURE TRAIL. [Fig. 25(17)] An easy, 1-mile loop interpretive trail.

HELTON CREEK FALLS TRAIL AND DRIVE

An easy .2-mile trail leads to the falls from a parking area on Helton Creek Road. About 1.1 miles south of Vogel State Park at Lark Gap, a rough dirt road (FS 118) goes down Helton Creek. After 1 mile, the road becomes gravel. With care, in 1.2 miles, you can reach the very beautiful Helton Creek Falls even in an average car.

To continue on to this road's terminus at the Russell Scenic Highway requires great care. Because of potholes and creek fordings, it is recommended only for four-by-four and high-clearance vehicles. There are actually two falls, one about 30 feet high and visible from the road; the other, twice as high, is about 150 feet upstream.

LEAST SHREW
(Cryptotis parva)
This mammal is also known as the "bee" shrew because it sometimes nests in beehives and feeds on bees and their larvae.

TULIPTREE OR YELLOW-POPLAR
(Liriodendron tulipifera)
Of eastern broadleaved trees, the tuliptree is one of the straightest and tallest and has one of the largest diameter tree trunks. Wind-borne seeds of the tulip poplar make their way into the openings in mountain forests to take over in areas denuded by heavy logging or disease.

SOSEBEE COVE SCENIC AREA AND HIKING TRAIL

[Fig. 24(6)] This 175-acre tract of hardwood timber, largely part of the Blood Mountain Wilderness, is a memorial to Arthur Woody, who served as a Forest Service ranger from 1911 to 1945. Ranger Woody, the "Barefoot Ranger," loved this peaceful cove and negotiated its purchase for the Forest Service. Rare and beautiful wildflowers and ferns abound. In the boulderfield above the road, there is rich, high-altitude herb flora, including Dutchman's breeches, squirrel corn, waterleaf, and others. Here also is found the rare yellowwood tree and representative northern hardwoods, such as yellow birch. A salamander-rich branch flows down the cove. There are several large buckeyes below the road, along with a stand of second-growth yellow poplar that followed heavy logging that reduced the diversity of the cove forest. A .3-mile trail consists of two linked loops.

Woody, with his own funds, brought the first deer back into the mountains after they had been extirpated. He always claimed his father killed the last deer in north Georgia in 1895.

Directions: Take US 129 south from Blairsville for 9.5 miles; turn right (west) on GA 180 and go 2 miles to the Sosebee Cove parking area on the right.

DUNCAN RIDGE TRAIL

[Fig. 24(3)] 20.4 miles and strenuous. On this blue-blazed trail, one can traverse the longest contiguous ridgeline leading off the main Blue Ridge. The trail's eastern terminus is to the west of Blood Mountain at Slaughter Gap [Fig. 24(9)], then crosses northwest through Wolfpen Gap [Fig. 24(4)] and Coosa Bald [Fig. 24(2)], then goes westward to Mulky Gap (*see* page 99) and intersects with the Benton MacKaye Trail (*see* page 241).

LAKE WINFIELD SCOTT RECREATION AREA

[Fig. 24] This lovely, clear, 18-acre mountain lake, which is owned and managed by the U.S. Forest Service, is the source of Cooper Creek and contains a large population of rainbow trout. A nice hiking trail circles the lake.

Activities: Camping, picnicking, swimming, boating (electric motors only), fishing, hiking.

Directions: Take US 19 south from Blairsville 9.5 miles; turn right (west) on GA 180 and go 7 miles. On US 19/GA 60 from Dahlonega, fork left on GA 60; in Suches, turn right onto GA 180 East, and go 4.5 miles to Lake Winfield Scott.

For more information: U.S. Forest Service, Brasstown Ranger District, 1881 GA Highway 515, Blairsville, GA 30512. Phone (706) 745-6928.

JARRARD GAP TRAIL AND SLAUGHTER CREEK TRAIL [Fig. 24(9,11)] 1.2 miles and 2.7 miles, respectively. These two easy-to-moderate trails provide access to the Appalachian Trail from Lake Winfield Scott Recreation Area. The Jarrard Gap Trail follows portions of an old logging road through cove hardwoods.

Directions: Follow directions to Lake Winfield Scott, (*above*). The trails begin on the right after crossing the head of the lake. Look for the trail sign near the head of the lake. The trails share the same path for a short distance. Parking is available on the left just before you cross the head of the lake.

WOODY GAP

[Fig. 24] The gap, with scenic vistas of Yahoola Valley, is marked with a large wooden sign. This is where the white-blazed Appalachian Trail crosses GA 60. A moderate, 1-mile hike to the north leads to a rock-outcrop overlook on the rocky face of Big Cedar Mountain (3,737 feet). A 1.5-mile hike to the south leads to a southerly view of the Yahoola Valley from atop Ramrock Mountain (3,200 feet). Both of these trail sections offer a pretty display of spring wildflowers on this richly wooded Blue Ridge Mountain range.

Directions: 14 miles north of Dahlonega on GA 60.

Facilities: Large parking area with chemical toilets and trash cans; picnicking areas with 10 tables located on both sides of the road.

PERSISTENT TRILLIUM
(Trillium persistens)
A rare flower, it grows under or near rhododendrons in Northeast Georgia.

CHESTATEE OVERLOOK

The overlook offers a scenic vista of Blood Mountain Cove and Blood Mountain. There are hiking trails in the area. The watershed in the foreground is the famous Waters Creek trophy trout stream [Fig. 24(19)].

Directions: Take GA 60 north from Dahlonega for 12 miles.

Facilities: 3 picnic tables.

DOCKERY LAKE RECREATION AREA

[Fig. 24(20)] Dockery Lake (2,388 feet), nestled within a large cove surrounded by ridgetops and small valleys, offers the forest visitor a wide variety of natural and scenic beauty.

Deer and grouse are common sights. Purple rhododendron blooms in May at higher elevations, while the white variety blooms in mid-June at lower elevations. Native trees such as dogwood, sourwood, locust, and laurel add more color to spring and brilliance to the fall leaf season. Trout fishing is available along the Pigeon Roost Creek and nearby Waters Creek, as well as in the 6-acre Dockery Lake, which is stocked on a regular basis.

Facilities: 11 campsites (no electrical or water hookups or showers), restrooms, drinking water, 6 picnic sites.

Activities: Hiking, fishing, picnicking.

Directions: Follow GA 60 for 12.3 miles north of Dahlonega and turn right onto FS 654 opposite the Dockery Lake sign [Fig. 24(20)].

For more information: U.S. Forest Service, Brasstown Ranger District, 1881 Highway 515, PO Box 9, Blairsville, GA 30512. Phone (706)745-6928.

DOCKERY LAKE TRAIL. [Fig. 24(18)] 3.4 miles. This moderate-to-strenuous trail provides access to the Appalachian Trail. It winds north 3 miles over portions of an old logging road and terminates at Miller Gap [Fig. 24(16)]. The trail parallels a portion of Pigeon Roost Creek and provides scenic views of nearby mountain ridges and peaks.

Twelve streams either parallel or cross the trail. Stands of hemlock, white pine, hickory, black walnut, and magnolia cling to the mountain slopes of granite and milky quartz. Delicate mosses and colorful lichens adorn the boulders bordering much of the trail. In spring, the trail comes alive with blooming magnolias and wildflowers including wild iris, trillium, bloodroot, and fleabane.

Directions: Follow the directions for Dockery Lake Recreation Area, (above). The trail begins at the parking lot.

LAKESHORE TRAIL. [Fig. 24(18)] .5 mile. This trail encircles Dockery Lake and is accessible to the handicapped. Footpaths provide access to fishing areas around the lake.

Directions: Follow directions for Dockery Lake Recreation Area, (above). The trail begins at the parking lot.

WATERS CREEK RECREATION AREA

[Fig. 24(21)] Located along a beautiful mountain stream. The headwaters is a trophy trout stream.

Directions: Take US 19 north from Dahlonega for 12 miles, turn left (northwest) onto FS 34, and go 1 mile.

Activities: Camping, hiking, fishing.

For more information: U.S. Forest Service, Brasstown Ranger District, 1881 Highway 515, PO Box 9, Blairsville, GA 30512. Phone (706)745-6928.

BLOOD MOUNTAIN FALLS

[Fig. 24(17)] This waterfall is located on Blood Mountain Creek, which flows approximately 20 feet through a rock cut, creating a churning sluice of water. An unmaintained footpath leads to the falls.

Directions: Follow the directions to Waters Creek Recreation Area, (above). After passing the game warden station, the road narrows; go 2.5 miles to Blood Mountain Creek. The falls are located on the right.

Map References: USGS 1:24,000 series: Neel's Gap–Coosa Bald.

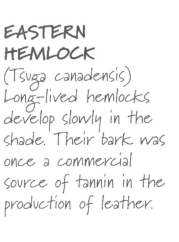

EASTERN HEMLOCK

(Tsuga canadensis) Long-lived hemlocks develop slowly in the shade. Their bark was once a commercial source of tannin in the production of leather.

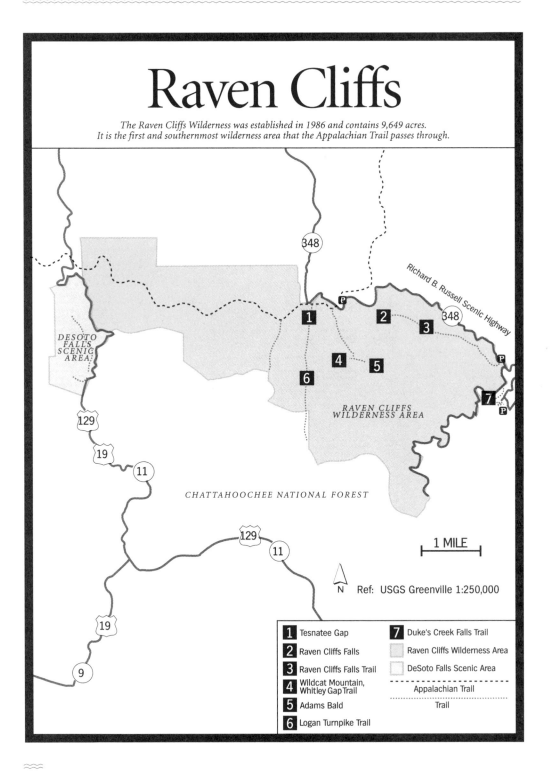

Raven Cliffs

The Raven Cliffs Wilderness was established in 1986 and contains 9,649 acres.
It is the first and southernmost wilderness area that the Appalachian Trail passes through.

348

Richard B. Russell Scenic Highway

348

1

2

3

DESOTO FALLS SCENIC AREA

4   **5**

6

7

RAVEN CLIFFS WILDERNESS AREA

129

19

11

CHATTAHOOCHEE NATIONAL FOREST

129

11

1 MILE

N   Ref: USGS Greenville 1:250,000

19

9

1 Tesnatee Gap	7 Duke's Creek Falls Trail
2 Raven Cliffs Falls	Raven Cliffs Wilderness Area
3 Raven Cliffs Falls Trail	DeSoto Falls Scenic Area
4 Wildcat Mountain, Whitley Gap Trail	----- Appalachian Trail
5 Adams Bald	.... Trail
6 Logan Turnpike Trail	

Raven Cliffs

Established in 1986, the Raven Cliffs Wilderness Area is located northwest of Cleveland, Georgia. A number of trails with beautiful mountain streams and waterfalls, mountaintops, a wide variety of natural community types, rock outcrops, and scenic vistas abound throughout the 9,115-acre area.

SMITHGALL WOODS CONSERVATION AREA

[Fig. 27(8)] Smithgall Woods Conservation Area was acquired by the state in 1994 as a gift-purchase from Charles A. Smithgall Jr. Governor Zell Miller dedicated the 5,562-acre area as a Heritage Preserve, ensuring that this spectacular, pristine area will remain protected for future generations. Duke's Creek runs through the property and is available for catch-and-release fishing with special regulations.

To observe hardwoods, streams, and wildlife, hikers can explore the area on trails and bikers can explore the area on roads. As we go to press, two hiking trails have been constructed, and a third is under construction. The Laurel Ridge Interpretive Trail is a moderately strenuous, 1.5-mile loop. The Cathy Ellis Memorial Trail is an easy, 1-mile walk. The Martin's Mine Historic Trail, which is under construction, will allow the hiker to see the site of the 1893 gold mine, where miners dug vertical shafts as deep as 125 feet and a tunnel 900 feet long to locate and follow the gold-bearing quartz vein. The Smithgall Woods Conservation Center also provides accommodations for executive and organizational conferences and getaways.

Directions: Located on GA 75-A, 3 miles west of Helen, and just south of the Richard B. Russell Scenic Highway (GA 348).

For more information: Smithgall Woods Conservation Area, 61 Tsalake Trail, Helen, GA 30545. Phone (706) 878-3087.

DUKE'S CREEK FALLS TRAIL

[Fig. 26(7)] About 1 mile, marked with blue blazes. The trail is the roadbed of the Byrd-Matthews Lumber Company logging railroad, operated circa 1914–15. The large falls seen from the trail and parking lot is called Duke's Creek Falls even though it is on Davis Creek. There are several smaller waterfalls in the area. The trail ends at the confluence of Davis Creek and Duke's Creek. Duke's Creek is a beautiful mountain waterway with large boulders and splashing water around foaming pools and riffles. Spray from the falls, which is about 250 feet high, cools the area and provides relief for the hiker.

Careful observers will notice the small wildflowers growing along the banks of the trail. Water seeps out of this bank at scattered locations and, with broken patches of sunlight, provides excellent habitat for a variety of flora. This is a west-facing slope with patches of mountain laurel and rhododendron all along the way. The upper part of the slope is drier, with mixed hardwoods, especially oaks, hickories, and tulip poplars, forming a tree canopy about 50 feet high. Toward the bottom of the trail and along Duke's Creek, a cove forest of young hemlock and white pine is developing. Several large hemlocks provide an accent along the stream bank.

Directions: Take GA 75 north from Helen for 1.5 miles; turn left on GA 356 (75 Alternate); go 2.3 miles to the Richard Russell Scenic Highway; turn right and go 2 miles to the Duke's Creek Falls parking area. An alternate access is to go approximately 1 mile farther north on Richard Russell Scenic Highway to FS 244, which intersects the highway to the southwest, and travel along the southern boundary of the Raven Cliffs Wilderness Area. Drive .6 mile, park, then follow an unmarked trail over a small ridge and down to the top of Duke's Creek Falls. The falls can be clearly heard from the FS road, and the hike is only about 1,200 feet from the road.

RAVEN CLIFFS FALLS TRAIL

[Fig. 26(3)] About 2.5 miles, easy to moderately difficult. This trail, like the Duke's Creek Falls Trail, is the roadbed of the Byrd-Matthews Lumber Company logging railroad, operated circa 1914–15. Dodd's Creek is one of the most beautiful mountain streams easily accessible in north Georgia. It splashes and winds through the mountain valley with an abundance of whitewater, riffles and pools, moss-covered seepages, and overhanging tangles of laurel. At numerous points along the trail, the hiker can approach the stream for a closer view. There are five or six lesser falls to observe along the way, and one of these is impressive enough to make many visitors think it is Raven Cliffs Falls itself.

Near the falls the trail climbs about 40 feet and moves a little away from Dodd's Creek, then returns at Raven Cliffs. Directly ahead, the visitor encounters a massive cliff face of solid rock that rises vertically from the landscape about 80 to 90 feet. The cliff appears from the trail as two large blocks with a narrow crevasse between. Raven Cliffs Falls results from the water of Dodd's Creek falling straight down between the blocks back inside the crevasse and into a dark pool at the bottom. Although the water flow is not great this high in the drainage basin, the sound of it is amplified by the cliff face and gives the visitor an overall impression of the powerful forces at work sculpting the mountain landscape.

Even though no signs identify the trail, it is a heavily visited area. On a November weekend, for example, 42 vehicles were parked at the trailhead and six camps were in use nearby. At Raven Cliffs, two mountain climbers were rappelling from the cliff face, and several hikers were sitting on top of the cliff. In spite of such a level of activity, this is one of the best trails anywhere for a great hiking experience with the whole family.

Directions: Take GA 75 north from Helen 1.5 miles; turn left on GA 356 (75 Alternate) and go 2.3 miles to the Richard Russell Scenic Highway; turn right and go 3 miles to the trailhead and parking area. Walk downstream 145 yards along the creek, cross a tiny stream, and turn right to pick up the trail.

WILDCAT MOUNTAIN, WHITLEY GAP TRAIL

[Fig. 26(4)] Whitley Gap Trail is about 1.1 miles long; if the visitor wants to visit Adams Bald [Fig. 26(5)], another .5 mile is added to the trip. The best part of the trail, however, is to the top of Wildcat Mountain, which is only about .5 mile. The climb up the north slope is about 300 feet. This trail is fun for children and adults alike. It ascends from the road first through a stand of sweet birch and some hardwoods, and then through a laurel thicket of rhododendron and mountain laurel. This type of heath growth is typical on the north-facing slopes of higher peaks in this area.

Whitley Gap Trail is an easily accessible example of this fairyland growth form. Children are amazed by this natural community type. Everything is their size and everything is green and pretty. There are moss-covered rocks, ferns, and wildflowers along the trail. Small, gnarled limbs of the laurel thicket arch over the path, making it a secret passageway. The trail emerges from the evergreen thicket near the ridgetop of Wildcat Mountain at an elevation just under 3,800 feet. This is the highest peak in the vicinity, and it provides an outstanding scenic view in all directions, especially west and south. The fairyland theme continues on the Wildcat Mountain ridgeline. White oaks, chestnut oaks, scarlet oaks, and several sweet birch, which normally grow into tall dominant trees, are gnarled and stunted on the mountaintop. Limbs start about 2 feet from the ground, and children can't resist climbing them to get an adult's view of the surrounding mountain ranges.

Directions: About 7 miles northwest of the junction of the Richard Russell Scenic Highway and GA 75 Alternate, north of Helen. The Appalachian Trail crosses Richard Russell Scenic Highway at Hogpen Gap. Whitley Gap Trail branches off the AT on the north slope of Wildcat Mountain. A parking area on the north side of the Russell Highway provides convenient access to Wildcat Mountain.

LOGAN TURNPIKE TRAIL

[Fig. 26(6)] About 2 miles, blue blazes. The Logan Turnpike is an abandoned toll road that was privately maintained and used during horse-and-buggy days as a corridor through the mountains. It is difficult to imagine anyone pulling an empty wagon, much less a fully loaded one, straight up this steep trail through Tesnatee Gap [Fig. 26(1)]. About .2 mile down the trail and near the bottom of the steep part of the slope, one of the most interesting aspects of this trail begins to appear. Here is an excellent location to observe firsthand the formation of a natural stream in the forest. Tiny springs of water begin to appear along the lower slopes to the right and left of Logan Turnpike. Crystal-clear water seeps up from points along the ground and flows so gently that it does not push aside the leaf litter to make a visible path. These small trickles would go unnoticed in the woods, except that several coalesce and travel along the trail underfoot.

Eventually, the small trickles join others, making small but noisy brooks less than a foot wide. Several of these turn and run along the trail before crossing it to the west side and forming the beginning of Town Creek. The beautiful stream which results contains clear, cold water with moss-covered rocks through the stream bed and no silt to be found. Contrast this with a stream in an urban/suburban community where after a rain, the warm muddy water rushes along gullies from the roadside and fills the streams first with a torrent of erosive force and then with mud and silt as the storm water subsides. The trail extends about 2 miles almost due south from the trailhead and drops about 1,270 feet in that distance—700 feet in the first .5-mile, a part of the trail that is steep and rocky.

Directions: On the Richard Russell Scenic Highway 7.6 miles from the junction with GA 75 Alternate, the scenic drive passes close to Tesnatee Gap, then turns due north. The Logan Turnpike goes south through Tesnatee Gap [Fig. 26(1)]. There is a marker here for the gap. A parking area provided on the south side of the Russell Highway provides easy access. The Logan Turnpike begins on the east side of the parking lot and goes south down the draw. To reach the southern trailhead for the turnpike, take US 19 north from Dahlonega for 13.5 miles to Turners Corner; turn right and proceed south on US 129 for 2.8 miles; turn left on Town Creek Road (gravel road) and go 2.5 miles. This road is very rough past the old toll-keeper's house near the trailhead; a high-clearance vehicle is recommended. The road ends at a small trailhead parking lot. The trail begins at the junction of the county road and the Forest Service property line. A historical marker on the approach road to the trailhead designates the toll-keeper's house.

RICHARD RUSSELL SCENIC HIGHWAY DRIVING TOUR

[Fig. 26] This scenic route crosses the Blue Ridge and provides scenic overlooks. It forms the northern boundary of the eastern half of the Raven Cliffs Wilderness, giving access to Raven Cliffs's trails, Duke's Creek Falls, and the Appalachian Trail at two places. To arrive at the start of the driving tour, take GA 356 (75 Alternate) out of Helen 2.3 miles. Watch for GA 348 turning west where it dead-ends into GA 356. Set the odometer on 0. The first overlook is at 1.4 miles. The entrance to Duke's Creek Falls parking is .8 mile farther, and the trail to Raven Cliffs about a mile beyond that. One encounters white pines about mile 2.4; the tree is common until mile 4.7, when deciduous (oak-hickory) forest continues to Tesnatee Gap. The road begins to climb steeply at 3.2 miles.

The Tray Mountain vista (*see* page 122) is to the right at 4.1 miles. The foreground ridge bears white pine mixed with hardwoods, while red maples grow close below the parking area. At mile 4.2 the road bank has a remarkable covering of Christmas fern and primitive club moss. Vistas to the left, such as at miles 5.1, 6, and 6.7, overlook the Raven Cliffs Wilderness. One is able to gaze across the flat Dahlonega Gold Belt to Yonah Mountain and the distant Piedmont. At milepost 6 one begins to see in the road cuts the structure of the most common rock of the Eastern Blue

Ridge, banded gneiss. This rock becomes more noticeable at mile 6.3 and at Hogpen Gap, just beyond the crossing of the Appalachian Trail. Here, at 7 miles, the large cut on the left offers a study in the wavy banding of dark and light that characterizes metamorphic rock.

Starting down the colder north slope of the Blue Ridge, there is parking at 7.5 miles and close access to the Appalachian Trail at Tesnatee Gap [Fig. 26(1)]. At this point one crosses the old Logan Turnpike, which came through Tesnatee Gap, one of the earliest crossings of the Blue Ridge by the early settlers. From this point the highway parallels the old Logan Turnpike, descending rapidly down the Nottely River headwaters—in this case, Lordamercy Cove. At 8.9 miles one encounters a hemlock-heath community along the creek, and at 9.4 miles in the floodplain south of the highway is a white pine–tulip poplar forest indicating the site of an abandoned field.

One should anticipate a settlement ahead, and after passing through a mix of white pine and Virginia pine, one reaches the first house at 10.5 miles. At mile 10.8, by looking across the flood-plain, one can see the extent of former hillside pastures so common in the early days of settle-ment. Note how the growth of white pines in the old pasture is sharply delineated from the hard-woods above it. Highway 348 dead-ends into GA 180 at 13.6 miles. Turn east on GA 180.

In about 4 miles, the road enters the ring of ultrabasic rock surrounding Brasstown Bald, rock in which Indian carvings are preserved at Track-

EASTERN WHITE PINE
(Pinus strobus)

rock Gap nearby. Continue and cross Jack's Gap, where the Jack's Gap Trail crosses and the road to Brasstown, begins its very steep ascent. Dropping down the east side from the gap, one descends Soapstone Creek, leaving the soapstone and other pecu-liar rocks at the Owl Creek road turnoff. Continue on and turn south onto GA 75. Almost immediately, the High Shoals Falls Scenic Area road turns east, and in another mile the very steep road to Indian Grave Gap and Tray Mountain (FS 283) also turns east. Continuing on GA 75, one reaches Unicoi Gap in approximately 3 more miles. Unicoi Gap was the boundary between Indian and white lands until the Dahlonega gold rush. It was one of the first gaps crossed by a highway. Continuing down the south side of the Blue Ridge, watch for the sign marking Andrews Cove on the left. Here Andrews Creek follows the westernmost part of the famed geologic anomaly, the Warwoman Shear, which cuts across Lake Burton to the Chattooga River country. Past Andrews Cove, GA 75 descends to the Chattahoochee headwaters and the starting point at Helen.

Map References: USGS 1:24,000 series: Cowrock–Neel's Gap.

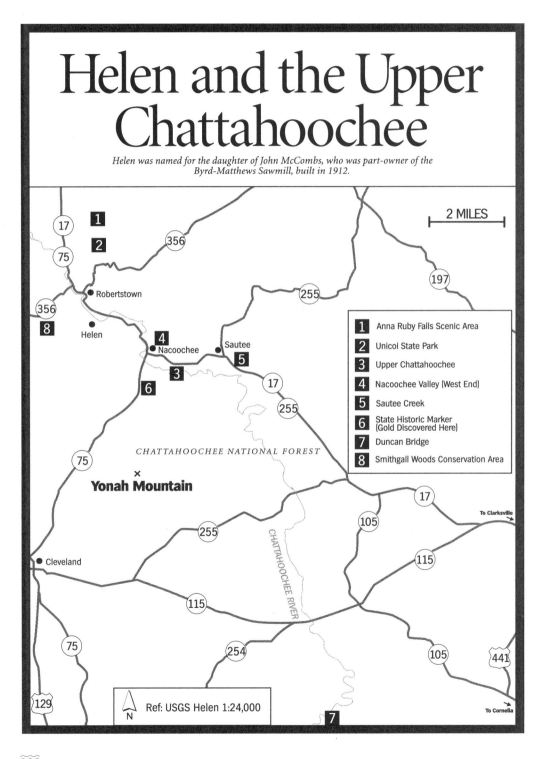

Helen and the Upper Chattahoochee

Helen was named for the daughter of John McCombs, who was part-owner of the Byrd-Matthews Sawmill, built in 1912.

2 MILES

17
75
356
75
356
8
Helen
Robertstown
197
255
4 Nacoochee
Sautee
5
3
17
6
255

1 Anna Ruby Falls Scenic Area
2 Unicoi State Park
3 Upper Chattahoochee
4 Nacoochee Valley (West End)
5 Sautee Creek
6 State Historic Marker (Gold Discovered Here)
7 Duncan Bridge
8 Smithgall Woods Conservation Area

CHATTAHOOCHEE NATIONAL FOREST

× **Yonah Mountain**

75

255

17

To Clarksville

105

115

Cleveland

CHATTAHOOCHEE RIVER

115

75

254

105

441

129

N
Ref: USGS Helen 1:24,000

To Cornelia

7

Helen and the Upper Chattahoochee

The north Georgia town of Helen [Fig. 27] developed around the Byrd-Matthews Sawmill, which was built in 1912. The town was named for the daughter of John McCombs, a prominent citizen of that era who was part owner of the mill and of the newly built railroad through the valley. The sawmill operated continuously until the late 1920s, when the virgin pines and hardwoods, once plentiful here, had been cut down and run through its blades. It was subsequently demolished.

For the next 40 years, Helen's fortunes declined. Bypassed by the major transportation routes through the mountains, it got little benefit from the steady increase in tourism that the mountain region as a whole experienced during that period, and the town's few citizens found jobs scarce. A new women's apparel plant, Orbit Manufacturing, was opened in the early 1960s and run by a man named Jim Wilkins, and a few people were hired. But the town was almost a ghost town in 1968, when the business district consisted of one rundown motel and 16 concrete block buildings, 9 of them empty. Then things began to change.

Three men were the prime movers behind born-again Helen. One of them was Jim Wilkins, the founder of Orbit Manufacturing, who owned most of the west side of the business district. Another was Pete Hodgkinson, who lived in nearby Clarkesville, worked with Wilkins in the management of Orbit, and also owned land in Helen. They added their ideas and resources to those of the third member of the triumvirate, John Kollock, an artist who lived nearby and had a passion for the architecture and landscape of the Bavarian Alps. Within a week of their first meeting, these three drew up the initial plan for putting a new face on Helen—one calculated to be alluring to the mountain tourists. Kollock drew a series of sketches depicting his vision of what the town would look like after its projected transformation, and the other two wasted no time in convincing their fellow businessmen and property owners in town to cooperate with the effort. Hodgkinson was later killed in 1976 in an accident while hot air ballooning, a sport he brought to Helen and which later developed into one of the area's major promotional attractions—the Helen-to-the-Atlantic Balloon Race.

In the years since, Helen has developed into a major north Georgia tourist attraction, drawing visitors from Atlanta and all over the Southeast. Although Orbit Manufacturing has closed, outside entrepreneurs have opened new businesses, all in keeping with the Bavarian Alpine theme, and have bought up slices of the surrounding woodlands for development as second-home sites.

Visitors to Helen can wander through the Alpine-style shops to browse for antiques, brownies, books, Indian jewelry, cigars, backpacks, and Christmas ornaments, or sit on a restaurant deck overlooking the Chattahoochee to dine on anything from pizza to knockwurst.

NACOOCHEE VALLEY

[Fig. 27(4)] Just north of the junction of GA 75 and GA 17, the Nacoochee Valley extends to the east. In the foreground is the Nacoochee Indian Mound, rising from the flat pastureland and crowned with a white latticework gazebo. A much larger, wooded mound stands in the floodplain to the east. At the time of the first European contact with this area—Hernando De Soto's 1540 expedition in search of gold—this was the center of civilization in the region, a Cherokee town called Guasili, or Guax-ale. The mound, however, predates even the Cherokees; it was built by their predecessors in this valley, the Uchee Indians. The name "Nacoochee," in fact, comes from the Uchee word for this small temple mound, *nagutsi*.

YELLOW BIRCH
(Betula alleghaniensis)
The unique bark of the birch is thin and shreddy. This bark is flammable even when wet, so it is useful for campsites.

WEST END

[Fig. 27(4)] Just north of the GA 75/17 junction is the impressive Italianate Victorian house known as West End. One of the oldest surviving structures in the valley, it was built in 1870 for retired Confederate colonel John Nichols and was later occupied by Lamartine Griffin Hardman, Georgia governor from 1927 to 1931.

DUKE'S CREEK GOLD MINING

The first bridge south of the Chattahoochee River crosses Duke's Creek on GA 75 [Fig. 27(6)]. This is the site of the first discovery of gold in White County (see state historical marker). In the floodplain east of the bridge, there is a series of narrow ponds. These are ponds associated with mining the placer deposits (gold in stream gravel). In some river floodplains, huge dredges were floated in ponds of their own digging, digging out in front and filling in behind.

CANOEING THE UPPER CHATTAHOOCHEE

The section of the Chattahoochee River above Helen is a tight, difficult, and rapidly descending mountain river. This section can usually be run only after a rain, and water levels vary almost hourly. It should be run in the spring only by experts paddling in small parties.

The Upper Chattahoochee, from Nacoochee Valley to GA 255, is a nice float on moderate rapids. Near the end of the valley, Sautee Creek [Fig. 27(5)] enters from the left. Many paddlers put their boats into Sautee Creek on Lynch Mountain Road, an unpaved county road next to the GA 17 bridge over the creek. This is a short float across the valley to the main stream of the Chattahoochee.

As noted in *North Georgia Canoeing*, by Bob Sehlinger and Don Otey, from the Sautee Creek junction down to GA 255 is one of the longest undisturbed stretches of the river. The terrain is heavily forested, with large white pines and frequent rock outcroppings. Rapids are fairly frequent but are of the mild Class I and II category.

The section between GA 255 and GA 115 contains some Class III water. From GA 115 to Duncan Bridge [Fig. 27(7)] is the section most appealing to whitewater buffs. None of the rapids are particularly difficult; but combined, they provide interesting and challenging canoeing.

Directions: In Helen there is a take-out point across from the Wildewood Outpost. There is a put-in spot where Sautee Creek enters the river from the northeast. One can also put in to Sautee Creek on Lynch Mountain Road, an unpaved county road next to the GA 17 bridge over the creek (*see above*).

Other put-in and take-out points: 1) The GA 255 bridge, on the left (Habersham County side) of the river only. The property owner on the right side should not be disturbed. Use the public highway right-of-way. 2) Duncan Bridge. The distance from Jasus Creek to Helen is about 8 river miles; approximately six hours should be allowed for the run. From Helen to the GA 255 bridge is approximately 13 miles; from the GA 255 bridge to the GA 115 bridge is 4.2 miles, and from there to Duncan Bridge is about 4 miles. The Wildewood Outpost runs a parking lot at Duncan Bridge; there is a fee.

UPPER CHATTAHOOCHEE RIVER AREA CAMPGROUND & PICNIC AREA

This campsite on the banks of the upper Chattahoochee provides access to the nearby Mark Trail Wilderness Area and Appalachian Trail.

Directions: From Helen, go north on GA 75, past Andrews Cove, about 8 miles. Just at the Whit County/Towns County line, turn left onto FS 44 and proceed 5 miles to campground.

Facilities: 34 campsites, sanitary facilities, drinking water, cooking grills, fire rings.

For more information: U.S. Forest Service, Chattooga District, 200 Highway 197, PO Box 1960, Clarkesville, GA 30523. Phone (706) 754-6221.

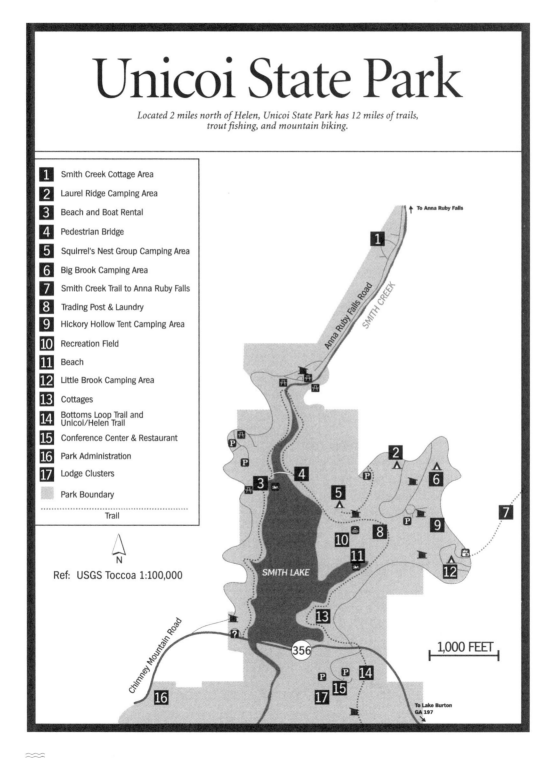

Unicoi State Park

*Located 2 miles north of Helen, Unicoi State Park has 12 miles of trails,
trout fishing, and mountain biking.*

1 Smith Creek Cottage Area
2 Laurel Ridge Camping Area
3 Beach and Boat Rental
4 Pedestrian Bridge
5 Squirrel's Nest Group Camping Area
6 Big Brook Camping Area
7 Smith Creek Trail to Anna Ruby Falls
8 Trading Post & Laundry
9 Hickory Hollow Tent Camping Area
10 Recreation Field
11 Beach
12 Little Brook Camping Area
13 Cottages
14 Bottoms Loop Trail and Unicoi/Helen Trail
15 Conference Center & Restaurant
16 Park Administration
17 Lodge Clusters
Park Boundary
Trail

N

Ref: USGS Toccoa 1:100,000

To Anna Ruby Falls

Anna Ruby Falls Road

SMITH CREEK

SMITH LAKE

Chimney Mountain Road

356

1,000 FEET

To Lake Burton
GA 197

UNICOI STATE PARK

[Fig. 28] Just 2 miles north of Helen, Unicoi is a 1,081-acre park with a beautiful 100-room lodge plus a wide range of other accommodations and a buffet-style restaurant. Popular activities include hiking on 12 miles of trails, trout fishing, mountain biking on a 7-mile trail, group camping and walk-in tent campsites, mountain culture programs, and a craft shop in the lodge. Special events at this site include the Fireside Arts and Crafts Show in February, the Wildflower Weekend in April, the Folk Life Festival in June, and the week-long Earthskills Workshop in the spring and in the fall.

Directions: Located 2 miles northeast of Helen via GA 356.

Facilities: 100-room lodge and conference center, 30 cottages, 80 tent and trailer sites, 53-acre lake and beach, 4 lighted tennis courts, buffet-style restaurant.

For more information: Unicoi State Park, PO Box 849, Helen, GA 30545. Phone (706) 878-2201 for office and group reservations. Call (800) 864-PARK, or (770) 389-PARK in metro Atlanta, for individual reservations.

HIKING TRAILS OF UNICOI STATE PARK

UNICOI LAKE TRAIL. This is an easy, 2.4-mile loop trail around Unicoi Lake, across the dam, and back to the lodge.

Directions: Follow directions to Unicoi State Park (above). The trail begins at the lodge.

BOTTOMS LOOP TRAIL. 2.1 miles. An easy, pleasant trail past streams, fields, low ridges, and wildflower displays.

Directions: Follow directions to Unicoi State Park (above). The trail begins near the lodge and conference center.

UNICOI/HELEN TRAIL. 3 miles one-way. A pleasant walk from the lodge to Helen.

Directions: Follow directions to Unicoi State Park (above). The trail begins near the lodge and continues to City Park in Helen.

YONAH MOUNTAIN

[Fig. 27] This landmark peak, located in Georgia's Piedmont region, is a monolith of granite gneiss. It and its companion, Pink Mountain, are highly visible from the Richard Russell Scenic Highway and stand as isolated peaks in the Dahlonega Gold Belt. Yonah's convenient cliffs provide mountaineering experience for U.S. Army ranger units as well as other climbers. Most of Yonah (meaning "bear" in the Cherokee language) is in the Chattahoochee National Forest.

Directions: The existing road to Yonah has been closed by private landowners. The Forest Service is currently acquiring land and a road easement for the Trust for Public Land in another location to provide public access. Call the Forest Service at (770) 536-0541 for updates on when access will be secured.

Map References: USGS 1:100,000 series: Toccoa.

Tray Mountain

This is rugged backcountry, located near Helen, Georgia, combined with some fine state parks and easy-to-reach waterfalls and hikes, including the Appalachian Trail. Access is available to most parts of this area by car. The Tray Mountain area includes unique sites such as the incomparable Ramp Cove, with the finest stand of giant buckeyes in Georgia (if not the Southeast) and a wildflower paradise. Exciting boulderfields are common here just under the Appalachian Trail (AT) and off the Kelly Ridge. The Kelly Ridge spur provides a superb hike similar to the great Duncan Ridge in the Blood Mountain area. The huge rock outcrop at the Mill Creek Roughs is worth exploring. Tray Mountain itself, with its superlative boulderfield, is one of the major overlooks in the Georgia Blue Ridge. The southern part of this area is the 9,702-acre Tray Mountain Wilderness.

Tray Mountain [Fig. 29] is the eighth highest Georgia peak (4,430 feet). Because of its elevation and its standing as a sentinel in a great sweeping arc of the Appalachian Trail from west to north, Tray Mountain is a magnificent grandstand from which to view the Nantahalas and the Georgia Blue Ridge. Southward one can see the Piedmont. On clear days, it is said that even Kennesaw Mountain and Stone Mountain are visible. Closer is the flat terrain of the Dahlonega Gold Belt, bordered on the west by the Hayesville Fault, from which the mountains of the Raven Cliffs Wilderness rise abruptly. In the foreground, also, is the lovely peak of Yonah Mountain. Yonah's abrupt cliffs provide the best, easily accessible area for rock climbing in the Georgia mountains.

MAIN ACCESS ROUTES TO TRAY MOUNTAIN

For the first route, take GA 356 east from Robertstown (1 mile north of Helen) for 5 miles. Turn left at Bethel Church onto Chimney Mountain Road and follow it for 2 miles to FS 79 (Tray Mountain Road) which is maintained for four-wheel-drive vehicles and pickup trucks. Travel FS 79 north for 7 miles to Tray Mountain Gap [Fig. 29(49)] at the intersection of FS 698 and the AT crossing. For the second route, a steep incline with switchbacks, take GA 75 north from Robertstown for 1 mile. Turn right on FS 79 across from the Hooch Trading Post. Travel in a northerly direction 6.5 miles to a fork. The left fork goes to a landmark called Indian Grave Gap [Fig. 29(54)], a high, wide saddle between Rocky Mountain (4,017 feet) and Tray. On either side are "hanging valleys" of great scenic beauty. Also crossing here are the Appalachian Trail and a trail from Andrews Cove [Fig. 29(60)]. Here the last remnant of the great gash of Warwoman Shear [Fig. 29(55)] makes its final appearance, lining up the head of High Shoals Creek with Andrews Creek [Fig. 29(41,48)]. The right fork goes past the little meadow [Fig. 29(52)] called "Cheese Dairy," the former site of a goat cheese factory. There is a spring here at this popular camping spot. Continue to Tray Gap [Fig. 29(49)], located at the intersection of FS 698 and the AT. Hikers can follow the AT to the top of Tray Mountain.

For the third route, the shortest, take GA 75 north from Helen 11 miles (2 miles north of Unicoi Gap). Turn right onto FS 283. Proceed in a southerly direction for about 4 miles. Turn east at the junction with FS 79 and go 2 miles to arrive at the intersection of FS 698 and the AT crossing. At 1.3 miles on FS 283, pass the High Shoals trailhead [Fig. 29(38)] to a bridge over High Shoals and a trail down to two sets of exceptional falls where, because of several deaths, viewing platforms [Fig. 29(37)] have been built.

APPALACHIAN TRAIL

It is an exhilarating experience to hike the .9-mile portion of the Appalachian Trail that climbs 600 feet to the summit of Tray Mountain. The ridges at Tray Gap and upward bear red oak ridge forest; near the summit, the oaks become dwarfed and gnarled. There are patches of lily of the valley and other interesting plants on the way. Near the top, there is a veritable garden of purple, or Catawba, rhododendron which—unlike the common or rosebay—blooms in spring rather than summer. It surrounds rock outcrops on which grow patches of high-altitude spike moss.

Just below the top of Tray on the north side is one of the best-developed boulder-fields in north Georgia [Fig. 29(46)]. It is hazardous walking, but one can drop down through it to Corbin Creek Road [Fig. 29(42)] or go up the third cove [Fig. 29(43)] 2 miles or more north of Tray Gap. It is characterized by two high-altitude maples—striped and mountain—together with holly and Catawba rhododendron. Two herbs here—the beautiful rosy twisted stalk and an elderberry—are at their southernmost limits. Just down the AT, north from the top a few hundred yards, there is a side trail to the south leading to an exceptional overlook [Fig. 29(50)] of the southern part of the Tray Mountain area and the headwaters of the Soque River.

SWALLOW CREEK

The northern portion of the Tray Mountain area is largely the watershed of Swallow Creek. While not designated wilderness, much of this area is wild and primitive. It has two outstanding high ridges—the Blue Ridge (from Dick's Gap to Kelly Knob—4,276 feet) and the Kelly Ridge. The walking along both is easy, and the scenery is rewarding. The Swallow Creek watershed, tucked away in the Blue Ridge, is hardly known at all. There is a high cove of huge old growth buckeyes (Ramp Cove) [Fig. 29(9)] and the heaviest growth of the fabled "mountain garlic" (ramps) in Georgia. The abundant north-facing coves offer boulderfields and wildflower assemblages. The advantage of this area is that one can hike up one creek, hit the ridge, go around and down another creek, and arrive back at the starting point, so you can create a hike suited to individual desires.

To approach the area, turn off US 76 2 miles east of where GA 17/75 dead-ends into it. Turning here [Fig. 29(1)] at the lower Hightower Church, drive several miles to the end of the pavement to park [Fig. 29(2)]. If the gate straight ahead is open,

Tray Mountain

Tray Mountain is one of Georgia's highest peaks.
On clear days, one may see Kennesaw and Stone Mountain to the south.

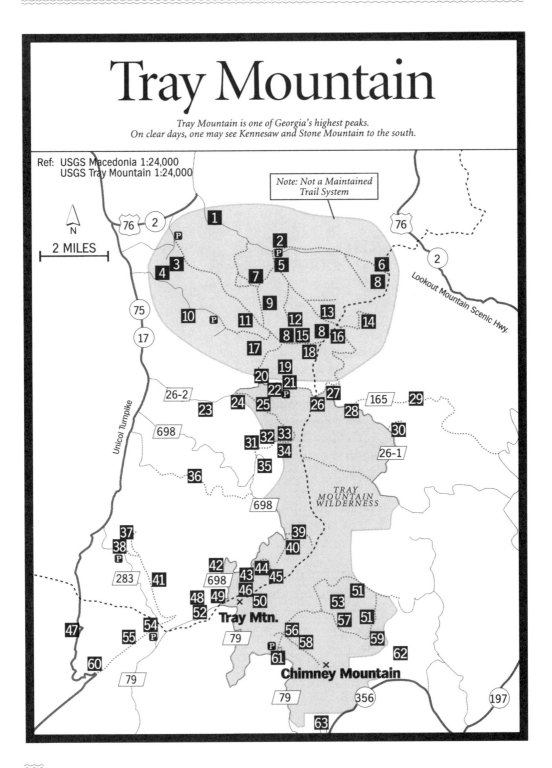

Ref: USGS Macedonia 1:24,000
USGS Tray Mountain 1:24,000

Note: Not a Maintained
Trail System

Lookout Mountain Scenic Hwy.

Unicol Turnpike

TRAY
MOUNTAIN
WILDERNESS

Tray Mtn.

Chimney Mountain

2 MILES

N

1 Lower Hightower Church

2 Gate at End of Raod to Swallow Creek

3 Schoolhouse Gap

4 Cynth Creek

5 Swallow Creek Ford

6 Swallow Creek

7 Ramp Cove Ravine

8 Boulderfields, Kelly Ridge & AT

9 Ramp Cove

10 Dyer Family Trout Farm

11 Kelly Ridge

12 Stroud Creek Falls & Cascades

13 Dismal Cove

14 White Oak Stamp

15 Stroud Cove

16 Deep Gap

17 Buzzard Knob

18 Kelly Knob

19 Roughs, Mill Creek

20 Gated Road – Sassafras Creek

21 Mill Creek Roughs

22 Waterfall, Mill Creek

23 Mill Creek

24 Sassafras Creek

25 Sassafras Branch Cove

26 Addis Gap

27 Addis Family Farm

28 Park's Gap

29 Moccasin Creek Trail

30 Fuller Gap

31 Tripp Gap

32 Rock Outcrop, High Top

33 Boulderfield, Yellow Birch, Dismal Mountain

34 White Oak Forest

35 Log Road to Tripp Gap

36 Corbin Creek

37 Viewing Platforms, Falls below High Shoals

38 High Shoals Trailhead to Blue Hole/High Shoals Falls

39 Double Branch to Steeltrap Gap

40 Blocked Log Road to Spring Cove

41 High Shoals Creek

42 Corbin Creek Road

43 Third Cove North of Tray Gap

44 Ridge Trail to Spring Cove

45 Spring Cove

46 Boulderfields, North Top of Tray Mountain

47 Spoil Cane Creek

48 Andrews Creek

49 Tray Mountain Gap

50 Overlook, South Tray Mountain & Soque River Headwaters

51 Trail to Soque River/Chimney Mountain

52 "Cheese Dairy"

53 Wolfpen Ridge

54 Indian Grave Gap

55 Warwoman Shear

56 Deep Gap

57 Waterfalls, Left Fork to Soque River

58 Ridgeline to Chimney Mountain

59 Old Tram Railroad up Soque River

60 Andrews Cove Recreation Area

61 Rich Cove Trail

62 Private Land – Blocks Access to Soque River

63 Buzzard Knob

Tray Mountain Wilderness

- - - - - - - - - - - - - - - - - - - Appalachian Trail

·· Trail

proceed another mile or so. Most visitors park at the end of the pavement. Of the two dirt roads to the right, select the left-hand (a jeep can drive another .25 mile on FS 300, but it is not recommended). From the end of the pavement, go up the dirt road and take the first old road to the right that fords the creek [Fig. 29(5)] (there are two old roads; take the one most traveled).

Follow this old logging road, which shortly climbs a long ravine [Fig. 29(7)]. High up in this ravine, one finds smooth-barked, black, and crooked trunks of the rare yellowwood tree. Cross a flat area, follow the road on up, and soon enter what may be the grandest old growth forest in the mountains [Fig. 29(9)]. The buckeyes here reach 4 feet in diameter and exceed those in Sosebee Cove. Moreover, the herbaceous ground is extremely rich in species, including abundant ramps for which the cove is named. The soil is rich black Porter's loam.

One can continue up to the top of Kelly Ridge [Fig. 29(11)], walk around and come down Stroud or Dismal Coves [Fig. 29(13,15)] (note that Stroud and Dismal are not marked on the ground and can be difficult to locate), or take the AT to Moreland Gap and come down Swallow Creek itself [Fig. 29(6)]. There is a series of small falls and cascades along Stroud Creek [Fig. 29(12)]. Kelly Knob itself is a high scenic point [Fig. 29(18)]. As one walks east along Kelly Ridge and on the AT, almost every cove has a boulderfield at its head [Fig. 29(8)]. Some can be seen from the AT.

One obvious, easy way to reach Kelly Ridge is from Dick's Gap on US 76, which cuts out some of the climbing. West on Kelly Ridge, one can drop off to a parking area on GA 88. Normally, one could drop off at Schoolhouse Gap [Fig. 29(3)], but a clear-cutting currently blocks the way. Another access to Kelly Ridge is by way of the Cynth Creek Road [Fig. 29(4)], which turns east at the first bridge over the Hiawassee River south of the GA 17/US 76 junction. This road passes around one of the Dyer family's four trout-rearing stations [Fig. 29(10)], which sell trout for stocking and as bait for striped bass in Lakes Burton and Lanier.

RUFOUS-SIDED TOWHEE
(Pipilo erythrophthalmus)
A loud "drink-your-tea" song coming from underbrush or thicket identifies the towhee.

South of Kelly Ridge is an area of interest. The western access is by the Mill Creek Road, which is 3.5 miles north of Indian Grove Gap Road or 3.4 miles south of the junction of GA 17 and US 76. The pavement ends above the Dyer Trout Farm on Mill Creek [Fig. 29(23)]. The road climbs through nice oak-hickory slope forest and passes a trailhead for Sassafras Creek [Fig. 29(24)] and a north-turning gated road [Fig. 29(20)] which can lead the hiker to Kelly Ridge. About .25 mile before a locked gate (9.1 miles from GA 17) on the main road, one crosses three small branches at the Mill Creek Roughs [Fig. 29(21)].

Just below the juncture of the last two branches is a beautiful waterfall [Fig. 29(22)]. Up the tiny branches are about .25 mile of "flats" ideal for picnicking. At the head of the flats, one encounters the "roughs" [Fig. 29(19)], and trails cease. A dense, unbanded rock outcrops here near the surface over many acres. Streams cascade off it through rhododendron thickets.

The huge area of rough is most unusual in northern Georgia. Soil has difficulty forming over this immense outcrop. Because of its roughness, it has not been logged since horse-logging days—and then perhaps sparingly. Some old trees might reward exploration. A rattlesnake den is reported in the vicinity of Buzzard Knob [Fig. 29(63)].

ADDIS GAP

[Fig. 29(26)] The gap cannot be reached by vehicle, as the old road has been gated. The gap was named for the Addis family who farmed the rocky slopes .25 mile east of the gap [Fig. 29(27)].

Directions: Addis Gap is reached from the east by the Wildcat Creek Road (26-1), which turns off GA 197 one mile north of LaPrades or 1.5 miles south of Moccasin Creek State Park (also GA 197). It is the first left road past Wildcat Creek going north on GA 197. It is marked FS 26. Just north of the old Addis homestead, a gated road, FS 675, serves as a trail at least as far as White Oak Stamp [Fig. 29(14)] on the head of Chastain Creek. There is an easy connection with the AT at Deep Gap [Fig. 29(16)], where the trail up an old logging road also terminates.

TRAILS

At Park's Gap [Fig. 29(28)], Dick's Creek Road begins. A gated road, it can be hiked to the Dick's Creek watershed. In just a short distance, the trail down Moccasin Creek [Fig. 29(29)] by the Moccasin Creek Falls begins. At Fuller Gap [Fig. 29(30)] another "trail," really an old log road, joins this one in the vicinity of the Moccasin Creek Falls. The Moccasin Creek Trail is a renowned hike of great beauty. It is actually the roadbed of the old railroad by which the watershed was logged in the early 1900s.

Approximately 4 miles back down the Wildcat Creek Road, a gated log road runs up Wildcat Branch.

NORTHERN ACCESS

The principal access to the northern half of the Tray Mountain area from the west is the Corbin Creek Road which turns east off GA 17/75 about 1 mile south of the Mill Creek Road. Take this gravel road (FS 698) 4.2 miles to where it crosses Miller Branch. One can park here and walk a gated log road (FS 698-A) to Tripp Gap [Fig. 29(31)]. There is an unmaintained footpath here that turns right up the ridge toward High Top, passing it to the north and continuing into and around the head of Sassafras Branch Cove [Fig. 29(25)].

On the northwest face of High Top is a very fragmented rock outcrop [Fig. 29(32)] with much lichen growth and occasional seeps of sphagnum moss and saxifrage. The flat on the south side [Fig. 29(34)] is a white oak forest. Many of the trees are quite old. On the north slope between the two tops of Dismal Mountain is a poorly developed boulderfield with some yellow birch [Fig. 29(33)]. About .5 mile south from Miller Branch, one encounters the terminus [Fig. 29(35)] of the old road up Corbin Creek [Fig. 29(36)]. The other end begins as a gravel road about .5 mile south of the main Corbin Creek Road.

The next footpath of consequence goes up Double Branch [Fig. 29(39)] to Steeltrap Gap.

SPRING COVE AREA

[Fig. 29(45)] Spring Cove has a nice spring surrounded by a stately 80-year-old forest with ash, buckeye, and hemlock with diameters up to 36 inches. It is reached on foot along a blocked log road [Fig. 29(40)], where Corbin Creek Road crosses Corbin Creek, or by walking up the ridge [Fig. 29(44)].

THE HEAD OF THE SOQUE RIVER AND CHIMNEY MOUNTAIN

The wilderness south of the AT is rough and steep terrain. It is not well known at all. Private land [Fig. 29(62)] currently blocks easy access up the Soque River. The most interesting hike is to the top of Chimney Mountain [Fig. 29(58)], reached by the ridgeline from a gap and an access trail up Rich Cove [Fig. 29(61)]. To get to this trailhead, one either comes down 4.4 miles on FS 79 east out of Tray Gap or up a similar distance from GA 356. A four-wheel-drive vehicle is advisable on FS 79. The views from Chimney Mountain (3,357 feet) are exceptional. The trail to the top passes through high-quality pitch pine and scarlet oak ridge forest and is very pleasant walking. The south and west faces of Chimney Mountain have extensive rock outcrops. The southern outcrop is surrounded by red cedar which appears to be quite old. It is unusual for red cedar to appear on mountaintops. The summit is a flat outcrop covered in lichen-sedge. There are three rather hollow rock cairns about 4 feet high on the summit of Chimney Mountain. They are of unknown origin.

The other access to this portion of the wilderness is by way of the Shelton Branch Road, reached by taking GA 197 to the first left turn after GA 356 dead-ends into it.

Go 2 miles on paved road and take the first main (paved) road to the left for .5 mile; there, take the right fork; then the first road to the left should be Shelton Branch. The best trail [Fig. 29(51)] crosses Wolf Pen Branch and strikes the north prong of the Soque, from which point one can go up the left prong to Deep Gap [Fig. 29(56)] or down the left fork to two waterfalls [Fig. 29(57)].

The old timers ranged cattle on the Wolfpen Ridge [Fig. 29(53)]. There was an old tram railroad up the Soque [Fig. 29(59)] during the early logging era. While one can find occasional large trees in the Soque watershed, most of the timber is young (around 30 years), owing to the disastrous Hickory Nut Ridge fire that swept 10,000 acres of the basin in 1953. Another fire ravaged the Wildcat watershed in 1958. Fortunately, the wetter north side of the Blue Ridge did not burn.

HIGH SHOALS TRAIL

1.2 miles. High Shoals Scenic Area is comprised of 170 acres with waterfalls, luxuriant banks of rhododendron and laurel, and sparkling mountain streams. The only way to see the two major waterfalls, Blue Hole and High Shoals Falls, is to hike the steep, moderately difficult, 1.2-mile trail [Fig. 29(38)]. The trail, marked by blue blazes, is in good condition, but reaching the trailhead can be difficult. The road may be rough, and fording the stream may cause trouble. When the road is frozen or very muddy, only a four-wheel-drive vehicle can negotiate it.

YELLOW BUCKEYE
(Aesculus octandra)
Growing as tall as 90 feet, the yellow buckeye has 4—6 inch leaves and yellow flowers and produces seeds protected inside smooth capsules. Buckeye seeds resemble chestnuts, but they are round while chestnuts have a pointed tip.

The trail descends from 2,880 feet to 2,560 feet with two switchbacks through a predominantly hardwood forest. After reaching the bottom, the trail follows High Shoals Creek downstream, crosses the water on a wooden bridge, then descends steeply more than 300 feet as the creek cascades downward in a series of five waterfalls. Side trails lead to two observation decks [Fig. 29(37)]. The first deck overlooks Blue Hole, a pool more than 20 feet deep created by the churning of the water and rock falling from 30 feet above. Farther downstream is the grander High Shoals Falls, which tumbles more than 100 feet over jagged rocks, splashing and spraying water into the air.

RED SALAMANDER
(Pseudotriton ruber)

Directions: Go 11 miles north of Helen on GA 75 to the rough dirt and gravel Indian Grave Gap Road, FS 283 (the first road to the right after Unicoi Gap); make a sharp right turn (east); proceed ahead, ford the usually shallow stream, and continue up the hill. Parking for the trail is approximately 1.3 miles from GA 75. Use four-wheel-drive vehicle in winter; two-wheel drive cars may also have difficulty with mud after rain.

ANNA RUBY FALLS SCENIC AREA

[Fig. 27(1)] Anna Ruby Falls, high on the slopes of Tray Mountain, is formed at the junction of Curtis and York creeks. Both creeks originate atop Tray Mountain and are fed by underground springs, rain, and snow. Curtis Creek then drops 153 feet, and York Creek drops 50 feet, forming the double falls. At the base of the falls, where there is an observation deck, the water becomes Smith Creek and tumbles downhill to Unicoi Lake.

The U.S. Forest Service purchased the land surrounding the falls in 1925. The 1,600-acre scenic area adjacent to and surrounding part of Unicoi State Park was established in 1964. The falls were named for Anna Ruby Nichols, the only daughter of Colonel John H. Nichols, who purchased the surrounding land in 1869. His Victorian-style mansion, West End, still stands at the junction of GA 17 and 75. He also built Crescent Hill Baptist Church and the gazebo atop the Nacoochee Indian Mound, both of which are still standing along GA 17.

An easy to moderately difficult, paved, .4-mile trail leads from the parking lot to the foot of the falls.

Directions: Take GA 75 north from Helen 1 mile; turn right onto GA 356 and go 1.5 miles; turn left at the entrance to the falls; follow this road 3.6 miles to the parking area, which accommodates 140 cars and 2 tour buses.

Activities: Hiking, picnicking, fishing.

Facilities: Drinking water, restrooms, trails, gift shop, parking, group tours by arrangement, vending machines, information.

For more information: Anna Ruby Falls Scenic Area, U.S. Forest Service, Chattooga Ranger District, PO Box 1960, Burton Road, Hwy 197, Clarkesville, GA 30523. Phone (706) 754-6221.

SMITH CREEK TRAIL

4.5 miles. This moderately difficult, blue-blazed trail provides hikers with a nice walk through dense patches of rhododendron, mountain laurel, hemlock, and fern. The trail goes up and over Hickory Nut Ridge through hardwood stands and crosses several small mountain streams before ending at Unicoi State Park Campground.

Directions: Follow the directions to Anna Ruby Falls Scenic Area, (*above*). The trail begins at the right of the observation bridge.

ANDREWS COVE RECREATION AREA

[Fig. 29(60)] This recreation area is located along a beautiful mountain stream in a heavily wooded area. It is 2 miles from Andrews Cove to the Appalachian Trail over a moderate trail.

Directions: On GA 75, 5 miles north of Helen and 14 miles north of Cleveland.

Activities: Camping, hiking.

Facilities: Toilets, drinking water pump.

For more information: Andrews Cove Recreation Area, U.S. Forest Service, Chattooga Ranger District, PO Box 1960, Burton Road, Highway 197, Clarkesville, GA 30523. Phone (706) 754-6221.

Map References: USGS 1:24,000 series: Macedonia–Tray Mountain.

MOUNTAIN
LAUREL
(Kalmia latifolia)

(For **DESOTO FALLS SCENIC AND RECREATION AREAS AND TRAIL**, *see* Blood Mountain section, page 101. For **UNICOI STATE PARK**, *see* Helen and the Upper Chattahoochee section, page 117.)

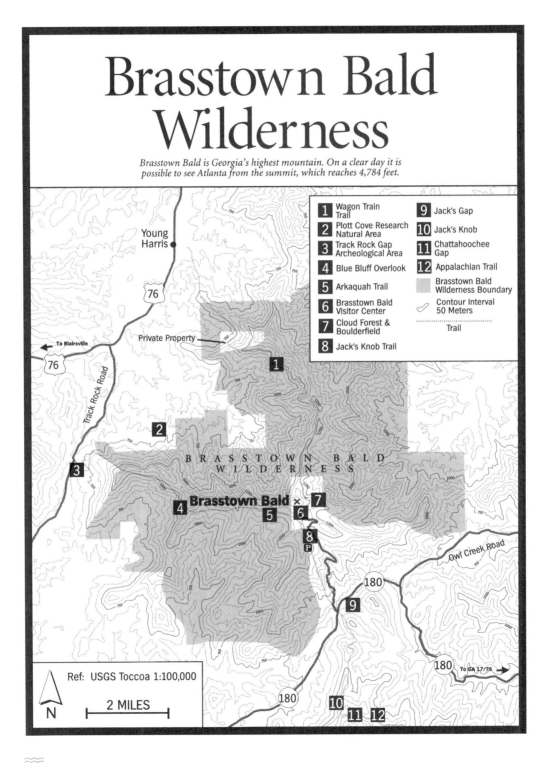

Brasstown Bald Wilderness

Brasstown Bald is Georgia's highest mountain. On a clear day it is possible to see Atlanta from the summit, which reaches 4,784 feet.

1 Wagon Train Trail
2 Plott Cove Research Natural Area
3 Track Rock Gap Archeological Area
4 Blue Bluff Overlook
5 Arkaquah Trail
6 Brasstown Bald Visitor Center
7 Cloud Forest & Boulderfield
8 Jack's Knob Trail
9 Jack's Gap
10 Jack's Knob
11 Chattahoochee Gap
12 Appalachian Trail

Brasstown Bald Wilderness Boundary

Contour Interval 50 Meters

Trail

Young Harris

76

To Blairsville

76

Track Rock Road

Private Property

BRASSTOWN BALD WILDERNESS

Brasstown Bald

Owl Creek Road

180

180

180

To GA 17/75

Ref: USGS Toccoa 1:100,000

2 MILES

N

Brasstown Bald and the Brasstown Bald Wilderness

Brasstown Bald is Georgia's highest mountain. From its summit at 4,784 feet, there are breathtaking views of four states. On a clear day, it is possible to see as far south as Atlanta.

In 1986, 11,823 acres within the Chattahoochee National Forest were designated by Congress as the Brasstown Wilderness. Since then, an additional 1,152 acres have been acquired. The bald itself, which is not within the wilderness area, is only .75 acre. The paved trails, parking areas, visitor center, etc., are outside of the wilderness.

A narrow ring of ultrabasic rocks (soapstone, dunite, and olivine) completely surrounds Brasstown Bald and the ridges leading to it. This is the southernmost habitat for many northern plant and animal species, including the red-back vole. A northern hardwood "cloud forest" of huge, old birches covers the north face. Rhododendron and mountain laurel are among the few shrubs that can survive on these thin, cold soils. The wildflower displays are particularly outstanding in the north-facing coves and down the east side of Wolfpen, one of the longest, highest ridges in Georgia.

Brasstown Bald was so named because of confusion between the Cherokee words *itse-yi*, meaning "new green place," and *untsaiyi*, meaning "brass."

Cherokee legend regarding bald mountains described a horrible, sharp-clawed, winged beast who attempted to steal and eat Indian children. The Cherokees cleared the forest to capture the monster and prayed to their Great Spirit, who killed the beast, restored the children, and has kept the mountaintops clear of trees ever since. A steep, paved .5-mile trail leads from the parking area to the visitor center [Fig. 30(6)] on the bald. For a fee, a shuttle bus carries visitors from the parking area to the visitor center, weekends during April and May then daily from Memorial Day through the end of October.

The trail from the parking area to the summit, the Wagon Train Trail [Fig. 30(1)], is well worth walking. The old wagon train road to Young Harris leads east then north into the fantastic "cloud forest" [Fig. 30(7)] of northern hardwoods on the north side of the mountain, below the visitor center. The huge, old yellow birch are festooned with old-man's beard lichen because of the continuous moisture from cloud condensation.

Rosebay rhododendron may be found near the parking lot, followed by purple rhododendron as the major heath shrub. As one ascends, the trees gradually get shorter. One soon enters a dwarfed red oak and white oak forest where the trees are very old, twisted, and limby. The top is a shrub bald with unique mountaintop species such as dwarf willow and red-berried mountain ash.

THE VISITOR CENTER COMPLEX

The center, built of stone, offers interpretive programs tracing human and natural history of the southern Appalachian region. The Mountaintop Theater features continuous video programs. An outside observation deck provides a 360-degree view of the surrounding area. Here visitors may be awed by the view but unprotected from the wind. Because of its height, Brasstown Bald gets much weather that misses the valleys. Strong wind, rain, and lower temperatures are not uncommon. In winter there is often snow and ice. The fire lookout tower is not open to the public.

Directions: From Cleveland take GA 75 north through Helen to GA 180; turn left (west) onto GA 180 (also GA 66); go 6 miles; turn right onto GA 180 spur; continue 3 miles to Brasstown Bald parking lot.

Facilities: Video show, picnic area, bookstore and gift shop, hiking trails, parking lot (fee), restrooms, exhibits, observation deck, brochures, concessions, shuttle bus.

For more information: Brasstown Bald, U.S. Forest Service, Brasstown Ranger District, 1881 Hwy 515, PO Box 9, Blairsville, GA 30514. Phone (706) 745-6928. Visitor center phone (706) 896-2556.

HIKING TRAILS FROM BRASSTOWN BALD

There are four hiking trails, including the paved summit-access trail. All start from the parking area at the bald. Simple maps and descriptions of all four trails are available in the Forest Service brochure "Trail Guide to the Chattahoochee-Oconee National Forests." The 1:24,000 scale topographical maps of the area (Hiawassee, Jack's Gap, and Blairsville quadrangles) show three of the trails—Arkaquah Trail, Wagon Train Trail, and part of Jack's Knob Trail.

JACK'S KNOB TRAIL. [Fig. 30(8)] About 4.5 miles. Built in the 1930s by the Civilian Conservation Corps and reconstructed in the 1980s by the Forest Service, Jack's Knob Trail is limited to foot traffic and is rated moderate to strenuous. Descending southward from the parking lot along a ridge following the boundary of Towns and Union counties, it crosses GA 180 in Jack's Gap [Fig. 30(9)] at an elevation of 3,000 feet and ascends Hiawassee Ridge past Jack's Knob [Fig. 30(10)], elevation 3,805 feet. Jack's Knob Trail joins the Appalachian Trail in Chattahoochee Gap near the source of the Chattahoochee River.

HIGHBUSH
BLUEBERRY
(Vaccinium corymbosum)

ARKAQUAH TRAIL. [Fig. 30(5)] About 5.5 miles. There is a difference of 2,500 feet in elevation as the trail descends westward along a ridgetop from its beginning in the Brasstown Bald parking area to its end at Track Rock Gap Archeological Area [Fig. 30(3)]. With a difficulty rating of moderate to strenuous, this is not considered a beginner's trail. Blue Bluff Overlook [Fig. 30(4)] is on the trail. Hikers pass Chimney Top Mountain and will be able to see Rocky Knob to the south. Plott Cove Research Natural Area [Fig. 30(2)], which is rich in herbs, wildflowers, and northern hardwoods, is north of the trail at Cove Gap. To reach the western end of the trail at Track Rock Gap, go east of Blairsville on US 76 for 6 miles, turn right onto Track Rock Road and go 3 miles.

BLUETS
(*Houstonia lanceolata*)
White to purple flowers.

WAGON TRAIN TRAIL. [Fig. 30(1)] The Brasstown Bald parking lot is the upper elevation entrance to this trail. To find the entrance, go between the bookstore and the concession stand located in the parking area. Take the paved trail and turn right (east) onto a dirt road. This trail is a wide path originally intended to be GA 66, and on some state maps it is still shown as such. Parts of the trail cross private property. It is a moderate, 5.6-mile walk with fine views. Near the summit, the trail passes remarkable cliffs and boulderfields [Fig. 30(7)] where rock tripe, lichens, reindeer moss, old-man's beard, and club moss flourish. In early spring, silverbell, serviceberry, mountain buttercups, white saxifrage, toothwort, cinquefoil, bluets, highbush and low-bush blueberries, white and purple violets, solomon's seal and plume, pussytoes, and four varieties of trillium can be seen blooming along the trail. The trail ends at private property 2 miles south of Young Harris.

▨ TRACK ROCK ARCHEOLOGICAL SITE

[Fig. 30(3)] Like the Mayan hieroglyphics of southern Mexico and Central America, the ancient petroglyphs carved into three large soapstone boulders on the west side of the road here have resisted translation. Referred to by the Cherokees, who inhabited the area at the time of the white settlement, as *degayelunha*, or "printed place," the rocks have been enclosed in metal cages to protect them from vandals and graffiti scrawlers. Though the stones are weathered, their mysterious inscriptions are still discernible to travelers who take time to stop here near the foot of Brasstown Bald.

Directions: On Track Rock Road off US 76, northwest of Blairsville and 4 miles southwest of Young Harris.

Map References: USGS 1:24,000 series: Jack's Gap–Hiawassee–Blairsville.

Southern Nantahala Wilderness

Most of the trails in the Hightower area of the Southern Nantahala Wilderness are old logging roads that are not maintained. There are plans for signs and management of trails in the future.

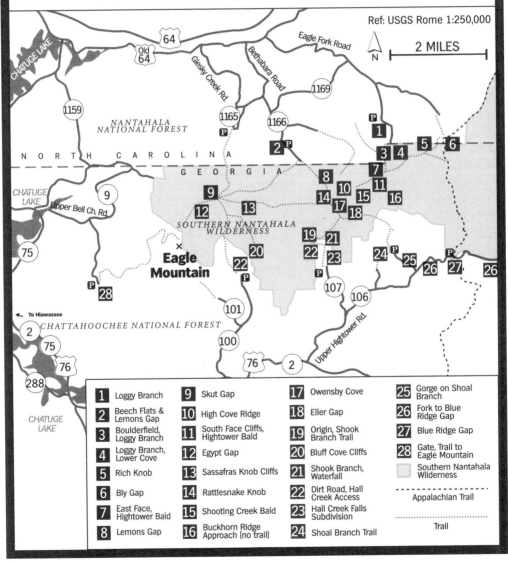

Ref: USGS Rome 1:250,000

2 MILES

1 Loggy Branch	**9** Skut Gap	**17** Owensby Cove	**25** Gorge on Shoal Branch	
2 Beech Flats & Lemons Gap	**10** High Cove Ridge	**18** Eller Gap	**26** Fork to Blue Ridge Gap	
3 Boulderfield, Loggy Branch	**11** South Face Cliffs, Hightower Bald	**19** Origin, Shook Branch Trail	**27** Blue Ridge Gap	
4 Loggy Branch, Lower Cove	**12** Egypt Gap	**20** Bluff Cove Cliffs	**28** Gate, Trail to Eagle Mountain	
5 Rich Knob	**13** Sassafras Knob Cliffs	**21** Shook Branch, Waterfall	Southern Nantahala Wilderness	
6 Bly Gap	**14** Rattlesnake Knob	**22** Dirt Road, Hall Creek Access		
7 East Face, Hightower Bald	**15** Shooting Creek Bald	**23** Hall Creek Falls Subdivision	Appalachian Trail	
8 Lemons Gap	**16** Buckhorn Ridge Approach (no trail)	**24** Shoal Branch Trail	Trail	

The Hightower Area of the Southern Nantahala Wilderness

As one drives US 76 between Hiawassee and Dick's Creek Gap, the east-west-trending high ridge to the north is the western portion of the Southern Nantahala Wilderness. The cliffs are visible near the top of Hightower Bald (4,568 feet), the highest peak in the area and the fourth highest mountain in Georgia. This long, high ridge links a series of peaks with stunning views both north and south. It is an area for the backcountry hiker and explorer. Getting up on the high ridge involves considerable climbing, beginning at the head of deep coves and flats.

On the northern approach there is a wealth of logging roads by which one can hike up to the edge of boulderfields in both Loggy Branch and Giesky Creek watersheds. The western approach up Sim's Branch passes east of the prominent Bell Knob, with its landmark quartz mine on top, visible for miles around. Of the eight access approaches, six are through private lands whose owners have been friendly to hikers and campers (though not necessarily to hunters), providing they are courteous and considerate. If possible ask permission. Both the Scataway (*see* page 140) and Shoal Branch (*see* Southern and Eastern Accesses, page 141) accesses, unlike Hall Creek access (*see* page 140), have a buffer area of Forest Service land before the wilderness boundary. Accordingly, both parking and camping areas are provided. These latter two accesses are recommended for the average visitor.

This area is not well known, and the old settler trails across Skut and Lemons gaps are hard to find, but sometimes that is half the fun. There is little evidence of logging roads above 4,000 feet in the zone of northern hardwoods.

Plans for the management of the Southern Nantahala Wilderness are in process and will include signs and trails. The trails throughout the area are largely old logging roads, currently unmaintained and unmarked, and are for the intrepid explorer only.

LOGGY BRANCH AND HIGHTOWER BALD

The easiest approach to Hightower Bald is the Loggy Branch access [Fig. 31(1)]. How far to drive on these rough roads will be a matter of personal judgment. A jeep road turns and goes south up the hillside west of Loggy Branch, swings right, and passes by an enormous red maple at the foot of a large boulderfield [Fig. 31(3)]. The road then extends to Loggy Branch [Fig. 31(4)] a short distance below the wilderness boundary. If so inclined, one can locate the famous Montgomery Corner and/or 30-mile post where the state line takes a large jog north and south.

Loggy Branch Cove itself is a botanical paradise. According to Georgia's eminent botanist Wilbur Duncan, it compares favorably with anything in the Smokies. Up and down Loggy Branch, one can find the black, twisted trunks of the rare yellowwood tree. This is Georgia's largest colony, and one of the largest aggregations of yellowwood in the Blue Ridge. Most of this area is privately owned.

Higher up in the cove, one encounters a northern hardwood forest of beech, sugar maple, and yellow birch. In and below mountain gaps, visitors find the southern limit of the "Beech Gap" phase of this community, where high altitude varieties of beech predominate. On the cold, high side of Hightower [Fig. 31(7)] just under the top, there is a refuge for two plants normally associated with the spruce-fir forest: a beautiful viburnum and a type of oxalis clover. This is the only place in Georgia where this particular viburnum (*Viburnum alnifolium*) is known to grow.

AMERICAN BEECH
(*Fagus grandifolia*)
This beech is identified by thin gray bark and papery leaves that may stay on all winter to twist and rustle in the wind.

The 150-foot cliffs on the south side [Fig. 31(11)] are dominated by moss and lichen, primitive rock spike moss, the rare Blue Ridge St. John's wort, and the federally listed and very rare Biltmore sedge. The boreal red-back vole, another Pleistocene relict, has been found here. On top is a dwarfed oak forest of white and red oak with a remarkably extensive growth of beaked hazelnut, which, with mountain raspberry, dominates the understory. Large hawthorn trees grow here and there. One can climb a dwarfed oak, as if walking up a ladder, and obtain fine views.

The ridgeline is supported by massive gneiss and amphibolite. A walk west down the ridge to Tom's Gap is rewarding; after a climb up a little cliff just west of Tom's Gap, one gets excellent vistas of the Hightower cliffs and the watershed below. Dwarf willow grows here in abundance on the cliff edge, and purple rhododendron is common.

The most difficult section of the ridgeline is between Shooting Creek Bald (4,317 feet) [Fig. 31(15)] and along the High Cove Ridge [Fig. 31(10)], an almost continuous series of rock outcrops, cliffs, and rhododendron. One can walk around under the cliffs; bear hunters prefer to burrow along the top. There is extensive rhododendron on the north face of Rattlesnake Knob. Otherwise the ridge is a fairly easy walk all the way to Eagle Mountain. Oak ridge forests to the east of Skut Gap [Fig. 31(9)] are dominated by northern red oak; those west are dominated by white oak. Just south of Egypt Gap [Fig. 31(12)], a series of small cliffs is covered with marginal wood fern, alum root, rock cap fern, and, nearby, monkshood.

The Sassafras Knob Cliffs [Fig. 31(13)] have bush honeysuckle. The coves, especially lower Owensby Cove and Loggy Branch [Fig. 31(4,17)], often have beautiful open stands of poplar or oak-hickory slope forest, waterfalls, and wildflower assemblages.

Much is to be learned from this relatively unexplored area. Early settlers lived remarkably high and far back in the mountain coves. On the Loggy Branch Road, a family named Davenport lived on rocky soil at about 3,000 feet. It is said that sled loads of mayapple, used for medicinal purposes, came out of Loggy Branch Cove and were sold for $.02 a pound. There are reported Indian petroglyphs on a rock on the trail to Lemons Gap [Fig. 31(8)].

ACCESS ROUTES

LOGGY BRANCH COVE ACCESS. Northern access to Loggy Branch Cove, Hightower Bald, and the eastern part of the wilderness. On old US 64 east, pass Bethabara Road .4 mile; turn right at a sign on paved Eagle Fork Creek Road; go 2.1 miles to the third bridge; turn left on a dirt road just before the bridge. At .4 mile a gated road turns left. (This is a very rough jeep road. If chosen, take all other right turns and eventually reach Bly Gap on the Appalachian Trail.)

Past this gated road go about 2 miles from the paved road and follow the most developed road (through some private lands) to reach a U.S. Forest Service sign. Do not cross the branch but turn up the ridge following an old logging road which goes by a huge red maple and on to Loggy Branch [Fig. 31(1)], well up in the cove. Whether four-wheel drive is needed will depend on logging activities and rain. Certainly past the government boundary one will need four-wheel drive, but at that point the short distance to the lower cove [Fig. 31(4)] can be hiked.

NORTHERN ACCESS. To Beech Flats, Lemons Gap, and the central part of the wilderness. From GA 75 north out of Hiawassee, dead-end at old US 64; turn east and go 4 miles; turn south at the sign for Bethabara Road (1166); go 2 miles; take the last road (dirt) to the right (west) just before the bridge; go about .4 mile through an apple orchard; turn left; ford a creek and park. Continue south about .6 mile to where the road is blocked at a branch.

Walk up the road on the left side of the branch. The wilderness boundary is very close. Climb southeast through Beech Flats until coming to the ridgeline where, with luck, one will be in the vicinity of Rattlesnake Knob [Fig. 31(14)]. To dodge difficult cliffs [Fig. 31(11)] of High Cove Ridge, avoid striking the ridge east of Lemons Gap. An old trail to, or close to, Skut Gap [Fig. 31(9)] leaves the entrance road (turns south) just past the last house after the creek ford.

OLD SKUT GAP TRAIL. Northern access to Old Skut Gap Trail and the western part of the wilderness. From the junction of GA 75 north, turn east on old US 64; go 3.2 miles to the Giesky Creek sign (NC 1165); turn right (south); at 2.4 miles, in a U-shaped curve, cross the bridge over Nattie Branch. The landowner here, John Robbins, lives just north of the bridge and says to park on the west side of the branch where the old log road follows the route of the old trail to Skut Gap by way of Burnt Cabin Cove.

EAGLE MOUNTAIN ACCESS. The western end of the wilderness. Off GA 75 north of Hiawassee, turn east on Upper Bell Creek Road (Road 9) just before a bridge crosses an arm of Lake Chatuge; go 1.2 miles; turn right (south) on SR 78. At about 1.6 miles, stop at a gate [Fig. 28(18)]; hike up the log road past Ben Gap (1.3 miles); reach another gate at 2 miles; walk up switchbacks to Eagle Mountain summit (about 3.2 miles total from the parking area).

SCATAWAY CREEK ACCESS. Southern entrance to the wilderness. Go north on GA 17/75 from Helen; turn right on US 76 and go 3.2 miles; turn north on a paved road (GA 100). At 1.2 miles, a paved road (GA 101) to the left goes up Jack Hooper Branch. It is possible to hike up to Eagle Mountain [Fig. 31] by this route, but there is no trail over the last mile of very steep terrain. The right fork (GA 100) continues toward the southern access trail to Skut Gap. After leaving the pavement, park and hike up an old log road trail [Fig. 31(22)] which does not follow the creek, but in .5 mile turns east up the slope and enters a clear-cut. Instead of turning east, head steeply uphill (north) through a small stand of pine trees, coming to an old road. This road climbs steeply, rounds the end of a ridge and joins a more open road. Approximately 1.2 miles from the U.S. Forest Service boundary, a trail turns right and goes southeast to the top of Bluff Cove Cliffs [Fig. 31(20)]. The old trail to Skut Gap [Fig. 31(9)] continues but is extremely hard to follow.

HALL CREEK ACCESS. This is the southern entrance to the central ridge of the wilderness and to the Maney Branch (Maney Cove) and Shook Branch (Owensby Cove) watersheds. It is the shortest route to the easternmost crossing of the main ridge by the old settlers' trail through Lemons Gap. A slightly longer hike is via the Shoal Branch access.

On the west side of the US 76 bridge over Hightower Creek, turn north on Upper Hightower Road. Take the first paved left, at 1.4 miles. The pavement ends in another .8 mile. After passing a flood-control reservoir on the right, be prepared to park along the gravel road anywhere south of the first mailbox on the left before reaching signs (another .2 mile) indicating private land, the Hall Creek Falls Wilderness community [Fig. 31(23)]. The public road ends a little south of these signs; walk up about 3,700 feet of graveled private road. Do not leave the road; it is a public right-of-way. After fording the creek twice, take the first old dirt road to the left [Fig. 31(22)], which leads to the red-blazed wilderness boundary. Follow the old road up the east side of the creek, Maney Branch. In less than 1,000 feet, watch for an old road or trail to turn eastward, sharply up a ridge [Fig. 31(24)]. This is the Shook Branch Trail. After about 1.25 miles on Shook Branch [Fig. 31(21)], Hall Branch Falls lies due east about 600 feet and barely within the wilderness boundary. About 1 mile up the Shook Branch Trail, Eller Gap Trail [Fig. 31(18)] intersects from the east. The "trail" up Owensby Cove [Fig. 31(17)] to Lemons Gap may be indistinct. Most trails in this area are currently unmaintained and unmarked. It is about 3,500 feet from the junction with the Eller Gap Trail to Lemons Gap, just east of Rattlesnake Knob [Fig. 31(14)].

SOUTHERN AND EASTERN ACCESSES. To go up Shoal Creek, continue east on the main Upper Hightower Road (GA 105, blacktop). At about 2 miles, past the Hall Branch Road, turn left on the narrow, paved Jack Branch Road. After crossing Hightower Creek, continue past the first house on the left, then turn abruptly left onto a dirt road that goes around and behind the house. This road is a public access to Shoal Branch. It passes through its narrow, scenic gorge [Fig. 31(25)], then by a flood control reservoir and through a meadow. At the meadow's end, enter the Forest Service boundary where parking and camping is permitted.

The Shoal Branch trail [Fig. 31(24)] continues northward 2,000 feet before swinging west to cross the creek and continue through Eller Gap [Fig. 31(18)] to intersect the Shook Branch Trail in Owensby Cove. For those who wish to climb to Hightower Bald, it is easy but steep bushwhacking due north from where the Shoal Branch trail turns west and crosses the creek. Upon encountering the base of the cliffs [Fig. 31(11)], turn left and work around to Tom Gap; then follow the ridgeline to the top or turn right and proceed until reaching Buckhorn Ridge [Fig. 31(16)]. Follow it to the summit. If the Buckhorn Ridge route is chosen, it may be necessary to crawl through heath thickets the last 100 yards or so before breaking out into the dwarfed "orchard" oak community on top.

A route with far less climbing but more walking is the eastern approach to Hightower Bald [Fig. 31(11)] via the Appalachian Trail. Past the Shoal Branch Road turnoff, the main road becomes gravel. About 2,000 feet beyond the Shoal Branch Road, bear right at a fork; go 1.2 miles to reach Blue Ridge Gap [Fig. 31(27)] (four-wheel drive recommended). At either Rich Knob [Fig. 31(5)] or Bly Gap [Fig. 31(6)], pick up the main ridge west to Hightower Bald.

Map References: USGS 1:24,000 series: Shooting Creek–Macedonia–Rainbow Springs–Hightower Bald.

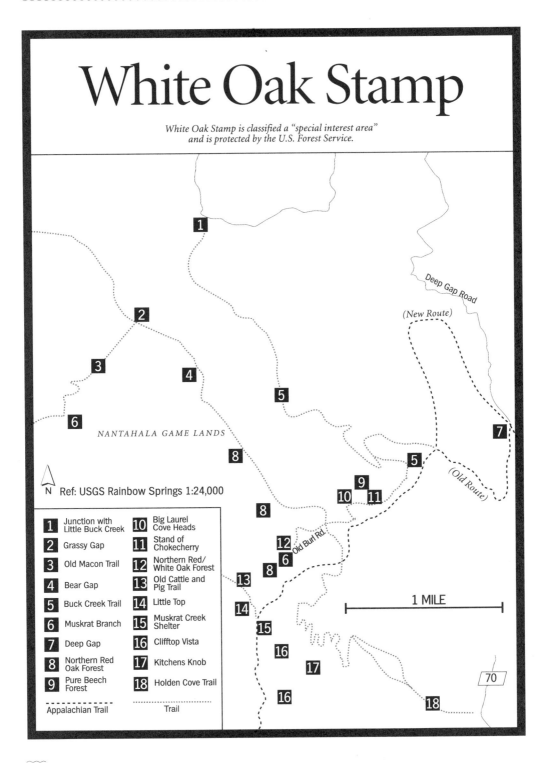

White Oak Stamp

*White Oak Stamp is classified a "special interest area"
and is protected by the U.S. Forest Service.*

Deep Gap Road

(New Route)

(Old Route)

NANTAHALA GAME LANDS

N   Ref: USGS Rainbow Springs 1:24,000

Old Buri Rd

1 MILE

70

1 Junction with Little Buck Creek	**10** Big Laurel Cove Heads
2 Grassy Gap	**11** Stand of Chokecherry
3 Old Macon Trail	**12** Northern Red/ White Oak Forest
4 Bear Gap	**13** Old Cattle and Pig Trail
5 Buck Creek Trail	**14** Little Top
6 Muskrat Branch	**15** Muskrat Creek Shelter
7 Deep Gap	**16** Clifftop Vista
8 Northern Red Oak Forest	**17** Kitchens Knob
9 Pure Beech Forest	**18** Holden Cove Trail

- - - - Appalachian Trail   .... Trail

White Oak Stamp

White Oak Stamp, together with Buck Creek and Chunky Gal Mountain (*see* page 145), is so unusual that parts of this area are classified and protected as "special interest areas" by the U.S. Forest Service. White Oak Stamp and adjacent areas of Chunky Gal and the Buck Creek watershed offer not only one of the very best examples of old growth, high-altitude forest areas to explore, but also vistas as exciting as any area within the scope of this book.

It is rare to find a large "flat" area such as White Oak Stamp at high elevations along the Blue Ridge. Most of the forest above 4,200 feet at White Oak Stanp is virgin old growth. A good part of it, especially on slopes and ridges, is high-altitude northern red oak forest [Fig. 32(8)], with many trees exceeding 2 feet in diameter. Shrubs here include flame azalea, several viburnums, and three species of blueberry. Mixed northern red oak–white oak forest occurs in certain areas [Fig. 32(12)]. Perhaps the most exciting environment is the area of northern hardwoods, especially in the Big Laurel cove heads [Fig. 32(10)], through which the Buck Creek Trail [Fig. 32(5)] passes. Here are giant, old, yellow birch between 2 and 3 feet in diameter. Subdomi-

WHITE OAK
(Quercus alba)
The leaves on a single oak tree may have different shapes, making identification a challenge. White oak leaves have deep or shallow clefts between lobes.

FLAME AZALEA
(Rhododendron
calendulaceum)

nants are buckeye and beech, the latter predominating on slight ridges with a rare pure beech forest lower down [Fig. 32(9)]. Just above it is a large stand of rare chokecherry [Fig. 32(11)].

The trail bisects one of the strikingly beautiful gneissic boulderfields. The northern herb-wildflower display is outstanding, with perhaps the largest colonies of the edible ramp and the poisonous large hellebore that visitors will ever see. This forest continues on the east side of Chunky Gal as far as Bear Gap [Fig. 32(4)].

In a low area not far from the Appalachian Trail—the old trail, now rerouted—lies a remarkable high-altitude heath bog on the head of Muskrat Branch [Fig. 32(6)]. While the dominant shrubs are rosebay rhododendron and mountain laurel, purple rhododendron does occur. This thicket is difficult to penetrate, but bears love it and native brook trout are common in the tiny, crystal-clear streams. Yellow birch, hemlock, and red maple make up a scattered overstory. The rare bog turtle may be present. Two small areas are open sedge marshes with cinnamon fern. Approaching the bog from the north is an old "burl road" formerly used to haul out rhododendron root burls. These burls were used in the manufacture of pipe bowls when supplies from the Mediterranean were cut off during World War II.

There is a spring at the Muskrat Creek shelter [Fig. 32(15)] on the Appalachian Trail. Not far south of it are two cliff-top vistas (no trails) that overlook the Tallulah watershed.

Hikers who walk west on the ridge opposite the shelter and are able to find the old cattle and pig trail [Fig. 32(13)] can follow it down, around, and north of a little top [Fig. 32(14)], then back out southeastward to the top of Raven Rock Cliff, which has fine vistas.

Directions: Four trails converge at White Oak Stamp. The easiest access may be from Deep Gap [Fig. 32(7)] via the old AT loop south of Yellow Mountain. Deep Gap Road is reached off old US 64, which is paved and turns off new US 64. Those who relish the exertion of a 2-hour climb can come up the scenic Holden Cove Trail [Fig. 32(18)] to where it crosses the Appalachian Trail and continues on down Buck Creek. The Buck Creek Trail [Fig. 32(5)] is reached off the Deep Gap Road near the junction of Buck Creek and Little Buck Creek [Fig. 32(1)].

Map References: USGS 1:24,000 series: Rainbow Springs.

Buck Creek and Chunky Gal Mountain

Like White Oak Stamp (*see* page 143), unique portions of Buck Creek, and Chunky Gal Mountain are classified and protected as "special interest areas" by the U.S. Forest Service. Buck Creek is a renowned site of ultrabasic rocks of great interest to those studying minerals, gems, or botany. Chunky Gal Mountain gets its name from the Cherokee legend of a plump Indian maiden who fell in love with a brave and followed him over this mountain after her parents had banished him from camp. With its long ridgetop scenic trail and noteworthy Riley Knob botanical area, Chunky Gal is considered by conservationists to be worthy of wilderness-area designation.

CHUNKY GAL MOUNTAIN

Chunky Gal is a long, 8-mile-high, remote, ridgelike mountain connecting the Blue Ridge and the Appalachian Trail with the Tusquittee and Fires Creek ranges. For hikers going north, there is a scenic overlook to the west from a cliff said to contain garnets and olivine. This is about 1.5 miles before Bear Gap. The trail's end south of Bear Gap [Fig. 33(19)] has most interesting vegetation in a near-original state. At Grassy Gap [Fig. 33(17)], a cove forest reaches the trail with lush herb flora including monkshood and purple-fringed orchid. A rare plant—wolfsmilk—occurs as far south as Grassy Gap, the southern limit of its growing range in the United States. Grassy Gap apparently was the crossing of the old Macon Trail [Fig. 33(18)] used by the Indians and was also a horse-back mail route before the construction of US 64. It was a shortcut from Shooting Creek to the headwaters of the Nantahala River. Accessible from Muskrat Branch [Fig. 33(20)], it may, nevertheless, be difficult to find.

THE RILEY KNOB/CHUNKY GAL SPECIAL INTEREST AREA

[Fig. 33(12)] This area covers 215 acres between 3,600 and 4,400 feet and is an outstanding example of an extensive old growth, high-altitude white oak forest. There is some cove forest and red oak ridge forest. Much of the rock in the Riley Knob area is amphibolite, which supports a rich herb flora. The knob and the Chunky Gal Ridge Trail are reached from US 64 at Riley Cove [Fig. 33(10)] or at a blue-blazed trail [Fig. 33(13)] from Glade Gap access point [Fig. 33(14)].

From this latter point, according to Allen de Hart's trail guide *North Carolina Hiking Trails*, one can cross US 64, turn left on old US 64, then turn right at .2 mile from Glade Gap on an old jeep road. Eventually one reaches Boteler Peak (also called Shooting Creek Bald, 5,010 feet) [Fig. 33(11)] at about 2.8 miles from Glade Gap. Here a blue-blazed trail descends northward to Perry Gap and continues on to link with the Rim Trail on the east rim of the Fires Creek Basin, a noted bear refuge.

Buck Creek & Chunky Gal Mountain

Chunky Gal Mountain gets its name from the Cherokee legend of a plump Indian maiden who fell in love with a brave and followed him over the mountain after the brave was banished from camp.

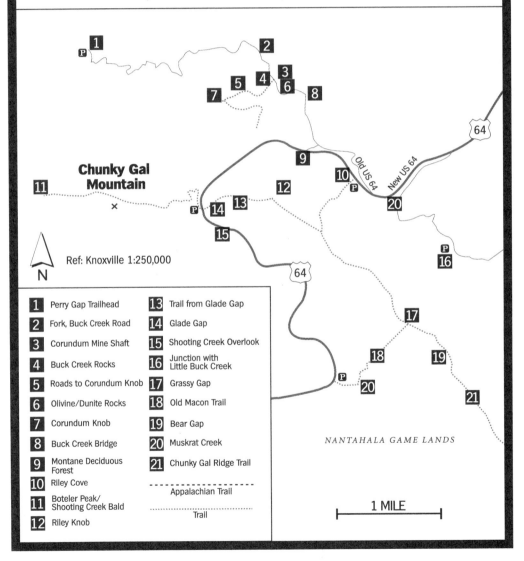

Chunky Gal Mountain

Ref: Knoxville 1:250,000

N

64

Old US 64

New US 64

NANTAHALA GAME LANDS

1	Perry Gap Trailhead	13	Trail from Glade Gap
2	Fork, Buck Creek Road	14	Glade Gap
3	Corundum Mine Shaft	15	Shooting Creek Overlook
4	Buck Creek Rocks	16	Junction with Little Buck Creek
5	Roads to Corundum Knob	17	Grassy Gap
6	Olivine/Dunite Rocks	18	Old Macon Trail
7	Corundum Knob	19	Bear Gap
8	Buck Creek Bridge	20	Muskrat Creek
9	Montane Deciduous Forest	21	Chunky Gal Ridge Trail
10	Riley Cove		
11	Boteler Peak/ Shooting Creek Bald		- - - - - - - Appalachian Trail
12	Riley Knob		·············· Trail

1 MILE

THE BUCK CREEK PINE BARRENS

These pine barrens in North Carolina are geologically and botanically unique. Basic magnesium-rich rocks such as olivine and dunite [Fig. 33(6)] predominate. At the first little creek [Fig. 33(4)], about .5 mile past the bridge [Fig. 33(8)], one is treated to an assortment of unusual rocks. The creek bed is littered with pieces of olivine, gabbro, chlorite schist, talc (with which one can write), and other mineral specimens—a smorgasbord of basic and ultrabasic rock. The Buck Creek Barrens contain the largest single outcrop of dunite in the Georgia and North Carolina olivine belt.

BLACK BEAR
(Ursus americanus)
This bear grows to 300 pounds.

Back .1 mile is a pullout by Buck Creek, a good place to picnic. Across the creek is a "tailings pile" or mine dump. The old corundum mine shaft [Fig. 33(3)] is above it in an area of dunite rock [Fig. 33(6)]. In the late 1800s, mining for the abrasive corundum, which has a hardness next to the diamond's, was carried out throughout the corundum belt. Old roads [Fig. 33(5)] go back to Corundum Knob [Fig. 33(7)], where corundum was also mined. Here it is possible to find tiny rubies in a matrix of green stone, a type of amphibole called smaragdite.

Because of the unique plant life here, 103 of the 346 acres in the Buck Creek Barrens have been proposed as a botanical preserve. Before leaving US 64, note the presence of a normal montane deciduous forest [Fig. 33(9)]. After crossing the bridge [Fig. 33(8)], one almost immediately enters an area dominated by pitch pine with scrubby, scattered white oak. The soil moisture and temperature are such that some prairie grasses have become established. The Forest Service recognizes three unique plant communities here: 1) pitch pine-witherod, 2) the only location of pitch pine bluestem grass and prairie dropseed south of Pennsylvania, and 3) one of two sites for pitch pine–little bluestem grass in North Carolina. Two unusual wildflowers are big-leaf grass of parnassus and fringed gentian.

The weird rocks, the unusual vegetation, and the chance of panning a piece of ruby corundum out of Buck Creek make this area a prized one. After passing through the mineralized zone, one quickly reaches a fork [Fig. 33(2)]. The left-hand turn goes 2.8 miles west to the Perry Gap trailhead [Fig. 33(1)]; the right-hand turn leads to what was the old Buck Creek Lodge, which is still private property. After a return to new US 64, it is 2.3 miles to the Shooting Creek Overlook [Fig. 33(15)] (with picnic tables). The next gated road on the left goes only a short distance up Muskrat Creek [Fig. 33(20)] where, with luck, one can locate the old Macon Trail [Fig. 33(18)].

Map References: USGS 1:24,000 series: Rainbow Springs–Shooting Creek.

The Nantahala Basin

Water flowing in the Nantahala Basin eventually winds
to the Mississippi River and flows into the Gulf of Mexico.

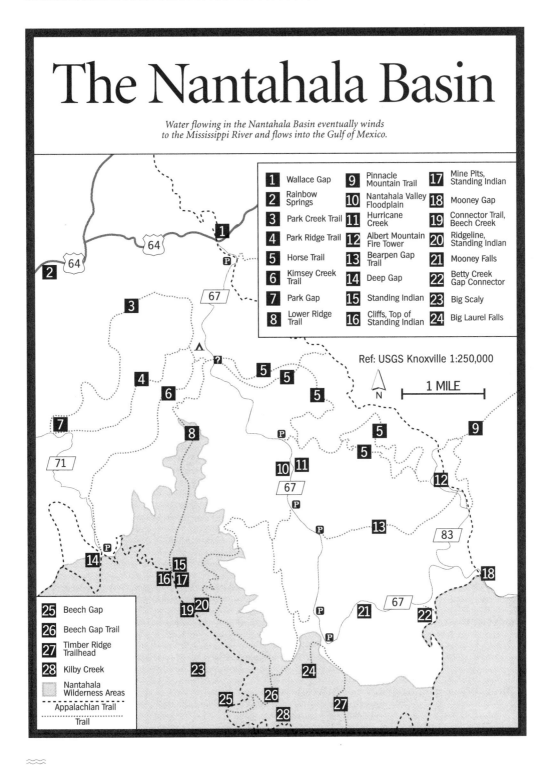

1 Wallace Gap	**9** Pinnacle Mountain Trail	**17** Mine Pits, Standing Indian
2 Rainbow Springs	**10** Nantahala Valley Floodplain	**18** Mooney Gap
3 Park Creek Trail	**11** Hurricane Creek	**19** Connector Trail, Beech Creek
4 Park Ridge Trail	**12** Albert Mountain Fire Tower	**20** Ridgeline, Standing Indian
5 Horse Trail	**13** Bearpen Gap Trail	**21** Mooney Falls
6 Kimsey Creek Trail	**14** Deep Gap	**22** Betty Creek Gap Connector
7 Park Gap	**15** Standing Indian	**23** Big Scaly
8 Lower Ridge Trail	**16** Cliffs, Top of Standing Indian	**24** Big Laurel Falls

Ref: USGS Knoxville 1:250,000

N

1 MILE

25	Beech Gap
26	Beech Gap Trail
27	Timber Ridge Trailhead
28	Kilby Creek
	Nantahala Wilderness Areas
	Appalachian Trail
	Trail

The Nantahala Basin

Rivers in the Nantahala and the Tallulah basins, separated from each other by the Eastern Continental Divide, run in opposite directions. Water flowing north in the Nantahala follows a much longer path via the Mississippi River to the Gulf of Mexico, while water in the Tallulah Basin reaches the Atlantic more directly via the Savannah River. Because the route to the Atlantic is a shorter, steeper one, downcutting is heavier on the south side of the Blue Ridge. This may be one reason why the Tallulah River is nearly 1,000 feet lower than the bed of the Nantahala River.

The Nantahala watershed has an extensive system of trails of different lengths and varying degrees of difficulty. There are at least three horse trails and a special horse camp. There are fascinating plant communities, including bogs and some virgin forest.

Because of its soils and elevation, the Nantahala watershed had original timber of a size and density that brought visitors from as far away as Asheville, even when virgin timber was widespread.

The area was logged until the 1920s. Ritter Lumber Company had its logging camp where the main campground for the area is today; and at Rainbow Springs [Fig. 34(2)], Ritter had a band-saw mill to saw the huge trees. Narrow-gauge railroads ran up and down the Nantahala River and went up its tributaries until stopped by waterfalls. The route of the dismantled railroad is marked on topographic sheets (USGS 1:24,000 map series: Rainbow Springs quadrangle).

The Nantahala is known for large brown trout, and its headwaters still support native brook trout populations. It has also been a black bear refuge for years. An additional attraction is Nantahala Lake, into which the Nantahala River flows. At 3,000 feet, it is one of the highest large lakes in the mountains.

Directions: Go north on US 441 to Franklin, NC; turn left onto US 64; go 12 miles and turn left onto old US 64; go 1.8 miles to Wallace Gap [Fig. 34(1)] and turn right onto FS 67, which is the road into the basin.

A DRIVING TOUR OF THE BASIN

For those interested in combining driving and short walks, there is a marvelous tour of the area to see an immense poplar tree, two waterfalls, and vistas from Pickens' Nose.

From the turnoff at Wallace Gap (*see* directions *above*), go .4 mile to a parking area on the left. It is directly adjacent to the Appalachian Trail (AT), so that one can park here for walks in either direction on the AT. This is also the trailhead for the short (1.4-mile round-trip) walk on a graded trail to the John Wasilik Memorial Tree, which is the second largest yellow poplar in the United States. It is 8 feet in diameter, 25 feet in circumference, and was 135 feet tall until topped by a storm. The tree is in one of a series of north-facing coves, called the Runaway Knob Special Interest Area, where over 100 plant species have been identified. Lying between 3,200 and 4,400 feet, the 140-acre area is the location of an exceptionally beautiful spring wildflower display. The forest below the Wasilik Poplar contains North Carolina's largest reproducing population of the rare yellowwood tree, which occurs in only a few localities in Georgia and North Carolina.

Continue about 1.1 miles on FS 67 to a fork; take the left fork, FS 67B, about .2 mile to the Backcountry Information Center. In the valley upstream are flat areas of floodplain and alluvial fill with some open areas [Fig. 34(10)]. Some of these are wildlife openings and others are rare wetland bogs—some as large as 20 acres, lying between 3,400 and 3,500 feet in elevation. This is the second largest bog complex in western North Carolina and the subject of paleobotanical studies of the peat underlying them. The bogs should not be entered.

Continue 4.7 miles on FS 67 to the parking area for Big Laurel Falls [Fig. 34(24)] (1.2 miles round-trip), an easy hike for the whole family. This is also the trailhead for the Timber Ridge Trail [Fig. 34(27)], which connects with the AT.

Continue on FS 67 for .8 mile to the pull-off area for Mooney Falls. The trail is a .2-mile round-trip to the falls [Fig. 34(21)].

Continue on FS 67 until its intersection with FS 83. Turn right and continue past Mooney Gap [Fig. 34(18)], a station for acid rain studies by Coweeta Hydrologic Laboratory, and a crossing of the Appalachian Trail. At .7 mile past Mooney Gap, park on the north side of the road and walk south 1 mile to Pickens' Nose (5,000 feet). Vistas are to the east, west, and south into the Betty Creek Basin. An optional walk is to Albert Mountain. Backtrack on FS 83 as far as it will go north, then hike up to the Albert Mountain fire tower [Fig. 34(12)], which provides an exceptional 360-degree view. (Pickens' Nose and Albert Mountain can also be reached by Buck Creek Road through the Coweeta Hydrologic Laboratory off US 441 north of the Georgia/North Carolina state line). At Big Spring Gap, the Pinnacle Mountain Trail [Fig. 34(9)] descends to the northeast.

KILBY CREEK

The best virgin timber in the area lies above the falls of Kilby Creek [Fig. 34(28)], a challenge for wild-country devotees. This is largely cove hardwood with big hemlock-rhododendron forests along the streams. Above the falls there are brook trout, the only native species. This is wild and rough country, a true wilderness. Visitors to it should take no chances.

STANDING INDIAN

[Fig. 34(15)] At 5,499 feet, this is the highest peak in the Nantahala Mountains. Its Indian name translates literally "the place where man stood." Cherokee mythology relates the story of a winged monster that stole a child and carried him to the cliffs on top of the mountain [Fig. 34(16)]. The Indians prayed to the Great Spirit, who answered their prayers by sending a lightning bolt that destroyed the monster and the trees on the summit, but the lightning also killed a lone Indian sentry and turned him to stone.

The easiest way to reach the summit is via US 64 and FS 71, a long gravel road to Deep Gap [Fig. 34(14)]. Along this road is dense roadside growth of an extremely primitive plant, a species of horsetail, or scouring brush, whose silica content was useful to the early settlers for scrubbing pots. From Deep Gap it is a 2.5-mile walk to the summit, climbing 1,200 feet and passing a good spring and shelter about one-third of the way up. The first large northern loop of this trail goes over

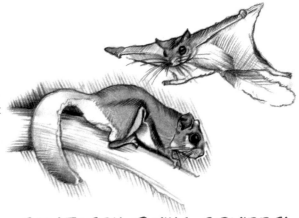

SOUTHERN FLYING SQUIRREL
(Glaucomys volans)
This squirrel doesn't fly but glides through the air.

and around a flat, wet, sheltered ridge with deep, stable soil, which may explain the white oak ridge forest here with flame azalea and fern understory. The trail also shows the effect of exposure. The white oak goes downslope only 30 feet to the more exposed east, but it goes down the western slope 120 feet. The summit of Standing Indian is heath or shrub bald, principally of purple rhododendron. Formerly, a fire tower stood here and a telephone wire ran up from the Tallulah Valley. The Fraser fir nearby were planted.

There are two springs northeast of the summit. South of the ridgeline in the ridge forest (not on the Appalachian Trail) are some pits [Fig. 34(17)], relics of the period when mica was mined in the area. These may be discovered by diligent explorers. The Appalachian Trail here tunnels through rhododendron and flame azalea and is quite dramatic in early summer. Traveling on down the 1.5-mile ridgeline, one sees Little Bald directly south and passes through several environments, principally red oak ridge forest and areas of shrub bald vegetation [Fig. 34(20)] dominated by mountain laurel, with some purple rhododendron. Some drier areas have grasses, while other almost-bare soil areas are covered with a rare tundra species—the three-leaved cinquefoil, a threatened species at the southern periphery of its range. The effects on the soil of ice heavage—that is, the repeated freezing and thawing of the earth—and the results of wind shear on the shrubs are evident.

There has been much scientific debate on the origin of balds such as those which cap many of the Appalachians' highest peaks. Here on the southwest slope, one can see the bald area grading into dwarf northern red oak–evergreen heath, which within several hundred feet grades into northern red oak–deciduous heath (azaleas and blueberries). On the opposite side (the northeast slope), the bald areas grade into a beautiful northern red oak-fern community that in turn grades into a northern hardwood forest. To the west lies Big Scaly (5,200 feet) [Fig. 33(23)] in the immediate foreground. The Girl Scouts had a connector trail [Fig. 33(19)] leading down to Beech Creek through the rhododendron and virgin red oak ridge forest with flame azalea understory, but the entrance is difficult to find. There are two other accesses to Beech Creek—one an old log road, the other a steep trail (*see* Tallulah Basin, page 154)—both beginning at Beech Gap. The upper portion of the Big Indian Loop horse trail passes through a succession of cove hardwoods, northern hardwoods, and boulderfields. Loop-trail possibilities are numerous. If two vehicles are available, a shuttle can be set up. For example, one vehicle may be left at Deep Gap [Fig. 34(14)] and another at either Standing Indian Campground or at the Beech Gap Trail junction with FS 67. Then one could hike to the summit of Standing Indian and down the Lower Ridge Trail [Fig. 34(8)], or down the long spine of Standing Indian to Beech Gap [Fig. 34(25)] and down the Beech Gap Trail [Fig. 34(26)], with a side visit to the Kilby Creek virgin forest [Fig. 34(28)].

HIKING TRAILS IN THE NANTAHALA BASIN

There are seven trails from the valley up to the Appalachian Trail (AT). They can be combined in a number of ways to create interesting loop hikes. One warning: the weather here can change rapidly. In particular, the hiker should beware of afternoon thunderstorms on the high ridges and peaks in the summer months.

KIMSEY CREEK TRAIL TO STANDING INDIAN. 10 miles round-trip. One favorite hike is to walk to Standing Indian Mountain starting from the Backcountry Information Center on the Kimsey Creek Trail [Fig. 34(6)], a wonderfully varied path along creeks and through wildlife meadows with many wildflowers. The trail connects with the AT at Deep Gap [Fig. 34(14)]. Follow the AT to the top of Standing Indian, which is a strenuous climb. There is a junction at which one spur goes from the AT to the top for a vista. Return to the AT and continue a very short distance (10 yards or so) to the Lower Ridge Trail [Fig. 34(8)], which returns to the Backcountry Information Center in 4 miles.

LOOP TRAIL. 10.9 miles round-trip. Another loop might be to hike up the AT on the Long Branch Trail from the Backcountry Information Center (1.9 miles). Hike south (to the right) 3.1 miles on the AT to the Albert Mountain lookout tower (5,280 feet) [Fig. 34(12)] for views in all directions. Continue on the AT. .3 mile to Bearpen Gap Trail [Fig. 34(13)]; descend 2.4 miles on Bearpen Gap Trail to FS 67/2; turn right and return 3.2 miles to the Backcountry Information Center.

PARK CREEK AND PARK RIDGE TRAILS. 10-mile loop. This interesting hike away from the AT (which means it is less crowded) combines the Park Creek [Fig. 34(3)] and Park Ridge trails [Fig. 34(4)]. One begins at the Backcountry Information Center. This beginning is the same as for the Lower Ridge Trail and the Kimsey Creek Trail. About .5 mile from the bridge in the campground, the Park Ridge Trail goes left up the ridge and climbs to Park Gap [Fig. 34(7)] at FS 71/1. Cross the road and descend on Park Creek Trail along a lovely stream to the Nantahala River; turn right and walk about 1.5 miles to the junction with Park Ridge Trail and retrace the path to the Backcountry Information Center.

ACCESS TO DAY HIKES. Another access to day-hike trailheads is from FS 71/1. Take US 64 west from Franklin, past the turnoff at 12 miles onto old US 64; go about 2.5 miles and turn left onto FS 71; go about 2.5 miles to reach Park Gap [Fig. 34(7)]; park in this area and walk the Park Ridge and Park Creek loop trails. Driving another 3 miles past this parking area, one reaches the end of the road at Deep Gap. Here is access to the Kimsey Creek Trail, the AT east to Standing Indian Mountain (2.8 miles one-way), a primitive trail south to the Tallulah River, and the AT west to White Oak Stamp and Bly Gap.

THREE-DAY WALK. 24 miles. A good backpacking trip starts at the Backcountry Information Center, on the Long Branch Trail to the AT. Turn right (south) onto the AT and follow it over Albert Mountain [Fig. 34(12)], through Bear Pen Gap, over Big Butt, down to Mooney Gap [Fig. 34(18)], passing Carter Gap and Beech Gap [Fig. 34(25)], climbing Standing Indian Mountain, and descending to Deep Gap [Fig. 34(14)]. Turn right on Kimsey Creek Trail and return to the Backcountry Information Center. This is a pleasant three-day walk. There are shelters at Big Spring Gap, Carter Gap, and Standing Indian (near Deep Gap). This is a popular loop, so shelters may be filled. Walked in early June, the stretch up Standing Indian Mountain is a botanical garden. The Catawba rhododendron and mountain laurel arch over the trail to form a floral tunnel.

OTHER TRAIL POSSIBILITIES. Many other combinations are possible using the following trails in conjunction with the Appalachian Trail: Kimsey Creek Trail [Fig. 34(6)], Lower Ridge Trail [Fig. 34(8)], Long Branch Trail, Beech Gap Trail [Fig. 34(26)], and Betty Creek Gap connector [Fig. 34(22)].

HORSE TRAILS IN THE NANTAHALA BASIN. A series of special horse trails [Fig. 34(5)] covers the Long Branch and Hurricane Creek watersheds. There is a horse camp near the mouth of Hurricane Creek [Fig. 34(11)]. For further information, ask the ranger. There is also a long horse trail on the east slopes of Standing Indian.

For more information: The U.S. Forest Service has prepared a recreational opportunities guide (which they refer to as ROG) in which many of the hiking trails in the area are summarized along with directions to the trailheads. The public may view this guide at the Wayah Ranger District Forest Service office or order copies of the pages of the guide for the cost of copying and mailing. Topographical maps of the area are also available here. U.S. Forest Service, Wayah Ranger District, 90 Sloan Road, Franklin, NC 28734. Phone (704) 524-6441.

Map References: USGS 1:24,000 series: Prentiss–Rainbow Springs.

The Tallulah Basin

If one had to select a national park site in Georgia, this land of gorges, waterfalls, and scenic splendor would be it. Hunters of bear and hog have used the area for years. Only now are horseback riders and hikers discovering this watershed and its myriad trails, many of them connecting with the Appalachian Trail. There was no easy way for the early settlers to reach the remote valley called Tate City, a pastoral setting rimmed by a great northward flex of the Blue Ridge. Tate City was once a busy corundum mining community and later a logging town with stores and churches. Now only two churches and a handful of homes remain. Most of the original mountain people who lived by subsistence agriculture are gone. The bears and perhaps even the cougar have returned.

UPPER TALLULAH BASIN SCENIC DRIVE

[FS 70 to Fig. 35(17)] This drive up the Tallulah's upper gorge is spectacular. It begins at the bridge over the Coleman River. At this bridge is the trailhead for an exciting, short (less than a mile) trail up the gorge of the Coleman River through the Coleman River Scenic Area [Fig. 35(44)], described on a sign just north of the bridge. FS 70 dead-ends in the heart of the Southern Nantahala Wilderness. The major access point for the Tallulah River basin, FS 70 follows beside the Tallulah through the 3-mile-long Rock Mountain Gorge [Fig. 35(43, 41)], on the old railroad bed, which was blasted out of solid rock by the lumber company logging the valley in virgin timber days. This lovely road crosses the Tallulah four times. The picturesque gorge has been the site of television commercials and postcard vistas. One can picnic on the rocks or fish the pools stocked weekly with eating-size rainbow trout. In the gorge grow a number of the beautiful and rare flowering tree, the mountain camellia, or Stewartia, which blooms in June and July. The best place to see the tree is in a stand at a wide place in the road at the extreme southern end of the Tate Branch Campground [Fig. 35(39)]. At Line Branch, one can look back, high up at the Flat Branch Falls [Fig. 35(42)]. Just below the Tate Branch Campground, Charlie's Creek Road fords the river. When this road emerges on a flat

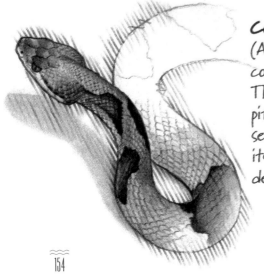

COPPERHEAD
(Agkistrodon contortrix)
The copperhead is a pit viper with a sensory pit between its eyes that detects prey.

near the AT, a north-turning fork [Fig. 35(36)] leads one to the main Charlie's Creek. Across the creek and up the road a few hundred yards, there is a trail up to an amethyst mine [Fig. 35(34)] that has produced some of the finest gem amethysts in the United States.

▨ THE BEECH CREEK–CHIMNEY ROCK LOOP

[Fig. 35(28)] This 12-mile loop hike has been a favorite of scout groups for many years. Skirting private property, the lower trailhead is at the "Glory Patch" [Fig. 35(28)] and crosses a low gap in Scaly Ridge before descending to the Beech Creek log road trail at an old homesite. Shortly thereafter, this main road crosses Bull Cove Branch. A striking cliff and falls with rich herb growth lies just out of sight upstream [Fig. 35(26)].

CATAWBA RHODODENDRON
(Rhododendron catawbiense)
This shrub forms dense thickets on mountain slopes.

The road then fords Beech Creek [Fig. 35(25)] to enter the stunningly beautiful Beech Creek Gorge [Fig. 35(23)] (a trail to the left [Fig. 35(24)] leads to Bear Gap). In about 2 miles, the log road trail reaches an old ore-crusher foundation of packed rock [Fig. 35(22)] and begins switchbacks up through the vast cliffs [Fig. 35(19)] on the face of Big Scaly Mountain. At about the second switchback left, a prominent trail goes off east and down to the creek, where it reaches beautiful High Falls [Fig. 35(21)], probably 200 feet high. Trail length is less than .25 mile.

The old Tate corundum mine is high in the cliffs [Fig. 35(20)], and the remains of the old oxen haul road (made of dead-packed, or mortarless, rock) up to the mine may be found to the left (west) at about the third switchback to the east. If one goes west through the cliffs, there are perhaps 50 acres of virgin slope forest. It is possible to hike through this to Chimney Rock. Bears raise and den in these cliffs [Fig. 35(19)] and are often seen in the gorge below if the visitor can remain quiet. After gaining the "top" of the cliffs on the main road, one enters an incredibly long "flat" [Fig. 35(13)]. After 1.5 miles arrive at the Beech Creek Spring [Fig. 35(8)], once the site of an Adirondack shelter. Approaching the spring on the left, pass through an unusual climax variety of northern hardwood forest of beech with yellow birch and hop hornbeam [Fig. 35(11)]. This is possibly a relict Ice-Age forest of the Pleistocene era, 15,000 to 20,000 years ago.

At this point, the hiker is about 4,600 feet above sea level. Upslope, at about 4,700

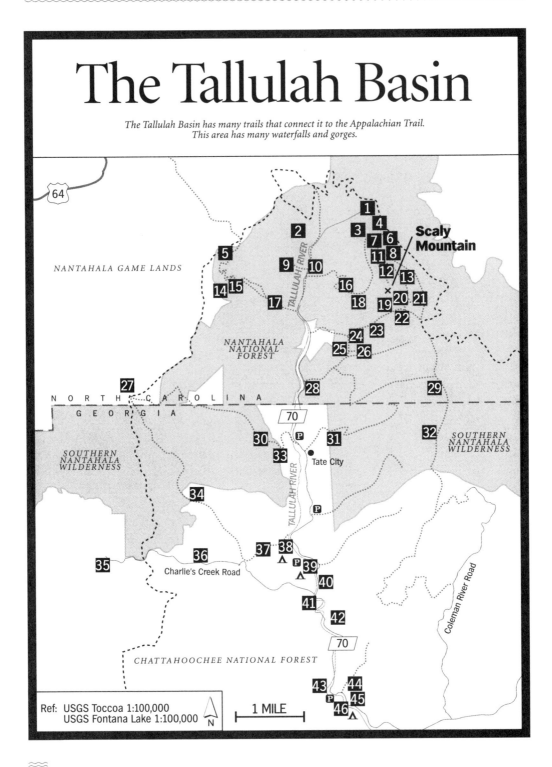

The Tallulah Basin

The Tallulah Basin has many trails that connect it to the Appalachian Trail.
This area has many waterfalls and gorges.

64

NANTAHALA GAME LANDS

Scaly Mountain

TALLULAH RIVER

NANTAHALA NATIONAL FOREST

NORTH CAROLINA

GEORGIA

70

SOUTHERN NANTAHALA WILDERNESS

SOUTHERN NANTAHALA WILDERNESS

Tate City

TALLULAH RIVER

Charlie's Creek Road

Coleman River Road

70

CHATTAHOOCHEE NATIONAL FOREST

Ref: USGS Toccoa 1:100,000
USGS Fontana Lake 1:100,000

1 MILE

N

1	Standing Indian Mountain	**29**	Little Bald
2	New Falls	**30**	Bly Gap Trail
3	Boulderfield	**31**	Denton Creek Falls
4	Shrub Bald Area	**32**	Dick's Knob
5	White Oak Stamp	**33**	Fall Branch Falls
6	Appalachian Trail Connector Trail	**34**	Amethyst Mine
7	"Indian Stomp Ground"	**35**	Western Approach Up Hightower
8	Beech Creek Spring	**36**	Road to Charlie's Creek Headwaters
9	Thomas Falls	**37**	Powerline Trail
10	Girl Scout Former Camping Area and Deep Gap Trail	**38**	Sandy Bottom Campground
11	Beech, Yellow Birch & Hop Hornbeam Forest	**39**	Tate Branch Campground
12	Trail to Big Scaly Mountain	**40**	New Falls
13	Beech Creek Flat	**41**	Rock Mountain Gorge (end)
14	Brush Mountain Cliff	**42**	Flat Branch Falls
15	Chimney Rocks	**43**	Rock Mountain Gorge (start)
16	Gap Overlook – Waterspout Water Shed	**44**	Coleman River Scenic Area
17	Holden Cove Trail	**45**	Mini-Gorge Containing the "Strainer Hole"
18	Chimney Rock	**46**	Tallulah Campground
19	Big Scaly Mountain Cliffs		Nantahala Wilderness Areas
20	Tate Corundum Mine		
21	High Falls		---- Appalachian Trail
22	Rock Crusher		····· Trail
23	Beech Creek Gorge		
24	Bear Creek Falls		
25	Beech Creek Ford		
26	Bull Cove Branch Falls		
27	Bly Gap		
28	Beech Creek – Chimney Rock Loop		

feet, enter a totally different environment—a high-altitude or northern oak ridge forest which can best be experienced on the trail [Fig. 35(12)] to the top of Big Scaly. Near Beech Creek Spring, the forest of rich black soil was once principally northern red oaks. Trees were wide apart, and the area resembled an orchard. Trunks were short and limby. One can find a few of these ancient specimens missed by loggers. There are numerous small chestnut sprouts. Fraser firs are also here, planted, as they are on top of Standing Indian [Fig. 35(1)]. The Beech Creek Flat [Fig. 35(13)] is a mecca for wildflower lovers. The highly prized ramps, or "mountain garlic," grow in profusion and are found near to Bear Creek Falls in the gorge below.

Just north of the spring is an area of naked red earth, clay-rich soil that deer eat. This is the "Indian Stomp Ground" [Fig. 35(7)]. It is certainly possible that the Indians danced here, but early settlers may have invented this name as an explanation for the naked ground. Several hundred yards beyond, a log road turns left. Here, a gentle nature trail [Fig. 35(12)] leads through virgin northern red oak ridge forest to the rocky summit of Big Scaly (5,200 feet), surrounded by dense purple rhododendron and yielding magnificent vistas to the northwest and southwest.

One can take the very steep and poorly marked Appalachian Trail connector trail [Fig. 35(6)] to the AT, where one will find areas of shrub bald [Fig. 35(4)]. To the left (north) is Standing Indian Mountain (5,499 feet) [Fig. 35(1)]. To the right (south) is Little Bald (5,015 feet) [Fig. 35(29)], which one can also reach from the loop trail [Fig. 35(28)]. Just south of Little Bald is Dick's Knob [Fig. 35(32)], the third highest peak in Georgia. Just before Case Knife Gap, a few feet past the turnoffs of the Big Scaly and AT connector trails, the north-facing cove to the right has a boulderfield [Fig. 35(3)] with some northern hardwoods. Go down past a spring and follow the small branch.

Down the loop road and through Case Knife Gap is the Chimney Rock watershed. This section is not nearly as steep as the Beech Creek section. Descending, watch carefully the ridgeline that comes down westerly from Big Scaly. Sticking slightly above it will be Chimney Rock [Fig. 35(18)]—a climbable (with great care) rock formation that affords a tremendous view of the watershed and is reached by a short (less than .25 mile), indistinct trail winding up through huge, scenic rocks. The trail turns south in a flat about 200 yards below the last fork of Chimney Rock Branch that is forded. The main log road trail continues down, passing through a gap [Fig. 35(16)] overlooking the Waterspout watershed and then meeting the Deep Gap Trail in an old pasture now full of saplings. The Girl Scouts's primitive camping area was located here [Fig. 35(10)]. A trail leads to Thomas Falls from the Deep Gap Trail [Fig. 35(9)], and New Falls [Fig. 35(40)] is at the bluff where Wateroak Creek leaves Collary Cove.

Facilities: Three campgrounds are located on the upper Tallulah River: Tallulah [Fig. 35(46)], 17 campsites; Sandy Bottom [Fig. 35(38)], 12 campsites; and Tate Branch [Fig. 35(39)], 19 campsites and 10 picnic shelters.

Fees: There is a fee at each of these areas.
For more information: U.S. Forest Service, phone (706) 782-3320.

WATERFALLS
Many of the streams entering the Tate City Valley have waterfalls.
DENTON CREEK FALLS. [Fig. 35(31)] A sheer drop easily reached about .25 mile upstream from the first ford (where the road is blocked). *See* Fig. 35.
FALL BRANCH FALLS. [Fig. 35(33)] Best visited from the top by way of the Bly Gap Trail [Fig. 35(30)], a long trail which at Bly Gap [Fig. 35(27)] intersects both the Appalachian Trail and a road down into the Shooting Creek Valley. Park at the trailhead.

GOLDEN-CROWNED KINGLET
(Regulus satrapa)
A restless, flitting movement and a high, thin "ssst" identify the kinglet.

THE HOLDEN COVE TRAIL
[Fig. 35(17)] This trail offers a number of smaller falls. Generally moderate, it is difficult in one place. Halfway up, a logging road intercepts the trail, making the rest of the climb easy and providing a view of Chimney Rocks [Fig. 35(15)], the formidable Brush Mountain Cliff [Fig. 35(14)], and rhododendron slicks. It proceeds to intersect both the AT and the Chunky Gal Trail at White Oak Stamp [Fig. 35(5)].

COLEMAN RIVER ROAD
This road provides access to the wilderness and to the Coleman River headwaters.
Directions: Take the Persimmon/Patterson Gap road to the right off US 76 7.5 miles west of Clayton. Continue .5 mile past the Tallulah River Road (FS 70) and turn left onto FS 54.

COLEMAN RIVER SCENIC AREA
[Fig. 35(44)] This picturesque 330 acres encompassing the lower Coleman River was dedicated in 1960 to "Ranger Nick" Nicholson following his 40 years of public service. A 1-mile-long trail passes up the gorge with its pools, cascades, and shoals. Some large examples of evergreen trees, especially hemlock, can be seen. Fraser magnolia is common and Stewartia occurs. Carolina rhododendron is unusually abundant. Between the Tallulah Campground and the Scenic Area trailhead is a mini-gorge containing the "strainer hole" [Fig. 35(45)] which, prior to dynamiting,

had a hydraulic, or "keeper," at its input which drowned several people.

Directions to Upper Tallulah River Basin: From the center of Clayton, proceed west on US 76 7.5 miles; turn right (north) on a paved road and in 2.2 miles pass a cemetery in the community of Persimmon. Continue 1.8 miles and turn left at the first paved road. Follow this road (FS 70), which becomes gravel. Go 1 mile past parking area for canoe put-in (to float down to Lake Burton). The Forest Service's Tallulah River Campground is only .3 mile farther. The Coleman River Scenic Area and bridge are .1 mile past the campground. The drive up the Rock Mountain Gorge begins .2 mile past the Coleman River bridge and continues for about 1.9 miles. The gorge ends just south of a shallow ford across the Tallulah which leads to the four-wheel-drive road to Charlie's Creek. Continuing up the main road, it is .3 mile to the second Forest Service campground at Tate Branch. From Tate Branch it is .8 mile to the third official campground at Sandy Bottoms. From there it is .5 mile to Mill Creek (and its trail) and another 1 mile to Denton Creek then another .5 mile to the Beech Creek Bridge. Shortly north of this bridge is the North Carolina state line. From there it is about .4 mile to the parking area and trailhead for the Beach Creek gorge trail. Watch for a flat, cleared area on your left. The road ends about .2 mile farther and is the other end of the Beech Creek/Chimney Rock Loop Trail. Holden Cove Branch and its trail are several hundred yards back down the road from the dead end.

▓ TALLULAH GORGE

[Fig. 36, Fig. 38(1)] At 600 feet in depth, Tallulah Gorge is one of the deepest and most spectacular gorges in the East. It is geologically unique, being cut down in resistant quartzite, quite unlike the gneisses and schists of the surrounding mountains. It is a textbook example of stream capture. Originally, both the Chattooga and Tallulah rivers were headwaters of the Chattahoochee River. The Savannah River, down-cutting more rapidly, eventually cut back and robbed the Chattahoochee of these two streams. Over millions of years, the river has carved out the gorge.

The rare, persistent trillium and a wealth of other flora are found in the gorge. So is the green salamander, a rare crevice-dweller. The bird density is low, consisting mainly of vultures, phoebes, and swallows. Both the rare Carolina hemlock and table mountain pine grow around the gorge rim. Carolina rhododendron is unusually abundant. This is one of the few areas where the rare fringed polygala may be found.

Until the turn of the nineteenth century, Tallulah Falls and Tallulah Gorge were relatively unchanged by man. For centuries, only the Cherokee Indians inhabited the area, and few whites penetrated the wilderness. The few white hunters and traders who wandered through the area told stories about the gorge and its mysterious thundering waters. Even the Cherokees seldom ventured into the gorge, believing it to be inhabited by a strange race of "little people" who were alleged to live in the nooks and crannies of the cliffs overlooking the falls. The Cherokees also believed that one of the caves in the gorge was the entrance to the "Happy Hunting Grounds"; if an Indian ever entered, he would never return.

TURKEY VULTURE
(Cathartes aura)
The vulture's wings
form a V when gliding.

After the Cherokees were driven out in 1819, white adventurers began to explore the region. Within a year of the Cherokees' departure, spectacular accounts were circulated concerning this natural wonder in the northeast Georgia mountains. Although great stamina was required to make the trip, tourists began forging their way through the mountains to see this curiosity of nature. Clarkesville was the closest point where pack horses could be obtained to begin the 12-mile trek through the mountains to the gorge.

Interest in Tallulah Falls and Gorge had spread beyond Georgia. During the 1830s and 1840s, foreign and American dignitaries began to make pilgrimages to the region. The area's attraction is not hard to understand. The gorge itself is a 3-mile-long gash in the earth that reaches a depth of almost 600 feet, bordered by rocky, vertical walls. The Tallulah River carries runoff from a watershed area of over 200 square miles. In those days, this mighty river roared into the gorge over a series of spectacular cataracts, creating a continuous, thundering sound that echoed through the gorge day and night.

At the head of the gorge, the bed of the Tallulah River suddenly became narrow, creating a swift current headed toward the first falls. Tourists named this narrow bed Indian Arrow Rapids. The first of the great falls over which the Tallulah poured into the gorge was named Ladore; then came the 76-foot-high Tempesta Falls; then, the 96-foot Hurricane Falls. The fourth of the great falls was named Oseana. Next was Bridal Veil Falls, with a drop of 17 feet. And last was Sweet Sixteen Falls, with a 16-foot fall. Beyond the falls, deep in the canyon, was a great bend in the river called Horseshoe Bend, from which visitors liked to gaze upward to guess the height of the towering cliffs. Many streams and creeks poured over the canyon rim into the gorge below and were given appropriate names—no one knows exactly by whom. The pool at the bottom of Ladore Falls was named Hawthorne Pool, in memory of a man who fell to his death there. A natural water slide on the side of the gorge was named Hank's Sliding Place, in memory of a native of the region who slipped and fell more than 100 feet into the raging river below and lived to tell about it. The thundering waters beneath an overhanging rock reminded someone of the voice of Satan, so that rock was named Devil's Pulpit—probably the most popular tourist site at the gorge, then and now. An outcropping that reminded someone of a profile was given the name Witch's Head and was a popular spot for photographers in the nineteenth century.

As tourists grew impatient with making the long trek from Clarkesville and with having to camp at the gorge, inns sprang up near the attraction. Fine hotels were built, able to accommodate as many as 300 guests. Tallulah Gorge became a mecca for summer vacationers, offering cool temperatures, great views, and accommodations for rich and poor.

The old Tallulah Falls Railroad, which reached the gorge in 1882, ran along its western rim. The cuts may still be seen, and the old train station at Tallulah Falls Dam is now a craft store. This railroad, which ran from Cornelia to Franklin, was the principal means of bringing visitors to the gorge in the early years. Before the right-of-way was sold in the 1950s and the many wooden trestles were demolished, it was the setting for Walt Disney's film *The Great Locomotive Chase*.

On July 24, 1886, a crowd estimated at 3,500 to 6,000 people assembled to watch Professor Leon walk across the gorge on a tightrope. His historic feat began on the north rim at Inspiration Point, the highest point in the gorge at 1,200 feet. When he was near the center, one of his guy lines broke and the professor fell. Luckily, he caught the cable and sat on it for 25 minutes, before completing his walk.

In 1905, the state legislature made an effort to buy and preserve the land around Tallulah Gorge, but could not raise the $100,000 needed to make the purchase. Three years later, what was to become Georgia Power Company was organized by E. Elmer Smith of York, Pennsylvania, and Eugene Ashley of Glens Falls, New York. In 1909, these two men obtained the $108,960 necessary to purchase the strategic tract of land around the head of the gorge.

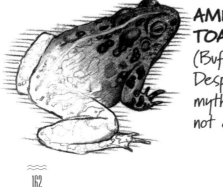

AMERICAN TOAD
(Bufo americanus) Despite popular myth, toads do not cause warts.

Efforts were made to rescue the Tallulah River and Gorge from development. In the first large environmental battle in the state's history, a group of citizens led by the widow of Confederate general James Longstreet appealed to officials of Rabun County, to the state legislature, to the governor, to the Georgia Supreme Court, and even to President Taft. But it was too late. Work on Tallulah Dam began.

Throngs of people came to the gorge area to watch this remarkable engineering feat. But more came in 1912 to view Tallulah Falls for the last time.

From its mile-high beginnings on the southwest slopes of Standing Indian Mountain in North Carolina, the Tallulah had bounded southward through the north Georgia mountains for centuries, falling more than 4,700 feet during the 46-mile journey to its confluence with the Chattooga beyond the end of Tallulah Gorge, at the South Carolina border. Its last 4 miles, beginning at the falls, had been the most dramatic. Over these falls the river had plunged downward a total of 600 feet in less than 1 mile.

In September of 1913, with the dam at the head of the gorge completed and the river diverted through its powerhouses, electricity flowed for the first time over the wires to Atlanta—to run the city's trolley cars. The "terrible" Tallulah River, as the Cherokees had called it, had been tamed and reduced to a trickle, dripping through Tallulah Gorge.

The decline of Tallulah Gorge as a tourist attraction was rapid thereafter. Many hotels closed. Others were burned in a fire of 1922 that almost destroyed the little tourist town of Tallulah Falls. Two years later, the construction of US 441 bypassed the town of Tallulah Falls altogether.

The moaning of the wind is the only sound that comes from the gorge now, although the place has enjoyed a few brief moments of notoriety. On July 18, 1970, Karl Wallenda duplicated Professor Leon's tightrope walk across the gorge, completing the distance in under forty minutes and breaking the professor's record for speed, if not for distance. In 1972, scenes for the movie *Deliverance* were shot in the canyon.

Today, almost a century after the first unsuccessful effort to turn the gorge into a state park, a unique partnership between the state of Georgia and the Georgia Power Company has done just that (*see* Tallulah Gorge State Park, *below*). Hiking trails, scenic overlooks, and an interpretive center will help lure tourists back to this remarkable area. As part of the park development plan, the Georgia Department of Natural Resources, in conjunction with state and national environmental organizations and the Georgia Power Company, has come up with a plan for water releases from Tallulah Dam, which addresses a wide range of practical, recreational, and scenic considerations.

While the details of this plan may change due to practical experience, it presently allows for a continuous water flow of 35 cubic feet per second (CFS) into the gorge. This slight volume of water is similar to the 12 CFS that flows through the gorge now and allows hikers to explore the bottom of the gorge. On 14 weekends per year during daylight hours, the flow will be increased to 200 CFS, or what's termed as "aesthetic flow." (As this book goes to press, aesthetic flows of 200 CFS are scheduled to occur every weekends: the third weekend in April–Memorial Day weekend, Labor

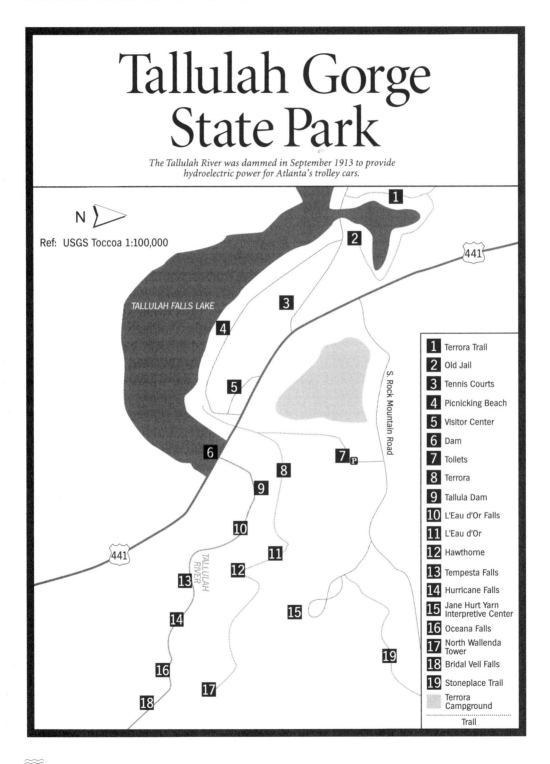

Tallulah Gorge State Park

The Tallulah River was dammed in September 1913 to provide hydroelectric power for Atlanta's trolley cars.

N

Ref: USGS Toccoa 1:100,000

441

TALLULAH FALLS LAKE

S. Rock Mountain Road

441

TALLULAH RIVER

1 Terrora Trail
2 Old Jail
3 Tennis Courts
4 Picnicking Beach
5 Visitor Center
6 Dam
7 Toilets
8 Terrora
9 Tallula Dam
10 L'Eau d'Or Falls
11 L'Eau d'Or
12 Hawthorne
13 Tempesta Falls
14 Hurricane Falls
15 Jane Hurt Yarn Interpretive Center
16 Oceana Falls
17 North Wallenda Tower
18 Bridal Veil Falls
19 Stoneplace Trail
   Terrora Campground
   Trail

Day weekend–the last weekend in October. "Aesthetic flow" raises the water in the gorge to approximate pre-dam levels and allows visitors to witness the scenic beauty of the waterfalls as well as the whitewater flowing through the rest of the gorge. Hikers may be prohibited from entering the gorge when water is at the 200 CFS level.

On five weekends per year (now scheduled for the first two weekends in April and the first three weekends in November), the flow will be increased to between 500 and 700 CFS, significantly increasing the whitewater drama of the gorge. During these periods, a limited number of canoeists and kayakers may challenge the rapids of the 2-mile canyon. Hiking in the gorge is likely to be prohibited at the 500 CFS level. Call the state park for a current schedule of water releases, rules of access, and information about boating in the canyon.

TALLULAH GORGE STATE PARK

Created through a partnership between the Georgia Department of Natural Resources and the Georgia Power Company, Tallulah Gorge State Park is the most recent addition to the Georgia state park system. The park includes 3,048 acres in and around Tallulah Gorge.

Directions: In Tallulah Falls, between Clarkesville and Clayton on US 441. Just north of the bridge, turn east on South Rock Mountain Road, proceed about 1 mile, and follow the signs.

Facilities: 50 tent and trailer sites, picnic area and shelter, 2 lighted tennis courts, 63-acre lake with sand beach, bath house with hot and cold showers and washing machines, visitor information center, interpretive center.

For more information: Tallulah Gorge State Park, PO Box 248, Tallulah Falls, GA 30573. Phone (706) 754-7970. For camping reservations, phone (706) 754-7979.

HIKING TRAILS IN TALLULAH GORGE

There are three hiking trails for exploring the gorge. South Walenda Trail and Hurricane Falls trails both descend to the bottom of the rugged area, but only South Walenda Trail is open to hikers. Hurricane Falls Trail is planned to be open to boaters. The South Rim and North Rim trails border the edge of the gorge, affording some very dramatic views.

Hiking to the bottom of the gorge is strenuous but rewarding. It can also be dangerous, especially when the rocks are wet. A strict permitting policy is in effect for hikers using South Walenda Trail and boaters using Hurricane Falls Trail. Only 100 hikers per day are allowed in the gorge, and no advance reservations are taken. For permits and detailed trail directions, go to the Jane Hurt Yarn Interpretive Center on South Rock Mountain Road in the park (*see* Tallulah State Park directions, above).

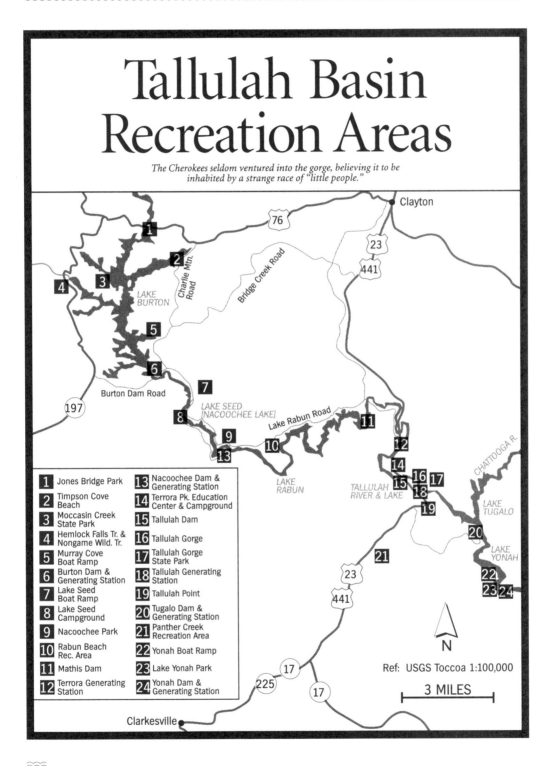

Tallulah Basin Recreation Areas

The Cherokees seldom ventured into the gorge, believing it to be inhabited by a strange race of "little people."

Clayton

76

23

441

Charlie Mtn. Road

Bridge Creek Road

LAKE BURTON

Murray Cove Boat Ramp

Burton Dam Road

197

LAKE SEED (NACOOCHEE LAKE)

Lake Rabun Road

LAKE RABUN

CHATTOOGA R.

TALLULAH RIVER & LAKE

LAKE TUGALO

LAKE YONAH

23

441

21

17

225

17

Clarkesville

N

Ref: USGS Toccoa 1:100,000

3 MILES

1 Jones Bridge Park
2 Timpson Cove Beach
3 Moccasin Creek State Park
4 Hemlock Falls Tr. & Nongame Wild. Tr.
5 Murray Cove Boat Ramp
6 Burton Dam & Generating Station
7 Lake Seed Boat Ramp
8 Lake Seed Campground
9 Nacoochee Park
10 Rabun Beach Rec. Area
11 Mathis Dam
12 Terrora Generating Station
13 Nacoochee Dam & Generating Station
14 Terrora Pk. Education Center & Campground
15 Tallulah Dam
16 Tallulah Gorge
17 Tallulah Gorge State Park
18 Tallulah Generating Station
19 Tallulah Point
20 Tugalo Dam & Generating Station
21 Panther Creek Recreation Area
22 Yonah Boat Ramp
23 Lake Yonah Park
24 Yonah Dam & Generating Station

ROCK CLIMBING IN TALLULAH GORGE

Tallulah Gorge contains a variety of popular rock-climbing sites for all skill levels. A strict permitting policy is in effect and only 20 permits per day are issued. No permits are issued during inclement weather and no advance reservations are taken. To apply for a permit, go to the Jane Hurt Yarn Interpretive Center on South Rock Mountain Road in the park (*see* Tallulah State Park directions, page 165).

CANOEING GUIDE & DRIVING TOUR OF THE TALLULAH RIVER BASIN

The destinations below, whether reached by car, canoe, foot, or a combination thereof, provide a rare opportunity for visitors to view the mountains from scenic lakes, run the rapids of what remains of Tallulah Gorge, and pay tribute to what was once one of the mightiest rivers in Georgia. The guide that follows provides directions for canoeing 31.5 miles of the Tallulah River, including its scenic impounded lakes and sections of the river where Class I–IV rapids provide hints of what the river once was. The trip can be divided into six parts or done as one long trip. The driving directions to put-ins and take-outs provide an opportunity for visitors to see much of the same terrain by car.

THE FIRST 10 MILES. Although the first 10 miles of the Tallulah are uncanoeable, driving streamside is worthwhile for the mountain scenery alone. *See* directions for the Upper Tallulah Basin Drive, page 154.

THE UPPER TALLULAH—SECTION 1. This section begins 10 miles from the source of the river. It offers miles of Class I–III whitewater paddling on a relatively untouched area of the river beside the Coleman River Wildlife Management Area, and 2 miles of paddling on the backwaters of Lake Burton.

Directions: The put-in for Section I is at the Tallulah River Recreation Area Campground. Put in either at the campground or just up the road at the Coleman River Bridge. The takeout is on US 76, 9.2 miles west of Clayton on Jones Bridge over the Tallulah River finger of Lake Burton. The best take-out point is not at Jones Bridge itself but .2 mile up Vickers Road, which starts at the northwest corner of the bridge.

LAKE BURTON—SECTION II. Lake Burton, the largest of the five reservoir lakes on this trip, impounds almost 10 miles of the Tallulah River in its 2,775 acres. A many-fingered mountain lake with 62 miles of shoreline, Burton serves as a reservoir, controlling the water flow to Lakes Seed, Rabun, Tallulah, and Tugalo below. It is a favorite spot for fishermen. Impounded in 1919 upon completion of Burton Dam, it was named after the town of Burton, which once occupied the site on which the lake now stands. Lake Burton is a large, deep lake, and canoeists must be alert for rapidly rising winds and thunderstorms. Paddling near the banks is recommended. Follow the map carefully to avoid making a wrong turn into one of its dead-end fingers.

Directions: This section is a 4.5-mile paddle down the lake's main Tallulah River channel from the Jones Bridge put-in to the Murray Cove take-out, the nearest public landing to Burton Dam. To reach Murray Cove from Jones Bridge, go east on US 76 for 2.2 miles and turn right (south) onto paved Charlie Mountain Road. Follow this road for 3.5 miles and turn right onto paved Bridge Creek Road. Go .3 mile and turn right onto Murray Cove Road.

LAKE SEED—SECTION III. Lake Seed, sometimes called Lake Nacoochee, offers a canoeing experience entirely different from that offered by Lake Burton. Burton's wide and many-fingered layout provides breathtaking views of distant mountains. Seed, on the other hand, is tight and narrow and follows the original bed of the Tallulah River quite closely. Seed is 4.5 miles long, impounded by the 75-foot-high Nacoochee Dam, completed in 1926. The lake has a 13-mile shoreline. The canoe route goes 3.5 miles, from the put-in at the base of Burton Dam to the public boat ramp on Lake Seed. Georgia Power Company offers primitive campsites at Lake Seed on a first-come, first-served basis.

Directions: Put-in for this 3.5-mile trip is at the base of Burton Dam (mile 12.7 on the map). Take Murray Cove Road to its intersection with Bridge Creek Road, turn right, and go 1.6 miles to Lake Rabun Road. Turn right (west) and go .5 mile to the bridge over the Tallulah River at the base of Burton Dam.

For more information: Phone (706) 754-7923.

LAKE RABUN—SECTION IV. Lake Rabun has been a popular recreation area for many years. Houses and cottages were built on its shores as early as the 1930s, and today its 25-mile shoreline is dotted with homes. Georgia Power Company, which owns most of the shoreline and leases land for homes, limits development, so sprawling motel complexes are not present. This 8-mile trip is winding and scenic, offering a stop at the popular Rabun Beach Recreation Area located just off Lake Rabun Road. On the lake, stick close to shore to avoid heavy motorboat traffic. The Nacoochee Park Recreation Area offers picnic tables and restrooms.

Directions: Put-in for Lake Rabun is at the base of the dam on Lake Seed at the Nacoochee Park Recreation Area just off Lake Rabun Road. Take-out is at Hall's Boat House in the little town of Lakemont.

TALLULAH RIVER AND LAKE TALLU-LAH—SECTION V. The special feature of this

WILD TURKEY (Meleagris gallopavo) Turkeys can fly well for short distances but prefer to run.

5.5-mile stretch is that it follows for 4 miles the original bed of the Tallulah River, offering significant rapids, including a Class IV. The final 1.5 miles are on a lake complete with waterfalls and mountain streams trickling along its banks. This small lake, only 63 acres, is impounded by the 130-foot-tall Tallulah Dam. Completed in 1912, it was the first dam built on the Tallulah River. Its construction on the rim of Tallulah Gorge cut off most of the water for Tallulah Falls. Unlike its sister lakes, Lake Tallulah is full of yellow perch.

Directions: The take-out for this stretch is in Terrora Park behind the Terrora Visitor Center off US 441 at Tallulah Dam. To reach the put-in, leave Terrora Park, turn left onto old US 441 and go 4 miles to the put-in bridge. At 1.6 miles into the shuttle, old US 441 joins the current US 441 for about 100 yards; turn left at this intersection. Stay on old US 441, which leaves the new road at the signs pointing to Lake Rabun. The put-in, located 1 mile downstream from Mathis Dam at the junction of the Tallulah River and Tiger Creek, is steep. Best access is at the northwest corner of the bridge.

To scout the river, take the road that leads across the river to the Terrora Generating Station .8 mile from Terrora Park and to a bridge over the Tallulah River .9 mile beyond the park. These are good places from which to scout the four dangerous rapids in this section, one of them rated Class IV.

TALLULAH GORGE AND LAKE TUGALO—SECTION VI. The last 2 miles of canoeable water on the Tallulah River are in Tallulah Gorge, on the west finger of Lake Tugalo [Fig. 38(3)]. This section is canoed as a 4-mile round-trip, using the same point as put-in and take-out. The Tugaloo River begins where the Tallulah and Chattooga rivers meet, and its name, in Cherokee, means "fork of a stream." Lake Tugalo was formed with the completion of the Tugalo Dam [Fig. 38(5)] and Hydroelectric Plant on the Tugaloo River in 1922.

Lake Tugalo covers 597 acres and has 18 miles of shoreline. The property around the lake is undeveloped. Tugalo is surrounded by a mixed pine-and-hardwood forest that has been relatively undisturbed by logging because of its steep shoreline. Tugalo is a beautiful lake for both fisherman and canoeist. Catfish and bass fishing are good. Tugalo is one of the few lakes in Georgia where canoeing and slow boat traffic are the norm (boat motors are restricted to 10 HP or less). On a leisurely day's paddle around the lake, a canoeist can explore many spots accessible only by water. Paddling up the Tallulah River arm of the lake leads into the Tallulah Gorge; paddling on the eastern side leads into the Chattooga Gorge [Fig. 38(4), Fig. 47].

Waterfalls cascade into the lake at several points, and spring and summer wildflowers are abundant. Wildlife in the area include deer and turkey. There are plenty of places to stop along the shore to stretch, have a picnic, or explore. Fires and camping are allowed only in Tugalo Park.

The South Carolina side of the ramp [Fig. 38(3), Fig. 47(25)] is very steep and difficult to navigate with a big boat and trailer. The parking lot here is often full

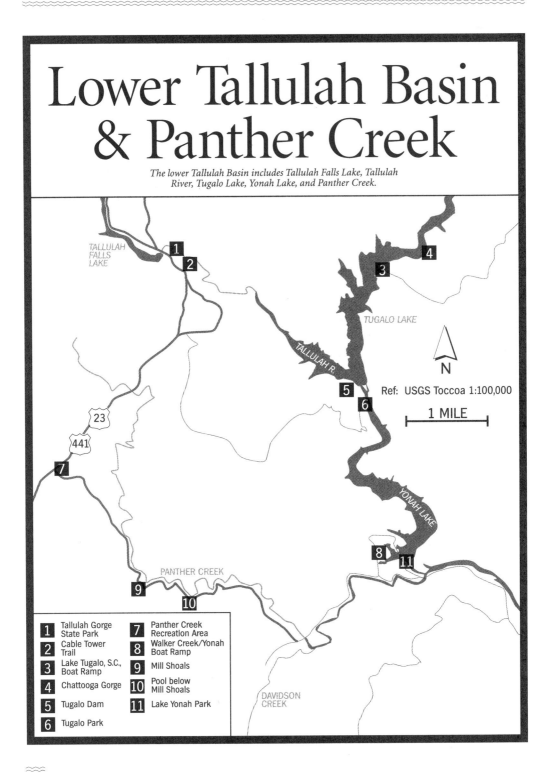

Lower Tallulah Basin & Panther Creek

The lower Tallulah Basin includes Tallulah Falls Lake, Tallulah River, Tugalo Lake, Yonah Lake, and Panther Creek.

TALLULAH FALLS LAKE

TUGALO LAKE

TALLULAH R.

N

Ref: USGS Toccoa 1:100,000

1 MILE

YONAH LAKE

PANTHER CREEK

DAVIDSON CREEK

1 Tallulah Gorge State Park		**7** Panther Creek Recreation Area	
2 Cable Tower Trail		**8** Walker Creek/Yonah Boat Ramp	
3 Lake Tugalo, S.C., Boat Ramp		**9** Mill Shoals	
4 Chattooga Gorge		**10** Pool below Mill Shoals	
5 Tugalo Dam		**11** Lake Yonah Park	
6 Tugalo Park			

during rafting season, this being a popular take-out point for rafters completing Section IV of the Chattooga River. Tugalo Park [Fig. 38(6)] has primitive campsites level and big enough for a tent or small trailer. There is no reservation system.

The boat ramp in the park is level and graveled, giving access to the northern end of Lake Yonah.

Directions: Access to Lake Tugalo from the South Carolina side is at Long Creek SC. Take US 76 east from Clayton approximately 10.7 miles to Long Creek; go south on Orchard Road for 2.6 miles to Battlecreek Road; turn right and go 2.5 miles to Damascus Church Road; turn right again. Just past Damascus Church (1.2 miles), turn right on Tugalo Lake Road (gravel); go 3.9 miles (the last mile is paved) to the boat landing on Lake Tugalo below the Chattooga River [Fig. 38(3), Fig. 47(25)].

For access from Georgia to Tugalo Park, turn east onto GA 15 Scenic Loop off US 23/441 south of Tallulah Falls. Turn south onto Tugalo Plant Road (the sign says "Georgia Power No. Ga. Hydro Group Hdqs. Office"). Go 3 miles, then turn left through a gate onto a gravel road (sign says "Tugalo Plant"). The park is approximately 2 miles ahead on a steep, winding, gravel road.

For directions and a U.S. Forest Service map of the Chattooga River Corridor (fee), stop at the Chattooga Whitewater Shop on US 76 in Long Creek.

Facilities: Primitive camping, picnic tables, nonflush restrooms, boat ramps, parking.

Dates: Check with the Georgia Power office, phone (706) 754-6036.

For more information: Georgia Power Company, Terrora Park, US 23/441, PO Box 9, Tallulah Falls, GA 30573. Phone (706) 754-6036.

RECREATION AREAS AND HIKING TRAILS

MOCCASIN CREEK STATE PARK. [Fig. 37(3)] This is a small park, 32 acres, built on a floodplain flat at the mouth of Moccasin Creek on the shore of Lake Burton. It is an excellent base of operations for area sight-seeing, hiking, and other recreational activities. Daily interpretive programs are offered June through August. Annual special events include the Lake Burton Fun Run, All About Mountain Trout, and Lake Burton Arts and Crafts Festival.

Directions: Located 20 miles north of Clarkesville on GA 197 and 17 miles west of Clayton (take US 76 west to GA 197).

Facilities: 53 campsites, boat ramp and dock, handicapped-accessible fishing pier, stream and lake fishing, lakeside picnic area, playground open-air pavilion, trout hatchery, laundry facilities, comfort stations.

For more information: Moccasin Creek State Park, Georgia Department of Natural Resources, Route 1, Box 1634, Clarkesville, GA 30523. Phone (706) 947-3194. Phone (800) 864-PARK, or (770) 389-PARK, in metro Atlanta for individual reservations.

NON-GAME WILDLIFE TRAIL. [Fig. 37(4)] 1.2-mile loop trail. Along the way are grassy fields, areas of old field pines—that is, white, Virginia, and pitch pine—

and old field scrub lacking a tree canopy. There is an extensive area of deciduous hardwoods with poplar, red oak, and occasional sycamore. In this community along Moccasin Creek, alders dominate the creek bank along with dog hobbles and some American holly. Yellowroot, a mountain medicinal herb, occurs along the stream.

Directions: Trailhead is at the trout-hatchery intake across the highway from the Moccasin Creek State Park entrance (*see above*).

HEMLOCK FALLS TRAIL. [Fig. 37(4)] This easy, 1-mile trail follows Moccasin Creek, a beautiful trout stream with cascades and a waterfall. A hardwood-rhododendron community with hemlock and white pine prevails along the creek. The canopy is mostly poplar, red oak, white pine, black birch, and hemlock. Fraser magnolia occurs. Hemlock Falls marks the end of the trail.

Directions: The trailhead is .5 mile up the gravel road that begins at the parking area for the Non-Game Wildlife Trail, (*above*).

RABUN BEACH RECREATION AREA AND HIKING TRAIL. [Fig. 37(10)] Located amidst lovely mountain scenery of 934-acre Lake Rabun, the hiking trail starts from camping area number two on Joe Branch and goes .5 mile to Panther Falls and 1 mile to Angel Falls. From late spring until July, the trail travels through an outstanding display of flowering rhododendron.

Directions: From the Tallulah Gorge bridge, go 1.7 miles north on US 441 and turn left on old 441. Go 2.5 miles and turn left on Lake Rabun Road. It is 5 miles to the campground.

Facilities: two camping areas on the opposite side of the road from the beach contain 80 campsites, restrooms.

Activities: Hiking, boating, fishing, swimming.

For more information: Rabun Beach Recreation Area, Chattahoochee National Forest, Tallulah Ranger District, 825 Highway 441 South, PO Box 438, Clayton, GA 30525. Phone (706) 782-3320.

MINNEHAHA TRAIL. This .2-mile trail follows Fall Branch until it dead-ends at 50-foot-high Minnehaha Falls.

AMERICAN MOUNTAIN-ASH

(Sorbus americana)
Found along swamp borders as well as on mountainsides, the mountain-ash produces clusters of orange-red fruit for birds and rodents.

Directions: From the Rabun Beach Recreation Area above, continue past the recreation area for 1 mile and turn left, crossing the river below Lake Seed Dam. Follow the left fork of the road for 1.7 miles to a sign marking the trail on the right side of the road.

YONAH LAKE

[Fig. 38] Lake Yonah, one of six lakes managed by Georgia Power Company, was formed when the Yonah Dam and Hydroelectric Plant was completed on the Tugaloo River between Georgia and South Carolina in 1925. Yonah, meaning "big black bear" in Cherokee, is immediately south of Lake Tugalo and covers 325 acres.

The land adjacent to the lake being very steep, there has been little timber harvested here. Happily, there remains an undisturbed heavy forest of pines and hardwoods. This area has a great diversity of plant life, including many wildflowers. Other than the common Georgia wildlife, including deer and turkey, there is an occasional bear. Private homes are built around the 9 miles of shoreline, leaving the only public access to the lake at the boat ramps. The Lake Yonah boat ramp is paved and level. There is a small dock. The parking lot will hold approximately 15 cars and trailers. A dumpster is provided for trash. There are no restroom facilities.

The lake is popular year-round for canoeing and fishing for catfish and bass and in the summer for water-skiing. Canoeists must use caution on the lake in warm weather because of the fast and constant ski traffic. The lake can be paddled easily in a day. A put-in spot to the right of the dam has many seasonal wildflowers and is good for picnicking.

LAKE YONAH PARK

[Fig. 37(23), Fig. 38(11)] Located below the dam overlooking Tugaloo River. The river banks are steep and overgrown, making access to the river difficult.

Directions: Yonah Dam road turns off GA 184 near its intersection with GA 17. Follow signs to Walker Creek boat ramp, Yonah boat ramp [Fig. 37(22)], and Lake Yonah Park [Fig. 37(23), Fig. 38(11)].

Facilities: Picnic tables, limited parking, boat ramp, trash cans, dumpsters, nature trail access.

For more information: Georgia Power Company, Terrora Park, US Hwy 23/441, PO Box 9, Tallulah Falls, GA 30573. Phone (706) 754-6036.

PANTHER CREEK RECREATION AREA AND HIKING TRAIL

[Fig. 37(21), Fig. 38(7)] Panther Creek originates on the southern slope of Stony Mountain at an elevation of 2,440 feet, meanders down 940 feet before crossing US 23 and 441 at the recreation area, and empties into the Tugaloo River, which forms the border between Georgia and South Carolina. According to scientists who have studied the area, the natural features of Panther Creek Gorge have changed little during the past million years.

The 6-mile Panther Creek Trail, marked with blue blazes, begins at the Panther Creek Recreation Area [Fig. 38(7)]. It winds through a forest of poplar, hemlock, white pine, oak, hickory, and red maple, with an occasional birch, as it follows the steep, rocky bluffs of the creek. The trees, some of which are over 100 feet tall, provide shade in the summer and a display of colorful foliage in the fall. There are many rock cliffs with mosses and ferns growing in the moist crevices. In early spring, trout lilies appear, followed by violets and trillium. Trailing arbutus, dwarf iris, and gay-wings grow low to the ground. Spring flowering shrubs along the trail include serviceberry and horse sugar. There are masses of mountain laurel blooming in May, and the white and pink blossoms of the rhododendron are present well into June. The flowers of the dogwood and silverbell trees add to the beauty of the spring display.

The creek itself drops in a series of cascades. Little Panther Creek enters Panther Creek .6 mile before the stream turns sharply east at Mill Shoals, a former mill site [Fig. 38(9)]. Approximately .5 mile farther, 3.6 miles from Panther Creek Recreation Area and 2.4 miles from the eastern end of the trail, the creek falls 60 to 70 feet into a pool [Fig. 38(10)]. The trail leads down to the pool where there is a grand view of the falling water. This waterfall is preceded by an impressive Mill Shoals Falls, which could be mistaken for the more dramatic falls farther on. The trail ends at a dirt road near the point where Davidson Creek joins Panther Creek. The road continues for 2 miles to Lake Yonah Dam and Park.

SHOWY ORCHIS (Orchis spectabilis) Bees and dragonflies thrust tongues into the spur of this blossom for pollen.

The eastern, or lower, end of the trail is designated a Protected Botanical Area by the U.S. Forest Service because of the richness and diversity of its plant life. This area is unique because it is within the Brevard Fault Zone. A relatively narrow band of limestone within the fault supports vegetation not commonly found in north Georgia. The soil allows calcium-loving plants, such as chinquapin oak, to thrive here. The herbs, in particular, are remarkable.

Overnight camping areas are limited, and water along the trail is not safe for drinking. The trail is moderately difficult to hike, with a few steep places. Hikers carrying heavy packs should be aware of the rocky overhangs and narrow trails.

Panther Creek, home to rainbow trout and redeye bass, is classified as a secondary trout stream. Fishing schedules are available on Georgia fishing licenses, which are renewable annually.

Directions: Panther Creek Recreation Area is 9 miles north of Clarkesville and 3.6 miles south of Tallulah Falls on US 23/441.

For access to the eastern end of Panther Creek Trail drive .6 mile from Yonah Dam Park on Yonah Dam Road to a dirt road and turn to the left. This road follows the creek approximately 2 miles to the small parking area at the end of the trail (no sign, but blue blaze marks the trail). The road is hard-packed dirt but is rocky and requires a four-wheel-drive vehicle in wet weather. *See* Fig. 38.

Facilities: Recreation area, parking, restrooms, picnic tables with some shelters, hand pump for water, blazed hiking and nature trail.

RED-TAILED HAWK
(Buteo jamaicensis)
This hawk hunts for small animals from the air or from exposed perches.

For more information: Panther Creek, U.S. Forest Service, Chattahoochee National Forest, Burton Road, Clarkesville, GA 30523. Phone (706) 754-6221.

Map References: USGS 1:24 000 series: Tallulah Falls–Tugalo Lake–Rainbow Springs–Hightower Bald.

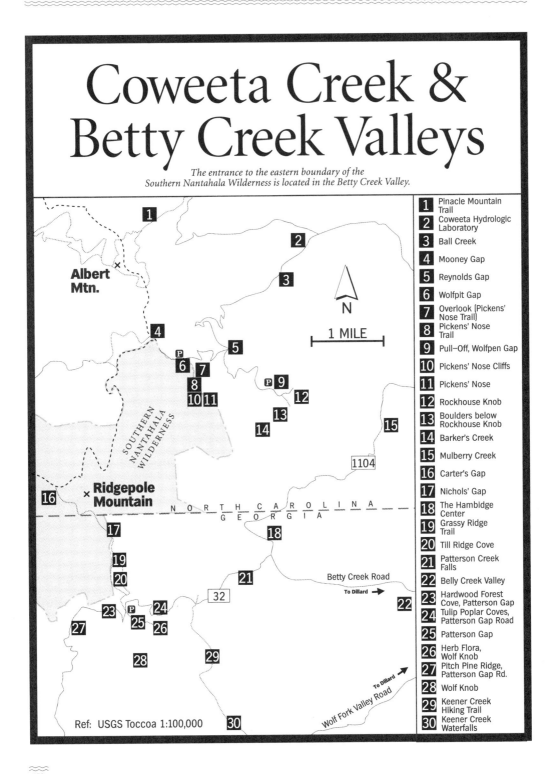

Coweeta Creek & Betty Creek Valleys

The entrance to the eastern boundary of the
Southern Nantahala Wilderness is located in the Betty Creek Valley.

1. Pinacle Mountain Trail
2. Coweeta Hydrologic Laboratory
3. Ball Creek
4. Mooney Gap
5. Reynolds Gap
6. Wolfpit Gap
7. Overlook (Pickens' Nose Trail)
8. Pickens' Nose Trail
9. Pull–Off, Wolfpen Gap
10. Pickens' Nose Cliffs
11. Pickens' Nose
12. Rockhouse Knob
13. Boulders below Rockhouse Knob
14. Barker's Creek
15. Mulberry Creek
16. Carter's Gap
17. Nichols' Gap
18. The Hambidge Center
19. Grassy Ridge Trail
20. Till Ridge Cove
21. Patterson Creek Falls
22. Belly Creek Valley
23. Hardwood Forest Cove, Patterson Gap
24. Tulip Poplar Coves, Patterson Gap Road
25. Patterson Gap
26. Herb Flora, Wolf Knob
27. Pitch Pine Ridge, Patterson Gap Rd.
28. Wolf Knob
29. Keener Creek Hiking Trail
30. Keener Creek Waterfalls

Ref: USGS Toccoa 1:100,000

Coweeta Creek and Betty Creek Valleys

▨ BETTY CREEK VALLEY

[Fig. 39(22)] This entrance to the eastern boundary of the Southern Nantahala Wilderness is one of the most beautiful valleys in north Georgia. Combining good hiking, scenic views, and pleasant driving tours with the possibility of visits to the Hambidge Center or the Coweeta Hydrologic Laboratory, it will appeal to visitors with recreational, scientific, or cultural interests.

Betty Creek Road offers a scenic drive through this serene valley. The total distance from the turnoff at Dillard to the North Carolina state line where the pavement ends is about 6 miles. The continuation of the road (NC 1104) crosses Beasley Gap and descends Mulberry Creek [Fig. 39(15)] to a beautiful, early spring wildflower area that is accessible by car. It eventually comes out on US 441 south of Otto, North Carolina.

▨ THE HAMBIDGE CENTER

[Fig. 39(18)] The center is the creation of Mary Hambidge, a feminist, environmentalist, and preserver of mountain culture who was 50 years ahead of her time. She helped her husband, Jay Hambidge, codify his ideas pertaining to classical-art design principles, which they labeled Dynamic Symmetry. Their work gained international recognition.

Mary encouraged local crafts, particularly dyeing and weaving, done in the large loom room at the center. She perfected a range of vegetable dyes that has never been duplicated. She decorated President Truman's yacht, designed costumes for dancer Isadora Duncan, and opened a successful shop on Madison Avenue in New York. Eliot Wigginton, who went on to found Foxfire, a hugely successful series of publications dedicated to the preservation of mountain culture, was a protégé of hers. In later years she became reclusive.

Today the Hambidge Center, which consists of an office building, gallery, workshop, dining hall, and a number of cabins on 600 picturesque acres, organizes workshops, seminars, and film and concert series. Approximately 20 different programs are offered during the months of May to October. In addition, each year the center awards 20 to 25 resident fellowships to encourage creative exploration and inner self-renewal.

Visitors are asked to register in the office and are welcome to walk the center's nature trails. There is also a water-powered gristmill known as the Barker's Creek Mill, restored for the third time in 1988. It is usually open on Fridays and Saturdays for grinding grains brought by local residents.

Directions: On Betty Creek Road approximately 4 miles west of Dillard.
Dates: Open Mon.–Fri.

For more information: The Hambidge Center, PO Box 339, Rabun Gap, GA 30568. Phone (706) 746-5718.

PATTERSON GAP
[Fig. 39(25)] The road to Patterson Gap (FS 32) turns left off Betty Creek Road about 3.5 miles from US 441 and crosses a bridge. As one climbs a steep grade, off to the left is Patterson Creek Falls [Fig. 39(21)]. FS 32 passes through Moon Valley. After entering U.S. Forest Service land, the road is steep but scenic through great coves of tulip poplar [Fig. 39(24)] which have come in after the death of the chestnut because of a blight in the 1930s and following logging in the early 1900s. Crossing Patterson Gap, one circles a cove hardwood forest [Fig. 39(23)], then descends along a pitch pine ridge [Fig. 39(27)]. Along the road banks grows the rare sweetfern. This road eventually joins Persimmon Road, which dead-ends at US 76.

GRASSY RIDGE TRAIL
[Fig. 39(19)] At Patterson Gap [Fig. 39(25)], a well-known trail goes up Grassy Ridge, forking off to the right to Till Ridge Cove [Fig. 39(20)], considered by many to be one of the finest botanical areas in the state. From more than 1,000 trillium nodding their heads in the spring to dazzling displays of golden witch hazel blooms in late October, the cove offers a constant pageant of wildflowers. The left fork eventually crosses the west side of the ridge at Nichols' Gap [Fig. 39(17)] and encounters the Appalachian Trail at Carter's Gap [Fig. 39(16)]. Hikers along this trail can look up at Ridgepole Mountain (5,007 feet), with its heath thickets out of which emerge some evergreens. South of Patterson Gap stands Wolf Knob [Fig. 39(28)] (3,329 feet). North-facing coves in this area have lush and interesting herb flora [Fig. 39(26)].

KEENER CREEK HIKING TRAIL
[Fig. 39(29)] At or near the U.S. Forest Service boundary, a nice trail goes up Keener Creek from the Wolffork Valley loop road past two waterfalls [Fig. 39(30)] in a gorge to the left. Adventurous hikers equipped with topographic maps (the Dillard quadrangle) will notice a large flat area at the head of Keener Creek—an area which should be interesting botanically. This area can be reached either from Patterson Gap or up an old log road turning off the paved Wolf Fork Valley Road just east of the junction with the graveled Blue Ridge Gap Road.

COWEETA HYDROLOGIC LABORATORY
[Fig. 39(2)] The Coweeta Hydrologic Laboratory, site of a long-term ecological research program, is studying several watersheds for the effects of logging and other forest-management practices on water yields and quality. Roadside signs indicate the experimental areas and explain the experiments. It is advisable to stop at the office to

obtain a map of the area before beginning any exploration. The 14-mile driving tour past the station continues as a loop to US 64 via the Standing Indian Campground and takes approximately 1 hour.

Directions: From Dillard, go north on US 441 4.3 miles to Coweeta Hydrologic Laboratory sign. Turn left and follow signs 2.9 miles to the parking lot.

Dates: The laboratory is open Mon.–Fri., closed holidays. The road to hiking trails, Pickens' Nose, and Cherokee Cave is closed intermittently during periods of bad weather between January 1 and March 15.

DRIVE UP BALL CREEK TO PICKENS' NOSE TRAILHEAD

[Fig. 39(3)] This long and curvy climb leads first to Reynolds Gap [Fig. 39(5)]. Take the left fork at Reynolds Gap to the first place one can see down the slope both north and south of the road. From the pull-off [Fig. 39(9)] here at Wolfpen Gap, a short and fairly level trail leads south to the famed Cherokee Cave, a huge overhanging rock ledge on the west side of Rockhouse Knob [Fig. 39(12)]. Mountain legend holds that three Cherokees hid out here to avoid being driven to Oklahoma during the Indian removal known as the Trail of Tears. Below is a veritable rock city [Fig. 39(13)] of gigantic boulders fractured and fallen from the cliff above. Growing on them are some plants characteristic of boulderfields—a vinelike gooseberry, for example. Farther down the cove of Barker's Creek [Fig. 39(14)] is a rich area with spring seeps and abundant herbs such as Turk's cap lilies. This is a nice hike, but the lower end is private, so visitors should inquire.

The right fork at Reynolds Gap leads to Wolfpit Gap [Fig. 39(6)], where parking is obvious on the right. The Pickens' Nose Trail [Fig. 39(8)] begins here on the left. It is a relatively gentle climb of less than a mile to the top [Fig. 39(11)]. The vegetation and views make it a very attractive hike. At .3 mile, watch for a short spur trail to a rock cliff on the left [Fig. 39(7)], with a great view to the east. The trail runs through northern red oak ridge forest but the surroundings gradually change more to rhododendron and shrubs. Watch for purple rhododendron and the rarer minniebush, *Menziesia*, along with the common mountain laurel. At the Pickens' Nose Cliffs [Fig. 39(10)] is one of the best views in the eastern part of the wilderness as one gazes out over the vast Betty Creek valley, 2,000 feet below, to Ridgepole and beyond. Outward Bound and others teach cliff climbing here. With care, exploration is possible down, around, and under the cliffs. Plants that grow exclusively on cliffs are found here. One, St. John's wort, is found only on high rock outcrops in the southern Appalachians.

Albert Mountain can be reached by continuing on FS 83 with a short hike on the Appalachian Trail. It affords fine views.

Map References: USGS 1:24,000 series: Prentiss–Dillard.

Black Rock Mountain State Park

Black Rock Mountain State Park is Georgia's highest elevated state park, and it has more than 1,800 acres.

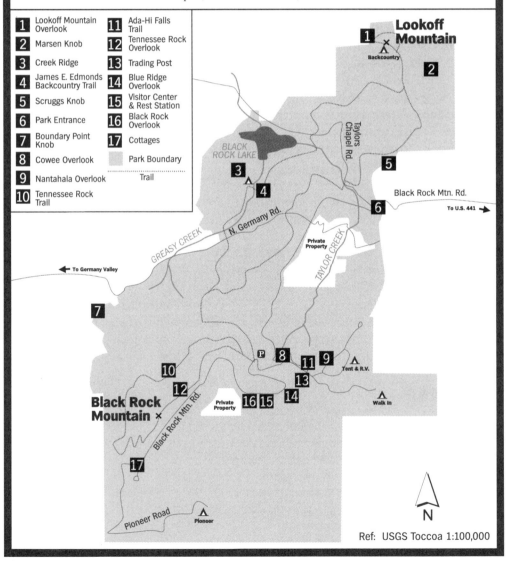

1. Lookoff Mountain Overlook
2. Marsen Knob
3. Creek Ridge
4. James E. Edmonds Backcountry Trail
5. Scruggs Knob
6. Park Entrance
7. Boundary Point Knob
8. Cowee Overlook
9. Nantahala Overlook
10. Tennessee Rock Trail
11. Ada-Hi Falls Trail
12. Tennessee Rock Overlook
13. Trading Post
14. Blue Ridge Overlook
15. Visitor Center & Rest Station
16. Black Rock Overlook
17. Cottages

Park Boundary

Trail

Lookoff Mountain

Backcountry

Black Rock Lake

Taylors Chapel Rd.

Black Rock Mtn. Rd.

To U.S. 441

Greasy Creek

N. Germany Rd.

Taylor Creek

Private Property

To Germany Valley

Tent & R.V.

Walk In

Black Rock Mountain

Black Rock Mtn. Rd.

Private Property

Pioneer Road

Pioneer

N

Ref: USGS Toccoa 1:100,000

Black Rock Mountain State Park

Black Rock Mountain State Park [Fig. 40], named for its sheer cliffs of dark granite, has the distinction of being Georgia's highest state park. It stretches over 3 miles along the Eastern Continental Divide, the spine of the southern Blue Ridge Mountains. Containing six different peaks above 3,000 feet in elevation, it covers more than 1,800 acres. From park overlooks on a clear day, visitors may enjoy views extending for more than 80 miles. Among the areas of the southern Appalachians visible are the Nantahala Mountains, the Cowee Range, and, on especially clear days, the Great Smoky Mountains.

The park is noted for its many spring wildflowers, including several varieties of trillium, violets, bloodroot, and flame azalea. In early summer, masses of mountain laurel and rhododendron are in bloom. In the fall, leaves of oak, maple, sourwood, and other deciduous trees and shrubs create a spectacular blaze of yellow, orange, and red. Evergreens present a contrasting note. Goldenrod and other fall blooms add to the show. The most common natural environment in the park is a deciduous hardwood slope forest with red oaks dominant. Chestnut oaks in drier places and white oaks in certain areas lend diversity.

Animals in the park include gray squirrels, chipmunks, opossums, black bears, foxes, woodchucks, bobcats, skunks, and occasional deer. There are wild turkey, ruffed grouse, and, in season, many songbirds.

The park's visitor center features an observation deck, wildlife exhibits, a log cabin exhibit, trail maps, and handicapped-accessible re-strooms. Nature guides, raised-relief maps, hiking-trail guides, and books about mountain culture and area attractions are also available. Park rangers are on duty to answer visitors' questions. Special events include a spring wildflower program in May or June and an overnight backpacking trip in the fall.

Directions: In Mountain City, 3 miles north of Clayton via US 441.

Facilities: 1,803 acres,

BOBCAT (Lynx rufus)
The bobcat is the most common wild feline in North America. A solitary animal, the bobcat's preys are usually rabbits and mice.

48 tent and trailer sites, 11 walk-in sites, pioneer campground for organized groups, 10 rental cottages, playground, 2 picnic shelters, 17-acre lake, 6 scenic overlooks, and 10-mile trail system.

For more information: Black Rock Mountain State Park, PO Drawer A, Mountain City, GA 30562. Phone (706) 746-2141. Call (800) 864-PARK, or (770) 389-PARK in metro Atlanta, for individual reservations.

TENNESSEE ROCK TRAIL

[Fig. 40(10)] 2.2 miles. In a relatively short distance, this trail passes through several distinct environments. The entire trail is above 3,000 feet in altitude, and the first mile is located on the north side of the Blue Ridge. This cool, moist environment nourishes the growth of a variety of wildflowers, including lady slippers and umbrella leaf. Three poplar coves are found along this section of the trail. As it passes through the second of these coves, the trail lies immediately below the summit of Black Rock Mountain (3,640 feet), which is just high enough to have on its north face a small boulderfield containing herbs, such as blue cohosh, that are indicative of moist, high elevations. The trees among the rocks are primarily basswood and black birch, and the area provides fine wildflower displays in the spring and summer. After leaf fall, clumps of intermediate wood fern and alum root are visible.

Near the western border of the park, the trail passes through an almost pure stand of white pine which seeded in after intensive logging of hardwoods prior to the establishment of the park. After leaving this pine forest, the trail climbs rather steeply to the summit of Black Rock Mountain, then follows the Blue Ridge crest to Tennessee Rock Overlook [Fig. 40(12)]. This entire section of trail is above 3,600 feet in altitude. There is much rock, and the red oaks are stunted and lichen-covered; rosebay rhododendron is prevalent. Beyond Tennessee Rock, the trail remains on the crest of the ridgeline for several hundred yards before descending back to the trailhead parking area. Numbered posts along the entire length of the trail correspond to a fully illustrated, 32-page trail guide which interprets various aspects of the park's natural features. This booklet is available at the park visitor center for a small fee.

JACK-IN-THE-PULPIT

(Arisaema triphyllum) This common biennial grows to 3 feet tall and produces bright red clusters of berries.

HIGHBUSH BLACKBERRY
(Rubus allegh"eniensis")
This bramble produces a delectable fruit that is popular food for wildlife.

JAMES E. EDMONDS BACKCOUNTRY TRAIL

[Fig. 40(4)] 7.2 miles. Along this trail there are two patches of hemlock forest and more extensive areas of red oak–rhododendron in moist places, with mountain laurel replacing rhododendron in drier locations. Where the rhododendron is thin, large patches of evergreen galax, or coltsfoot, are present.

A short side trail leads hikers to the summit of 3,162-foot Lookoff Mountain, the northernmost peak in the park. Several granite cliffs are visible from the trail, and the scenic overlook on Lookoff Mountain [Fig. 40(1)] is atop a similar outcrop. Cliff faces drop several hundred feet straight down, and granite surfaces are often surprisingly slippery. Hikers are cautioned to remain on the trail and not be tempted to explore more closely these beautiful, but potentially deadly, cliff faces.

While the name "Greasy Creek" may not be particularly poetic, the section of trail that follows this mountain stream is nonetheless very scenic, with numerous small shoals and cascades framed with rhododendron and hemlock.

ADA-HI FALLS TRAIL

[Fig. 40(11)] .2 mile. *Ada-Hi* (pronounced Uh-dah`he) is the Cherokee word for "forest." This hike begins in the most common natural environment in the park—a deciduous hardwood slope forest dominated by red, chestnut, and white oaks. This forest then phases into a red oak–rhododendron environment with huge patches of the evergreen galax in open places. The trail ends in a cove of tulip poplars at a wooden overlook platform which allows hikers to view the falls safely and easily.

Because Ada-Hi Falls is located so high in the Taylor Creek watershed, the falls are small; during extended periods of dry weather the flow of water diminishes to a trickle. Even so, with dense thickets of rhododendron arching over the trail and colorful displays of wildflowers to view, most hikers find the trail quite enjoyable.

Map References: DNR Black Rock State Park map.

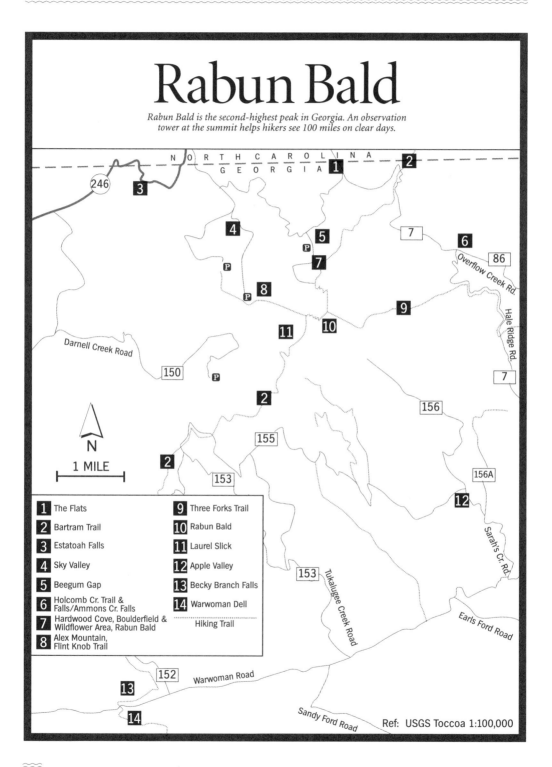

Rabun Bald

Rabun Bald is the second-highest peak in Georgia. An observation tower at the summit helps hikers see 100 miles on clear days.

NORTH CAROLINA
GEORGIA

246

Overflow Creek Rd.

Hale Ridge Rd.

Darnell Creek Road

150

N

1 MILE

155

153

156

156A

1 The Flats
2 Bartram Trail
3 Estatoah Falls
4 Sky Valley
5 Beegum Gap
6 Holcomb Cr. Trail & Falls/Ammons Cr. Falls
7 Hardwood Cove, Boulderfield & Wildflower Area, Rabun Bald
8 Alex Mountain, Flint Knob Trail

9 Three Forks Trail
10 Rabun Bald
11 Laurel Slick
12 Apple Valley
13 Becky Branch Falls
14 Warwoman Dell

....
Hiking Trail

153

Tulalugee Creek Road

Sarah's Cr. Rd.

152

Warwoman Road

Earls Ford Road

Sandy Ford Road

Ref: USGS Toccoa 1:100,000

Rabun Bald

Rabun Bald (4,696 feet) [Fig. 41(10)] is the second-highest peak in Georgia; only Brasstown Bald (4,784 feet) is higher. An observation tower on the summit provides hikers with what many people believe is the most spectacular view from any one point in the Georgia mountains. Into the Georgia and South Carolina Piedmont, views on clear days extend for more than 100 miles. In other directions, the views of the Blue Ridge, Nantahala, Cowee, and Great Smoky mountains are outstanding.

Rabun Bald's main ridgeline, which is indicated by the Bartram Trail on the map, is the Eastern Continental Divide, dividing waters draining northward into the Tennessee/Mississippi Gulf system from those draining southward to the Atlantic Ocean. Most of Rabun Bald's streams are located on the mountain's southeast flank and drain via Warwoman Creek to the Chattooga River, then to the Savannah River, and finally to the Atlantic.

The Rabun Bald area rates among Georgia's leading botanical sites; spring wildflowers are exceptional. Near the summit is a zone of dwarf oak heath (mainly scarlet oak and purple rhododendron). Look for the striking red berries of mountain ash. In some places there is a thick ground cover of blueberries. Together with the Chattooga River to the southeast and the Cowee Mountains to the north, the region is a prime habitat for deer, black bear, wild boar, and, reportedly, even mountain lion.

Directions: Take US 441 north from Clayton for 1 mile past Dillard; turn right onto GA 246 toward Highlands, NC; continue on GA 246 and NC 106 for 7 miles; turn right onto Hale Ridge Road (FS 7), which is beside the Scaly Post Office; go 2.1 miles and take the right fork (FS 7 goes left); go 1.3 miles and take a left fork on a steep dirt road toward Beegum Gap [Fig. 41(5)]; after 1.6 miles, park and walk 2 miles to Rabun Bald. There is an observation platform on the summit. Note the northern hardwood cove, boulderfield, and wildflower area [Fig. 41(7)].

SCENIC DRIVES
WARWOMAN ROAD. A scenic drive which follows Warwoman Shear, a geologic "path" that provided Indians and early settlers in the region with their principal east-west trading route.

Directions: From US 441 in Clayton, go east at the light where US 76 turns left.
TUKALUGEE CREEK ROAD (FS 156) AND SARAH'S CREEK ROAD. [Fig. 41] All-weather roads providing a 10-mile scenic loop drive. Gate closed December through March.

DARNELL CREEK ROAD (FS 150). [Fig. 41] This scenic drive is especially pretty after leaf fall, when cascading Darnell Creek and surrounding mountains are more visible. The all-weather road is rough in spots, but certainly passable. While travel is not limited to trucks or four-wheel-drive vehicles, cars with low ground clearance should be driven with care.

OVERFLOW CREEK ROAD (FS 86). [Fig. 41] This very scenic, all-weather road is open year-round. The lower sections of the road run parallel to the West Fork of the Chattooga River, providing access at several places for fishermen, hikers, and campers.

SANDY FORD ROAD. [Fig. 41] One of only two unpaved road access points to the Chattooga River on the Georgia side (Earl's Ford, below, being the other). Good canoe put-in point for Section III of the river. Not a four-wheel-drive road, but difficult in bad weather.

EARL'S FORD ROAD. [Fig. 41] Old county road that once provided major access from South Carolina to Georgia by crossing the Chattooga River. It parallels and crosses Warwoman Road. Four-wheel-drive vehicle is advisable.

POINTS OF INTEREST

WARWOMAN DELL. [Fig. 41(14)] This recreation area was developed in the 1930s by the Civilian Conservation Corps. Cuts of the old Blue Ridge Railroad can be found here. This railroad was partially constructed but never operated before the Civil War. An interpretive trail with 25 numbered posts and an accompanying pamphlet identify many plants common to the region. Several rare ferns, including the walking fern, are found in the area.

BOG TURTLE
(Clemmys muhlenbergi)
This turtle is only 4
inches long.

Facilities: 2 picnic pavilions, outdoor restrooms with facilities for handicapped.

Dates: Open Memorial Day–Labor Day. Gate locked Fri. and Sat. at dark.

APPLE VALLEY. [Fig. 41(12)] Popular, dispersed camping and fishing area managed by the U.S. Forest Service. Sarah's Creek is heavily stocked with trout. Off GA 246.

SKY VALLEY. [Fig. 41(4)] Georgia's highest valley (3,100 feet), Sky Valley, is one of the highest incorporated cities in the eastern United States, with elevations inside the city limits exceeding 4,200 feet. Sky Valley Resort includes an 18-hole golf course, swimming pool, restaurant, and condominiums, as well as year-round and rental homes. Sky Valley is best known as Georgia's only ski area, with runs up to 2,200 feet in length and a vertical drop of 250 feet. A rope tow serves the "bunny hill," and a double chairlift serves intermediate and advanced slopes. Located just off GA 246.

ALEX MOUNTAIN, FLINT KNOB TRAIL. [Fig. 41(8)] From the summit of 4,080-foot Alex Mountain are good vistas to the west and southeast. A Georgia Power microwave tower is located on the northern end of the mountain.

Directions: From Flint Gap on the Bartram Trail, or take the Sky Valley Exit from

GA 246 and take either the Alex Mountain or Flint Knob forks.

THE FLATS. [Fig. 41(1)] A remarkable, high, flat area forming the western rim of the Highland Plateau. Formerly this was the location of a number of unique peat bogs. Among the rarest of mountain environments, these bogs occur at the heads of valleys where seeps and springs keep the soil consistently wet and produce rare plants such as bog laurel, swamp pink, and cotton grass. Unfortunately, most of the bogs here have been drained or bulldozed.

Directions: *See* Alex Mountain, Flint Knob Trail (*above*).

LAUREL SLICK. [Fig. 41(11)] Very dense thickets of rhododendron are found at the 4,000-foot level of Rabun Bald's southwestern flank.

🌿 WATERFALLS

BECKY BRANCH FALLS. [Fig. 41(13)] This 20-foot-high cascade is reached by a .25-mile trail that crosses Warwoman Road just upstream from the Warwoman Dell Recreation Area.

ESTATOAH FALLS. [Fig. 41(3)] This wide falls, located just inside the western city limits of Sky Valley, is best viewed from GA 246, approximately 1 mile east of Dillard.

HOLCOMB CREEK TRAIL AND FALLS AND AMMONS CREEK FALLS. [Fig. 41(6)] The .5-mile trail to Holcomb Creek Falls and Ammons Creek Falls is rated easy to moderate. At .3 mile, the very impressive Holcomb Creek Falls, approximately 120 feet in height, comes into view from a footbridge over the creek. The trail continues approximately .2 mile to Ammons Creek Falls, where an observation deck allows easy viewing.

Directions: Take Warwoman Road east from Clayton for 10 miles. Turn left (north) on FS 7 (Hale Ridge Road), or south on Hale Ridge Road from NC 106, and go 9 miles.

🌿 HIKING TRAILS

THREE FORKS TRAIL. [Fig. 41(9)] 9.5 miles from Rabun Bald to Holcomb Creek, or 1.4 miles from John Teague Gap to Holcomb Creek. While the Three Forks Trail originates on Rabun Bald, it is most often hiked from John Teague Gap (*see* page 196).

BARTRAM TRAIL. [Fig. 41(2)] This National Recreational Trail stretches from the Georgia/North Carolina line over the summit of Rabun Bald to the Chattooga River. It is named for William Bartram, a naturalist who explored and wrote about this area in the 1770s. *See* Long Trails, Bartram Trail, page 245.

Directions: Take US 441 north from Clayton for 1 mile past Dillard; turn right onto GA 246 toward Highlands, NC. Continue on GA 246 and NC 106 for 7 miles, then turn right onto Hale Ridge Road; go 2.1 miles, then take FS 7 for 1.1 miles.

Map References: USGS 1:24,000 series: Rabun Bald.

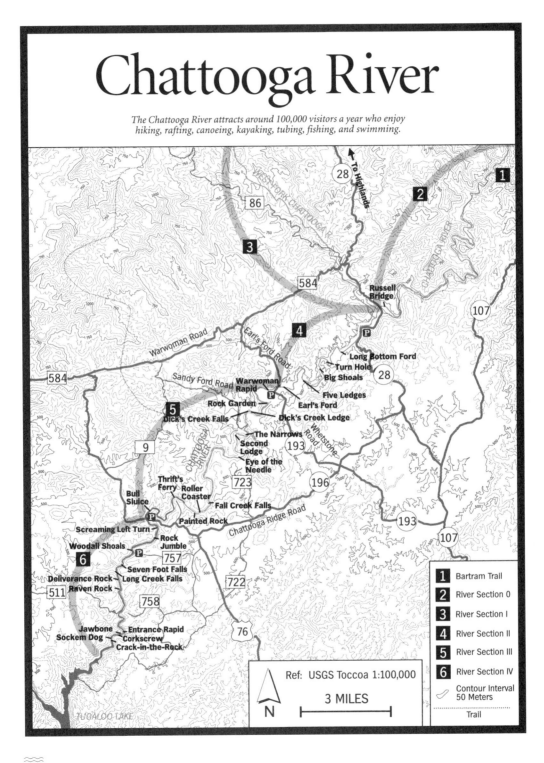

Chattooga River

The Chattooga River attracts around 100,000 visitors a year who enjoy hiking, rafting, canoeing, kayaking, tubing, fishing, and swimming.

28 To Highlands

WEST FORK CHATTOOGA R.

86

CHATTOOGA RIVER

1

2

3

584

Russell Bridge

107

Warwoman Road

Earls Ford Road

4

P

Long Bottom Ford
Turn Hole
Big Shoals

584

Sandy Ford Road

Warwoman Rapid P

Five Ledges

28

Rock Garden

Earl's Ford

5

Dick's Creek Ledge

Dick's Creek Falls

Whetstone Road

9

The Narrows
Second Lodge

193

Eye of the Needle

CHATTOOGA RIVER

Thrift's Ferry

Roller Coaster

723

196

Bull Sluice

Fall Creek Falls

P

Painted Rock

Chattooga Ridge Road

193

Screaming Left Turn

Rock Jumble

107

Woodall Shoals

P

757

6

Seven Foot Falls
Long Creek Falls

758

722

Deliverance Rock
Raven Rock

511

Jawbone
Sockem Dog

Entrance Rapid
Corkscrew
Crack-in-the-Rock

76

1	Bartram Trail
2	River Section 0
3	River Section I
4	River Section II
5	River Section III
6	River Section IV
	Contour Interval 50 Meters
	Trail

Ref: USGS Toccoa 1:100,000

3 MILES

N

TUGALOO LAKE

The Chattooga River

The Chattooga River is the crown jewel of southern whitewater rivers and a symbol for wilderness river lovers throughout the United States and Canada. Its high rainfall, unusual geology (with many cliffs, gorges, and waterfalls), and steep gradient place it in the "world class" category of rivers. Most remaining rivers of the Chattooga's quality are tucked away in western gorges or West Virginia mountains. The river is arguably the area's prime single natural attraction, luring some 100,000 visitors a year for hiking, rafting, canoeing, kayaking, tubing, fishing, swimming, or plain and simple river watching.

Headwaters of the Chattooga are in the Nantahala National Forest and private lands in North Carolina. Flowing southward out of North Carolina, they form approximately 40 river miles of boundary between Georgia and South Carolina. The river drops from approximately 3,000 feet elevation at its headwaters to 950 feet at its termination into Lake Tugalo. It is under the control and protection of the Sumter National Forest in South Carolina, the Chattahoochee National Forest in Georgia, and the Nantahala National Forest in North Carolina.

The names of the river's rapids and other landmarks bear witness to the area's early inhabitants. Indian names translated into English have become Sock'em Dog, Shoulder Bone, and Cutting Bone Creek. Local settlers' humor shows in the names of two feeder creeks—Bad Creek and Worse Creek—both now covered by Lake Tugalo. Between those two streams is Sinking Mountain, named because of the instability of the soil and underlying decayed rock.

The Chattooga was designated a National Wild and Scenic River by Congress in May of 1974. As a result, no motorized vehicles are allowed within a .25 mile of its banks. In addition, man-made facilities are minimal, consisting primarily of maintained hiking trails. Primitive toilet facilities and water are available at camping areas. As a result of the minimal disturbance by man, the Chattooga and its corridor provide a clean, litter-free hiking or rafting experience. However, the growth in population in the mountain areas and resulting activities could pose a multifaceted danger to the river in the future.

The Chattooga is divided into five sections, Section 0–Section IV. Section 0 includes the entire headwaters region from Whiteside Mountain southward to Russell Bridge (GA 28). Sections I–IV cover the portions of the river open to boating, including the West Fork (Section 1) southward to Section IV and the river's end at Lake Tugalo.

EASTERN
CRAYFISH
(Cambarus bartonii)

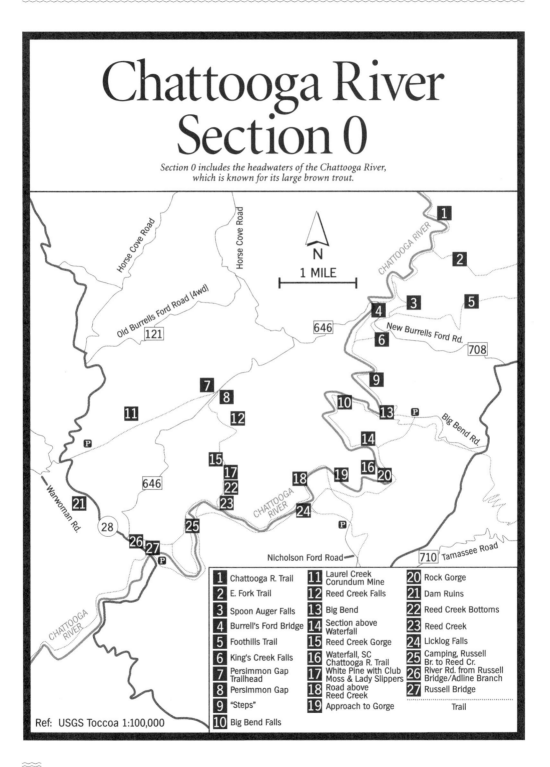

Chattooga River Section 0

Section 0 includes the headwaters of the Chattooga River, which is known for its large brown trout.

Horse Cove Road

Horse Cove Road

N

1 MILE

CHATTOOGA RIVER

Old Burrells Ford Road (4wd)

121

646

New Burrells Ford Rd.

708

Big Bend Rd.

Warwoman Rd.

646

CHATTOOGA RIVER

28

Nicholson Ford Road

710 Tamassee Road

CHATTOOGA RIVER

1 Chattooga R. Trail	11 Laurel Creek Corundum Mine	20 Rock Gorge
2 E. Fork Trail	12 Reed Creek Falls	21 Dam Ruins
3 Spoon Auger Falls	13 Big Bend	22 Reed Creek Bottoms
4 Burrell's Ford Bridge	14 Section above Waterfall	23 Reed Creek
5 Foothills Trail	15 Reed Creek Gorge	24 Licklog Falls
6 King's Creek Falls	16 Waterfall, SC Chattooga R. Trail	25 Camping, Russell Br. to Reed Cr.
7 Persimmon Gap Trailhead	17 White Pine with Club Moss & Lady Slippers	26 River Rd. from Russell Bridge/Adline Branch
8 Persimmon Gap	18 Road above Reed Creek	27 Russell Bridge
9 "Steps"	19 Approach to Gorge	········ Trail
10 Big Bend Falls		

Ref: USGS Toccoa 1:100,000

Section 0–The Headwaters

ACCESS TO RIVER CROSSINGS

BURRELL'S FORD BRIDGE. [Fig. 43(4), Fig. 48(11)] FS 646 begins .5 mile west of Russell Bridge (GA 28). Follow FS 646 for approximately 5.5 miles to Burrell's Ford Bridge. *See* Ellicott Rock section, Foothills Trail (page 210); Spoon Auger Falls (page 211); and King's Creek Falls (page 211).

BULL PEN BRIDGE. [Fig. 48(2), Fig. 50(6)] Follow SC 107 south from the intersection of US 64 in Cashiers, North Carolina. Turn west on Bull Pen Road and follow it to the bridge. *See* Highlands section, Horse Cove Road and Bull Pen Road, (page 216).

HIKING TRAILS AND ACCESS POINTS

CHATTOOGA RIVER TRAIL. The southern end of the Chattooga River Trail begins in Georgia in the parking area at the west end of the US 76 bridge [Fig. 42] and continues north for 10 miles, where it intersects and combines with the Bartram Trail. The combined trails continue another 10 miles to the GA 28 bridge, where the hiker must cross the bridge and pick up the trails on the South Carolina side. At a point 3.7 miles above the bridge, the Bartram Trail branches off to the east with the Foothills Trail, while the Chattooga River Trail joins with the Foothills Trail and parallels the river closely for another 6.7 miles to Burrell's Ford Campground and Burrell's Ford Road. In this section trails split and come together again many times; a trail map is useful. One-half mile north of Burrell's Ford Road, the trail enters the Ellicott Rock Wilderness. Here the hiker must register. The Foothills Trail branches off to the east at this point and the trail to Ellicott Rock continues upstream for 2.1 miles, where it joins with the East Fork Trail and continues 2.5 miles to Walhalla Fish Hatchery. The East Fork Trail continues 1.7 miles upstream to Ellicott Rock where Georgia, North Carolina, and South Carolina's boundaries meet [Fig. 48(5), Fig. 50(9)]. Ellicott Rock can also be reached by foot from North Carolina (*see* Ellicott Rock Wilderness, page 209). The only camping area with restroom and water facilities is the Burrell's Ford Campground. Other camping areas are primitive, and in some areas in the Ellicott Rock Wilderness camping is forbidden.

THE CHATTOOGA ABOVE BULL PEN ROAD. The upper Chattooga River harbors some of the river's most scenic and rugged stretches. Closed to boats, the area must be reached by foot.

This section of the river is known for the steep, remote Chattooga Cliffs [Fig. 50(3)] and for a small gorge area called the Upper Narrows. Both areas can be reached from the Bull Pen Road Bridge [Fig. 48(2), Fig. 50(6)], known locally as the "metal" or "government" bridge. It is recommended that the hiker have a car waiting at the bridge before beginning the walk upstream. Major access points are Bull Pen

Road and primitive roads off Whiteside Cove Road. Both Bull Pen Road and Whiteside Cove Road are gravel and accessible by car.

Along this stretch the Chattooga is narrow and wild. Farther upriver, the grade is relatively flat, but the adjacent cliffs and overhangs provide constant interest. Here the rare Biltmore sedge, a northern club moss, and forests of giant mountain laurel up to 30 feet tall are present at the base of the cliffs. Farther downstream one reaches the Upper Narrows, where the rushing water is compressed into a stream about 6 feet wide. Only the most skilled rock climber can maneuver through the gorge. For a safer route, it is recommended that the hiker walk the gorge's edge. Downstream from the Upper Narrows, a loop trail is reached. This trail consists of a lower and upper section. The lower section affords good views of the boulder-strewn gorge which is found just upstream from the Bull Pen Road Bridge. Car-sized boulders and unusual potholes are present, as well as several nice swimming pools.

Below the bridge the river is less scenic but still worth the visit. Two trails off Bull Pen Road lead to Ellicott Rock.

THE CHATTOOGA HEADWATERS FROM GA 28, BURRELL'S FORD BRIDGE TO RUSSELL BRIDGE. [Fig. 48(11)] Unlike some parts of the river, this section is relatively accessible. Old log roads up the East Fork and the splendid trail up the entire South Carolina side afford all degrees of hiking and fishing experiences (*see* Ellicott Rock section, page 209).

While the river itself is not constant whitewater, areas are breathtakingly wild and scenic. The area between the Big Bend [Fig. 43(10)] and Lick Log Falls [Fig. 43(24)] is a challenge for the most intrepid fisherman, since there are no riverside trails. Crossing the river back and forth is essential and is risky in winter and spring high water. The wild isolation of the Rock Gorge [Fig. 43(20)] and the magnificence of the Big Bend Falls make it worthwhile. Prior to the construction of FS 646 (New Burrell's Ford Road), major accesses were at the Russell Bridge [Fig. 43(27), Fig. 44(29)] and from SC 28 near Big Creek (Old Burrell's Ford Road, 7 miles of torturous mountain road). This was part of the "mystery river" (*see* West Fork section, page 195), the area known for large brown trout. The river is open for fishing year-round.

For easy hiking and fishing, the section of the Chattooga between Russell Bridge and Reed Creek [Fig. 43(23), Fig. 44(26)] is hard to beat, for there is a trail (or log road) on either side. At the north side of the Russell Bridge, one looks out over a marsh with ponds and wood-duck boxes. This was the old Whitmire place, formerly a fertile cornfield. When it was acquired by the Forest Service, beavers promptly dammed up Mose Branch, creating a marsh dominated by alder shrub, sedges, and marsh grasses. One can go up the river by climbing down the bridge riprap or, more easily but less speedily, by taking the (gated) first road [Fig. 43(26), Fig. 44(28)] that turns off west of the bridge. About a mile up this road (1.75 miles by river) are some beautiful pools and camping places [Fig. 43(25), Fig. 44(27)]. Farther on there is an old field, called Reed Creek Bottoms, planted in loblolly pine [Fig. 43(22), Fig.

44(25)], which is rare in the mountains unless planted. Here one can turn up a trail on the west side of the field that leads up Reed Creek. Soon there will appear one of the most beautiful stands of white pine in north Georgia, with abundant patches of club moss and pink lady slippers [Fig. 43(17), Fig. 44(24)]. Farther on one enters Reed Creek Gorge [Fig. 43(15), Fig. 44(22)]. There are no trails in this section. The cascades, falls, and pools are extremely scenic and not too difficult to negotiate. With luck the visitor will see the highest of the falls, Reed Creek Falls [Fig. 43(12), Fig. 44(21)], before a more tranquil section leading up to Persimmon Gap [Fig. 43(8), Fig. 44(19)].

On the main river above Reed Creek there is more entrancing scenery, especially beginning at Lick Log Falls [Fig. 43(24)]. This area is most easily reached from the old Nicholson Ford Road. Above this, around a long "square" bend, the road is fairly high above the river [Fig. 43(18)]. The observant visitor may see signs of wild hogs rooting. This is truly backcountry, in spite of the old log roads that turn up the mountain, skipping the rock gorge entirely. On the approach to the gorge [Fig. 43(19)] one may see the beautiful mountain camellia, whose large, white blossoms appear in late summer. This is a plant found in streamside zones and on most bluffs.

It is difficult to negotiate the gorge [Fig. 43(20)], even with nonslip shoe soles. This can be a dangerous section. Towering cliffs appear, and the only way out is at least 1 mile farther upstream, reached by wading and rock hopping. Where the main Chattooga River Trail on the South Carolina side comes down to the river after going high around the gorge, there is a waterfall with a beautiful falls and pool below [Fig. 43(16)]. Although unnamed, this falls and the section above it [Fig. 43(14)] are alone worth the trip. At the next huge pool upstream there is a trail leading up to an east-west ridge. Big Bend Road leads off to SC 107, the easiest access to the river above the rock gorge. Above this pool (and branch) is another 1.5-mile section that has no trail. The main trail cuts across a ridge and comes down just above Big Bend Falls [Fig. 43(10)]. A side trip down to the falls is worth the exertion. At the Big Bend [Fig. 43(13)], one will see pieces of truck axle sticking out of the rock, evidence of a former logging bridge. As unlikely as it may seem, trucks with light loads were able to haul logs up the steep ridge on the South Carolina side, now an access trail. Farther upstream, the remaining several miles of river up the "Steps" [Fig. 43(9)] are a pleasant, beautiful riverside hike, with more whitewater and fewer huge pools than above Burrell's Ford Bridge.

CANOEING AND BOATING
All boating is prohibited upstream of the GA 28 bridge [Fig. 43(25), Fig. 44(29)].

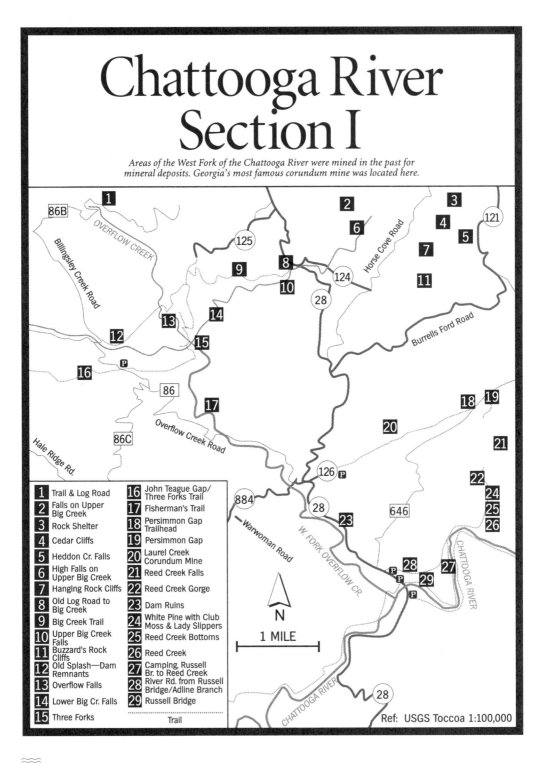

Chattooga River Section I

Areas of the West Fork of the Chattooga River were mined in the past for mineral deposits. Georgia's most famous corundum mine was located here.

1	Trail & Log Road	16	John Teague Gap/Three Forks Trail
2	Falls on Upper Big Creek	17	Fisherman's Trail
3	Rock Shelter	18	Persimmon Gap Trailhead
4	Cedar Cliffs	19	Persimmon Gap
5	Heddon Cr. Falls	20	Laurel Creek Corundum Mine
6	High Falls on Upper Big Creek	21	Reed Creek Falls
7	Hanging Rock Cliffs	22	Reed Creek Gorge
8	Old Log Road to Big Creek	23	Dam Ruins
9	Big Creek Trail	24	White Pine with Club Moss & Lady Slippers
10	Upper Big Creek Falls	25	Reed Creek Bottoms
11	Buzzard's Rock Cliffs	26	Reed Creek
12	Old Splash—Dam Remnants	27	Camping, Russell Br. to Reed Creek
13	Overflow Falls	28	River Rd. from Russell Bridge/Adline Branch
14	Lower Big Cr. Falls	29	Russell Bridge
15	Three Forks		

Trail

N

1 MILE

Ref: USGS Toccoa 1:100,000

Section I–The West Fork

The West Fork of the Chattooga River begins at Three Forks [Fig. 44(15)], the intersection of Holcomb, Overflow, and Big creeks. From there the West Fork flows 7 miles to the southeast to meet with the Chattooga. The entire West Fork, plus 1 mile upstream along Overflow Creek, is included within the boundaries of the Chattooga National Wild and Scenic River.

The upper portion of the West Fork is one of the most beautiful river sites in Georgia—a river of low falls and deep green pools hemmed in by bluffs and steep forested slopes. From Overflow Creek Road bridge down to the junction with the Chattooga, the river is relatively calm with long, deep pools ideal for lazy floating or swimming. Fine picnic and strolling sites are accessible and reached by road.

This is a country of beautiful but unknown waterfalls. One is on Overflow creek just above Three Forks. There are three falls on Big Creek; the middle one is outstanding. It is along the West Fork's headwaters that the last remnants of the old splash-dam logging system can be seen.

Formerly, Old Burrell's Ford Road offered the only former access to the Chattooga's East Fork, which, in the 1940s, was discovered to be Georgia's famed "mystery river." Large brown trout kept turning up, but no one would reveal their source until it was found that the inaccessibility of both the East and West forks had protected a remarkable fishing resource.

The West Fork is also an area rich in mining lore. The ultrabasic deposits along the lower river below Pine Mountain have yielded asbestos and soapstone and were the site of Georgia's most famous corundum mine at Laurel Creek. Most maps show that Laurel Creek, Reed Creek, and Warwoman Valley form one of north Georgia's most remarkable geologic features, a straight line or lineament, the "Warwoman Shear," that continues to control topography as far west as Tray Mountain.

After float logging divested the West Fork of much of its hardwood timber, white pine seeded in. Abundant by 1950, it was subsequently harvested, this time via log roads.

Directions: From US 441 in Clayton where US 76 turns west, turn east onto paved Warwoman Road; once on Warwoman, turn right (not hard right) at the stop sign; proceed past the Georgia Power building; follow Warwoman Road for about 14 miles to the intersection with Overflow Creek Road (FS 86). From Highlands, North Carolina, take NC 28 south to the intersection of Warwoman Road; turn right onto Overflow Creek Road (FS 86). Beaver dams can be seen below the road.

ACCESS TO RIVER CROSSINGS

WARWOMAN ROAD BRIDGE. Follow Warwoman Road 14 miles east from Clayton.

OVERFLOW CREEK ROAD BRIDGE. Follow Warwoman Road 14 miles east from Clayton. Cross the West Fork, then turn left onto FS 86 (Overflow Creek Road) and follow approximately 1.3 miles to a one-lane bridge.

🞖 HIKING TRAILS AND ACCESS POINTS

JOHN TEAGUE GAP AND THREE FORKS TRAIL. [Fig. 44(16)] While the Three Forks Trail originates on Rabun Bald (*see* page 187), it is most often hiked from John Teague Gap. From there it gently descends through a forest typical for the area—oak-hickory slope forest with scattered patches of white pines. At .7 mile the path crosses the blue-blazed boundary of the Chattooga National Wild and Scenic River. Three-tenths of a mile farther, it dips to a three-way intersection with an old jeep road. Here the Three Forks Trail, occasionally blazed with white diamonds, turns left and heads downhill following the road to a slab of bedrock overlooking a cascade on Holcomb Creek. This is the end of the designated trail. The remainder of the route down this gorge is on the north side of Holcomb Creek (cross the creek) down a ravine with potholes and falls that reach all the way to Three Forks (about .25 mile). It is not difficult bushwhacking, but one must pick a path through hemlock-rhododendron heath which, along with white pine, forms the bulk of the streamside zone of vegetation.

Directions: Take Warwoman Road east from Clayton for 16 miles to Overflow Creek Road (FS 86); turn left (northwest) and go 4 miles to John Teague Gap.

FISHERMAN'S TRAIL. [Fig. 44(17)] The trail passes rock shelters and cliffs harboring colonies of wood rats.

Directions: Upstream on north side of West Fork from where FS 86 crosses West Fork.

OLD SPLASH DAM REMNANTS. [Fig. 44(12)] Around the turn of the century, loggers in this area built what were termed "splash dams" across creeks like Holcomb and Overflow. Cut logs were dragged down to the creeks and backed up behind the dam. At a prearranged signal, dams on several creeks were broken at one time, sending water and logs raging down the stream. Called "float logging," this method was used to harvest many of the slope forests, including streamside hemlocks. Logs from the West Fork were destined for Madison, South Carolina.

Directions: About .25 mile below where Billingsley Creek Road crosses Holcomb Creek. Cross the bridge and go down the north side of the creek.

BILLINGSLEY CREEK ROAD. Built by the Forest Service so that Overflow Creek watershed could be logged.

TRAIL AND LOG ROAD. [Fig. 44(1)] Joins with Blue Valley and Clear Creek road system.

THREE FORKS. [Fig. 44(15)] The intersection of Holcomb Creek, Overflow Creek, and Big Creek divides the forest landscape into four neat quadrants and rewards determined hikers with the light, sound, and color of one of the most delightful scenes in Georgia. Other than by the Three Forks Trail route (*see* above),

Three Forks can be reached via GA 28. *See* directions to High Falls on Upper Big Creek, *below*.

OVERFLOW FALLS. [Fig. 44(13)] Waterfall about .5 mile above Three Forks.

LOWER BIG CREEK FALLS. [Fig. 44(14)] Waterfall on Big Creek [Fig. 44(9)] and Upper Falls on Big Creek [Fig. 44(10)]. Old log road [Fig. 44(8)] provides a good hike to Big Creek.

FALLS ON UPPER BIG CREEK. [Fig. 44(2)]

HIGH FALLS ON UPPER BIG CREEK. [Fig. 44(6)]

Directions: Proceed on GA 28 to Satolah, Georgia, at the bridge over Big Creek. Just north of the bridge, turn off and park on the west side of the highway. Find a Forest Service log road which crosses a little branch immediately, and follow this

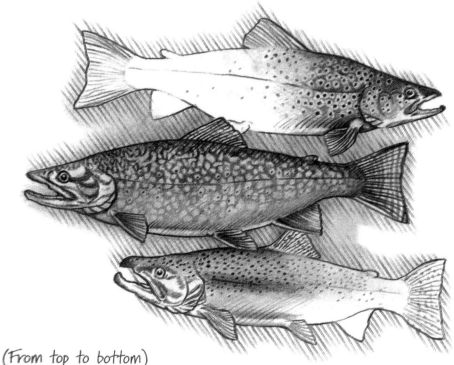

(From top to bottom)
BROWN TROUT (Salmo trutta)
BROOK TROUT (Salvelinus fontinalus)
RAINBOW TROUT (Oncorhynchus mykiss)
The brook trout is the only fish of these three that
is native to the Appalachians; the others are stocked.

easy, graded road all the way to Three Forks. The middle and upper Big Creek Falls can be found either by walking the creek or by listening for their roar. The lower Big Creek Falls is a rugged series of cascades that plummets all the way to Three Forks and is only for hardy adventurers.

BURRELL'S FORD ROADS. In the 1940s reports filtered out of the north Georgia mountains of giant brown trout from a "mystery river." Eventually it was discovered that the mystery river was the Chattooga above Burrell's Ford, reached from Georgia only by Old Burrell's Ford Road (FS 121) [Fig. 43], which turns east off GA 28. The new Burrell's Ford Road (FS 646) turns north off GA 28 just before the Russell Bridge.

RIVER OTTER
(Lutra canadensis)
Sociable animals, river otters wrestle, play tag, and roll around riverbanks and in water. Their streamlined bodies, webbed toes, and eyes and ears that can be closed underwater make them well suited for life in and around water.

BUZZARD'S ROCK CLIFFS [Fig. 44(11)], **HANGING ROCK CLIFFS** [Fig. 44(7)], and **CEDAR CLIFFS** [Fig. 44(4)]. These are a series of high cliffs reached only by bushwhacking. Georgia's only location for sand myrtle is found on Cedar Cliffs. These cliffs are adorned with a picturesque spike moss, which forms thick, photogenic mats with twisted, hairlike spines. On Cedar Cliff Mountain is a rock shelter [Fig. 44(3)] containing evidence of both goats and the rare wood rat.

HEDDON CREEK FALLS. [Fig. 44(5)] This falls on Heddon Creek Road is accessible only by four-wheel drive. Just beyond the falls is a flat, swampy area, the site of a shrub bog.

Directions: Take FS 121 east off GA 28 about 2 miles south of Big Creek Bridge. About 4 miles down FS 121 the road fords Heddon Creek. To reach the falls, turn left up the creek.

LAUREL CREEK CORUNDUM MINE. [Fig. 43(11), Fig. 44(20)] Georgia's most famous corundum mine, unworked since 1894 when a huge block of peridotite fell, closing the tunnels. In addition to corundum, which is the second hardest mineral (only diamond is harder) and is used in the manufacture of abrasives for grinding and smoothing, the mine produced excellent specimens of blue and red corundum, though seldom of ruby and sapphire quality.

The peridotite outcrop covers several hundred acres including two rough, barren hills. The owners of the private land at the road terminus have not objected to hikers and parking. The trail can also be reached at the opposite end from Persimmon Gap on New Burrell's Ford Road (FS 646).

Directions: Laurel Creek is the first creek crossed going south from the junction of Warwoman Road and GA 28. After crossing the creek (about 1 mile), turn east.

PERSIMMON GAP TRAILHEAD. [Fig. 43(7), Fig. 44(18)]

DAM RUINS. [Fig. 43(21), Fig. 44(23)] Water was dammed to power a turbine which turned machinery for milling asbestos ore. The ore came from a mine just across the river on Dockins' Mountain. A nearby soapstone deposit at Adline Branch [Fig. 43(26), Fig. 44(28)] was cut into blocks with crosscut saws and used to build the blacksmith forge at the Laurel Creek Corundum Mine and to line local fireplaces.

CANOEING AND BOATING

The lower section of the West Fork, from Overflow Creek Road Bridge to the junction with the Chattooga, is a slow-moving, gentle stream suitable for the novice canoeist. Two Class II rapids, Dam Sluice and Big Slide, provide excitement for the beginner. The take-out is at Long Bottom Ford [Fig. 45(3)].

Map References: USGS 1:24,000 series: Satolah–Tamassee.

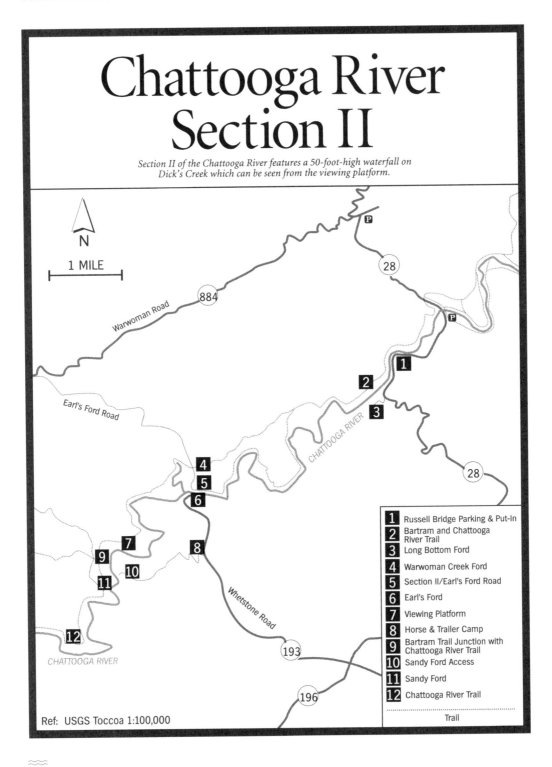

Chattooga River Section II

Section II of the Chattooga River features a 50-foot-high waterfall on Dick's Creek which can be seen from the viewing platform.

N

1 MILE

Warwoman Road

884

28

Earl's Ford Road

CHATTOOGA RIVER

28

Whetstone Road

193

196

CHATTOOGA RIVER

1 Russell Bridge Parking & Put-In
2 Bartram and Chattooga River Trail
3 Long Bottom Ford
4 Warwoman Creek Ford
5 Section II/Earl's Ford Road
6 Earl's Ford
7 Viewing Platform
8 Horse & Trailer Camp
9 Bartram Trail Junction with Chattooga River Trail
10 Sandy Ford Access
11 Sandy Ford
12 Chattooga River Trail

Trail

Ref: USGS Toccoa 1:100,000

Sections II, III, and IV

These sections of the Chattooga accommodate those who enjoy the thrills of whitewater boating or watching others negotiate dangerous rapids. On the Georgia side of the river, a good hiking trail, the Chattooga River Trail, later joined by the Bartram Trail, parallels the river between the US 76 and SC 28 bridges. Below US 76 there are very limited trails along the river, and the gorge is navigable only by floating. At normal water levels, Section III is a good Class III run. At low water, outfitters avoid Section III and run Section IV, which extends from the US 76 bridge downriver to Lake Tugalo.

▓ ACCESS TO RIVER CROSSINGS

RUSSELL BRIDGE. [Fig. 44(29), Fig. 45(1)] Follow Warwoman Road 14 miles east from Clayton, cross the West Fork of the Chattooga, and go to the junction with GA 28. Turn right (south) on GA 28 and go approximately 3 miles to the bridge.

HIGHWAY 76 BRIDGE. [Fig. 47(3), Fig. 46(21)] Located 9 miles east of Clayton on US 76. This is the take-out for Section III and put-in for Section IV.

▓ ACCESS TO RIVER

RUSSELL BRIDGE, LONG BOTTOM FORD PUT-INS. On SC 28, 1.25 miles south of the Russell Bridge is a parking and put-in area [Fig. 45(1)]. One-half mile below here a dirt road turns off south to Long Bottom Ford [Fig. 45(3)], where a low-water bridge and ford were the major river crossings for the early settlers around Pine Mountain on the West Fork. Boaters can put in here. Most cars can travel the road.

SOUTH CAROLINA ACCESS TO EARL'S FORD AND SANDY FORD. Downstream, Earl's Ford is the next point of access. At Mountain Rest, about 3.75 miles, turn right (south) on FS 196 and go 3.25 miles to a four-way stop at Whetstone; turn right (west) and go off pavement at 1.75 miles on a good gravel road for 1.25 miles. There is a camp specially designed to accommodate horses and horse trailers, and from it radiate horse trails that explore the area [Fig. 45(8), Fig. 46(4)]. If one turns left here on FS 721A, in 1.25 miles the river corridor is reached, and a trail leads .25 mile to the river. This is the Sandy Ford access [Fig. 45(10), Fig. 46(8)] from the South Carolina side. Continuing straight on Whetstone Road 1 mile past the horse camp, one reaches a parking area and trail to Earl's Ford [Fig. 45(6),Fig. 46(3)].

GEORGIA ACCESS TO EARL'S FORD AND SANDY FORD. Georgia has access to both Earl's Ford and Sandy Ford, but the roads in are long, sometimes muddy, and are not used by the commercial outfitters. The Georgia Earl's Ford Road access [Fig. 45(5), Fig. 46(2)] can be reached by ordinary car, except that in high water, Warwoman Creek [Fig. 45(4), Fig. 46(1)] cannot be forded. (It is possible to drive, with care, to Sandy Ford.) In both cases, roads go to the river's edge, unlike those in South

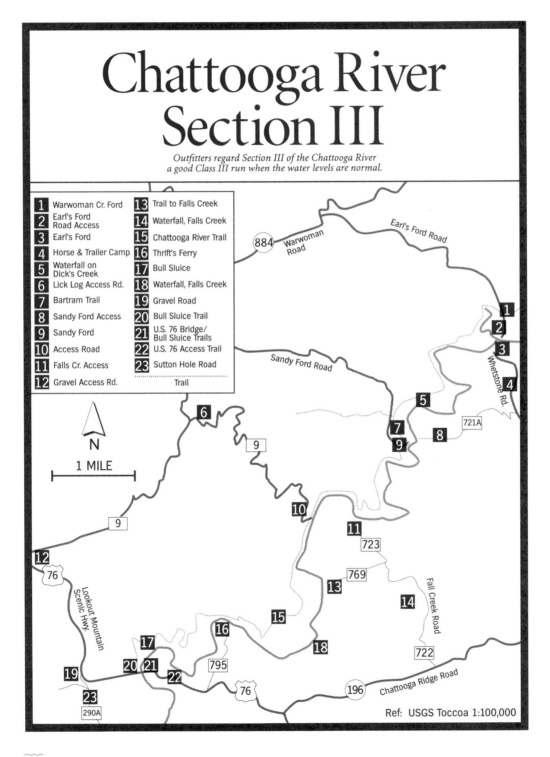

Chattooga River Section III

Outfitters regard Section III of the Chattooga River a good Class III run when the water levels are normal.

1	Warwoman Cr. Ford	13	Trail to Falls Creek
2	Earl's Ford Road Access	14	Waterfall, Falls Creek
3	Earl's Ford	15	Chattooga River Trail
4	Horse & Trailer Camp	16	Thrift's Ferry
5	Waterfall on Dick's Creek	17	Bull Sluice
6	Lick Log Access Rd.	18	Waterfall, Falls Creek
7	Bartram Trail	19	Gravel Road
8	Sandy Ford Access	20	Bull Sluice Trail
9	Sandy Ford	21	U.S. 76 Bridge/ Bull Sluice Trails
10	Access Road	22	U.S. 76 Access Trail
11	Falls Cr. Access	23	Sutton Hole Road
12	Gravel Access Rd.		Trail

N

1 MILE

884 Warwoman Road

Earl's Ford Road

Whetstone Rd.

Sandy Ford Road

721A

Lookout Mountain Scenic Hwy.

723

769

Fall Creek Road

722

795

76

196 Chattooga Ridge Road

290A

Ref: USGS Toccoa 1:100,000

Carolina. However, the protective corridor extends .25 mile from the river. All vehicle traffic is required to stay well away from the riverbanks.

On the Georgia side above Sandy Ford [Fig. 45(11), Fig. 46(9)] is a beautiful 50-foot-high waterfall on Dick's Creek. Take the Bartram Trail north [Fig. 45(9), Fig. 46(7)] about .5 mile past the Dick's Creek Ford to a side trail and viewing platform constructed by the U.S. Forest Service [Fig. 45(7), Fig. 46(5)].

FALLS CREEK ACCESS. This access is best approached off US 76. Two miles east of the US 76 bridge turn left (north) onto the Chattooga Ridge Road (FS 196), the first paved road to the left. Go 2 miles, take the gravel road (FS 722) left (west). At the second fork (2 miles), the right hand fork (FS 723) goes to an access point [Fig. 46(11)] with a very steep trail to the river (.25 mile). The left fork (FS 769) leads to a less steep but longer trail [Fig. 46(13)]. There are two lovely waterfalls on Falls Creek [Fig. 46(14)].

THRIFT'S FERRY. The next access is at Thrift's Ferry [Fig. 46(16)], reached by a gravel road that turns north about 1 mile east of the US 76 bridge.

US 76 SHOULDER ACCESS. Farther downriver, there is a special short access trail (parking is on US 76 shoulder) [Fig. 46(22), Fig. 47(4)] where some outfitters put in for short runs over Bull Sluice [Fig. 46(17), Fig. 47(1)].

BULL SLUICE TRAILS. There are two trails upriver to Bull Sluice, at high water levels a very dangerous, roaring, Class V rapid. Some visitors choose to walk up the better trail on the east (South Carolina) bank [Fig. 46(21), Fig. 47(3)] from the US 76 bridge parking area to watch the rafters come through the sluice. Photographers often prefer to walk up the west bank (Georgia) trail [Fig. 46(20), Fig. 47(2)], which is less well maintained but offers better views of the falls from below. (This is not the Chattooga River Trail. One has to walk too far on the Chattooga River Trail to reach Bull Sluice, while this trail is a short hike.)

WOODALL SHOALS. [Fig. 47(10)] This is a beautiful spot for picnicking and for swimming in the pool below the rapids. Do not attempt to swim or body surf Woodall Shoals. Rated a Class VI rapid, it is considered the most dangerous on the river. Given proper water levels, it can be run by or with professionals, but normally it should be portaged. Visitors should be content to explore below the rapid. On the east side of Woodall Shoals is one of the best places in north Georgia to see how Blue Ridge Mountain rocks have been metamorphosed by heat and pressure, as compared to the sedimentary- or "layer cake"- type mountains of the Cumberland Plateau in the northwestern part of the state. In fact, this site is said to be the "Rosetta Stone" for the interpretation of the changes that have taken place in the rocks of the Eastern Blue Ridge. Most of the rock at Woodall Shoals is a gneiss with black mica, but in it are dark bands and lumps of calcium-rich amphibolite, which furnishes good nutrition for nearby plant communities. Fresh rock is exposed here, courtesy of Mr. Woodall, who apparently dynamited the west side of the river several decades ago so his logs would not be trapped by the rapids along the east bank. Woodall Shoals is

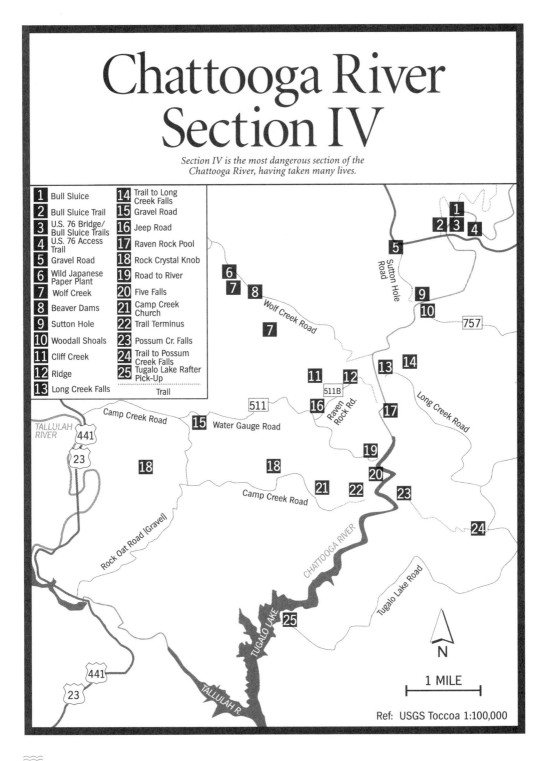

Chattooga River Section IV

Section IV is the most dangerous section of the Chattooga River, having taken many lives.

1 Bull Sluice
2 Bull Sluice Trail
3 U.S. 76 Bridge/ Bull Sluice Trails
4 U.S. 76 Access Trail
5 Gravel Road
6 Wild Japanese Paper Plant
7 Wolf Creek
8 Beaver Dams
9 Sutton Hole
10 Woodall Shoals
11 Cliff Creek
12 Ridge
13 Long Creek Falls
14 Trail to Long Creek Falls
15 Gravel Road
16 Jeep Road
17 Raven Rock Pool
18 Rock Crystal Knob
19 Road to River
20 Five Falls
21 Camp Creek Church
22 Trail Terminus
23 Possum Cr. Falls
24 Trail to Possum Creek Falls
25 Tugalo Lake Rafter Pick-Up

Trail

Ref: USGS Toccoa 1:100,000

1 MILE

reached by turning right (south) 2.5 miles east of the US 76 bridge, and again right at the first gravel road to the right. It is about 2 miles to the parking and camping areas. Note that camping is prohibited here within the Wild and Scenic corridor.

LONG CREEK FALLS. [Fig. 47(13)] Below Woodall Shoals there is a beautiful falls on Long Creek, where most rafts stop for a swim and photographs. It can also be reached by a trail [Fig. 47(14)]. Turn south off US 76, 4.5 miles east of the US 76 bridge. After turning at Long Creek, go 2.5 miles, turn right (west) on FS 758, and go 1.25 miles; turn left onto a gravel road, which in 1.5 miles becomes a jeep road, and proceed until the trailhead is reached. This is Long Creek Road.

POSSUM CREEK FALLS. The Possum Creek Falls [Fig. 47(23)] is reached by a 1.5-mile trail which turns south in a bend [Fig. 47(24)] .5 mile off the paved road at Battle Creek, the same access to Long Creek Road.

TUGALO LAKE ROAD. The last access road on the South Carolina side is off Long Creek Road about 4 miles south of US 76. Turn right (west) onto the gravel Tugalo Lake Road. Be cautious in wet weather. This is the road used by buses to pick up rafters who have made the Section IV trip [Fig. 47(25)]. Length is 3.5 miles.

LICK LOG. Coming down the river on the Georgia side below Sandy Ford is the Lick Log access road [Fig. 46(6)]. It is reached by turning south off Warwoman Road at the Antioch Church turn-off to Sandy Ford, bearing left at the first fork (.5 mile), then bearing right at the second fork (about .25 mile). Then take the next left-hand road (FS 9). (*See* Rabun Bald, page 185, for road access from Warwoman Road.) These are gravel roads suitable for all vehicles.

FS 9 APPROACH. Another Georgia approach is off US 76 east from Clayton, 2.8 miles past the Willows. Turn north (left) on gravel road [Fig. 46(12)], go 3.5 miles, and take FS 9 [Fig. 46(6)] east (right) 3.8 miles to a gate. An old road [Fig. 46(10)] goes down a ridge to the river.

SUTTON HOLE ROAD. About .75 mile west of the US 76 Bridge, a gravel road (FS 290) turns south [Fig. 47(5), Fig. 46(19)]. Within .5 mile the short Sutton Hole Road (290A) [Fig. 46(23)] goes down to the river corridor, where the outfitters overnight their two-day-trip customers at Sutton Hole [Fig. 47(9)]. This is a jeep or pickup truck road, not for ordinary cars.

WOLF CREEK ROAD. This route requires about a 1-mile walk to the river. To reach it, turn right (east) off US 441, 4 miles north of Tallulah Falls Bridge, onto the second paved road to the right. Keep straight for about 3 miles (the road turns to gravel). Turn right (east) at the Wolf Creek Church sign (FS 515). This is an interesting area. From above the church along Wolf Creek, the strange, introduced Japanese paper plant grows wild [Fig. 47(6)]. Farther down Wolf Creek below the church are at least a dozen beaver dams [Fig. 47(8)]. A jeep can go down to within 1 mile of the Chattooga (stay on the right-hand road). This road leads to two potentially exciting areas which have not been much explored or apparently logged. The gorge of Cliff Creek [Fig. 47(11)] and lower Stekoa Creek (refer to Rainey Mountain quadrangle) are excellent places to explore.

CAMP CREEK ROAD. This is one of the most exciting access points to the Chattooga. It is a paved road 2.9 miles north of the Tallulah Falls Bridge, or 8.25 miles south of US 76, on US 441. After 1.5 miles, Water Gauge Road (FS 511) forks to the left off Camp Creek Road. Water Gauge is a good gravel road that dead-ends at a turnaround area at the river corridor after 4 miles. Drive with care; logging trucks and buses carrying rafters also use the road. There is an old road down to the river's edge [Fig. 47(19)]. Walking downstream along a thickly overgrown trail, one soon comes to the first of a series of Class V rapids [Fig. 47(20)] with names like Corkscrew, Jawbone, and Sock'em Dog. In good weather, it is quite a show to watch river runners go through this whitewater. A ford at or near the mouth of Camp Creek was evidently the main old settlers' route to South Carolina, a wagon road reportedly down which herds of hogs were driven to market.

Back about a mile from the terminus of Water Gauge Road (FS 511), Raven Rock Road (FS 511B) turns north, terminating at the Raven Rock trailhead [Fig. 47(12)]. A trail drops down .75 mile to the Raven Rock Pool [Fig. 47(17)], a grand, scenic place to have lunch, fish, and watch the rafters go by. Four-wheel drive is recommended for Raven Rock Road.

The trail terminates across the river from Raven Rock Cliffs, a 200-foot escarpment. Just upstream, Raven's Chute, a solid Class IV drop, challenges boaters.

The main Camp Creek Road continues south. At 2.6 miles N. Rock Mountain Road turns and comes out at Terrora Park on Tallulah Falls Lake. Camp Creek Road passes Camp Creek Church at 4.5 miles. Just west of it is a ridge that has yielded rock crystals, which also occur on a rocky knob several miles to the west [Fig. 47(18)]. On these rocky ridges and southward around Tallulah Gorge, the dominant pine is often the rare table mountain pine, with cones so prickly that it can hardly be handled. The Camp Creek paved road ends .3 mile past the church [Fig. 47(21)]. A jeep can go only another .5 mile; then one takes a trail. In this area, as in the area southward around Tallulah Gorge, the dominant heath is Carolina rhododendron, which has a purple bloom, as well as abundant azalea. At the terminus of the trail [Fig. 47(22)], one will be able to gaze off into the gorge of the Chattooga. This is the fabled "Sinking Mountain," where the visitor who stands long enough in one spot can feel the ground giving way underfoot. Bulldozers left overnight have been known to sink a foot or two. An Indian myth attributes this to a race of spirit people or "little people" who mined beneath the mountain, which is now caving in on their tunnels.

CANOEING AND BOATING

The Chattooga River is an outstanding whitewater experience that attracts boaters from all over the United States and Canada. While it is one of the finest recreational resources Georgia has to offer, it can be extremely unsafe—even deadly—for those who approach it unaware of its hazards. Many individuals, experienced as well as inexperienced boaters, have lost their lives in the river, particularly on Sections III and IV. A variety of books and maps details the river's boating pleasures and its dangers, and one or more of these resources should be consulted before attempting to navigate any section of the river. Reliable river guidebooks are listed in Appendix D. In addition, a number of outfitters provide canoeing and rafting expeditions on the Chattooga (*see* Commercial Rafting Trips, *below*). No one should attempt Sections III and IV of the Chattooga without first going with an experienced guide.

The Forest Service requires a minimum of two boats in any boating party, and each party boating on the Chattooga must register and provide proof of that registration on the river. *Rangers frequently check for registrations at the take-out points and issue $50 fines if the registration is not produced.* Registration booths are located at the Russell Bridge parking and put-in area, the Earl's Ford parking area, the US 76 bridge parking area, and the Woodall Shoals parking area. Boaters entering the river at a put-in location without a registration booth must first register at a site with such a booth.

SECTION II - GA 28 TO EARL'S FORD. [Fig. 45(5)] One Class III rapid (Big Shoals) and other shelflike rapids make Section II an excellent area for novice to intermediate whitewater boaters.

SECTION III - EARL'S FORD TO THE US 76 BRIDGE. [Fig. 47(3), Fig. 46(21)] At this point the river becomes much more dangerous, requiring greater expertise in negotiating boulders, gorges, and ledges. There are several Class III and IV rapids and one Class V at Bull Sluice, just above the take-out point near the US 76 bridge.

SECTION IV - FROM THE US 76 BRIDGE TO TUGALO LAKE. [Fig. 47(25)] The infamous Woodall Shoals, a Class VI rapid that has taken many lives, is located on this section a short distance below the bridge. From here on, the river narrows and concentrates into several Class IV and V rapids before entering Lake Tugalo where a 1.5-mile paddle across the lake to take out is required. Both Sections III and IV are dangerous and should be attempted only by experienced boaters.

COMMERCIAL RAFTING TRIPS

Guided river trips are available from three local rafting companies—Southeastern Expeditions, Wildwater Limited, and Nantahala Outdoor Center, all carefully regulated by the federal government. These outfitters conduct canoe clinics and raft trips lasting from a half day to two days, with an overnight camp-out available. Commercial operations usually run from late March through October, depending on stream flow and weather. For a listing of outfitters, see Appendix C.

Map References: USGS 1:24,000 series: Cashiers–Highlands Satolah–Tamassee–Rainy Mountain; USFS Chattooga River Corridor map.

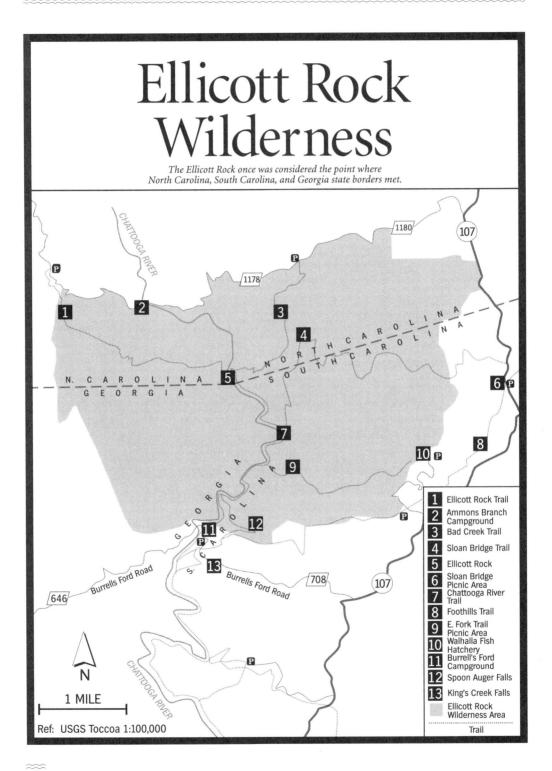

Ellicott Rock Wilderness

*The Ellicott Rock once was considered the point where
North Carolina, South Carolina, and Georgia state borders met.*

Legend:

1. Ellicott Rock Trail
2. Ammons Branch Campground
3. Bad Creek Trail
4. Sloan Bridge Trail
5. Ellicott Rock
6. Sloan Bridge Picnic Area
7. Chattooga River Trail
8. Foothills Trail
9. E. Fork Trail Picnic Area
10. Walhalla Fish Hatchery
11. Burrell's Ford Campground
12. Spoon Auger Falls
13. King's Creek Falls

Ellicott Rock Wilderness Area

Trail

N

1 MILE

Ref: USGS Toccoa 1:100,000

The Ellicott Rock Wilderness

This is a 8,274-acre tract of unspoiled mountain land that surrounds the point at which Georgia, North Carolina, and South Carolina come together. The first boundary, a small scenic area, was identified and established in 1966. It and a much larger area were made a part of the National Wilderness System in 1975 and thus became fully protected by guidelines of the 1964 National Wilderness Protection Act.

This primitive land is isolated and well protected, allowing a wilderness experience within its rocky, mountainous terrain.

The National Wild and Scenic Chattooga River flows through the wilderness, cascading from 2,381 feet to 2,100 feet within its boundaries. Fork Mountain, 3,294 feet above sea level, is the second-highest point in South Carolina.

This wilderness has several unique plant communities, a number of rare and endangered plants growing alongside the trails, evergreen forests with dense understory of mountain laurel, streamside rhododendron which defies human penetration, a diverse population of large and small animal life, and many fish, including the eastern brook trout.

Hiking is the only method available for exploring the interior of Ellicott Rock Wilderness. The automobile-access roads merely provide a way to get to the trailheads. No horses, bicycles, or motorized vehicles are permitted. Camping is allowed within the wilderness, but campsites must be over .25 mile from an approach road and 50 feet from a stream or maintained trail.

The Forest Service has recommended a 2,000-acre addition to this wilderness in the Sumter National Forest in South Carolina. The addition would be bounded by SR 107 on the east and the New Burrell's Ford Road on the south.

▓ TRAILS

CHATTOOGA RIVER TRAIL. [Fig. 43(1), Fig. 48(7)] This portion of the Chattooga River Trail within the wilderness is over 3.4 miles of old Indian trail. It runs beside the east bank of the Chattooga River from a Burrell's Ford trailhead near the river to an intersection with the East Fork Trail (1.5 miles), then to Ellicott Rock (1.6 miles) [Fig. 48(5), Fig. 50(9)] to join Bad Creek Trail [Fig. 48(3), Fig. 50(7)] and Ellicott Rock Trail [Fig. 48(1), Fig. 50(5)] (.3 mile). The trail is a moderately easy climb through patches of rhododendron and old growth stands of hemlock, white pine, and mixed hardwood. Bad Creek is easily crossed during low water but may have to be waded when water is high.

Directions: To reach the trailhead from the intersection of US 64 and NC 107 in Cashiers, go south on NC 107 to New Burrell's Ford Road (FS 708); turn right (west) and proceed to the trailhead near the river.

ELLICOTT ROCK TRAIL. [Fig. 48(5), Fig. 50(9)] *See* trail information in the Highlands section, (p. 217).

BAD CREEK TRAIL. [Fig. 48(3), Fig. 50(7)] *See* trail information in Highlands section (p. 217).

SLOAN BRIDGE TRAIL. [Fig. 48(4), Fig. 50(8)] This is a moderately difficult trail in good condition. From Sloan Bridge Picnic Area [Fig. 48(6), Fig. 50(10)], it joins Bad Creek Trail (6.3 miles), then proceeds to Ellicott Rock (1.4 miles). Sloan Bridge Trail is perhaps best used for overnight camping after leaving a car at some other trailhead, such as the Walhalla Fish Hatchery [Fig. 48(10)].

Also called Fork Mountain Trail, it crosses SC 107 and approaches the wilderness from the east. The trail ascends and descends, steeply at times. It climbs to near the top of Fork Mountain and falls to streamside, where it passes opulent woodland flora. Ornithologists find the trail of interest because of the diverse species of bird life related to altitude and flora. Hawks and eagles are often seen in this most remote area of the wilderness.

Directions: To reach the trailhead from the intersection of US 64 and NC 107 in Cashiers, go south on NC 107 to about .75 mile south of the North Carolina/South Carolina border. Ample parking is available at Sloan Bridge trailhead north of the picnic area.

EAST FORK TRAIL. [Fig. 48(9)] Sometimes called the Fish Hatchery Trail, this path immediately enters the wilderness and runs downstream alongside the East Fork of the Chattooga for 2.5 miles until it intersects the Chattooga River Trail. The renowned "Forty Thousand Dollar Bridge" which spans the mouth of the East Fork is located here. To reach Ellicott Rock, follow the river upstream 1.7 miles.

Many water-carved rocks, cascades, and deep pools in the Chattooga combine with the streamside hemlock and white pine forest to make this a particularly appealing area. There is a stand of old growth hemlock preserved near the hatchery. The trail is marked with black blazes, and the round-trip of about 8.1 miles is easily covered on a full-day hike.

HELLBENDER
(*Cryptobranchus alleganiensis*)

The hellbender grows to 29 inches.

Directions: To reach the trailhead from the intersection of US 64 and NC 107 in Cashiers, go south on NC 107; turn right on the road to the Walhalla Fish Hatchery [Fig. 48(10)]. The trailhead is at the parking area of the Chattooga Picnic Area, next to the hatchery.

FOOTHILLS TRAIL. [Fig. 43(5), Fig. 48(8)] 6.6 miles. This is a long, well-marked, and well-maintained South Carolina trail. It approaches the Ellicott Rock Wilderness Area across the road from Burrell's Ford Campground parking area [Fig. 43(4), Fig. 48(11)] and skirts the southeastern boundary of the wilderness to leave the area at Sloan Bridge Picnic Area on SC 107. Unlike the other trails in this section, it does not penetrate the interior of the wilderness. After leaving the Burrell's Ford parking area, the trail climbs Medlin Mountain, passes the Fish Hatchery Road (3.3 miles) on the Chattooga Ridge escarpment, and proceeds to the Sloan Bridge Picnic Area (3.3 miles). The Medlin Mountain climb is moderately difficult, but other areas of the trail are traveled with ease. The trail has segments which may be chosen for day hikes, overnight camping, or extended visits along the wilderness border and/or into the Chattooga River corridor.

Directions: To reach the Burrell's Ford trailhead from the intersection of US 64 and NC 107 in Cashiers, go south approximately 13.5 miles on 107 and turn right on New Burrell's Ford Road; go to the parking area and trailhead.

To reach the place where the trail crosses Fish Hatchery Road from the intersection of US 64 and NC 107 in Cashiers, go south on NC 107 approximately 12 miles and turn right on Fish Hatchery Road; go to the trail crossing, which is plainly marked.

To reach the Sloan Bridge trailhead from the intersection of US 64 and NC 107 in Cashiers, go south on NC 107 approximately 10 miles to the Sloan Bridge Picnic Area.

WATERFALLS

SPOON AUGER FALLS. [Fig. 43(3), Fig. 48(12)] This picturesque, cascading falls can be visited by taking an easy loop trail starting across from the entrance to Burrell's Ford Campground parking lot [Fig. 43(4), Fig. 48(11)]. The trail climbs gradually through lovely hardwoods and rhododendron for about .5 mile to the falls, crosses the creek, and continues on about 1.7 miles until it interconnects with the Chattooga River Trail [Fig. 43(1), Fig. 48(7)]. Returning to the parking lot via the Chattooga River Trail and New Burrell's Ford Road is a walk of about 1.5 miles.

KING'S CREEK FALLS. [Fig. 43(6), Fig. 48(13)] Located on a beautiful mountain stream surrounded by dense hardwoods and an undergrowth of hemlock and rhododendron. At the falls, water can be seen freely falling for approximately 80 feet into a picturesque pool. The falls is located about .5 mile from the Burrell's Ford Campground parking lot [Fig. 43(4), Fig. 48(11)]. It is easily reached on a loop trail starting at the display board on the east side of the parking lot. The trail crosses King's Creek and follows the creek upstream about 300 yards to the base of the falls. One can then backtrack .7 mile to the parking lot, continue downstream .5 mile to the campground, or go down the loop trail to its intersection with the Chattooga River Trail. The return to the parking lot on the Chattooga River Trail is about 2 miles.

Map References: USGS 1:24,000 series: Tamassee–Satoloh Highlands–Cashiers; USFS Chattooga Corridor map.

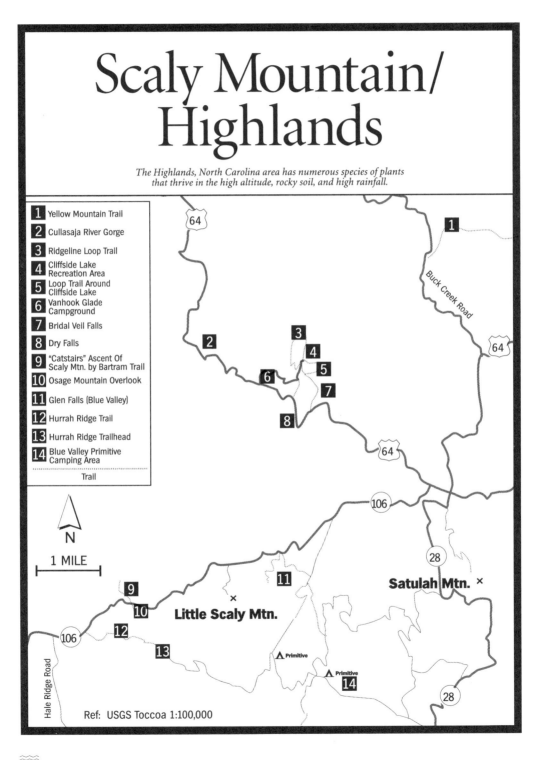

Scaly Mountain/ Highlands

The Highlands, North Carolina area has numerous species of plants that thrive in the high altitude, rocky soil, and high rainfall.

1 Yellow Mountain Trail
2 Cullasaja River Gorge
3 Ridgeline Loop Trail
4 Cliffside Lake Recreation Area
5 Loop Trail Around Cliffside Lake
6 Vanhook Glade Campground
7 Bridal Veil Falls
8 Dry Falls
9 "Catstairs" Ascent Of Scaly Mtn. by Bartram Trail
10 Osage Mountain Overlook
11 Glen Falls (Blue Valley)
12 Hurrah Ridge Trail
13 Hurrah Ridge Trailhead
14 Blue Valley Primitive Camping Area

....
Trail

N

1 MILE

Buck Creek Road

Little Scaly Mtn.

Satulah Mtn.

Hale Ridge Road

Primitive

Primitive

Ref: USGS Toccoa 1:100,000

Highlands, North Carolina

Central to this remarkable and highly scenic area is an unusually high (4,000-foot) plateau on the southern edge of the Blue Ridge. Numerous mountains with steep granite cliffs—a unique feature in the southern Appalachians—create imposing scenery in this area. These cliffs may be seen from NC 106 and US 64 and, indeed, throughout the area; but they are best observed from the tops of two remarkable mountains, Whiteside and Satulah. Both of these summits are reached by short, easy trails.

The cliffs and rock outcrops are botanical treasure houses showcasing the southernmost distribution of numerous rock-loving plants which need a combination of altitude, bare rock, and high rainfall to survive. These cliffs are excellent places to see peregrine falcons, ravens, and wintering golden eagles.

This region encompasses the headwaters of the famed Chattooga River and is the major northern access to the Ellicott Rock Wilderness. Streams such as the Cullasaja fall off the plateau in steep gorges. Waterfalls are frequent. Vistas of the Rabun Bald country and Blue Valley, now an experimental forest, are visible from NC 106, especially at the Osage Mountain [Fig. 49(10), Fig. 49(9)] and Blue Valley overlooks.

🪨 THE MOUNTAIN (LITTLE SCALY)

A short but narrow road leads to the summit, which is privately owned and affiliated with the Unitarian Church. It is an excellent example of a rock bald with an unusual forest of ancient, "krummholz" (wind-sheared) white oak, along with evergreen heath. This may be the oldest white oak stand in the world. Many trees have been dated between 400 and 500 years of age. A viewing tower is present. This is one of the very few instances in which one can drive to the summit of a granite dome.

Directions: About midway between Highlands and Scaly Mountain on the south side of US 64, a sign designates "The Mountain."

🪨 SATULAH MOUNTAIN

The summit of Satulah (4,543 feet) is classified as a heath bald. From here the visitor can view the mountains of three states. Ascending the trail, one first encounters a forest comprised of northern red oak, white oak, and chestnut oak. At the first switchback there begins a remarkable stand of mountain pepperbush overhanging the trail. Both chinquapin and witch hazel are common shrubs here. Soon hikers pass into a stunted, virgin oak forest. At the trail fork, go right. As one approaches the summit, the forest becomes heath (rhododendron) with stunted white oak. At the summit are scattered, dwarfed white oak, some 200 years old.

This is a zone with dwarfed pitch pine where a 200-year-old tree may be only 10 inches in diameter. The first purple rhododendron is encountered along with the first pines. Chinquapin is abundant.

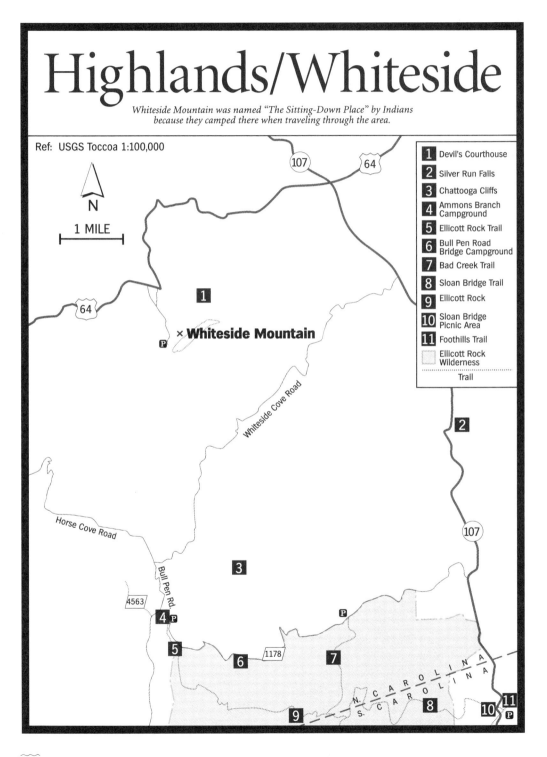

Highlands/Whiteside

Whiteside Mountain was named "The Sitting-Down Place" by Indians because they camped there when traveling through the area.

Ref: USGS Toccoa 1:100,000

N

1 MILE

Whiteside Mountain

Whiteside Cove Road

Horse Cove Road

Bull Pen Rd.

4563

1178

64

107

64

107

N. CAROLINA
S. CAROLINA

1	Devil's Courthouse
2	Silver Run Falls
3	Chattooga Cliffs
4	Ammons Branch Campground
5	Ellicott Rock Trail
6	Bull Pen Road Bridge Campground
7	Bad Creek Trail
8	Sloan Bridge Trail
9	Ellicott Rock
10	Sloan Bridge Picnic Area
11	Foothills Trail
	Ellicott Rock Wilderness
	Trail

The summit provides the best look at unusual plants growing only on the bare granite rock so characteristic of the cliffs of this area and extending into Georgia only on similar cliffs along the Chattooga headwaters. One of the most fascinating, the twisted hair spike moss, forms large, thick mats on the upper cliffs. Another, sand myrtle, grows only at the outer edge of the ground cover extending onto the rocks. A rare juniper forms low-spreading, wind-pruned growth. Exploring the summit, one can find curious potholes, the basement of a former fire tower, and patches of soil forming in moist depressions in the naked rock. Often on other outcrops, the niche of the pitch pine is filled by the rarer table mountain pine, and hemlocks might include the rare Carolina hemlock. In the spring the evergreen heaths on these balds present unequalled wildflower displays. The mountain summit is protected and offered for public use and education by the Satulah Summit and Ravenel Park, Inc.

Directions: From downtown Highlands, turn south on NC 28 and proceed up Fourth Avenue to Satulah Road. Park, with permission, in the rear section of Nick's Restaurant parking lot at the intersection of Satulah Road and South Street. Follow the Satulah Summit signs, bearing right at the fork. Walk about .5 mile to the end of the pavement and continue another .3 mile to a set of steep wooden stairs just before the road dead-ends into a gated private drive. The stairs begin the trail to the summit. When the trail forks, take the right fork.

THE HIGHLANDS NATURE CENTER

The center offers daily programs for children and adults, including lectures, nature classes, tours of the botanical gardens, and outings. The center offers exhibits on local archeology, geology, and biology, including live salamanders, snakes, and fish. Fresh wildflower arrangements are available to help visitors identify local plants. Next door is the Appalachian Environmental Art Center, where one may enroll in classes in nature and landscape photography.

Directions: On Horse Cove Road, an extension of East Main Street, in Highlands.

Dates: Open Jun.–Labor Day, Mon.–Sat.

For more information: The Highlands Nature Center, phone (704) 526-2623.

THE HIGHLANDS BIOLOGICAL STATION

Founded in 1929, the Highlands Biological Station hosts about 20 scientists and students annually for research in the field of biology of the southern Appalachians. On 20 acres, it maintains a rhododendron trail as well as one of the finest wildflower "gardens" in the Appalachians. The garden is a series of loop trails through the forest, with plants labeled along the way.

Directions: Either park at the Highlands Nature Center (*above*) and walk around back of it, or drive around (Sixth Street off Horse Cove Road, turn right at sign) to where the trails actually start at the parking area of the biological station.

HORSE COVE ROAD AND BULL PEN ROAD

This very scenic drive is a major entrance to the Ellicott Rock Wilderness from the north.

In Highlands, East Main Street becomes Horse Cove Road shortly before the Highlands Nature Center. Follow this winding paved road into beautiful Horse Cove. As one enters the cove, Rich Gap Road is on the right. Approximately 200 feet up Rich Gap Road on the right is the path to a giant poplar, the second largest in North Carolina and one of the three largest in the country. There is a direction sign to the tree. Back to Horse Cove Road, continue east to the fork at the end of the pavement. The right fork is Bull Pen Road, a beautiful, one-lane, gravel road that is something of a hiking trail for cars. Bull Pen Road crosses the Chattooga on an iron bridge. By the bridge is a good place to stop and view the river. The water has worn basins in the rocks from the size of a thumb print to larger than washtubs.

From Bull Pen Road there is access to Chattooga River Cliffs Trail [Fig. 50(3)], Chattooga Loop Trail, the Chattooga Wild and Scenic River, Bad Creek Trail, Ellicott Rock Trail [Fig. 48(1)], and Ammons Branch Campground [Fig. 48(2), Fig. 50(4)]. The road returns to NC 107 south of Cashiers.

The left fork from Horse Cove Road is Whiteside Cove Road. A fine view from the bottom of Whiteside Mountain can be found in Whiteside Cove. This road returns to NC 107 in Cashiers.

CARDINAL FLOWER (Lobelia cardinalis) A favorite stop for hummingbirds, this flower grows up to 5 feet tall.

CULLASAJA RIVER GORGE

[Fig. 49(2)] US 64 runs between Highlands and Franklin, North Carolina, following the gorge cut by the Cullasaja River through the granite gneiss mountain and passing a number of waterfalls and scenic areas.

BRIDAL VEIL FALLS. [Fig. 49(7)] This falls cascades from a height of 120 feet over the highway, 1.2 miles west of Highlands. Basswood and yellow birch trees, characteristic of northern hardwood forests, are found in the vicinity.

DRY FALLS. [Fig. 49(8)] 2.1 miles from Highlands. There is limited parking, and the short trail down the cliff to the 75-foot falls is well marked. Those who do not mind getting a bit wet can walk under the falls to view the gorge. Mountain laurel is abundant. In the area around both Bridal Veil and Dry falls, visitors will see Fraser magnolia, white pine,

Eastern hemlock, and red maple, along with dog-hobble, rosebay rhododendron, and wild hydrangea. These falls nurture some extremely rare ferns.

LOWER CULLASAJA FALLS. Eight miles west of Highlands, this falls cascades about 250 feet. It is unmarked, but there is a pullover area in which to park and view the falls. The trees in this area include tulip poplar, yellow birch, red oak, and chestnut oak. Also present are grape, Virginia creeper, and wild hydrangea.

HIKING TRAILS IN THE HIGHLANDS AREA

Trail guides, maps, brochures, and books about the area are available at the Forest Service's Highlands District Visitor Center in Wright Square near the intersection of US 64 and NC 106 in Highlands. Open May through November with limited hours in May and November. Similar information is available at the U.S. Forest Service District Office on Flat Mountain Road east of Highlands off US 64. The turnoff is well marked.

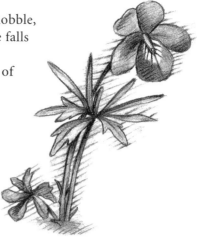

BIRDFOOT VIOLET
(Viola pedata)
This violet is identified by its bird's-foot shaped leaves.

ELLICOTT ROCK TRAIL. [Fig. 48(1)] About 3.5 miles. One of the oldest trails in the area, Ellicott Rock Trail runs from the trailhead [Fig. 50(4)] to the surveyor's rock marking the intersection of Georgia, North Carolina, and South Carolina. It follows an old roadbed for over 2 miles, makes a left turn at a fork, and descends to the Chattooga River corridor. It then climbs steeply, crosses the Chattooga River, and joins the Chattooga River Trail and Bad Creek Trail. Ellicott Rock is downstream on the far bank, inscribed with a simple "NC" [Fig. 48(5)]. The rock that most people find is actually Commissioner's Rock—the true intersection of the three states. It is located 10 feet downstream from Ellicott Rock and inscribed "LAT 35 AD 1813 NC SC." Both rocks were named for surveyors who marked state boundaries. The return hike is more difficult than the hike in; the climb requires 2 hours or more.

Directions: Follow the directions to Bull Pen Road (page 216). Go on this road past a primitive campground and look for a bulletin board that marks the trailhead.

BAD CREEK/FOWLER CREEK TRAIL. [Fig. 48(3)] Similar in terrain to the Ellicott Rock Trail (*above*). This trail follows an old roadbed for about .75 mile to where an old road, now blocked off, led down to Bad Creek. The main trail continues with gentle ascents and descents for 1.5 miles, where it intersects the Sloan Bridge Trail. It then continues down steeply, with switchbacks for 1.5 miles, to the river

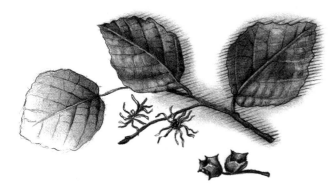

WITCH-HAZEL
(Hamamelis virginiana)
This plant blooms after its leaves fall.

level. Here it joins the Ellicott Rock Trail and Chattooga River Trail. Ellicott Rock is .125 mile downstream.

Directions: The head of the Bad Creek Trail is about 3 miles east of the Bull Pen Road Bridge. Limited parking is available about 50 yards away across Fowler Creek Bridge. A bulletin board identifies the trailhead.

YELLOW MOUNTAIN TRAIL. [Fig. 49(1)] About 9.6 miles round-trip. The longest trail in the Highlands area leaves Cole Mountain Gap (4,300 feet) and traverses two peaks—Cole Mountain (4,600 feet) and Shortoff Mountain (5,000 feet)—and ends with a 360-degree panoramic view on Yellow Mountain (5,127 feet). The gneissic, oak ridge forest is dominated by white oak (formerly mixed with chestnut) with unusually abundant serviceberry as a subcanopy. Offering trailside snacks in late summer and fall are two abundant heaths, deerberry and buckberry. In April to June there are floral displays. Masses of hayscented and New York fern offer pleasing vistas.

Directions: From the junction of US 64 and NC 28 in Highlands, go east on US 64 for 2.7 miles to Cole Mountain Road (also called Buck Creek Road); turn left at the Shortoff Baptist Church sign; go 2.3 miles to Cole Cap and park on the left side of the road. The trail sign is to the right.

GLEN FALLS (BLUE VALLEY). [Fig. 49(11)] A gravel, one-lane, Forest Service road approximately 1.5 miles southwest of Highlands on the south side of NC 106 leads to Glen Falls. Follow this road about a mile to the parking area and a sign for Glen Falls Scenic Area. It is a short, .5-mile walk to the falls. Glen Falls is a series of three falls, approximately 60 feet each, on the east fork of Overflow Creek. A steep, 1-mile trail with steps and places to rest along it goes down to the bottom of the falls, where the view is better. Be cautious, as the trail has washed away in some places. The trail continues down into Blue Valley Campground (primitive). Blueberries and rhododendron grow in the area. Glen Falls offers a magnificent vista over northeastern Georgia and northwestern South Carolina, the Chattooga River valley.

HURRAH RIDGE/WEST FORK LOOP TRAIL. About 1.5 miles long and fairly steep. In the Highlands/Cashiers area and eastward, corundrum deposits have yielded many sapphires of gem quality. One community near US 64 is, in fact, named Sapphire. Several old mines are quite close to the highway. This trail leads to the old Tiffany sapphire mine.

Directions: Follow the Blue Valley Road (FS 79) 6 miles west of NC 28 to the trailhead. At a broken culvert in the west fork of Overflow Creek, cross the creek and take the right-hand trail [Fig. 49(12)], which was once used to drive livestock up to the grazing grounds in the "flats" between Scaly Mountain and Rabun Bald.

WHITESIDE MOUNTAIN

[Fig. 50] Whiteside is an outstanding example of the isolated, cliff-sided mountains characteristic of the Highlands/Cashiers area. Its summit offers fine views from a high ridgetop amidst the beauty and solitude of the forest. To the north is Devil's Courthouse [Fig. 50(1)], a huge rock outcropping, and the headwaters of the Chattooga River. To the south are Whiteside Cove and a long view back into Georgia and South Carolina.

Whiteside Mountain is a magnificent and popular spot. Technical rock climbers test their skills here. The mountain was known by the Indians as "the sitting-down place" because they camped there when traveling through the area. Legend says that Spanish explorers also visited the mountain as they passed through this part of the country.

The U.S. Forest Service acquired Whiteside in 1974. The old road is now closed to motorized vehicles. The visitor can hike part or all of the 2-mile loop trail to the 4,930-foot summit for a view of the valley floor, lying 2,100 feet below the surrounding mountains. The Whiteside Mountain Trail is designated a National Recreation Trail and is a component of the National Trail System.

Both the north and south faces of Whiteside contain sheer cliffs ranging from 400 to 750 feet in height. These cliffs were formed from igneous rock commonly called "whiteside granite" (actually a quartz diorite gneiss). This rock contains a high content of feldspar, quartz, and mica, along with such minerals as pyrite and rare monazite. Due to the weathering and drying

DWARF GINSENG
(Panax trifolius)
Believed by some to be an aphrodisiac, ginseng has been overcollected.

effects of wind and sunlight, the cliffs on the south side have little vegetation. Their blue-gray hue is the natural rock color. The very noticeable white streaks that decorate this side are veins of feldspar and quartz.

The north face, which receives less sunlight and more moisture, has a darker appearance due to the mosses and lichens that are able to grow in this more favorable environment.

Two distinct plant communities are present on Whiteside. First is the forest where oaks—particularly northern red oaks—are dominant. Also commonly found in the forest are Fraser magnolia, black birch, yellow birch, striped maple, and witch hazel. Before the chestnut blight in the early 1900s destroyed all of the large chestnut trees, there was a concentration of chestnut here.

There is an abundance of chestnut sprouts in the area, but they seldom reach more than 3 inches in diameter before dying.

The second community exists in the rock outcrops along the cliffs' edges and along trails. An abundance of flowering and nonflowering plants and shrubs grows here—some rare, all beautiful. The common shrubs include rosebay rhododendron, mountain laurel, and flame azalea. Plants include false lily of the valley, several species of trillium, summer bluets, wild strawberry, sand myrtle, mats of spike moss on outcrops, and the rare Carolina hemlock.

COMMON
FOXGLOVE

(Digitalis
purpurea)
This is
the source
of digitalis,
a drug
used to
treat
heart
disease.

Directions: From downtown Highlands, go east on US 64 for 5.5 miles to the Whiteside Mountain Road sign; turn right on paved road NC 1600 and go .6 mile; bear left at the Wildcat Ridge Road sign and go .35 mile; turn left into a gravel parking lot.

Facilities: Parking lot, toilet.

CAMPGROUNDS AND RECREATIONS AREAS
BLUE VALLEY PRIMITIVE CAMPING AREA.
[Fig. 49(14)] Go 6 miles south of Highlands on NC 28, turn right (west) on a road into Blue Valley and then go 3 miles. The campground is on the right. There is a pit toilet. The water supply is from streams and should be boiled or treated before using. This camp area is recommended for small groups.

VANHOOK GLADE CAMPGROUND. [Fig. 49(6)] About 4.3 miles west of Highlands (elevation 3,300 feet). The campground is open from about early April until late October, depending on the weather. Each of the 20 quiet, secluded, small campsites has a parking space, grill/fireplace, table, and tent pad. Small trailers will fit into some parking spaces; RVs are allowed. A volunteer host is on site to answer questions. No group larger than family-size is permitted to camp. There are five water spigots and a flush toilet. The area is 1.5 miles from Cliffside Lake by either road or trail. Campers have free access to Cliffside Lake Recreation Area, (*below*).

CLIFFSIDE LAKE RECREATION AREA. [Fig. 49(4)] Located 4.4 miles west of Highlands and 1.5 miles off US 64, Cliffside is open year-round as a day area but no water is available from the end of October until early May. There are picnic tables and shelters, a bathhouse with cold

GARTER SNAKE
(Thamnophis sirtalis)
Garter snakes have three stripes, one on back and one on each side. They're often found near water.

showers and flush toilets, and a cliff-top vista shelter. Cliffside Lake provides good trout fishing and a swimming beach. There are six marked hiking trails in the area ranging from .5 mile to 1.5 miles in length, including a loop trail around the lake [Fig. 49(5)] and another longer loop [Fig. 49(3)] which includes the crest of a nearby ridge. White pine and Eastern hemlock trees, rhododendron, blackberry, and mountain laurel grow in the campground.

AMMONS BRANCH CAMPGROUND. [Fig. 48(2), Fig. 50(4)] Located on the right about 1.5 miles from the fork at the beginning of Bull Pen Road (*see* page 216), marked with a Forest Service sign. This little-used, small campground may not be accessible by car after heavy rains. The only water supply is from streams and must be boiled or treated. There is one picnic table, a grill, and a pit toilet. A connector trail leaves from the campground, parallels Bull Pen Road, and joins the Ellicott Rock Trail about .2 mile from its head on Bull Pen Road, 1 mile west of the bridge. There is limited parking at the trailhead.

For more information: Highlands Ranger District, U.S. Forest Service, 2010 Flat Mountain Road, Highlands, NC 28741. Phone (704) 526-3765.

Map References: USGS 1:24,000 series: Highlands–Cashiers Sealy.

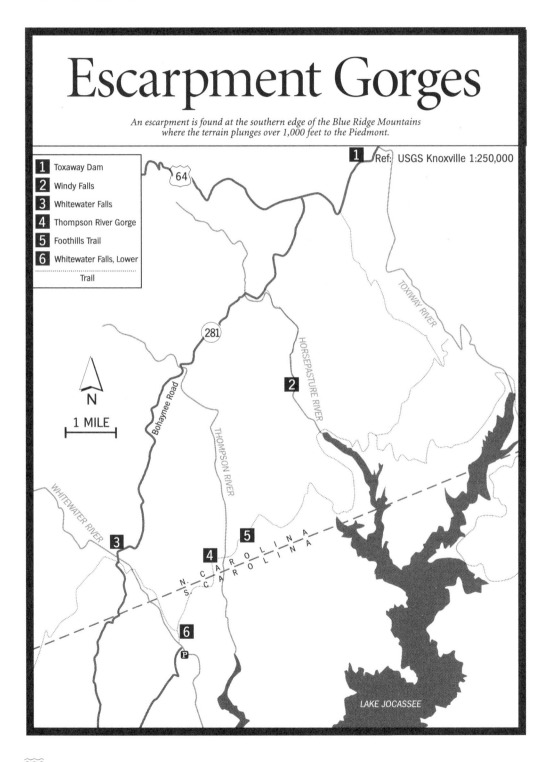

Escarpment Gorges

*An escarpment is found at the southern edge of the Blue Ridge Mountains
where the terrain plunges over 1,000 feet to the Piedmont.*

1 Ref: USGS Knoxville 1:250,000

1 Toxaway Dam
2 Windy Falls
3 Whitewater Falls
4 Thompson River Gorge
5 Foothills Trail
6 Whitewater Falls, Lower
Trail

64

281

TOXAWAY RIVER

HORSEPASTURE RIVER

Bohaynee Road

THOMPSON RIVER

WHITEWATER RIVER

N
1 MILE

N. CAROLINA
S. CAROLINA

P

LAKE JOCASSEE

The Escarpment Gorges

At the southern edge of the Blue Ridge Mountains, the terrain suddenly plunges in a steep escarpment to the Piedmont, over 1,000 feet below. In this area rivers form deep gorges and dramatic waterfalls—some near roads and easily seen, others requiring hikes of varying lengths over rugged terrain.

WHITEWATER FALLS

[Fig. 51(3)] At 411 feet, this is one of the highest waterfalls in the eastern United States. A five-minute walk on a paved path takes visitors to an overlook with a dramatic view of the falls.

To the right, about 100 steps down the gorge, is another excellent view. This is also a good place to see the rock-loving Carolina hemlock. Along the trail, just as it descends from the overlook, large colonies of the uncommon faded trillium may be found blooming in early May. The trail descends to Whitewater River in the bottom of the gorge. There, Gleason's white trillium occurs. The rare green salamander is known to inhabit crevices below the falls.

To the left of the overlook, the visitor can follow the Foothills Trail (*see* page 210), which passes through this point to the head of the falls about .5 mile away. Use extreme caution. Fifteen people have fallen to their deaths at this location.

Directions: From the intersection of US 64 and NC 281 (Bohaynee Road, go south on NC 281. From I-85 north take SC 11 (Cherokee Scenic Foothills Highway), north to SC 130/171; turn left and go to the entrance of Whitewater Falls picnic area (SC 130/171 becomes NC 281). Note that NC 281, or Bohaynee Road, crosses Horsepasture, Thompson and Whitewater rivers on the edge of the escarpment.

Facilities: Parking area, picnic area, toilets, bulletin board with trail information, paved path to overlook.

HORSEPASTURE RIVER

Includes Drift Falls, Turtleback Falls, Rainbow Falls, Stairstep Falls, and Windy Falls [Fig. 51(2)]. These are a series of dramatic waterfalls along Horsepasture River, which has been designated a Wild and Scenic River. *Caution: This is extremely rugged and dangerous country. Do not walk or wade close to the rim of any falls. Rainbow Falls alone has claimed a number of lives.*

Directions: To reach Horsepasture River from the intersection of US 64 and NC 107, go east on US 64 and turn right (south) on NC 281 (Bohaynee Road); go about 2.2 miles to a small off-road parking area just north of the bridge over Horsepasture River. Several paths and rough roads follow the river downstream and do not consolidate into one identifiable trail until below the first waterfall, Drift Falls. In the summertime this falls becomes a thrilling water slide for adventurous daredevils. A quarter to half mile downstream from Drift Falls is Turtleback Falls, where the river turns sharply right.

Another .25 mile beyond that is Rainbow Falls, which drops a stunning 150 feet over darkened, resistant Cashiers gneiss. A broad spray zone supports interesting bog and seepage-area plants. The white water against the dark rock, and the blast of spray, make's a trip to Rainbow well worth the short hike. Continue past Rainbow Falls another .5 mile to a campsite by a stream. Cross the stream at the right end of the campsite and follow the trail up the hill several yards to a path that goes down the ridge to the river. Take the path to the river, where there is another campsite. To the left of the campsite is a trail following the river downstream. Hike along it to see the aptly named Stairstep Falls. Backtrack to the main trail on the ridge and then turn right and continue walking old primitive roads.

At each possible turn, go to the right. After about 2 miles, come to the top of Windy Falls [Fig. 51(2)]. Here the Horsepasture is a roaring, windy, rushing, boulder-strewn river in a remote gorge. Some boulders at the top of the falls are the size of small cabins. Only Whitewater Falls [Fig. 51(3)] equals Windy Falls in scenic beauty. Do not try to reach the bottom of Windy Falls from the top. It is simply too treacherous. Instead, on a separate overnight trip, follow the Horsepasture River upstream from the Foothills Trail [Fig. 51(5)] to the base of the falls. It is a 3- to 4-hour hike, well worth the time. Windy Falls may also be reached from the bottom by way of a primitive road from Rosman, North Carolina, using a four-wheel-drive vehicle.

TOXAWAY DAM

[Fig. 51(1)] This is the best place in all of Appalachia to see how vulnerably thin and shallow mountain soil is and to witness the fragility of the mountain soils and vegetation.

As recounted in *The Floods of 1916* by the Southern Railway Company, on July 5 and 6, 1916, a tropical cyclone came inland from the Gulf of Mexico, reaching the western Carolinas around July 8. A second storm came in from the Atlantic, and there were tremendous rains on July 15 and 16 in the same area.

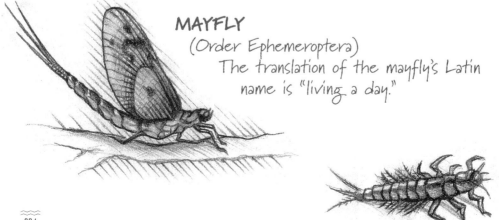

MAYFLY
(Order Ephemeroptera)
The translation of the mayfly's Latin name is "living a day."

The French Broad River was at 4 feet, or flood stage, on the morning of July 15. It had come down from 8.8 feet on July 11. But with the new rains on July 15, the river rose to 13.5 feet at 8 a.m. on July 16. By 9 a.m. on the same day, the river rose to 18.6 feet. At 10 a.m. the bridge on which the height of the river was measured washed away. The crest of the flood was estimated to be 21 feet.

It was this rain that washed away the dam at Lake Toxaway in 1916 and sent waters rushing down 16 miles of the Toxaway River Gorge. The dam was not rebuilt until 1960. The force of the flood removed all vegetation from the streamside zone, leaving a remarkable scene of exposed bedrock clearly evident to the visitor today. The dam creating Lake Toxaway is just on the north side of the US 64 bridge over the Toxaway River [Fig. 51(1)].

SLOAN BRIDGE HIKING TRAIL

To Whitewater Falls via the Foothills Trail [Fig. 48(8), Fig. 51(5)]. At the Sloan Bridge Picnic Area [Fig. 48(6), Fig. 50(10)], the Foothills Trail goes south toward the Fish Hatchery Road and east to Whitewater Falls, while another trail goes west to Ellicott Rock (see Ellicott Rock section, page 209).

The Foothills Trail to Whitewater Falls provides an interesting and different approach to the falls. This well-marked trail is only moderately difficult, 4.4 miles each way. Approaching the top of Whitewater Falls from upstream gives the hiker a fine view of the South Carolina Piedmont and the gorge. One could hike another .3 mile to the picnic area in the parking lot.

Directions: The beginning point for the hike, the Sloan Bridge Picnic Area, is on NC 107 about .2 mile north of SC 413.

Facilities: Picnic tables, a chemical toilet, parking.

FOOTHILLS TRAIL

To Thompson River Gorge [Fig. 51(4)]. About 5 miles one-way. From the White-water Falls Overlook [Fig. 51(3)] (see Whitewater Falls directions, page 223), descend into the gorge to the river and walk the Foothills Trail to Thompson River Gorge and the bridge crossing it. The trail follows Whitewater River downstream for about 1.6 miles. It then crosses over ridges and follows old roads for part of the way to Thompson River.

Look for wild bergamot and several small falls. There is an especially nice slide just off the trail to the left about 10 yards before the trail makes a sharp right turn from an old road to descend into Thompson River Gorge. The rushing water, huge boulders, and steep-sided gorge provide a sense of remoteness from civilization seldom found. Some adventurous hikers may wish to rock-hop upriver to Thompson High Falls, one of the most beautiful falls in the Escarpment Gorge region. Allow 2 or more hours for this trip.

This is also one of the few areas where shortia, or oconee bells, can be seen.

According to *Wildflowers of the Southeastern United States* by Wilbur Duncan and Leonard Foote, this flower is found in only seven counties in Georgia, South Carolina, and North Carolina.

On the other side of Whitewater River, a nature trail is marked at the point where the Foothills Trail leaves the river at 1.6 miles. Old trail books by Allen de Hart describe a cable bridge that crosses the river to the Coon Branch Natural Area. The bridge is not there now, and the river may be too high to ford. The Duke Power folder also describes a road to this area with a parking lot and access to lower Whitewater Falls [Fig. 51(6)]. This access to the lower falls, however, is blocked by the Duke Power Bad Creek Reservoir Project. One can hike to the top of the lower falls, but it is not recommended, as it requires scrambling on unmarked fishermen's paths.

▧ BACKPACKING ALONG THE FOOTHILLS TRAIL

One of the best ways to understand and learn about the Escarpment Gorges would be to backpack the Foothills Trail from Whitewater Falls to Toxaway River boat access or to US 178 at Laurel Valley. One could set up two cars, one at White-water Falls Picnic Area and the other at Laurel Valley. The distance would be 32.7 miles one-way along the Foothills Trail. The hiker would visit the gorges of the Whitewater River, Thompson River, Bear Camp Creek, Horsepasture River, and Toxaway River.

Directions: For driving to Whitewater River Picnic Area, see directions page 223.

For more information: The Foothills Trail Conference publishes an excellent guide to the Foothills Trail. Contact the Foothills Trail Conference, PO Box 3041, Greenville, SC 29602. Phone (864) 233-9403.

▧ SILVER RUN FALLS

[Fig. 50(2)] Silver Run is one of the creeks merging into Whitewater River to create Whitewater Falls. The falls drops 30 feet into a marvelous open pool with its own beach. Sitting on a rock in this pool, one would imagine it to be very far from the road.

Directions: To reach the falls from the junction of US 64 and NC 107, go south 4 miles on NC 107. There will be a dirt parking area on the left side of the road. There are 2 such areas along this stretch; the one with the telephone pole is the correct one. The trail to Silver Run Falls starts by the pole and is an easy, graded trail for .14 mile.

Map References: USGS 1:24,000 series: Cashiers–Reid; Duke Power Company Foothills Trail Brochure; Forest Service handout map with falls marked.

The Cowee Gem Region

During the late 1800s, corundum—a mineral second in hardness only to diamond—was mined extensively in north Georgia and North Carolina. Corundum was valuable in the manufacture of abrasives such as sandpaper. Impurities in the mineral also resulted in gem-quality sapphires and rubies, which were sometimes found during the course of mining corundum ore. In fact, the mineralized zone running northeast and southwest through Georgia and North Carolina was second only to the Mogok region of Burma as a source of high-quality rubies and sapphires. After the discovery that, with plentiful electricity, aluminum oxide could be artificially fused to make corundum, the commercial mining operations quickly closed down, and the economics of gemstone mining never made it a viable industry in the area. Presently, Thailand seems to be the main source of gem-quality rubies and sapphires. In more recent years, serious rock hounds and those just simply curious have discovered that the Cowee gem region and a number of locations around Franklin, North Carolina, still produce valuable gems, primarily for the tourist market. Most mines in Macon County are placer or gravel deposits. The gems weather out of decomposing bedrock higher in the watershed and are washed down by streams. Most of the gem mines furnish equipment, shovels, screens, and running water to wash the gravel. Either there is a flat fee, or one pays for the processed gravel.

FRANKLIN GEM AND MINERAL MUSEUM

[Fig. 52(5)] Located in the 15-year-old brick jail, the museum displays a variety of Macon County minerals, including a 48-pound corundum crystal. This is a good first stop on a visit to the area to become familiar with the appearance of the minerals and gems mined nearby.

Directions: Located on Phillips Street in Franklin, North Carolina.

Dates: Open May 1–Oct. 31.

MINING OPERATIONS

A number of these mines lie along Caler's Fork [Fig. 52(1)] on Cowee Creek [Fig. 52(2)]. Many of these mines, as well as others in the area, have native gems such as rubies, sapphires, and garnets. Some also sell "enriched" gravel by the bucket, meaning that exotic (and inexpensive) stones from all over the world have been added to the raw material.

Facilities: Facilities vary at each mining location, but most have restrooms and picnic and play areas. Some have campsites with showers, and most provide assistance in learning how to search for gems.

Dates: Most mines are open 6 or 7 days a week. Season is generally Apr.–Oct.

Directions: Go 6 miles north of Franklin on NC 28; turn right at West's Mill [Fig. 52(2)]; take the first road south, then the first road east (S1340), and follow that as it becomes S1341 and eventually S1343 along Caler's Fork. Watch for signs.

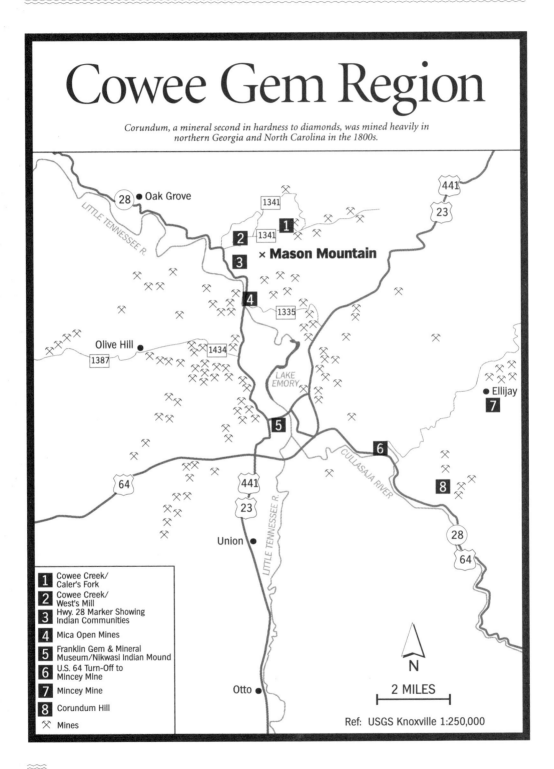

Cowee Gem Region

Corundum, a mineral second in hardness to diamonds, was mined heavily in northern Georgia and North Carolina in the 1800s.

Oak Grove

Mason Mountain

Olive Hill

LAKE EMORY

Ellijay

Union

Otto

CULLASAJA RIVER

LITTLE TENNESSEE R.

1 Cowee Creek/
   Caler's Fork
2 Cowee Creek/
   West's Mill
3 Hwy. 28 Marker Showing
   Indian Communities
4 Mica Open Mines
5 Franklin Gem & Mineral
   Museum/Nikwasi Indian Mound
6 U.S. 64 Turn-Off to
   Mincey Mine
7 Mincey Mine
8 Corundum Hill
✕ Mines

N

2 MILES

Ref: USGS Knoxville 1:250,000

CORUNDUM HILL

[Fig. 52(8)] This famous corundum mine has yielded some fine gems, including sapphires in orchid, green, yellow, pink, and blue, as well as 587- and 760-carat rubies. This deposit is associated with the ultrabasic rocks serpentine and dunite, as is the corundum at the Buck Creek olivine pine barrens.

Directions: Just north of US 64, about 5.5 miles east of the US 44/164 interchange in Franklin, North Carolina.

MINCEY MINE

[Fig. 52(7)] This is another well-known deposit of unusual bronze sapphires which "star." No equipment is furnished here.

Directions: Go 2.4 miles east of the US 44/164 interchange on US 64, turning left [Fig. 52(6)] just before the first bridge and proceeding 5.8 miles to Ellijay, Georgia. Inquire there.

MASON MOUNTAINS

The Franklin area is also noted for the occurrence of a splendid rose-pink variety of pyrope garnet called "rhodolite," first discovered on Mason Mountain. One can visit the Mason Mountain Rhodolite Mine or screen or pan for garnets in the gravels of Mason's Branch, Cowee Creek, and Caler's Fork. With luck, amateur miners might recover a piece of ruby or sapphire corundum. Mason Mountain is just south of Caler's Fork. Watch for signs.

OTHER MINES

A look at the map [Fig. 52] will indicate the stunning number of old or active mines in the area around Franklin (mine symbols). All are not gem mines. Some are giant, open cuts where mica or other minerals were mined [Fig. 52(4)]. This particular mine has enormous amounts of almost pure-white quartz. Unfortunately there are no good maps to the location of Macon County mines, nor is there information as to what is or was mined at particular sites. A few mines are no longer on revised 7.5-minute topographical maps. Inquiring of local residents seems to be one of the most productive means of finding interesting localities.

NIKWASI INDIAN MOUND

[Fig. 52(5)] The Franklin area is rich in Indian history and prehistory. Practically in the center of Franklin is an Indian mound on the south bank of the Little Tennessee River at the bridge. Near West's Mill there is a marker on NC 28 showing the location of the major Indian communities of Cowee [Fig. 52(3)] on the floodplain of the Little Tennessee River. Explorer and naturalist William Bartram passed through the Franklin area in the late 1700s.

Long Trails

There are three long trails in Georgia—the Appalachian, the Benton MacKaye, and the Bartram—covering nearly 400 miles.

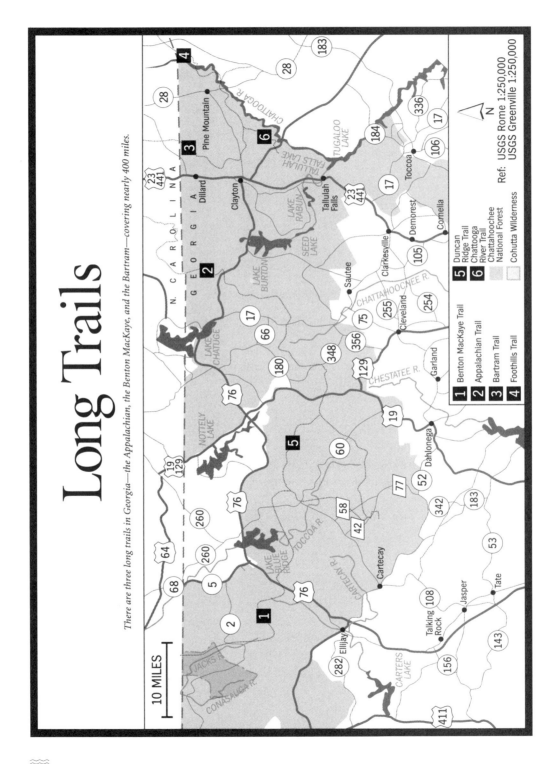

Long Trails

Three long trails—the Appalachian, the Benton MacKaye, and the Bartram—provide hikers with an opportunity to cover long distances entirely by foot. In addition, by combining these three trails with the Foothills Trail in South Carolina, the resourceful hiker could travel between 360 to 400 miles across some of the most varied and dramatic scenery in the Southeast. The Appalachian Trail (AT) is probably the most famous hiking trail in the world. Most hikers experience only certain portions of the trail such as from where the trail crosses a public road to the top of a mountain. Other hikers take several months off and hike the entire length. The Benton MacKaye is not as traveled as the AT and is more popular with some hikers who seek more privacy on their backpacking trips. The Bartram Trail winds through the northeastern corner of Georgia, tracing the footsteps of famous 18th-century naturalist William Bartram.

[*Above*: Beautiful Waterfalls of the Georgia Mountains]

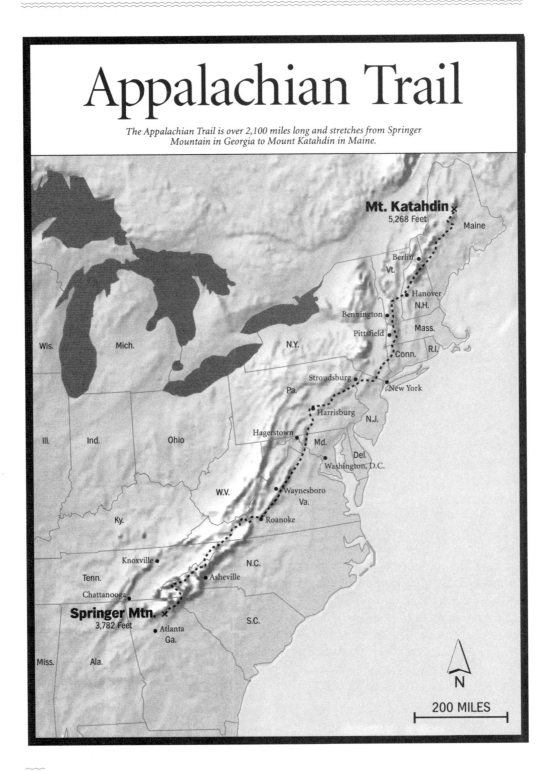

Appalachian Trail

The Appalachian Trail is over 2,100 miles long and stretches from Springer Mountain in Georgia to Mount Katahdin in Maine.

Mt. Katahdin ✗
5,268 Feet
Maine

Berlin
Vt.

Hanover
N.H.

Bennington
Pittsfield
Mass.

Wis.
Mich.
N.Y.
Conn.
R.I.

Stroudsburg
New York

Pa.
Harrisburg
N.J.

Hagerstown
Md.

Ill.
Ind.
Ohio
Del.
Washington, D.C.

W.V.
Waynesboro
Va.

Ky.
Roanoke

Knoxville
N.C.

Tenn.
Asheville

Chattanooga

Springer Mtn. ✗
3,782 Feet
Atlanta
Ga.
S.C.

Miss.
Ala.

N

200 MILES

The Appalachian Trail

The Appalachian National Scenic Trail is a wilderness footpath that winds over 2,100 miles along the crest of the Appalachian Mountains. It runs through 14 eastern states, stretching from Springer Mountain in Georgia to Mount Katahdin in Maine. The "AT," as it is called, is known throughout the world, each year attracting hikers from many different countries.

The trail began over 70 years ago with a "grand vision" articulated in 1921 by Benton MacKaye—forester, regional planner, and conservationist. MacKaye, now known as the "Father of the Appalachian Trail," proposed a "long trail over the full length of the Appalachian skyline, from the highest peak in the North to the highest peak in the South." His proposal, not just a detailed trail plan, envisioned the long trail as an escape for people in the crowded cities of the eastern seaboard, a place for regeneration of the human spirit through what he termed "harmony with primeval influences." The work on the trail was to be done primarily by volunteers. Trail enthusiasts, some of whom had also suggested a "grand trunk" trail along the Appalachian ridges, were galvanized into action by MacKaye and his inspiring article. The establishment of the Appalachian Trail was to be the culmination of many years of their hopes and dreams. Early hiking clubs in New England and New York had laid the foundations for this new trail; parts of their existing trails were used to form the first sections of the AT. In 1925 the Appalachian Trail Conference was formed as a confederation of clubs that would build and maintain the trail.

In the South little was known of the mountain areas, and a trail route was chosen largely from maps. In 1929 Roy Ozmer, a Georgian and accomplished woodsman, was chosen to scout the entire trail from Virginia through Georgia. Once a route was decided upon, volunteers were recruited, maintenance clubs were formed, and, with the help of U.S. Forest Service and Civilian Conservation Corps crews in some places, the trail was built. The last section to be completed was in Maine in 1937.

The trail in Georgia was completed in 1931 through the combined efforts of members of the newly organized Georgia Appalachian Trail Club and the U.S. Forest Service. The original southern terminus of the trail was Mt. Oglethorpe, near Tate, but development and chicken farming on private land between Amicalola Falls and Mt. Oglethorpe intruded on the wilderness experience of hikers, forcing the terminus to be moved in 1958 to Springer Mountain.

In 1968 Congress authorized the AT as the first National Scenic Trail; in 1978 Congress appropriated funds to acquire lands along the route to protect the trail from encroaching development. Maintenance of the trail rests with the Appalachian Trail Conference (ATC). In 1984, the secretary of interior signed a delegation agreement with the ATC assigning to it unprecedented responsibilities for operation, development, monitoring, and maintenance of the trail. Volunteers in AT clubs carry out these duties.

The Georgia portion of the AT [Fig. 55] extends some 75.6 miles through primitive areas of the Chattahoochee National Forest. Although rising at times to elevations of over 4,400 feet, the trail is mostly along ridges at elevations around 3,000 feet. Ascents and descents are sometimes steep but often reward hikers with grand views from rocky outcrops and open summits.

Most of the AT goes through deciduous hardwood forest—largely hickory, oak, and poplar. Rainfall is heavy and frequent, especially in the spring; ridges are often snow-capped or ice-covered in the winter. Mid-April through mid-May is the peak wildflower season. Flowers found along the trail include trillium, bloodroot, mayapple, bluets, wild azalea, and sometimes pink and yellow lady slippers. In June many sections are covered with flowering rhododendron and mountain laurel. The heavy rains ensure lush vegetation during the summer months; ferns are found in abundance all along the trail. The last two weeks of October are usually the best time to find autumn colors at their height. In winter when the leaves are off the trees, the trail offers ever-present scenic vistas of the surrounding countryside and of the mountains to the north and west.

The Georgia portion of the trail is managed and maintained by the Georgia Appalachian Trail Club, through a cooperative agreement with the U.S. Forest Service, Chattahoochee National Forest. Members of the club may be found on the trail almost every weekend cutting weeds, clearing blowdowns, painting blazes, repairing shelters, reconstructing portions of the trail, or participating in recreational hikes.

The trail's southern terminus is located atop Springer Mountain, near FS 42. Since this area is difficult to reach by automobile, an 8.1-mile approach trail begins at Amicalola Falls State Park on GA 52. Mountains along the trail with outstanding scenic views include Big Cedar, Blood, Cowrock, Rocky, and Tray. One of the many side trails leads from Chattahoochee Gap to the highest point in Georgia, Brasstown Bald. The trail passes through five of Georgia's wilderness areas: Raven Cliffs Wilderness between Neel's Gap and Tesnatee Gap; Tray Mountain Wilderness between Tray Gap and Addis Gap; the Southern Nantahala Wilderness north of Blue Ridge Gap; Mark Trail Wilderness between Unicoi Gap and Hogpen Gap; and Blood Mountain Wilderness from Neel's Gap to Woody Gap. Bly Gap on the Georgia/North Carolina border is the northern end of the AT in Georgia.

The trail is marked throughout its length with rectangular white blazes and is generally easy to follow. Double blazes indicate caution, usually meaning a turn in the trail. Side trails and trails to water are blue-blazed; signs are placed at road crossings, shelters, and other important intersections. There are 11 shelters on the Georgia AT, placed more or less at intervals permitting easy day hikes. All but one of these shelters are three-sided, open-front types with floors. Springs are reasonably close by. The exception is the stone, two-room structure atop Blood Mountain. It has four sides, a fireplace, windows, and a sleeping platform. There is no water on top of Blood Mountain.

▩ REACHING THE TRAIL

There is no public transportation to the AT in Georgia. The trail can be reached via the six main highways that traverse the mountains; usually the trail crosses at the highway's highest point, where a large hiking trail sign should be visible. Ample parking is available.

▩ ROAD CROSSINGS

Approximate distances from the nearest town and distance by trail to the next paved road crossing:

AMICALOLA FALLS STATE PARK APPROACH TRAIL ON GA 52. 15 miles west of Dahlonega, 15 miles northwest of Dawsonville, 20 miles east of Ellijay; 28.8 miles by AT to Woody Gap.

WOODY GAP ON GA 60. 15 miles north of Dahlonega; 11.3 miles by AT to Neel's Gap.

NEEL'S GAP ON US 129/19. 15 miles south of Blairsville, 19 miles northwest of Cleveland, 22 miles north of Dahlonega; 5.7 miles by AT to Tesnatee Gap, 6.6 miles to Hog Pen Gap.

TESNATEE GAP AND HOG PEN GAP ON GA 348. (Richard Russell Scenic Highway). 12 miles northwest of Helen, 15 miles southeast of Blairsville; 14.9 miles by AT from Tesnatee Gap to Unicoi Gap, 14 miles from Hog Pen Gap to Unicoi Gap.

UNICOI GAP ON GA 75. 10 miles north of Helen, 14 miles south of Hiawassee; 16.6 miles by AT to Dick's Creek Gap.

DICK'S CREEK GAP ON US 76. 11 miles east of Hiawassee, 18 miles west of Clayton; 8.7 miles by AT to Bly Gap on North Carolina border (no road access).

NOTE: The approach to Springer Mountain by automobile involves traveling on rough, unpaved Forest Service roads. One such road, FS 42, which runs from the town of Suches (enter from GA 60 next to Tritt's Store, 1.6 miles north on the highway from Woody Gap), provides access to several points along the trail, passing through Gooch Gap, Cooper Gap, Hightower Gap, and Springer Mountain. It also connects with FS 58 to Three Forks. An approach from GA 52 is through the Nimblewill community on FS 2811 and FS 77 across Winding Stair Gap and then on FS 58 down to the AT at Three Forks.

▩ SUGGESTED DAY HIKES

SPRINGER MOUNTAIN–THREE FORKS AREA. Highlights are views from a rocky outcrop atop Springer Mountain, southern terminus of the AT; the magnificent stand of virgin hemlock along Stover Creek; and three beautiful mountain streams that converge at Three Forks. From Springer Mountain, both the AT and the Benton MacKaye Trail (marked by diamond-shaped white blazes) lead by different routes to Three Forks, intersecting twice to form either two 5-mile loop trails or one 10-mile, figure-eight loop trail. Access to Springer Mountain is on unpaved FS 42 and to

THE APPALACHIAN TRAIL IN GEORGIA

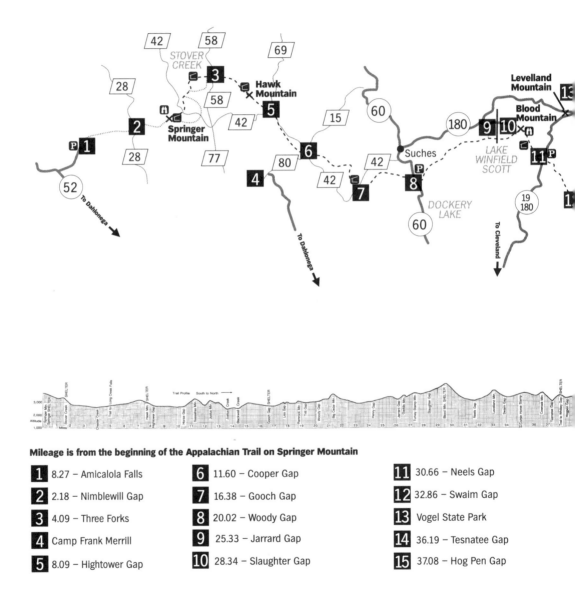

Mileage is from the beginning of the Appalachian Trail on Springer Mountain

1 8.27 – Amicalola Falls	**6** 11.60 – Cooper Gap	**11** 30.66 – Neels Gap
2 2.18 – Nimblewill Gap	**7** 16.38 – Gooch Gap	**12** 32.86 – Swaim Gap
3 4.09 – Three Forks	**8** 20.02 – Woody Gap	**13** Vogel State Park
4 Camp Frank Merrill	**9** 25.33 – Jarrard Gap	**14** 36.19 – Tesnatee Gap
5 8.09 – Hightower Gap	**10** 28.34 – Slaughter Gap	**15** 37.08 – Hog Pen Gap

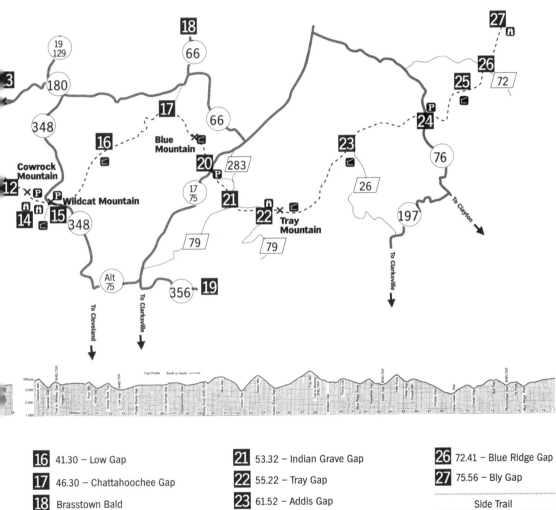

16 41.30 – Low Gap	**21** 53.32 – Indian Grave Gap	**26** 72.41 – Blue Ridge Gap
17 46.30 – Chattahoochee Gap	**22** 55.22 – Tray Gap	**27** 75.56 – Bly Gap
18 Brasstown Bald	**23** 61.52 – Addis Gap	⋯⋯⋯⋯⋯⋯ Side Trail
19 Unicoi State Park	**24** 66.80 – Dicks Creek Gap	– – – – Appalachian Trail
20 50.72 – Unicoi Gap	**25** 71.15 – Plum Orchard Gap	

Three Forks, on unpaved FS 58. Both are moderate climbs.

BIG CEDAR MOUNTAIN. Views from rocky overlook; 2-mile round-trip hike north on AT from Woody Gap.

BLOOD MOUNTAIN. Grand views from rocky summit and rock outcrops below summit; 4.2-mile round-trip to top; south on AT from Neel's Gap; 1,300-foot climb.

LAKE WINFIELD SCOTT LOOP. Blue-blazed trail leads from the west side of the camping area, 1 mile to Jarrard Gap on the AT, and, from the east side, 2.2 miles to Slaughter Gap on the AT. By following the AT between Jarrard and Slaughter Gaps, one can make a loop hike. An additional 2.2-mile round-trip hike can be made from Slaughter Gap to the summit of Blood Mountain.

NEEL'S GAP TO TESNATEE GAP. 5.7 miles one-way or 11.4 miles round-trip along ridge trail, with viewpoints from Levelland, Turkey Pen, and Cowrock mountains. At Neel's Gap the trail passes through the archway between two buildings at Walasi-Yi Inn, a hiking/craft store; moderate climbs.

WILDCAT MOUNTAIN. Viewpoints on summit and on top of ridge out blue-blazed side trail. One-mile round-trip to summit plus 1-mile round-trip on blue-blazed trail; south on AT from Hog Pen Gap; easy to moderate climb.

ROCKY MOUNTAIN LOOP. Six-mile loop or 3-mile round-trip to summit; north on trail from Unicoi Gap. Fine views lie southward along the summit trail. For loop hike, continue along summit on AT; descend 1.3 miles to Indian Grave Gap; turn left (north) on forest road following blue blaze for approximately 1 mile; turn left off road into woods and follow blue blaze back to junction with AT (approximately 1 mile); 1,200-foot climb.

TRAY MOUNTAIN. Views from an open, rocky summit. A 10.8-mile round-trip north on the trail from Unicoi Gap; or a 1-mile round-trip north on the trail from Tray Gap on FS 79 (access from GA 75, 2 miles north of Helen or 2 miles north of Unicoi Gap).

TRAIL DESCRIPTIONS

APPROACH: AMICALOLA FALLS STATE PARK. From visitor center, trail goes 8.1 miles north to summit of Springer Mountain. Frosty Mountain at mile 4.8 of approach trail; Nimblewill Gap at mile 6.2 of approach trail.

0 MILE. Springer Mountain (3,782 feet). Southern terminus of the AT. Plaque on rock, mailbox with register under summit plaque. Mount Katahdin in Maine is 2,100 miles north via the white-blazed trail.

.2 MILE. Springer Mountain shelter with seasonal spring. Located down side trail to right of AT, 2.5 miles. Stover Creek shelter with all-season stream nearby. Located to left of AT, down old logging road.

5 MILES. Long Creek Falls.

7.7 MILES. Hawk Mountain shelter; water from nearby stream.

8.2 MILES. Hightower Gap (gravel FS 42).

16.7 MILES. Gooch Gap shelter to right; good spring .2 mile south on AT.

20.3 MILES. Woody Gap (paved GA 60); parking.

21.3 MILES. Big Cedar Mountain; good rock ledges and views.

29.5 MILES. Blood Mountain (4,461 feet); highest point on the Georgia AT. Fine views are afforded on clear days. Blood Mountain shelter is located on the summit. Closest water is in Slaughter Gap, 1 mile and 660-foot descent south on AT.

31.6 MILES. Neel's Gap (paved US 19); parking at Byron Reece, north on highway.

32.9 MILES. Levelland Mountain; views to right and left.

35.2 MILES. Wolf Laurel Top; views to right in clearing.

36.5 MILES. Cowrock Mountain; views on rocks via side trail to right.

37.3 MILES. Tesnatee Gap on GA 348, Russell Scenic Hwy.; parking.

38 MILES. Wildcat Mountain; views. Side trail leads right 1.1 miles to Whitley Gap shelter with dependable spring.

38.2 MILES. Hog Pen Gap on GA 348; parking.

42.6 MILES. Low Gap shelter, right via side trail into cove; spring and stream nearby.

47.6 MILES. Chattahoochee Gap with spring, right via side trail, being the headwaters of the Chattahoochee River.

49.4 MILES. Site of former Rocky Knob shelter, recently torn down. New shelter .5 mile north on trail; spring downhill below old shelter site.

50 MILES. Blue Mountain shelter via side trail to left; spring on AT just before turnoff to shelter.

52.2 MILES. Unicoi Gap (paved GA 75); parking.

57.6 MILES. Tray Mountain (4,430 feet); outstanding views from summit. On descent going north, obscure trail to right leads out an arm to pinnacle.

58.1 MILES. Tray Mountain shelter left via side trail; good spring behind and down from shelter.

63.3 MILES. Deep Gap shelter to right, .3 mile down via side trail. Spring and stream nearby.

63.8 MILES. Dick's Creek Gap (paved US 76); picnic tables; seasonal stream.

73.1 MILES. Plum Orchard Gap shelter located to the right of the gap down side trail. Spring near shelter, but better spring down ravine to left of AT.

77.5 MILES. Bly Gap; the Georgia/North Carolina state line. There is no road access to this gap except by four-wheel-drive vehicles. The gap is often missed by hikers because as one comes from the south, the gap is climbed into instead of descended into. Hikers know they have arrived when there is a gnarled tree to the right and a sweeping vista to the left.

80.7 MILES. Muskrat shelter in North Carolina to right; stream and privy next to shelter.

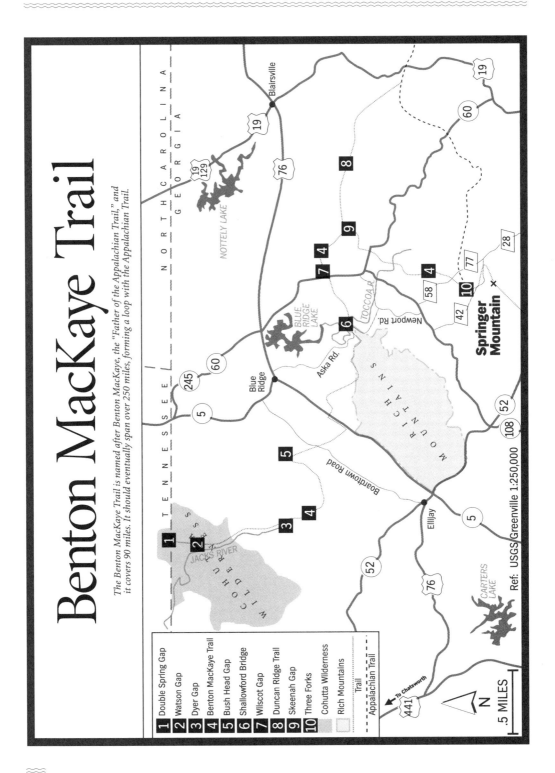

Benton MacKaye Trail

The Benton MacKaye Trail is named after Benton MacKaye, the "Father of the Appalachian Trail," and it covers 90 miles. It should eventually span over 250 miles, forming a loop with the Appalachian Trail.

Ref: USGS Greenville 1:250,000

.5 MILES

Legend:

1. Double Spring Gap
2. Watson Gap
3. Dyer Gap
4. Benton MacKaye Trail
5. Bush Head Gap
6. Shallowford Bridge
7. Wilscot Gap
8. Duncan Ridge Trail
9. Skeenah Gap
10. Three Forks

Cohutta Wilderness
Rich Mountains

Trail
Appalachian Trail

The Benton MacKaye Trail

On October 14, 1989, many volunteers, along with a number of U.S. Forest Service employees with whom they had worked jointly on the endeavor, celebrated the opening of the Georgia section of the interesting and diverse Benton MacKaye (pronounced Mac-Eye) Trail (BMT). From its beginning at Springer Mountain, the trail's distance covers 90 miles to US Hwy 64 in Tennessee. The trail should eventually wind through Tennessee and North Carolina, forming a 250-mile loop with the Appalachian Trail and providing an alternative long-distance footpath in the Southeast.

Named for Benton MacKaye, the "Father of the Appalachian Trail" (*see* Appalachian Trail, page 233), this trail grew out of the need to develop an alternative to the popular Appalachian Trail and also to develop a trail that more closely adhered to MacKaye's original trail plan—a plan that envisioned a path reaching to the Cohuttas in the north central portion of Georgia.

Volunteers have already documented much of the variety along the trail. Two beautiful waterfalls, Long Creek Falls and Fall Branch Falls, are scenic attractions. Atop Rhodes Mountain in the winter, one is afforded a 360-degree view of the surrounding countryside. A striking man-made attraction is the suspension bridge across the beautiful Toccoa River. The terrain varies from laurel- and rhododendron-covered walks along creeks to timbered land to ridgetop pathways to walks through thick forests. There are areas with quick access to major highways through Georgia, as well as quite remote areas within and south of the Cohutta Wilderness as well as in the Big Frog Wilderness. There is a 26-mile stretch of trail with only two road crossings.

The BMT is blazed with an off-white diamond symbol. The blazes are located at intervals of approximately 200 feet. There may be other blazes present, such as the white, vertical, 2-by-6-inch stripe of the AT or the 2-by-6-inch, vertical, blue blaze of the Duncan Ridge Trail. These blazes are present only along the first 20 miles of the BMT and will not be seen west of Rhodes Mountain. See below for other trail blazes in the Rich Mountain area and in the Cohutta Wilderness area.

For more information: Write the Benton MacKaye Trail Association, PO Box 53271, Atlanta, GA 30355-1271.

▨ TRAIL DESCRIPTIONS

SECTION 1: SPRINGER MOUNTAIN TO THREE FORKS. Fig. 56(10)] 5.8 miles. Easy. This section essentially traverses the pre-1977 corridor of the AT. It is well constructed and well blazed. Access roads are FS 42 and FS 58 (Noontootla Creek Road).

SECTION 2: THREE FORKS TO GA 60. [Fig. 56(10)] 11.4 miles. Moderate. This section is contiguous in part with the AT and entirely with the Duncan Ridge Trail. It

PITCH PINE
(Pinus rigida)

is essentially an overnight hike. Highlights of this section are the dramatic Forest Service suspension bridge over the Toccoa River and the newly created wildlife opening where many animals and plants may be readily seen. Access roads are FS 58 and GA 60.

SECTION 3: GA 60 TO SKEENAH GAP. [Fig. 56(9)] 5.7 miles. Difficult. This section is the most strenuous part of the BMT. The view from the top, however, after the character-building climb up the south face of Wallhalah Mountain, is worth the effort. Note that at Rhodes Mountain the Duncan Ridge Trail turns east-northeast, while the Benton MacKaye Trail regains its own identity and proceeds westward. Access roads are GA 60 and Skeenah Gap Road.

SECTION 4: SKEENAH GAP TO WILSCOT GAP. [Fig. 56(7,9)] 5.3 miles. Moderate. An up-and-down hike through general forest area. This is a very nice day hike, especially in winter, with views of the adjacent ridges and pastoral valleys. Access roads are Skeenah Gap Road and GA 60 at Wilscot Gap.

SECTION 5: WILSCOT GAP TO SHALLOWFORD BRIDGE. [Fig. 56(6,7)] 7.1 miles. Moderate. The most difficult part of this hike is the initial climb up Tipton Mountain. After this portion, the trail undulates over Brawley Mountain and Garland Mountain before descending to the beautiful Toccoa River. The climbs are challenging, and the beauty of the forest is rewarding. Access is by GA 60 and adjacent Forest Service roads, Dial Road and Aska Road. The number of access points allows for shorter hikes if desired.

SECTION 6: SHALLOWFORD BRIDGE TO GA 5. [Fig. 56(6)] 11.4 miles. Moderate. This is an obvious overnight trek, but it may be shortened to a very pleasant day hike by skipping 3.2 miles of road walk on the eastern end and 1.6 miles of road walk on the western end, taking only the 6.6-mile trail from Fall Branch to Laurel Creek. This section provides many sites atop Rocky and/or Davenport mountains or Scroggin Knob to stop, rest, and enjoy the views. Fall Branch Falls is a highlight right at the start, and the view from Scroggin Knob near the end of the hike is also pleasurable. It is here, climbing Rocky Mountain, that the BMT begins to follow the western arm of the Blue Ridge. White square blazes designating the contiguous Rich Mountain Trail will also be seen here. Access to the forested portion is via Stanley Gap Road, 3.2 miles west of where it and Aska Road intersect, and the Weaver Creek Road at its southwest end at the USFS boundary line.

SECTION 7: GA 5 TO BUSH HEAD GAP. [Fig. 56(5)] 6.5 miles. Easy. First part of this section uses an easement on private property. Hikers will encounter superb spring wildflowers and a picturesque creek with picnic table. This section also contains the only shelter on the BMT. The remaining 2.5 miles are on Gilmer County roads to Bush Head Gap.

SECTION 8: BUSH HEAD GAP TO DYER GAP. [Fig. 56(3,5)] 12.6 miles. Moderate. A long day hike or a very pleasant overnight trip, this part of the BMT is located entirely along the Tennessee Valley Divide. This is general forest land and many activities of the multiuse forest, such as logging, will be seen here. Road access is by the Bush Head Gap Road and FS 64 south of Watson Gap at the northern end.

SECTION 9: DYER GAP TO WATSON GAP. [Fig. 56(3,10)] 4.5 miles. Easy. A very short segment of the BMT, this footpath traverses riverside forest timber management activity areas, and then climbs a mountain with views of the Cohutta Wilderness before returning to the trailhead. Road access is by FS 64 at Dyer Gap and the old GA 2 at Watson Gap.

SECTION 10: WATSON GAP TO DOUBLE SPRING GAP. [Fig. 56(1,2)] 8.5 miles. Moderate. This section along the high ridge is located primarily within the Cohutta Wilderness boundary. It is minimally blazed and semiprimitive in construction. The BMT is contiguous with the Hemptop Trail north of Dally Gap. The blazing changes once again, but the former Forest Service road provides an easily followed path. Road access is at Watson Gap. Double Spring Gap is at the Georgia/Tennessee state line in the middle of the wilderness. A trail here leads north.

SECTION 11. DOUBLE SPRING GAP TO THUNDER ROCK CAMPGROUND. 11.2 miles. Strenuous. This newly opened section leads to the Ocoee River in Tennessee and lies primarily within the Big Frog Wilderness. Trail ascends Big Frog Mountain, a very steep climb, then descends on a network of old trails and Forest Service roads, along with the new trail, before reaching Thunder Rock Campground in the Cherokee National Forest and Ocoee #3 powerhouse on US 64. The 1996 Summer Olympic venue for whitewater events is just east on the Ocoee River.

RACCOON

(Procyon lotor)
The raccoon often appears to wash its food, resulting in its Latin name, "lotor," meaning "a washer."

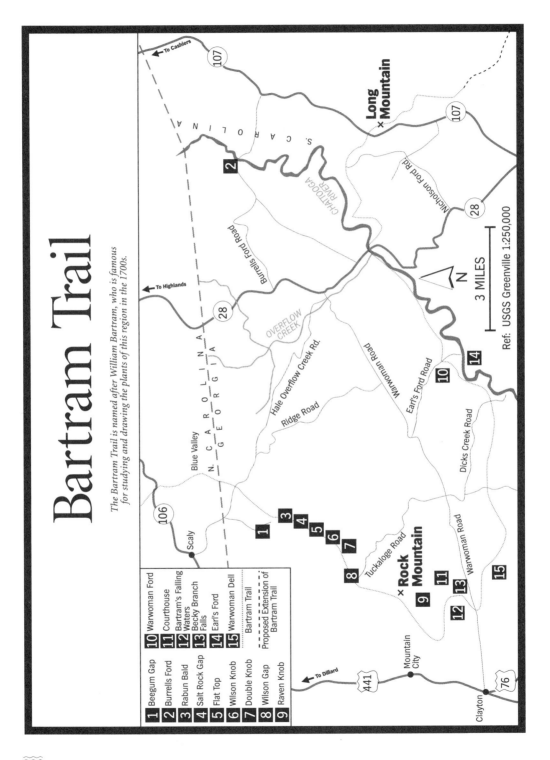

Bartram Trail

The Bartram Trail is named after William Bartram, who is famous for studying and drawing the plants of this region in the 1700s.

Ref: USGS Greenville 1:250,000

3 MILES

1 Beegum Gap	**10** Warwoman Ford
2 Burrells Ford	**11** Courthouse
3 Rabun Bald	**12** Bartram's Falling Waters
4 Salt Rock Gap	**13** Becky Branch Falls
5 Flat Top	**14** Earl's Ford
6 Wilson Knob	**15** Warwoman Dell
7 Double Knob	— Bartram Trail
8 Wilson Gap	⋯ Proposed Extension of Bartram Trail
9 Raven Knob	

The Bartram Trail

William Bartram was a native Philadelphian from a prominent family boasting kinship with Benjamin Franklin. In his early 30s, Bartram first traveled with his father, John Bartram, in Florida and coastal Georgia, becoming enamored with the southern wilderness—a fascination which was to launch him on a career that would lead to worldwide fame. An instinctive naturalist and explorer, he roamed through Georgia, North Carolina, South Carolina, Florida, Alabama, Mississippi, and Louisiana from 1773 until 1778, studying and drawing the plants and animals of the region and collecting plant specimens for his livelihood. His voluminous illustrated journals of those trips serve as the basis for the Bartram Trail, a portion of which now winds through the north Georgia mountains.

The north Georgia portion of the Bartram Trail begins about 1 mile east of Commissioner's Rock on the Georgia/North Carolina line, where it crosses NC 106 at the Osage Mountain overlook. It heads southwest for approximately 3 miles across the headwaters of Holcomb Creek. It then joins an old jeep road at Beegum Gap and follows it up a ridge 2 miles to Rabun Bald—Georgia's second highest mountain at 4,696 feet. At Rabun Bald, an old, abandoned Forest Service fire tower was converted by the Youth Conservation Corps into an observation deck, utilizing a natural rock base built by the Civilian Conservation Corps in the 1930s. The trail goes southwest for about 7 miles, following the Tennessee Valley Divide, and provides several beautiful vistas of the surrounding Blue Ridge Mountains. At Courthouse Gap, the trail turns southeast and follows Finney Creek and Martin Creek for about 3 miles; a turn back to the west here takes the trail to the crossing of Warwoman Road and into Warwoman Dell Picnic Area. From Warwoman Dell [Fig. 57(15)], it winds in a general easterly direction until it reaches Sandy Ford Road, where the trail turns north along the Chattooga River.

Another section is the portion that continues from Warwoman Creek to the confluence of the West Fork of the Chattooga River with the Chattooga River. In the future, a suspension bridge will carry the trail across the West Fork, where it will continue up the Chattooga to the GA 28 bridge and across into South Carolina.

Although there are extremely large white pines and hemlocks where the trail passes through Warwoman Dell, the vegetation of the Bartram Trail is not spectacular. It does, however, expose hikers to a representative cross section of north Georgia plant life. Changes in elevation, with a steady drop from Rabun Bald to Warwoman Road, and somewhat abrupt directional changes from shady north-facing slopes to sunny west and south exposures, provide habitat for many distinct plant communities. Sourwood, sugar maple, red maple, sweet birch, hemlock, white pine, pitch pine, Fraser magnolia (discovered by Bartram), and a variety of oaks and hickories make up the second-growth tree population. Spicebush, sweetshrub, dog-hobble, and blueberries inhabit the shrub level. The trail cuts through large colonies of galax growing under massive mountain laurel and rosebay rhododendron thickets. On the north-facing slopes and near the small streams and springs that cross the trail, grow numerous fern species, including Christmas, northern maidenhair, royal, cinnamon, interrupted, marginal shield wood, lady, and New York fern. Running ground pine, a club moss, grows in abundance in some areas. Typical wildflowers include Vasey's and Catesby's trilliums, trailing arbutus, partridge-berry, rattlesnake plantain, and wild ginger.

For additional information on the Bartram Trail, *see* the North Carolina Bartram Trail listing in Appendix F.

Other Long Trails & Cross-Georgia Hike

The Foothills Trail, the Duncan Ridge Trail, and the Chattooga River Trail are among the longer trails found throughout the Georgia mountains. They are described throughout this guide.

It has been suggested that one can hike across Georgia on first-class trails from the Cohutta Wilderness to Table Rock State Park in South Carolina. The new Benton MacKaye Trail goes from the Cohuttas to Springer Mountain, where it connects with the Appalachian Trail. The Appalachian Trail can then be hiked to Wayah Bald in North Carolina, at which point it connects with the Bartram Trail. The hiker can then turn east on the Bartram Trail and travel through North Carolina and Georgia (Rabun Bald) to the Chattooga River in South Carolina, where the Bartram Trail intersects with the Foothills Trail. The Foothills Trail can then be hiked to its terminus at Table Rock. It is estimated that the total distance would be 360 to 400 miles, depending on where the Benton MacKaye and Bartram Trails are completed. Spur trails and outstanding features are numerous.

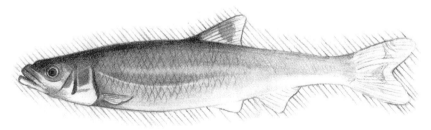

WARPAINT SHINER
(Luxilus coccogenis)
Deriving its name from its bright red cheeks,
this shiner grows to 5 inches long.

Appendixes

A. Map Sources

The enjoyment and usefulness of this guidebook will be greatly enhanced by the employment of maps in conjunction with the text. A vast amount of information is available from the following sources:

TOPOGRAPHICAL MAPS OF ALL STATES

Powers Elevation Co., Inc., PO Box 440889, Aurora, CO 80044. Phone (800) 824-2550. All USGS topos: $6, plus postage and handling charge from $2 to $10 per order. VISA, MasterCard, and American Express accepted. Allow 5–10 days.

Timely Discount Topos, Inc., 9769 West 119th Drive, Suite 9, Broomfield, CO 80020. Phone (800) 821-7609. All USGS topos: $6, plus postage and $1 handling charge per order. Checks only. Allow 5–10 days.

The U.S. Geological Survey, Map Sales, Box 25286, Denver, CO 80225. Phone (303) 236-7477. Call (800) USA-MAPS first for a free index with order form. Cost: $2.50 for 1:24,000, $4 for 1:100,000. Allow 6–8 weeks.

TOPOGRAPHICAL MAPS OF GEORGIA

Enpro Engineering Reprographics, 1800 Peachtree Street, Suite 210, Atlanta, GA 30309. Phone (404) 355-8520. Cost: $3 for 1:24,000, $4.50 for 1:100,000, plus postage and $1.89 if maps are rolled rather than folded. Allow 5–8 days.

The Georgia Geological Survey, Agriculture Building, Room 406A, 19 Martin Luther King Jr. Drive SW, Atlanta, GA 30334. Phone (404) 656-3214. Cost: $2.50 for 1:24,000; $4 for 1:100,000, plus 6 percent sales tax and postage. Allow 3–5 days.

TOPOGRAPHICAL MAPS OF WESTERN NORTH CAROLINA AND OF TOWNS COUNTY AND RABUN COUNTY, GEORGIA

Macon County Supply Company, 190 Depot Street, Franklin, NC 28734. Phone (704) 524-4428. Cost: $3.75 for 1:24,000. Raised relief maps of GA, NC, SC, and TN: $14.95 for 1:125,000.

Black Rock Mountain State Park, Mountain City, GA 30562. Phone (706) 746-2141. Raised relief maps of central and southern Appalachian areas (AL through PA): $16.95 for 1:125,000 quads. USA raised relief maps: $12.95–$19.95. Raised relief maps of Shenandoah and Great Smoky Mountain National Parks: $8.95.

STATE PARK MAPS

The Georgia Department of Natural Resources, Parks, Recreation, and Historic Sites Division, Floyd Tower East, 205 Butler Street SE, Suite 1352, Atlanta, GA 30334. Phone (404) 656-3530. To make reservations, call the appropriate park at the number listed in Appendix B.

FOREST SERVICE MAPS

The U.S. Department of Agriculture, Forest Service, Information Center, Room 154, 1720 Peachtree Road NW, Atlanta, GA 30309-2417. Phone (404) 347-2384. Or, in limited quantities, from USFS district offices throughout Georgia. Cost: free, $1, $6. Maps used for this guidebook included the Cherokee National Forest, the Appalachian Trail, the Chattahoochee National Forest, the Chattooga National Wild and Scenic River, the Cohutta Wilderness, the Nantahala Wilderness, and the Southern Nantahala Wilderness and Standing Indian Basin.

TVA MAPS OF LAKES BLUE RIDGE, CHATUGE, AND NOTTELY

The Tennessee Valley Authority, Maps and Surveys Department (HB1A), 1101 Market Street, Chattanooga, TN 37402-2801. Phone (615) 751-6277. Cost: $1.50 each.

ARMY ENGINEERS' LAKE MAPS OF CARTERS LAKE AND LAKE ALLATOONA

Allatoona Lake, PO Box 487, Cartersville, GA 30120-0487. Phone (770) 382-4700, fax (770) 386-6758.

Carters Lake, PO Box 96, Oakman, GA 30732-0096. Phone (706) 334-2248, fax (706) 334-2213.

STATE HIGHWAY MAPS AND COUNTY ROAD MAPS

Alabama Highway Department, 1409 Coliseum Boulevard, Room R-103, Montgomery, AL 36130. Phone (205) 261-6071.

Georgia Department of Transportation, Map Sales Division, 2 Capitol Square, Atlanta, GA 30334. Phone (404) 656-5336.

North Carolina Department of Transportation, Map Section, Public Affairs Unit, PO Box 25201, Raleigh, NC 27611. Phone (919) 733-7600.

South Carolina Department of Transportation, Map Sales Division, PO Box 191, Columbia, SC 29202. Phone (803) 737-1501.

Tennessee Department of Transportation, Map Sales Office, Suite 300, James K. Polk Building, 505 Deaderick Street, Nashville, TN 37243-0345. Phone (615) 741-2195.

Note: Information on road conditions in Georgia is available from the Georgia Department of Transportation at (404) 624-7890.

B. State Parks in the Mountains

Georgia's state parks are operated by the Parks, Recreation, and Historic Sites Division, Georgia Department of Natural Resources, Floyd Tower East, Suite 1352, 205 Butler Street SE, Atlanta, GA 30334. The following state parks are in the mountain region covered by this guidebook.

Amicalola Falls, Star Route, Box 215, Dawsonville, GA 30534. Phone (706) 265-8888.

Black Rock Mountain, PO Drawer A, Mountain City, GA 30562. Phone (706) 746-2141.

Cloudland Canyon, Route 2, Box 150, Rising Fawn, GA 30738. Phone (706) 657-4050.

Fort Mountain, 181 Fort Mountain Road, Chatsworth, GA 30705. Phone (706) 695-2621.

James H. "Sloppy" Floyd, Route 1, Box 291, Summerville, GA 30747. Phone (706) 857-0826.

Moccasin Creek, Route 1, Lake Burton, GA 30523. Phone (706) 947-3194.

Red Top Mountain, 653 Red Top Mountain Road SE, Cartersville, GA 30120. Phone (706) 975-0055.

Tallulah Gorge, PO Box 248, Tallulah Falls, GA 30573. Phone (706) 754-7970.

Unicoi, PO Box 849, Helen, GA 30545. Phone (706) 878-2201.

Vogel, Route 1, 7485 Vogel State Park Road, Blairsville, GA 30512. Phone (706) 745-2628.

Georgia's state parks offer excellent opportunities to enjoy a variety of natural environments. There is much to see and do, including hiking, swimming, camping, fishing, boating, and picnicking.

All state parks in the Georgia mountains offer tent and trailer camping, and all but two ("Sloppy" Floyd and Moccasin Creek) offer cottages for rent. Day-use picnicking is not allowed in the camping areas. No fees are charged for fishing in park lakes, rivers, and streams, but a valid Georgia fishing license is required of all residents 16 or older. Nonresidents must have a valid, nonresident license. Trout stamps are required for fishing in streams. Canoes, fishing boats, and boats with motors are available for rent at many state parks.

▓ CAMPGROUNDS

Campgrounds are open from 7 a.m. to 10 p.m. and require registration and payment of a fee before setting up camp. Permits to set up camp should be obtained by 8 p.m.; checkout deadline is 3 p.m. Arrivals at campsite after hours will be asked to pay the following morning.

Camping rigs plus two boat trailers and one pup tent are allowed on each site. Park campgrounds have picnic tables with benches, electrical hookups, water faucets, charcoal grills, playground equipment, garbage pickup, and restrooms with hot and cold water, showers, and lavatories. Some have sanitary dumping stations, coin-operated laundromats, public telephones, and refreshment vending machines. Maximum occupancy of any particular site is 14 days. Campers under age 18 must be accompanied by a responsible adult.

Organized groups are expected to use group campsites or pioneer camping areas rather than individual, developed, tent and trailer camping areas. No RVs are allowed in these areas.

Group camps, available only to groups with a camp director or official supervising committee, offer sleeping quarters, kitchen, dining/assembly room, craft shops, activity field, and swimming area.

Reservations for stays of two days or more can be made up to 30 days in advance by calling the numbers listed below. There is a small, nonrefundable registration fee. MasterCard and VISA are honored for all camping fees.

▓ COTTAGES

All cottages in the state parks are fully equipped with stoves and refrigerators, necessary cooking and serving equipment, linens, and blankets. All are heated; most are air-conditioned. Maximum period of occupancy is 14 days.

Check-in time for cottages is between 4 and 10 p.m.; checkout time is 11 a.m. No pets are allowed in cottages and there are no kennels available. The cottages are not available to organized groups.

Cottage reservations are accepted no more than 11 months in advance. For June 1 to Labor Day, reservations made more than 30 days in advance must be for a minimum of one week. Otherwise, and during the remainder of the year, reservations must be made for two nights. A minimum 72-hour cancellation notice is required for a refund. There is a $10 per-unit cancellation fee.

Reservations: Phone (800) 864-PARK, or (770) 389-PARK in metro Atlanta, for individual reservations.

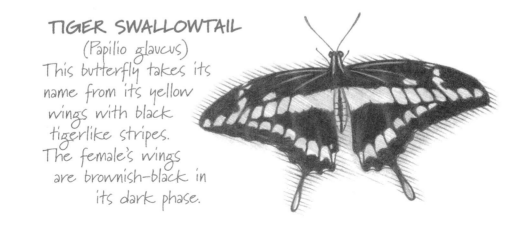

TIGER SWALLOWTAIL
(Papilio glaucus)
This butterfly takes its name from its yellow wings with black tigerlike stripes. The female's wings are brownish-black in its dark phase.

C. Outfitters, Guides, and Suppliers

The following is a listing of some of the outfitters providing specialized equipment and/or guided expeditions in the Georgia mountains and beyond.

Bargain Barn. Sales of hunting, fishing, archery, camping, and backpacking equipment. 3343 Highway 53 East, Jasper, GA 30143. Phone (770) 735-3340.

Blue Ridge Mountain Sports. Sales of backpacking, camping, and climbing equipment, and rental of backpacking and camping equipment. Lenox Square Mall, 3393 Peachtree Road NE, Atlanta, GA 30326. Phone (404) 266-8372.

Call of the Wild. Sales of backpacking, camping, canoeing, and rock-climbing equipment, and rental of backpacking and camping equipment. 425 Market Place, Roswell, GA 30075. Phone (770) 992-5400.

Cartecay River Bicycle Shop. Great source of mountain biking information. Sales, rental, and repair of bicycles. Group rides. Located 3 miles east of Ellijay on GA 52. Rt. 5, Box 244B Ellijay, Georgia 30540. Phone (706) 635-BIKE.

Chattooga Whitewater Shop. Sales and rental of canoeing, kayaking, and rafting equipment. Instruction in canoeing, kayaking, and rafting. Shuttle service on the Chattooga River. 14239 Long Creek Highway, Long Creek, SC 29658. Phone (864) 647-9083, fax (864) 647-4459.

Go With The Flow. Retail sales of canoes, kayaks, and sea kayaks; instruction, rentals, repairs. Provides information on water levels for area rivers. 4 Elizabeth Way, Roswell, GA 30075. Phone (770) 992-3200. 2597 Atlanta Highway, Athens, GA 30606. Phone (706) 613-8600.

High Adventures provides whitewater rafting on the Ocoee and Hiawassee Rivers, sea kayak lake excursions, rope courses, adventure hikes for children, cabin rental, campground, volleyball, picnic pavilion, and catering. Call (800) 233-8594 for information and reservations.

High Country Outfitters, Inc. Sales of hiking, backpacking, rock climbing and paddling gear, rugged sportswear, plus books and maps. Rental of backpacking gear at location #1. Rock climbing clinics, backpacking clinics, and whitewater rafting. Location #1: 3906 Roswell Road, Atlanta, GA 30342. Phone (404) 814-0999. Location #2: 440 Ashford Dunwoody Road, 1412 Perimeter Mall, Atlanta, GA. Phone (770) 391-9657. Location #3: Riverchase Galleria, 2000-147A, Birmingham, AL. Phone (205) 985-3215.

The Hometown Book Store. Sales of maps and books on southern Appalachia, official U.S. geological surveys, topography maps, guidebooks, and field guides. 114 North Park Street, PO Box 358, Dahlonega, GA 30535. Phone (706) 864-7225.

Mountain Crossing. Sales of camping and backpacking equipment. 9710 Gainesville Highway, Blairsville, GA 30512. Phone (706) 745-6095.

Mountain Crossing at Walasi-Yi Center. Sales of backpacking and camping gear, specializing in long-distance trips. Operation of seasonal hostel (Mar. 1–May 31) on Appalachian Trail. Advice and information on local trails and campsites. Highway 129, Route 1, Box 1240, Blairsville, GA 30512. Phone (706) 745-6095.

Mountaintown Outdoor Expeditions. Sales and rental of canoeing, kayaking, camping, backpacking, and mountain biking equipment. PO Box 86, Ellijay, GA 30540. Phone (706) 635-2524.

Mountain Ventures. Sales of camping, backpacking, rock climbing, caving and canoeing equipment, and rental of camping and backpacking equipment. 3040 N. Decatur Road, Atlanta, GA 30079. Phone (404) 299-5254.

Nantahala Outdoor Center. Sales of paddling, bicycling, backpacking, rock climbing, and camping equipment, and rental of canoeing, kayaking, and rafting equipment. Instruction in canoeing, kayaking, backpacking, and rock climbing. Guided raft trips on the Chattooga, Nantahala, Ocoee, French Broad, and Nolichucky rivers. Adventure travel expeditions to many destinations within and outside the United States. 13077 Highway 19 W, Bryson City, NC 28713-9114. Phone (704) 488-2175.

Outback Outfitters & Bikes. Sales of mountain bikes and accessories, backpacking and camping equipment and apparel. 1125 Euclid Avenue NE, Atlanta, GA 30307. Phone (404) 688-4878.

REI. A consumer cooperative offering sales of camping, backpacking, climbing, paddling, and cycling equipment. Comprehensive rental department. Two locations: 1800 NE Expressway, Atlanta, GA 30329 (intersection of Clairmont Road and I-85). Phone (404) 633-6508. 1165 Perimeter Center West, Dunwoody, GA 30346 (behind Perimeter Mall). Phone (770) 901-9200.

Rock Creek Outfitters. Sales of rock-climbing, camping, backpacking, canoeing, and kayaking equipment, and rental of backpacks and tents. 4825 Hixson Pike, Chattanooga, TN 37443. Phone (615) 877-6256.

Southeastern Expeditions. Guided raft trips on the Chattooga and Ocoee rivers. 50 Executive Park South, Suite 5016, Atlanta, GA 30329. Phone (404) 782-4331 (Chattooga) or (615) 338-8073 (Ocoee).

Wilderness Southeast. Nonprofit outdoor school offering adventure trips throughout the Southeast and to the Virgin Islands and Costa Rica. 711 Sandtown Road, Savannah, GA 31410. Phone (912) 355-8008.

The Wildewood Outpost. Sales and rental of canoeing and rafting equipment. PO Box 999, Helen, GA 30545. Phone (706) 865-4692.

Wildwater Ltd. Outdoor Adventures. Guided raft trips on the Chattooga and Ocoee rivers. Long Creek, SC 29658. Phone (803) 647-9587.

Wolfcreek Wilderness. Nonprofit outdoor school offering leadership training and instruction in backpacking, canoeing, and rock climbing. Route 1, Box 1190, Blairsville, GA 30512. Phone (706) 745-5553.

D. Books and References

The following books and booklets will help to illuminate the botany, geology, geography, commerce, and culture of the Georgia mountains.

Appalachian Whitewater, Volume I: The Southern Mountains by Bob Sehlinger, Don Otey, Bob Benner, William Nealy, and Bob Lantz, Menasha Ridge Press, Birmingham, AL 1986.

The Atlas of Georgia by Thomas W. Holder and Howard A. Schretter, University of Georgia Press, Athens, GA 1986.

Atlas of the Vascular Flora of Georgia: A Georgia Botanical Society Project compiled by Marie B. Mellinger and edited by Harriett L. Whipple, Studio Designs Printing, Milledgeville, GA 1984.

The Chattooga Wild and Scenic River by Brian Boyd, Ferncreek Press, Conyers, GA 1990.

Foxfire series edited by Eliot Wigginton, Anchor Press/Doubleday, Garden City, NY 1975.

Guide to the Foothills Trail, 2d edition. The Foothills Trail Conference, PO Box 3041, Greenville, SC 29602. (864) 233-9403.

The Hiking Trails of North Georgia by Tim Homan. Peachtree Publishers, Ltd., Atlanta, GA 1997.

Inns of the Southern Mountains by Patricia L. Hudson, EPM Publications, McLean, VA 1985.

More Mountain Spirits by Joseph Earl Dabney, Bright Mountain Books, Asheville, NC 1980.

Mountain Getaways by Rusty Hoffland, On the Road Publishing, Atlanta, GA 1988.

Mountain Singer: The Life and the Legacy of Byron Herbert Reece by Raymond A. Cook, Cherokee Publishing Company, Atlanta, GA 1980.

Mountain Spirits by Joseph Earl Dabney, Charles Scribner's Sons, New York, NY 1974.

The Natural Environments of Georgia by Charles H. Wharton, Georgia Department of Natural Resources, Atlanta, GA 1978.

North Carolina Hiking Trails, 2d edition by Allen de Hart, Appalachian Mountain Club Books, Boston, MA 1988.

Northern Georgia Canoeing by Bob Sehlinger and Don Otey, Menasha Ridge Press, Birmingham, AL 1980.

The Travels of William Bartram edited by Mark Van Doren, Dover Publications, Inc., New York, NY 1955.

Trees of the Southeastern United States by Wilbur H. Duncan and Mirion B. Duncan, University of Georgia Press, Athens, GA 1988.

Waterfalls of the Southern Appalachians by Brian Boyd, Ferncreek Press, Conyers, GA 1990.

Wildflowers of the Southeastern United States by Wilbur H. Duncan and Leonard E. Foote, University of Georgia Press, Athens, GA 1975.

E. Special Events, Fairs, and Festivals

Attendance at a select few annual events in the mountains will give the reader a good insight into mountain history, culture, and people. Following are some of the best of these events. Dates are subject to change.

Chiaha Harvest Fair and Heritage Holidays Festival—*Civil War reenactments, riverboat, wagon train and train rides. 80 southeastern artists and craftsmen. Late October in Rome. Phone (800) 444-1834 ext. 2 or (706) 235-4542.*

Dahlonega Blue Grass Festival—*At Blackburn Park on Old State Road 9E, 7 miles west of Dahlonega, in June. Phone (706) 864-3721 or (706) 864-7203.*

Fall Harvest Festival—*Country music, arts and crafts at fairgrounds in Hiawassee in October. Phone (706) 896-4191.*

Fasching Karnival—*In Helen in December and January. Phone (706) 878-2248.*

Georgia Apple Festival—*Crafts show in Ellijay in October. Phone (706) 635-7400.*

Georgia Mountain Fair—*12 days of crafts exhibits and entertainment at fairgrounds in Hiawassee in August. Phone (706) 896-4191.*

Harvest Festival—*Arts and crafts at farmer's market on US 441 in Dillard. Phone (706) 782-4812.*

Helen International Fest—*Dancing, food, music, crafts from all over the world. Late June, early July in Helen. PO Box 730, Helen, GA. Phone (706) 878-2181.*

Helen's Oktoberfest—*German food, beverages, and entertainment in Helen in October. Phone (706) 878-2521.*

New Salem Mountain Festival—*Quality arts and crafts atop Lookout Mountain on GA Highway 136 between Trenton and LaFayette. May and October, Box 600, Rising Fawn, GA 30738. Phone (706) 398-1988.*

Prater's Mill Country Fair—*Arts and crafts festival, GA Highway 2, 10 miles north of Dalton, in May and October. Phone (706) 275-MILL.*

The Reach of Song—*An Appalachian drama presenting the Georgia mountains through the life and words of native poet Byron Herbert Reece; in Hiawassee in June and July. Phone (706) 896-3388.*

Sorghum Festival—*In Blairsville in October. Phone (706) 745-5789.*

Spring Country Music Festival—*At fairgrounds in Hiawassee in May. Phone (706) 896-4191.*

Taste of Toccoa—*Family entertainment and a wide variety of country foods. In Toccoa in April. Phone (706) 886-8451.*

F. Conservation & Outdoor Organizations

All of the following are nonprofit organizations dedicated to the enjoyment and/or preservation of nature's bounty in the Georgia mountains and beyond.

Atlanta Audubon Society—*Box 29189, Atlanta, GA 30359. Phone (770) 955-4111. Conservation and environmental education, including bird study. Monthly programs on environmental concerns. News hotline concerning programs and bird sightings.*

Atlanta Whitewater Club—*PO Box 33, Clarkston, GA 30021. Phone (770) 299-3752. Whitewater canoeing and kayaking. Emphasizes improvement of outdoor skills, safety, and appreciation of river sports.*

Benton MacKaye Trail Association—*PO Box 53271, Atlanta, GA 30355. Enjoyment and maintenance of the Benton MacKaye Trail. Monthly construction hikes and trail maintenance along sections of the trail.*

The Dogwood City Grotto—*2457 Drew Valley Road, Atlanta, GA 30319. Atlanta chapter of the National Speleological Society. Cave protection, conservation, and exploration. Monthly outings to explore caves in the Southeast.*

Ens and Outs—*Unitarian Universalist Congregation of Atlanta, 1911 Cliff Valley Way NE, Atlanta, GA 30329. Preservation and enjoyment of nature. Weekly outings to a variety of destinations throughout the state.*

Friends of the Mountains—*Box 368, Clayton, GA 30525. Preservation and enjoyment of the southern Appalachian Mountain environment. Quarterly business meetings and conservation fair each spring. Monthly outings to natural areas in north Georgia and western North Carolina.*

Georgia Appalachian Trail Club, Inc.—*PO Box 654, Atlanta, GA 30301. Phone (404) 634-6495 (voice mailbox). Maintenance of the Appalachian Trail and approach trails in Georgia. Weekly hikes and outings. Monthly trail maintenance.*

Georgia Botanical Society—*7575 Rico Road, Palmetto, GA 30268. Furthering the appreciation of wildflowers. Monthly or semimonthly outings throughout Georgia and contiguous states.*

Georgia Canoeing Association—*PO Box 7023, Atlanta, GA 30357. River enjoyment and conservation. Training programs and weekly paddling trips in Georgia and contiguous states.*

The Georgia Conservancy, Inc.—*1776 Peachtree Street NW, Suite 400 South, Atlanta, GA 30309. Phone (404) 876-2900. 711 Sandtown Road, Savannah, GA 31410. Phone (912) 897-6462. Protection of Georgia's environment and the encouragement of responsible stewardship of our vital natural resources. Annual conference, naturalist trips, and chapter activities.*

Georgia ForestWatch—*1447 Peachtree Street NE, Suite 812, Atlanta, GA 30309. Phone (404) 872-9453. Fax (404) 872-8540. Protection of Georgia's Chattahoochee and Oconee national forests. Educational workshops and regular field trips to review timber* *cutting and related road construction on these forests and to propose areas for wilderness and other special management.*

Georgia Ornithological Society—*PO Box 1684, Cartersville, GA 30120. Furthering education about and understanding of birds. Semiannual statewide meetings for field study, fellowship, and information exchange. Publishes a quarterly newsletter, the Oriole. Call (770) 493-8862 for the society's rare-bird alert.*

Georgia Wildlife Federation—*1930 Iris Drive, Conyers, GA 30207. Phone (770) 929-3350. Conservation of wildlife and its habitat, and statewide environmental education programs. Sponsors the premier awards program to recognize conservation achievement in Georgia.*

The Nature Conservancy—*1401 Peachtree Street NE, Suite 236, Atlanta, GA 30309. Phone (404) 873-6946. Preservation of rare and endangered species and natural communities through protection of the ecosystems that sustain them. Annual general membership meetings and field trips throughout the year.*

North Carolina Bartram Trail Society—*Route 3, Box 406, Sylva, NC 28779. Development, maintenance, and enjoyment of the Bartram Trail.*

The Sierra Club, Georgia Chapter—*PO Box 46751, Atlanta, GA 30346. Exploration, enjoyment, and preservation of the nation's forests, waters, wildlife, and wilderness. Seven chapters throughout Georgia with monthly meetings and frequent outings to locations throughout the Southeast.*

Trout Unlimited, Georgia Council—*3836 Foxwood Road, Duluth, GA 30136. Protection, preservation, and enhancement of cold-water fisheries.*

The Wilderness Society—*1447 Peachtree Street NE, Suite 812, Atlanta, GA 30309. Phone (404) 872-9453, fax (404) 872-8540. Protection of natural areas on our federal lands, including national forests, national parks, and national wildlife refuges. Helps coordinate activities of the citizen group ForestWatch.*

EARLY MOREL
(Verpa bohemica)
Growing up to 4 inches tall, this morel is identified by a yellow-brown, bell-shaped cap atop a hollow, light-colored stem. It grows in wet areas.

G. Safety in the Mountains

ADVANCE PLANNING—Before setting out on a backpacking or canoeing trip into the mountains, do your homework. Become familiar with the maps of the area and learn to use a compass. Consider taking a short first-aid course to prepare for emergencies. Plan your trip in advance, let others know where you are going and when you expect to return, and travel with a companion.

EQUIPMENT AND SUPPLIES—Prepare a list of essentials, including the following:

WATER. Carry one or more unbreakable bottles of fresh water. Consider taking also a simple water-treatment system for emergency water purification.

FOOD. Carry enough food for the duration of the trip, plus extra for the unexpected. Include quick-energy items such as trail mix (gorp).

COMPASS AND MAPS. A good map allows for exploration of areas which otherwise might not be attempted. If lost without a map of the area, use the compass to walk in a straight line in the direction of a known landmark, such as a road.

FIRST-AID SUPPLIES. Carry a basic first-aid kit containing bandages, tape, aspirin, moleskin, disinfectant or antiseptic, analgesic tablets, a small mirror, and any personal medicines, as well as sunscreen, lip protection, sunglasses, and other supplies appropriate to the season and conditions.

FLASHLIGHT. A day outing may last longer than expected. Carry a reliable flashlight and an extra bulb and batteries.

POCKET KNIFE. A multipurpose knife is essential.

WATERPROOF MATCHES AND/OR LIGHTER. A fire for signaling, warmth, or cooking food may become necessary because of injury, delay, isolation, or sudden weather change.

SPACE BLANKET. This compact, lightweight material with a reflective side which helps to hold in body heat can be obtained at most sporting goods stores. It also can be used as a lean-to in emergencies.

TWINE OR FISH LINE. Twenty or 30 feet of twine or fishline and several safety pins can be useful for many types of emergencies or for repair to equipment or clothing.

CLOTHING AND RAINWEAR. Always prepare for the possibility of sudden weather change due to rain, snow, and wind storms. At a minimum, a lightweight, water-repellent windbreaker is recommended. A pair of gloves—wool or pile recommended—and head protection provide additional barriers to heat loss when cold. Dressing in layers of clothing suitable to weather conditions allows you to adjust for temperature changes more easily.

Wool will warm even when wet. Select shoes or boots, tents, sleeping bags, and other equipment to match your activity and the worst-case conditions you might expect to encounter.

RESCUE TEAMS—For your security, be advised that many mountain counties have a search and rescue team with a four-wheel-drive vehicle. In an emergency, pile up enough wood and light a fire for warmth or for a signal to a plane or helicopter passing overhead. While waiting for help, get under an overhanging rock if possible, and if cold, use whatever cover is available—even mounds of dry leaves. If possible, send a companion for help. Contact the sheriff's office or any Forest Service personnel.

GIARDIA—Years ago, one could safely drink from any stream in the mountains. In the last several decades, however, a protozoan parasite, giardia, has spoiled the purity of natural streams worldwide. Not even Alaska, Guam, and Colorado are safe. Unfortunately, the disease is difficult and expensive to cure. The parasite, spread by human feces, has been picked up by many mammals, such as beaver and deer, which in turn contaminate surface water. Only spring water is safe. The cysts of giardia are destroyed by prolonged boiling of water; by the application of iodine; or by the use of small, light, filtering devices available at outdoor supply stores. Another solution is simply to carry water in unbreakable containers.

HYPOTHERMIA—Perhaps the greatest real danger in the outdoors is the threat of death by hypothermia, or a prolonged lowering of body temperature. To prevent hypothermia, stay dry. Carry rain gear. Wet clothes wick away body heat and lead to rapid chilling. Swimming a few minutes too long in an icy mountain stream may produce hypothermia, even in summer—especially if combined with smoking cigarettes or drinking alcohol. A hiking companion who talks or walks slowly for no apparent reason may be experiencing hypothermia. To produce body heat, keep exercising, build a fire, drink hot liquids, and use a sleeping bag.

ROCKS AND MOSS—Probably more people are injured, or even killed, by slipping on wet or moss-covered rocks than by all of the snakes, bears, hornets, and other causes combined. Wet rocks, especially if covered with a thin moss, can be the equivalent of stepping on ice. Use a walking stick, wear shoes with gripping soles, and exercise extreme care. Stay away from the heads of waterfalls; several people have slipped on them and fallen to their deaths.

INSECTS—Few places in the world are as free of insects and pests as is north Georgia. Mosquitos and deer flies are nearly absent. In early spring, blackflies may be a temporary annoyance. The most common is the tiny "no-see-um," called "sandfly" on the coast. It can be troublesome in still and moist weather. Carry repellent. Check for and remove any ticks promptly.

CLOUDBURSTS—Violent rainstorms, called "cloudbursts" by mountaineers, are frightening. Take shelter under cliffs if possible. Do not stand under isolated or very tall trees, or on ridges or mountaintops, where lightening frequently strikes. Most sudden downpours are over quickly and pose no danger other than getting soaked. If, however, you anticipate fording a mountain river such as the Chattooga or Cooper Creek, keep your eye on water levels. Streams can rise suddenly and cut you off, or force you to swim across and be subject to possible hypothermia.

BEARS—Bears will always run, unless you stumble closely on a mother with cubs. Don't leave enticing foods around. If ever confronted, stop and slowly back away. Make lots of noise. You will be lucky to glimpse a bear in 10 years of hiking in the Georgia mountains.

HUNTING SEASONS—A far greater danger than bears is to be mistaken for a deer or turkey during the short but intensive hunting seasons. Check to see if there is a hunt in progress in a wildlife management area where you anticipate hiking. As with bears, whistle and shout at intervals. Wearing bright colors is advisable.

YELLOW JACKETS—Remarkably, yellow jackets—a ground-dwelling wasp—are probably the only injurious creatures that one will encounter in the mountains. If you hear or see more than one yellow and black "bee" buzzing around your feet, you have probably stumbled upon a nest. Move rapidly away. Usually 50 feet is adequate if you move fast. Do not fear yellow jackets or other species—just be ready to move quickly. Remember that a stung horse can make a sudden leap. Carefully examine the entire area around a tree where any animal is tied. It may be difficult to release an animal in panic state. When bushwhacking away from trails, shorts are not advisable for many reasons, including greenbriers.

POISONOUS SNAKES—One can easily hike 10 years in the mountains without seeing a poisonous snake. It is a good idea to talk to local "old timers" if you are exploring trail-less terrain. Our timber rattlesnake is one of the most inoffensive and calm of the world's venomous reptiles. Many do not rattle but lie quietly "hoping" they will be passed by unseen (and unmolested). Be cautious and respectful, but not afraid. Simply take care where hands and feet are placed, especially in rocky places and near logs. A walking stick is helpful for getting through thick overgrowth. Never walk at night without a flashlight. In fall and spring, snakes crawl to and from and concentrate around communal dens where they hibernate during the cold months. By the first serious frost, most snakes are underground. Like all animals, an occasional snake will be irritable—possibly due to illness, overheating, or shedding of its skin, which obscures its vision—and rattle or appear aggressive.

Timber rattlers come in both yellow and black colorations. Copperheads, the only other potentially dangerous snakes in the mountains, are more difficult to see in the leaves. Fortunately, they are more rarely encountered in the higher mountains.

In serious snake-bite cases, consider staying put and calling for evacuation by helicopter or by local search and rescue teams. A high-tech solution is a jolt to the bite from a stun gun; but get acquainted with this technique before attempting it. Electricity appears to destroy most venoms.

In summary, plan ahead so that you are wellequipped and prepared to deal with the expected, as well as the unexpected. This will not only enhance your enjoyment of the outing by lending peace of mind; it may also save lives.

H. Southern Appalachian Areas

In 1964, Congress passed the Wilderness Protection Act, creating the National Wilderness Preservation System. Wilderness areas designated by Congress consist of federally owned land preserved in its natural state. Thus, in areas designated as wilderness, certain activities such as road building, timber harvesting, motor vehicle use, mining, and dam construction are prohibited. Permitted uses include hiking, fishing, camping, nature study, canoeing, horseback riding, and, in Forest Service wilderness areas, hunting. Wilderness not only provides backcountry recreation opportunities, but also protects high-quality watersheds and fisheries, old growth wildlife habitat, and visual beauty.

The only two areas from the Southeast included in the Wilderness Act of 1964 were Shining Rock and Linville Gorge in western North Carolina's Pisgah National Forest. For a decade, these two areas were the Southeast's only national forest wildernesses. Other areas proposed for wilderness designation were not considered by the Forest Service as sufficiently primitive.

In response to broad grass-roots support, Congress passed the Eastern Wilderness Act of 1975, which established the principle that areas that regain their natural, primitive character can and do qualify as wilderness. This act also established the Cohutta and Ellicott Rock wildernesses in Georgia.

During a process called "RARE II" in the late 1970s, the Forest Service identified over 200,000 acres of additional eligible wilderness in the Chattahoochee National Forest. In 1984 and 1986, Congress established the Rich Mountain, Raven Cliffs, Tray Mountain, Southern Nantahala, and Brasstown wildernesses and expanded the Cohutta and Ellicott Rock wildernesses. In 1991 Congress passed the Chattahoochee Forest Protection Act, which added to the Brasstown Wilderness and created the Blood Mountain and Mark Trail wildernesses. This act also designated the 7,100-acre Coosa Bald National Scenic Area and established the 23,330-acre Springer Mountain National Recreation Area (which was later renamed after Ed Jenkins, the longtime Congressional representative from this mountain district and the bill's lead sponsor).

Many other outstanding areas need wilderness designation, especially since the Forest Service projects that demand for wilderness recreation will soon outstrip available opportunities in the southern Appalachians. As noted in the following appendix, the current forest plan opens up most of these potential wildernesses to possible timber production and related road construction that may degrade their wildland value. Fortunately, however, an upcoming revision to the forest plan this decade will study eligible areas for possible wilderness recommendations, which will result in continued protection. Some top candidates for future wildernesses or other special area designations include additions to Raven Cliffs and Southern Nantahala Wilderness, Mountaintown, Kelly Ridge, Rock Gorge, Wolf Knob, the Rocky Face and John's Mountain areas on the Armuchee Ranger District, and Rabun Bald.

North Georgia has 10 wilderness areas totaling 114,616 acres. One, the Cohutta, overlaps into Tennessee; its "sister" wilderness, Big Frog, has 89 acres in Georgia. The Southern Nantahala Wilderness is almost equally divided between North Carolina and Georgia. Ellicott Rock along the Chattooga Wild and Scenic River is split among Georgia, South Carolina, and North Carolina.

Check with the local ranger for regulations regarding the use of horses, normally permitted except on the Appalachian Trail. Problems of management such as signs, parking, trail maintenance, and emergency evacuation procedures are being addressed by local Forest Service rangers for each wilderness area.

WILDERNESS AREA	TOTAL ACRES	ACRES IN GEORGIA
Big Frog	8,082	89
Blood Mountain	7,800	7,800
Brasstown	12,975	12,975
Cohutta	36,977	35,268
Ellicott Rock	8,274	2,021
Mark Trail	16,400	16,400
Raven Cliffs	9,115	9,115
Rich Mountains	9,476	9,476
Southern Nantahala	23,714	11,770
Tray Mountain	9,702	9,702
Total		**114,616**

VIRGINIA CREEPER

(Parthenocissus quinquefolia) A cousin of grapes, the Virginia creeper climbs and sprawls as it grows up to 150 feet high. Leaves are green in summer and red in fall. The dark blue berries are poisonous to humans but are food for songbirds and other wildlife.

I. Forest Planning

In the National Forest Management Act of 1976, Congress specifically directed the U.S. Forest Service to reduce clear-cutting, provide for biological diversity, protect streams and water quality, limit uneconomic timbering, and provide for public input. Responding to these mandates, the Forest Service in 1985 issued a final management plan for the Chattahoochee-Oconee National Forests. Dissatisfied with the management plan, a coalition consisting of The Georgia Conservancy, the Wilderness Society, the Sierra Club, Friends of the Mountains, Georgia Botanical Society, Atlanta Audubon Society, and the Georgia Council of Trout Unlimited filed an appeal, or administrative lawsuit, of the plan with the Chief of the Forest Service in Washington, D.C. In return for changes in the plan regarding preservation of special areas and the use of herbicides, the conservation groups withdrew their appeal. They also set up a process for continued review of Forest Service projects by a new citizen group called Georgia ForestWatch. (For information on how to participate in Georgia ForestWatch, *see* Appendix F.)

The Chattahoochee-Oconee management plan provides for 10 to 15 years of specific management direction and will affect the future of the forests for decades to come. It sets high goals for increasing timber harvest over the levels sold prior to the plan and, as a result, opens over 70 percent of the forest to logging. Conservationists have had to appeal and even litigate a number of timber sales over the years that threatened popular recreation areas, sensitive ecological sites, and potential wildernesses.

Fortunately, the National Forest Management Act also requires that forest plans be revised every 10 to 15 years, which means that the Chattahoochee and Oconee forests must be thoroughly replanned by the year 2000 at the latest. As mentioned in the preceding appendix, Southern Appalachian Areas, the Forest Service will consider lands on the forests for possible wilderness recommendations or other protective designations.

To assist in the replanning, a coalition of conservation groups, including The Georgia Conservancy, has published a proposal for the protection of a network of wildlands across the Chattahoochee National Forest, encompassing 44 natural areas with a total of 235,700 acres. Evidence of the compelling need to change the existing forest plan is that only 20 percent of these outstanding wildlands is currently protected from timber production and related road construction. (To obtain a copy of the report *Georgia's Mountain Treasures: The Unprotected Wildlands of the Chattahoochee National Forest* (1995), contact the Wilderness Society, listed in Appendix F.)

To help protect valued wildlands and become involved in the forest (re)planning process, write to:

George Martin, Supervisor, Chattahoochee-Oconee National Forests, 508 Oak Street NW, Gainesville, GA 30501.

Ask to be put on the mailing list for planning. You will receive regular newsletters from the Forest Service about the process and be able to comment at key points on the drafting of the new plan.

Conservation groups are urging the Forest Service to make significant improvements in the flawed and outdated 1985 forest plan. For the full protection of the distinctive natural values of Georgia's national forests, the following changes are essential: an end to new logging road construction; a substantial reduction in the annual timber sales level; the elimination of below-cost timber sales; the protection of the wildlands in *Georgia's Mountain Treasures*, including ample wilderness recommendations, preservation of visual beauty, the establishment of well-distributed old growth forest restoration areas, a redirection of budget toward recreation, fish, and wildlife and land acquisition, wider no-cut buffers along streams, and more emphasis on unfragmented forest habitat for songbirds and other species of special concern; separate plans for these two dissimilar forests; and a reform in logging methods away from even-aged cutting.

BUTTERFLY WEED
(Asclepias tuberosa)
This plant is often found in home gardens because its bright orange, star-shaped flowers attract butterflies. The plant's roots have been used in India as a cure for pleurisy and for other pulmonary ailments.

J. Glossary of Plants

Alabama snow-wreath	*Neviusia alabamensis*
Alum root	*Heuchera* sp.
Arbutus, trailing	*Epigaea repens*
Ash, blue	*Fraxinus quadrangulata*
Ash, mountain	*Sorbus americana*
Azalea, flame	*Rhododendron calendulaceum*
Azalea, pinxterflower	*Rhododendron nudiflorum*
Basswood	*Tilia heterophylla*
Beech	*Fagus grandifolia*
Bent Trillium	*Trillium flexipes*
Biltmore Sedge	*Carex biltmoreana*
Birch, black	*Betula lenta*
Birch, sweet	*Betula lenta*
Birch, yellow	*Betula lutea*
Black locust	*Robinia pseudo-acacia*
Black walnut	*Juglans nigra*
Bloodroot	*Sanguinaria canadensis*
Blue cohosh	*Caulophyllum thalictroides*
Blue Ridge St. John's wort	*Hypericum buckleyi*
Bluebell, Virginia	*Mertensia vilginica*
Blueberries, highbush and low-bush	*Vaccinium* sp.
Bluestem grass	*Andropogon* sp.
Bluets	*Houstonia* sp.
Buckberry	*Gaylussacia ursinus*
Buckeye	*Aesculus octandra*
Buttercups, mountain	*Ranunculus* sp.
Camellia, mountain	*Stewartia ovata*
Carolina bells	*Halesia carolina*
Cedar, red	*Juniperus virginiana*
Cherry, black	*Prunus serotina*
Chestnut, American	*Castanea dentata*
Chinquapin	*Castanea pumila*
Chokeberry	*Sorbus melanocarpa*
Chokecherry	*Prunus virginiana*
Cinquefoil, three-leaved	*Potentilla tridentata*
Columbo	*Swertia caroliniensis*
Cotton-grass	*Eriophorum virginicum*
Cucumber tree	*Magnolia acuminata*
Deerberry	*Vaccinium stamineum*
Dog-hobble	*Leucothoe axillaris*
Dogwood	*Cornus florida*
Dogwood, alternate-leaf	*Cornus alternifolia*
Dropseed, prairie	*Sporobolus* sp.
Dutchman's breeches	*Dicentra cucullaria*
Elderberry, red	*Sambucus pubens*
False lily of the valley	*Maianthemum canadense*

Fern, bracken	*Pteridium aquilinum*
Fern, Christmas	*Polystichum acrostichoides*
Fern, cinnamon	*Osmunda cinnamomea*
Fern, hayscented	*Dennstaedtia punctilobula*
Fern, log	*Dryopteris celsa*
Fern, marginal wood	*Dlyopteris marginaIis*
Fern, New York	*Thelypteris noveboracensis*
Fern, rock cap	*Polypodium virginianum*
Fern, walking	*Asplenium rhizophyllum*
Fir, Fraser	*Abies fraseri*
Fleabane	*Erigeron philadelphicus*
Galax	*Galax rotundifolia*
Gay-wings	*Polygala paucifolia*
Gentian, fringed	*Gentiana crinita*
Ginger, wild	*Hexastylis* sp.
Ginseng	*Panax quinquefolius*
Goldenrod	*Solidago* sp.
Gooseberry	*Ribes* sp.
Grass of parnassus	*Parnassia asarifoIia*
Harbinger of spring	*Erigenia bulbosa*
Hawthorn	*Crataegus* sp.
Hazelnut, beaked	*Corylus cornuta*
Hellebore	*Veratrum viride*
Hemlock, Carolina	*Tsuga caroliniana*
Hemlock, Eastern	*Tsuga canadensis*
Hickory	*Carya* sp.
Holly	*Ilex opaca*
Hop hornbeam	*Ostrya virginiana*
Horse sugar	*Symplocos tinctoria*
Horsetail	*Equisetum* sp.
Hyacinth, wild	*Camassia scilloides*
Hydrangea, wild	*Hydrangea arborescens*
Iris	*Iris cristata* and *Iris verna*
Jack-in-the-Pulpit	*Arisaematriphyllum*
Japanese knotweed	*Polygonum* sp.
Japanese paper plant	*Edgeworthia papyrifera*
Kudzu	*Pueraria lobata*
Lady slipper, pink	*Cypripedium acaule*
Lady slipper, yellow	*Cypripedium calceolus*
Laurel, bog	*Kalmia angustifolia*
Laurel, mountain	*Kalmia latifolia*
Lily, Turk's cap	*Lillium superbum*
Lily of the valley	*Convallaria montana*
Locust	*Robinia* sp.
Lovegrass, weeping	*Eragrostis* sp.
Magnolia	*Magnolia* sp.

Magnolia, Fraser's	*Magnolia fraseri*	Solomon's seal	*Polygonatum biflorum*
Maple	*Acer* sp.	Sourwood	*Oxydendron arboreum*
Maple, mountain	*Acer spicatum*	Spike moss, rock	*Selaginella rupestris*
Maple, red	*Acer rubrum*	Spike moss, twisted-hair	*Selaginella tortipila*
Maple, striped	*Acer pensylvanicum*	Spikenard	*Aralia racemosa*
Maple, sugar	*Acer saccharum*	Spurge, nodding	*Euphorbia mercurialina*
Mayapple	*Podophyllum peltatum*	Squirrel corn	*Dicentra canadensis*
Minniebush	*Menziesia pilosa*	Strawberry bush	*Euonymus atropurpureus*
Mock-orange, hairy	*Philadelphus pubescens*	Strawberry, wild	*Potentilla* sp.
Monkshood	*Aconitum* sp.	Sweetfern	*Comptonia peregrina*
Moss, primitive club	*Lycopodium* sp.	Swamp pink	*Helonias bullata*
Moss, reindeer	*Cladonia* sp.	Toothwort	*Dentaria diphylla*
Moss, sphagnum	*Sphagnum* sp.	Trillium, faded	*Trillium* sp.
Mountain laurel	*Kalmia latifolia*	Trillium, Gleason's white	*Trillium* sp.
Nettle, hedge	*Stachys nuttallii*	Trillium, lanceleaf	*Trillium lancifolium*
Oak, chestnut	*Quercus prinus*	Trillium, large-flowered	*Trillium grandiflorum*
Oak, chinquapin	*Quercus muehlenbergii*	Trillium, painted	*Trillium undulatum*
Oak, Northern red	*Quercus rubla*	Trillium, persistent	*Trillium persistens*
Oak,. scarlet	*Quercus coccinea*	Trillium, Vasey's	*Trillium vaseyi*
Oak, white	*Quercus alba*	Twinleaf	*Jeffersonia diphylla*
Oconee bells	*Shortia galacifolia*	Umbrella leaf	*Diphylleia cymosa*
Orchid, purple fringed	*Habenaria psycodes*	Viburnum	*Viburnum* sp.
Orchis, showy	*Orchis spectabilis*	Violet, bird-foot	*Viola pedata*
Oxalis	*Oxalis acetosella*	Violet, common blue	*Viola papilionacea*
Pepperbush, mountain	*Clethra acuminata*	Virginia creeper	*Parthenocissus quinquefolia*
Pine, Eastern white	*Pinus strobus*	Watercress	*Nasturtium officinale*
Pine, loblolly	*Pinus taeda*	Waterleaf	*Hyrophyllum canadense*
Pine, pitch	*Pinus rigida*	Wild bergamot	*Monarda fistulosa*
Pine, short leaf	*Pinus echinata*	Willow, dwarf	*Salix humilis*
Pine, table mountain	*Pinus pungens*	Witch hazel	*Hamamelis virginiana*
Pine, Virginia	*Pinus virginiana*	Wolfsmilk	*Euphorhia purpurea*
Pine, white	*Pinus strobus*	Yellowwood	*Cladrastis lutea*
Polygala, fringed	*Polygala paucifolia*	Yellowroot	*Xanthorhiza simplicissima*
Poplar, tulip or yellow	*Liriodendron tulipifera*		
Poppy, celandine	*Stylophorum diphyllum*		
Pussy-toes	*Antennaria* sp.		
Ramp (wild mountain onion)	*Allium tricoccum*		
Raspberry, flowering	*Rubus odoratus*		
Rhododendron, Carolina	*Rhododendron minus*		
Rhododendron, catawba	*Rhododendron catawbiense*		
Rhododendron, rosebay	*Rhododendron maximum*		
Rosy twisted stalk	*Streptopus roseus*		
Sand myrtle	*Leiophyllum buxifolium*		
Saxifrage	*Saxifraga* sp.		
Serviceberry	*Amelanchier arborea*		
Silverbell	*Halesia carolina*		
Smoketree	*Cotinus obovatus*		
Solomon's plume	*Smilacina racemosa*		

NOTE: sp. = species, either not known specifically or several different ones represented.

K. Glossary

Anticline—Arching rock fold that is closed at the top and open at bottom. Oldest formation occurs in the center of an anticline.

Basement—Complex of igneous and metamorphic rock that underlies the sedimentary rocks of a region.

Biotic—Pertaining to plants and animals.

Boreal—Relating to the northern biotic area characterized by the dominance of coniferous forests.

Carbonate rock—Collective term including limestone and dolomite.

Coniferous—Describing the cone-bearing trees of the pine family; usually evergreen.

Continental drift—Theory that the continental land masses drift across the earth as the earth's plates move and interact in a process called plate tectonics.

Deciduous—Plants that shed their leaves seasonally and are leafless for part of the year.

Endemic—Having originated in and being restricted to one particular environment.

Escarpment—Cliff or steep rock face formed by faulting that separates two comparatively level land surfaces.

Extinct—No longer existing.

Extirpated—Extinct in a particular area.

Feldspar—Complex of silicates that make up bulk of the earth's crust.

Fold—Warped rock including synclines and anticlines.

Gneiss—Metamorphic granitelike rock showing layers.

Granite—Igneous rock composed predominantly of visible grains of feldspar and quartz. Used in building.

Igneous—Rock formed by cooled and hardened magma within the crust or lava on the surface.

Karst—Area of land lying over limestone and characterized by sinkholes, caves, and sinking streams.

Lava—Magma which reaches the surface of the earth.

Magma—Molten rock within the earth's crust.

Metamorphic—Rock which has been changed into present state after being subjected to heat and pressure from the crust, or chemical alteration.

Monadnock—Land that contains more erosion-resistant rock than surrounding area and therefore is higher.

Orogeny—A geologic process which results in the formation of mountain belts.

Outcrop—Exposed bedrock.

Overthrust belt—An area where older rock has been thrust over younger rock.

Rapids—Fast-moving water that flows around rocks and boulders in rivers; classified from I to VI according to degree of difficulty navigating.

Schist—Flaky, metamorphic rock containing parallel layers of minerals such as mica.

Sedimentary—Rocks formed by the accumulation of sediments (sandstone, shale) or the remains of products of animals or plants (limestone, coal).

Shale—Sedimentary rock composed of clay, mud, and silt grains which easily splits into layers.

Syncline—A rock fold shaped like a U that is closed at the bottom and open at the top. The youngest rock is at the center of a syncline.

Talus—Rock debris and boulders that accumulate at the base of a cliff.

Watershed—The area drained by a river and all its tributaries.

Index

About The Georgia Conservancy

The Georgia Conservancy is an independent, nonprofit organization of citizens, community groups, and businesses dedicated to protecting Georgia's environment and encouraging responsible stewardship of vital natural resources. In pursuing this mission, The Georgia Conservancy works to ensure a balance between environmental concerns and the demands of social and economic progress.

Since its founding in 1967, The Georgia Conservancy has built a solid reputation for its reasoned, pragmatic approach to environmental problem solving and its well-practiced ability to build consensus on difficult and complex issues. Through education and advocacy, The Georgia Conservancy plays a key role in developing public policy and enhancing environmental quality.

As Georgia continues its unprecedented growth, the pressures on our environment increase. The Georgia Conservancy is committed to its leadership role as the state's primary resource for environmental information and advocacy. The *Highroad Guide to the Georgia Mountains*, like our *Guide to the Georgia Coast*, celebrates our magnificent natural heritage and is a testament to the compelling need to protect it for present and future generations.

Thousands of citizens have decided to act positively for environmental quality and have joined The Georgia Conservancy. Make the natural decision and join The Georgia Conservancy today!

Call: (404) 876-2900
Mail: 1776 Peachtree Street NW, Suite 400 South, Atlanta, GA 30309
E-mail: tgc@mindspring.com
Visit our website at www.gaconservancy.org